Might, right, prosperity and consent

Manchester University Press

Might, right, prosperity and consent

Representative democracy and the international economy 1919–2001

HELEN THOMPSON

MANCHESTER UNIVERSITY PRESS
Manchester and New York
distributed exclusively in the USA by Palgrave

Published by Manchester University Press
Oxford Road, Manchester M13 9NR, UK
and Room 400, 175 Fifth Avenue, New York, NY 10010, USA
www.manchesteruniversitypress.co.uk

Distributed exclusively in the USA by
Palgrave, 175 Fifth Avenue, New York,
NY 10010, USA

Distributed exclusively in Canada by
UBC Press, University of British Columbia, 2029 West Mall,
Vancouver, BC, Canada V6T 1Z2

British Library Cataloguing-in-Publication Data
A catalogue record for this book is available from the British Library

Library of Congress Cataloging-in-Publication Data applied for

ISBN 978 0 7190 7750 0 *hardback*

First published 2008

17 16 15 14 13 12 11 10 09 08   10 9 8 7 6 5 4 3 2 1

Typeset in ITC New Baskerville 10.5/12.5 pt
by Servis Filmsetting Ltd, Manchester
Printed in Great Britain
by Antony Rowe Ltd, Chippenham, Wiltshire

For my parents, Christopher and Barbara Thompson

Contents

Preface   ix

Introduction   1

1   The modern democratic nation-state   18

2   The crises of the inter-war years   42

3   The Bretton Woods rescue   75

4   Crises and non-crises: financial liberalisation
    and the end of the Cold War   144

5   Conclusions   251

Bibliography   270
Index   287

Preface

I began this book in the late summer of 1998 when for a moment the post-Bretton Woods international economy appeared on the precipice of a political crisis. Whilst the moment passed, and three years later the world would be convulsed by a far more dramatic kind of international shock that would decisively turn political attention away from the consequences of financial liberalisation, the underlying political significance of the possibility of such international economic turbulence remains. As John Maynard Keynes understood perhaps more lucidly than anyone, there is no *a priori* reason why representative democracy and the kind of international economy that produced the crises of that year are compatible bedfellows. This book is an attempt to explain the implications of this for representative democracy's success and failure.

My debts to others in writing this book are many. I am grateful to everyone who has helped me at Manchester University Press, and to Mick Moran for first suggesting Manchester as a publisher. Joy Labern, the secretary to the Politics Department at Cambridge, has made it easier for me to give time to this manuscript at crucial moments. The students at Cambridge University who have taken my courses on the politics of the international economy over the past ten years have forced me to sharpen up my thinking on various issues and to think hard about why the subject matters. At moments when completing the book seemed beyond me, David Runciman gave me faith that I would make it. Intellectually, my debts are various. The late Jim Bulpitt taught me in his inimitable style that one could not make sense of modern politics without understanding the international economy and to see just how economic questions confront politicians in democracies. What he would have made of this book I don't know, but it owes something to what he imparted to me. John Dunn first showed me how the history of political thought illuminates some central issues in modern politics. David Runciman read an early version of the introduction, and chapters 1, 2 and 5, and Harald Wydra read chapter 2. Andrew Gamble read the manuscript twice and made some really invaluable suggestions. My greatest debt is to Geoffrey Hawthorn, who read the manuscript twice and gave me extraordinarily detailed comments. In doing so he held me sentence by sentence to the highest standards. For that compliment, for talking me out of various dead ends, and for helping me to endure through the more trying times when I have been writing this book, I am immensely grateful.

Introduction

This is a book about the external economic conditions that have shaped the success and failure of democratic states. The book begins from the premise that in the modern world the international economy is central to the problem of maintaining representative democracy as a pressure that can weaken it and a potential opportunity for strengthening it. In conception the book starts from a moment of departure in the world and moves backwards and forwards from that moment. In 1944, reflecting on the inter-war years, the architects of Bretton Woods began from the assumption that representative democracy was not easy to reconcile with a largely open international economy. To make the international economy safe for democracy, they created an international currency system that whilst encouraging multilateral trade negated short-term capital flows. After the United States ended that monetary order in the early 1970s, much of the world has gradually returned to an international economy of the kind that John Maynard Keynes and his colleagues feared, and appears to have done so without jeopardising representative democracy.

With these changes in the external economic world as its intellectual centre, this book analyses the part that the international economy has played in the success and failures of democracies since the beginning of the inter-war years; in their becoming established, not infrequently, in putting them at risk, and in sustaining or weakening the authority and power of the states on which democracy depends. The book assumes that the success of democracy cannot be pre-ordained, and that although it undoubtedly depends on other factors – how a democracy has fared in war and its relations with other states in times of peace, and the passions, interests and actions of its citizens – that success also depends on how at various important moments in time, and over time, democratic governments have dealt politically with the international economy.

This book tries to occupy an intellectual space that has been vacated by much scholarship and commentary on the modern political world.

Political theory has been reduced either to prescribing a morally better world without serious regard to how that might be brought about in the complex economic and political context in which this ethical transformation is supposed to take place, or recapturing the historical intentions of past thinkers who tended to be rather more intellectually engaged with the actual dynamics of the political world than those who now write about them. The dominant theoretical narratives of political science and international relations either are absorbed with discrete questions about separate aspects of modern politics, or try to generalise about the political world through abstract theory. By contrast, this book aims to capture something of the bigger picture of a central part of the political experience of the twentieth century developed through specific, and detailed, empirical analysis and a historically grounded conceptual framework.

Meanwhile, the narrative of globalisation has done little to advance our understanding of the relationships between economic and political life. As much recent empirical analysis has shown, it hid the truth that there are many things that states still do, in economic terms, that have significant political impact. It pushed attention away from the sheer coercive power of states during a time when a hugely powerful state was shaping many of the political parameters of today's world. It also gave rise to polemical discourses about the transformation of the political world, for good or for ill, which blinded much scholarship to significant continuities in political life over the past few centuries. In doing so it shut off intellectually much earlier political analysis that could help us better understand the political world in which we now live. Whilst the recent resurrection of the discourse of empire takes the state far more seriously and does connect the present era to the past, it also has its limitations as a general framework for analysis because it either aspires to explain American power in relation to only a number of the world's states, or it cannot sufficiently distinguish between the different impacts that American power has on a range of different states. This book stands back from the literature on globalisation and American empire and situates its analysis historically both in terms of the practical development of the international economy over time and in an earlier language of political analysis, reason of state, that stressed the importance of the external world to the endurance of state authority and power. The book is concerned with what states have been able to do under different kinds of international economic conditions, as much of the debate about globalisation is, but concentrates on the consequences of the degree of their discretion for the authority and power of democratic states rather than discretion for its own sake. The book is also very much concerned with the nature of American power but it is focused on the consequences of that power for the domestic politics of other states rather than for the United States and that power itself.

In its analysis of representative democracy, this book is normatively neutral, as economists would say, indifferent. It does not seek to justify democracy and neither does it assume that there is any *a priori* reason why democracy is more likely to succeed than any other form of government. The book is not concerned retrospectively to approve of those circumstances that have allowed democracy to flourish nor to endorse those which might allow it to do so in the future. Nor does the book assume, as many have done, that once democracy is in place, this form of rule will prove to be what all people in all circumstances will, or should, want. Too many scholars in the current debate about democracy either take the practical and imaginative success of democracy for granted because they assume that democracy is the natural form of government for the modern world and that exceptions to it are aberrations, or treat it as an abstraction that stands or falls on its ethical superiority. These grand narratives too easily produce claims about democracy that are driven by theoretical expectation or normative hope and which, consequently, are empirically dubious. What has got lost in the subsequent debate is any real sense of democracy's historical contingency and its development over time, and it is these issues that this book seeks to address.

Representative democracy

My interest in representative democracy in this book is as a form of government.[1] This is not to suggest that the only meaning the term democracy has in modern politics is as a form of government. Over the course of the nineteenth and twentieth centuries the word became invested with various of the normative claims that sprung from the French and American revolutions, and those claims, confused as they sometimes are, matter in understanding the fate of democracies because they play a part in shaping citizens' and politicians' willingness to support or acquiesce to a democratic form of government. But as a form of government, representative democracy does not itself instantiate any of the values associated with the word democracy, even, given the restrictions on the franchise in virtually all democracies, an equal right to vote, and it contains several features that are rather more aristocratic than normative democratic sensibilities allow.

In thinking about representative democracy, I begin with Schumpeter's minimalist definition that it 'is that institutional arrangement for arriving at political decisions in which individuals acquire the power to decide by means of a competitive struggle for people's vote'.[2] Some contest the efficacy of this definition as conveying too little about what they take to be distinctive about democracy.[3] However, it has several advantages for empirical purposes. Even though some think that peaceful and open elections are an insufficient condition for democracy, nobody disputes that they are a necessary one. Consequently, it provides a relatively easy means of distinguishing representative democracies from non-representative democracies without having to make contestable judgements about the quality of any particular democracy. This makes comparisons between democracies easier, and by eschewing assumptions about the outcomes produced by representative democracy leaves open at the point of enquiry the question of the conditions in which this form of government is likely to succeed.[4]

Much democratic theory tends to draw a sharp distinction between authority and power in representative democracy. It assumes that if legitimate procedures are successfully established, authority depends less on power than in other forms of government because having consented to authority, citizens will be more likely to trust governments and voluntarily comply with their decisions.[5] In part this is correct. States in representative democracies have frequently put rather less of the routine burden of securing acquiescence on coercion than did their monarchical predecessors. However, one of the main strategies they have used to this end is nation-building, which, as I explain in chapter 1, has historically involved the exercise of power on a vast scale. And even languages of nationhood stressing the provision of economic services depend on an ability to tax, which in no democracy is voluntary and always requires a large coercive apparatus.

Neither does power go away once some notion of shared nationhood has been apparently settled. As an increasing number of scholars of democracy in recent years have recognised, since representative democracy is a form of rule in modern politics, it is utterly dependent on a modern state.[6] Whatever influence groups of citizens can bring to bear on representatives by lobbying and direct action, elections provide no mechanism for voters as individuals or in groups to give their consent to particular decisions. Governments can choose to do things disapproved of by the majority of the electorate, and whether they lose the subsequent election will depend upon a host of contingencies beyond that decision, as the easy survival of the British Labour government after the Iraq war testifies. Individuals may break the law in protest at what they regard as immoral decisions, and some democratic theorists may claim that they have a theoretical right to do so,[7] but modern states in representative democracies in no way qualify their authority to punish those who disobey the law, or their practical capacity to do so.[8] As the histories of the various democracies I discuss in later chapters exemplify, representative democracy cannot succeed independently of a modern state that through its legal apparatus and coercive power can enforce the decisions taken by the representatives regardless of the preferences of citizens. Arguments for democracy must logically suppose that the state's authority and power already exist or can readily be created.

The assumption that representative democracy can be distinguished from other forms of government by the relative absence of a coercive state found its way into the frequent post-Cold War presumption that representative democracy is universally the best form of government. In recent years, the argument that democracy in developing and post-communist countries will not succeed without effective state-building, and therefore the exercise of power, has been made more frequently, even by Fukuyama, whose earlier thesis about the teological foundations of liberal democracy ignored questions of the state.[9] But the concept of 'democratic consolidation' that has become central to the debate about 'third-wave' democracies has tended to distract from this understanding because it assumes that issues around the state's authority can be successfully settled.[10]

In regard to the world's long-established democracies, the lack of analytical attention to power has drawn a curtain over some awkward truths. Even where the authority of the state appears relatively secure, and therefore the burden on power is reduced, that authority will invariably be contested by some, and will always remain open to question because in the absence of universally agreed values authority cannot have incontrovertible foundations. Historically, the cost in human suffering of creating such authority has been immense. As I explain in chapter 1, the political problems generated by the first moves to representative democracy in the nineteenth and the first half of the twentieth century were enormous, and they were frequently addressed by the brutal exercise of power. In Europe they helped push the continent into the nightmare of the First World War, and in the United States they precipitated a grisly civil war. We can, if we so wish, try to imagine a world in which issues of authority would be settled without the spectre of power, but we can only deny that questions of power have been at the centre of politics in democracies by refusing to face the world as it has thus far been.

Representative democracy, reason of state and the international economy

Recognising the contingency of the authority and power of states can usefully take us back into the history of political thought, which has become regrettably separated from much contemporary political science, and in particular to early modern debates about reason of state. Although he did not use the term, reason of state was Machiavelli's legacy to political understanding.[11] He insisted, as nobody in western political thought had previously, that preserving authority, because it required the imposition of order through the exercise of power on the unpredictable tides of circumstances and human wilfulness, had its own ethical precepts at odds with Christianity. For Machiavelli the political world was a world of its own, dominated by a contest between *fortuna* and *virtù*, between events and the insecurities that they generate and the human capacity to create order. Since *virtù* could not permanently keep *fortuna* at bay, time was the terrible enemy in politics and any state had a finite life. From within, the state could be destroyed by divisions, the pursuit of self-interest and demagoguery. But just as easily, Machiavelli contended, it could be destroyed by the power of other states in an external world beyond the reach of law. No state, therefore, could hope to endure without a foreign policy backed by military power shaped to preserve it in the particular external world it confronted.

In the face of these realities, those who ruled in principalities or republics required the quality of *virtù* channelled through a single-minded ability to comprehend changing circumstances, including in the world beyond the state. They needed to choose appropriate means for their particular ends, anticipate the consequences of their actions, and develop a persuasive language to justify the actions demanded by *necessità* even if that language was dishonest. Externally, they needed to be willing to deploy force, sometimes aggressively. Those who ruled, therefore, had to strive to maintain the *virtù* of armed citizens. If the state would not do battle, its citizens tamed by Christianity into 'humility, abnegation, and contempt for mundane things'[12] and its leaders driven by ignorance and corruption into mistaken judgements, its authority would be destroyed by external enemies.

If Machiavelli understood the centrality of the external world to the authority and power of states, the external world he described has long since become more complex, not least with the emergence of an international economy in which matters of trade and finance have a huge influence on relations between states, and their relative domestic success and failure. When the notion of reason of state was first applied to the world of self-conscious international economic competition, it produced the doctrine of jealousy of trade in which states tried to use their power to secure a competitive economic advantage. States motivated by such jealousy of trade created a new set of political dilemmas around debt, overseas empire and mercantile war. Some of the consequences of these problems drove some of the most profound political change of the eighteenth century, not least the American and French revolutions, and established many of the conditions of modern politics.[13] Yet in the decade after the First World War it became clear that the international economy also raised issues for the authority and power of states that went far beyond the competition between states for resources and comparative advantage that had preoccupied eighteenth-century politicians and intellectuals.

Most importantly, the inter-war years made clear just how politically potent short-term movements of capital could be for the authority and power of states. The eighteenth and nineteenth centuries had exposed how the competition for investment capital could constrain the possibilities of domestic politics as they had the fallout of unserviceable debt, but not the consequences of short-term capital flows driven by speculation and investor anxiety in conditions of political turbulence. By the end of the 1920s, short-term capital flows generated by currency speculation, portfolio investment and international bond markets were shaping the level of interest rates in states and with it the rate of employment in any economy. They were also placing limits on the amount of money that states could spend, especially on welfare provision, because when short-term investors lost confidence they expected governments to cut public expenditure to demonstrate a commitment to macro-economic orthodoxy. The desire to maintain the post-World War I gold standard provided the mechanism by which capital flight required governments to respond. Like any fixed exchange-rate system, the gold standard also imposed a severe discipline on wages in export sectors, and governments that presided over balance-of-payments deficits also risked short-term capital moving abroad, leaving themselves needing to raise interest rates or cut public expenditure to try to salvage their credibility. In different ways, short-term capital flows during the inter-war years bequeathed to governments a set of political problems that were potentially lethal for democracies because the economic outcomes that they produced regularly clashed with the expectations of leaders and citizens alike.

These domestic political problems were compounded by the international politics around the international economy created in the aftermath of the First World War. As the United States became the *de facto* centre of the reconstructed gold standard, it accumulated sufficient power to set the parameters for all other states' monetary policies at a moment when the political significance of monetary decision-making in all European democracies was becoming acute. Consequently, the political predicaments generated by the domestic outcomes of monetary policy were compounded by the damage that monetary subordination to another state did to the notion of national sovereignty, especially in states in which great-power status was central to the imaginative foundations of the state's authority. The inequality of monetary power relations exacerbated what were already fraught relations between the major powers. Inter-state debt between the First World War allies and German reparations to the European allies gave leverage to the United States to push European states towards actions they would not freely have chosen. Within Europe this simultaneously gave the United States and its war allies power over Germany, and Germany the incentive to debilitate its own economy to make payment impossible. The uncertainty, fury and fear bred by inter-state debt eventually helped to engender an aggressive international environment that threatened the security of Europe's democratic states. The international politicisation of debt repayment also reinforced all the domestic problems produced when private creditors lost confidence in a government's fiscal and current-account management. Whilst the fallout of the First World War generated some problems that were specific to the inter-war years, the core economic problems that the movement of short-term capital wrought during the inter-war years have endured when states have allowed, or indeed encouraged, capital flows across national borders, as has the fallout of one state establishing monetary hegemony under conditions of democratic politics. That the international economy mattered to the fate of democracy during the inter-war years is not a novel argument. But just how and why it mattered has profound implications for understanding the historically specific relationship between the international economy and democracy that has emerged over the past thirty years. Beginning in the inter-war period brings into sharp relief the contingencies that in parts of the world anyway have made representative democracy an enduring form of government.

This book explains how representative democracies have fared since these political problems emerged during the inter-war years through the attempt at Bretton Woods to foreclose them and the return of such capital movements over the past thirty years. It does so whilst recognising that the fate of any democracy is about far more than simply the question of how it endures in the international economy. As the inter-war years made clear, democracies can fail in different kinds of ways. They can fall to military coups, as did Poland's democracy in 1926, or be terminated by those who have risen to power via elections, as the Weimar republic was in 1933. They can succumb to civil war, which can involve other states offering support to those rebelling against a state's authority, as in Spain in 1936, and they can fall when a militarily victorious foreign power imposes a non-democratic regime, as did French democracy in 1940. When democracies do fail the international economy can be a direct causal agent of the failure, can matter directly in conjunction with other factors, or can directly explain little. For example, the rise to power of the Nazis was in good part the consequence of first German hyperinflation in 1923, which turned a significant section of the German middle class against Weimar, and then the crash of the international economy in 1929, which produced the misery of mass unemployment. But it also depended on the peace settlement imposed on Germany in 1919 and Hitler's ability to exploit the anger that reparations fuelled. Czechoslovakia's democracy, by contrast, simply fell to invasion by Nazi Germany in 1939 because it was a militarily weak state, abandoned by nominal allies to a militarily mightier one, independently of the impact of the international economy on Czech democracy during the previous years. Yet even the failure of Czechoslovakia's democracy is indirectly the story of what happened to the democracies of Europe as the international economy changed through the inter-war years. That the British and French governments would not go to war for Czechoslovakia was in part because under the international economic conditions of the 1930s they believed that they could not afford to rearm without pursuing radically different kinds of economic policies.

In writing about democracy, many democratic theorists have ignored the external economic conditions in which democracies have succeeded because their interest lies in institutions, civil society and values within democracy. In some of the more recent literature on democratic transitions and consolidation, external economic conditions have received much more attention.[14] But this literature tends to emphasise the simple issue of economic development, accepting Lipset's thesis[15] that states getting richer has a very strong positive effect on the likely success of democracy.[16] However, this argument is limited. It may be true that no democracy with a higher per capita income than Argentina had in 1975 has fallen,[17] but that doesn't tell us whether democracies are therefore any more secure than non-democratic regimes with comparable per capita incomes, or about the other ways in which economic questions interact with democracies. The exceptions to the claim that rich states are generally democratic, and poor states generally not, matter. Singapore's authoritarian regime has been stable for decades whilst India is the largest democracy in the world and has survived as one, except for a brief interruption in the mid-1970s, for nearly sixty years, despite abject poverty in parts of the country. China, meanwhile, has grown extraordinarily rapidly over the past two decades and contained the political consequences without moving anywhere near democracy.

Neither can participating in the international economy be treated as a fixed, wealth-generating external condition for democracies that is independent of the political consequences of states exercising power within this domain. The presumption that economic development is the path to democracy has now become bound up with the claim that the surest route for poor states to become first richer and then democratic is openness to the international economy.[18] However, once we recognise that states exercise power in the international economy and indeed determine its nature by doing so, then we have to see, as Weber understood, that how states participate in it will never just be a question of material benefit.[19] Openness to trade and investment may perhaps be the most reliable agent of growth for poor countries, but if the terms of that openness have consequences for the domestic authority and external power of a state then participation may sometimes endanger democracy regardless of economic gain. In thinking about the relationship between democracy and the international economy, democracy should not be treated in an ahistorical way either as an exceptionally successful form of government, or one that has a non-political relationship to economic development. In going back to the inter-war years where the kinds of political problems for democracy created by the present international economy originated and making comparisons over time and between democracies, we can see just how contingent democracy's success is, and the potential for failure, as well as success, that the international economy creates.

Approach

This book is a piece of comparative analytical political history. It does not purport to be conventional political science, international political economy or historical sociology. It does not start from theory nor does it test different theories against empirical evidence. It begins in the world at a contingent moment of time and explains what has changed over the subsequent eighty years in a range of democratic states, and it finishes by drawing some general conclusions about the changes in these contingencies over this time period. It does not offer a single thesis about the relationship between representative democracy and the international economy. Precisely because the contingencies of the international economy impact on democracy through other political contingencies and both sets of contingencies changed radically during the course of twentieth century, attempts to generalise about this relationship will not be especially illuminating. It is in understanding exactly what has changed over time that we can see the relative successes and failures of representative democracy today more clearly.

In my explanations of particular democracies, I begin with the politicians in power and the political circumstances in which they thought
and acted. I try to reconstruct the practical reasoning of these political
actors under the particular set of conditions in which they made choices.
Obviously these circumstances are in good part structural. Domestically,
these are created by the historical development of institutions, the kinds
of political arguments that do, or do not, resonate with citizens, the
pattern of class relations, the domestic organisation of economies, and,
where they exist, institutionalised relationships with economic actors.
But I don't in my explanations privilege any one of these structural conditions beyond the nature of representative democracy and the authority and power of the state in any particular place in time. Instead I look
at these conditions as constraints and opportunities around which those
with power have to manoeuvre and will sometimes want to change. To
do otherwise ends up attaching too little importance to the power of
states that politicians command and negates the crucial fact that politicians in representative democracies, as they have to compete for power
through elections, have a distinct set of motives and purposes that
cannot either be reduced to the interests or judgements of economic
actors or social classes, or be explained as the outcome of ideas, institutional incentives or economic structures divorced from the realities of
electoral competition. Since competition between and within parties is
the means by which governments acquire power in a representative
democracy and since power is what makes authoritative decision-making
in a democracy possible, I start in understanding the domestic conditions in which governments take decisions with that competition for
power, and the deeper difficulty of sustaining the source of that power
in the state's authority.

This is not to suggest that this is the only kind of approach that
can make sense of how democracies have succeeded and failed
during the twentieth century in the context of the international
economy, only that in starting with the dilemmas facing governments we
can recapture something of the way in which the problems generated by
the international economy actually appeared to those with power. For
example, Gregory Luebbert has shown for the inter-war years how a set
of positive and hostile relations between different classes strengthened
democratic forces in some states whilst weakening them in others.[20] But
this kind of argument can't explain why governments apparently representing similar classes chose to deal with the difficulties for democracy
created by the inter-war international economy in such different ways,
not least because it negates the interaction of the contingencies of
domestic politics with changes in the international economy and power

relations between states. If we start outside the relationship between the domestic and the international and the way that governments grapple with the dilemmas it generates, we will distort the historical truth, whatever we capture about the way that a particular variable works. Of course, the comparative composition of classes in Weimar Germany can reveal something about why that democracy failed, but it cannot itself explain why the decision by the United States in 1924 to reconstruct the international economy gave Weimar a chance to succeed, or why the way that the Brüning government pursued a deflationary policy after the international economy crashed did such damage to Weimar. If we say that these contingencies don't matter, we cannot explain why Weimar failed in 1933 and not ten years earlier, or understand just how for a period of time it held Hitler at bay. Neither the success nor the failures of democracies are determined by single variables, domestic or international.

Cases and organisation

The book considers a relatively large set of democracies in different periods of time in different parts of the world. Its detailed analysis begins in 1919 at the conjunction of a huge change in the external world, defined by the rise of the United States as an economic and political power and the, not causally disconnected, rise of representative democracy as the predominant form of government in Europe. Its detailed analysis ends in early 2001, before the Bush administration's response to the attacks on the United States dramatically reconstructed the external world in which other democracies have to endure, and before China began radically to change the terms of the international economy. The book takes the democracies it analyses historically rather than as case studies for theory-driven hypothesis-testing. In the specific democracies it analyses, it concentrates on cases where the fate of democracy has been historically significant either in international politics or because of the size of the state, and where it can be traced easily over time. I take representative democracy to be the prevailing form of government when competitive elections determine who exercises power at the centre. In democracies when the military or revolutionaries seize power, those who have won power either terminate scheduled elections or put restrictions on party competition, or defeat in war leads to military occupation, I take democracy to have broken down. To take the major cases of democratic failure the book considers, I take Italian democracy during the inter-war years to have ended with Mussolini's assumption of power, the Weimar republic with the Nazis' violence against their opponents during the elections of March 1933, Brazil's post-Second

World War democracy with the army's coup in 1964, and Indonesia's with Sukarno's coup and declaration of martial law in 1956.

The general conclusions in the book are limited to comparative judgements about the actual democracies studied, and do not presume to offer a theory of democracy or the international economy. In grounding its analysis in comparative history whilst trying to conceptualise the distinctly political dilemmas that confront democratic states, the book aspires to occupy a space between archival-based, single-country studies driven by narrative alone and the ahistoricism of much political science and international political economy that has abandoned in-time analysis for theoretical and methodological preoccupations.

Organisationally, the book begins in chapter 1 with the development of representative democracy as a form of government and the general political problems that accompanied it. This provides the analytical framework for the rest of the book, and sets out the terms of that discussion – the modern state, nationhood, representative democracy, and the phrase 'modern democratic nation-state' subsequently used to try to capture the relationship between the three. The chapter then examines the problem of the authority of the state in representative democracies as that began to be revealed by the partially formed democracies of Europe in the nineteenth and early twentieth centuries.

The book's method thereafter is historical and comparative between places and over time. Three chapters cover the eight decades from 1919 to 2001, reflecting the most significant watersheds in the international economy during that period. Chapter 2 covers the inter-war period, chapter 3 the Bretton Woods era, and chapter 4 the return from the 1970s to open short-term capital flows. This takes the discussion through three sharply contrasting historical periods, during one of which, the inter-war years, radically opposed international economic conditions prevailed at different times.

Chapters 2, 3 and 4 are written as analytical narratives. The discussion identifies the constraints and opportunities shaped by the external economic world and then traces the way that governments in a set of countries responded to those common constraints and opportunities and the consequences for each democracy of their doing so. For each case, the discussion begins with the particular circumstances of that representative democracy around the authority and power of the state, expectations of nationhood, electoral and institutional conditions, and its position in the international economy. The general argument in each of these chapters is structured in the first instance through the country-cases as they unfold in that story. This approach makes it possible to show how the cumulative consequences of the choices made by various governments continually reconfigured parts of the external environment around which future political judgements had to be exercised.

Whilst using a singular political vocabulary for discussing the dilemmas of representative democracy, the book seeks to explain how these have played out in states with both similar historical experiences and radically different ones. Since throughout the period covered the United States was the state with the most power to shape the international economy, the book does not discuss issues around the authority and power of the American state in relation to this world. Instead it analyses democracy in some of the states that have had to survive in an international environment shaped by the United States. Chapter 2, on the inter-war years, concentrates on Europe. It was here that the different kinds of pressures placed on democracies during this period were most acute, and where the failures of democracy were most dramatic in their consequences. This chapter considers in most detail the cases of the four European states – Germany, France, Italy and Britain – that had been great powers at the beginning of the First World War, only one of which survived as a democracy beyond 1940. It also more briefly discusses two cases – Poland and Yugoslavia – where democracy collapsed during the 1920s under external pressure; one – Spain – where it failed under the conjunction of domestic and external pressures; one – Czechoslovakia – where it failed as a consequence of the rise of Nazi Germany; and one – Sweden – where it succeeded.

Chapters 3 and 4 continue the analysis of the four large west European democracies, one now a long-standing democracy, one imposed by defeat and occupation, one reconstituted after military defeat, and one re-created in a mix of military defeat and internal rebellion, and through their different relations with the United States interacting differently with the Bretton Woods international economy. Chapter 3 introduces Japan, a democracy established by military occupation that effectively abandoned any claim to sovereignty in security, and whose economy became the second largest in the world. This chapter also extends the analysis to the developing world, where in several countries, first and foremost in Asia, those who inherited power from their imperial predecessors were faced with the enormously difficult burden of trying simultaneously to create an independent modern state and establish democracy. The chapter takes up two post-colonial cases, India and Indonesia, where, with large and diverse populations, the problems of securing consent to the authority of the state and democratic constitutional rules were potentially immense. In one instance democracy has survived almost continuously since 1947 and in another it failed within a decade of independence. Chapter 3 analyses the failure of Indonesian democracy during the 1950s, and the latter part of chapter 4 explains the difficulties that have bedevilled the reintroduction of democracy in Indonesia in the late 1990s. The final case is Brazil. As a relatively poor country in 1945, Brazilian democracy shared many of the economic difficulties of India and Indonesia. However, since the Latin American states had been independent since the nineteenth century and since the United States pursued a rather different policy towards Latin America than Asia for much of the Bretton Woods years, the political problems were rather different. Brazil's fate as a democracy has also been distinct from either of the Asian cases. Chapter 3 explains the weakness of Brazilian democracy during the postwar period, culminating in its demise in 1964. Chapter 4 considers the re-emergence of democracy during the 1980s and its subsequent predicaments in the post-Bretton Woods international economy.

The final chapter uses the preceding historical analysis to make some comparisons between democracies in the same states over time and between different democracies at the same time. On this basis it draws some conclusions about the central dilemmas of representative democracy as a form of rule at the beginning of the twenty-first century in different parts of the world. It shows that whilst democracy in Japan and European states has survived some potentially lethal developments in the international economy over the past thirty years, in the post-colonial states discussed in this book many of Keynes's fears for representative democracy in an international economy that was open to all kinds of capital flows still had force.

Notes

1 I sometimes use the word 'democracy' as shorthand for representative democracy but in doing so do not mean to conflate democracy as the ancient form of government with modern representative democracy.

2 J. A. Schumpter, *Capitalism, Socialism and Democracy* (London: Routledge, 1994), p. 269. For a good defence of Schumpeter's definition see A. Przeworski, 'Minimalist conception of democracy: a defense', in I. Shapiro (ed.), *Democracy's Value* (Cambridge: Cambridge University Press, 1999).

3 See, for example, L. Diamond, *Developing Democracy: Towards Consolidation* (Baltimore: Johns Hopkins University Press, 1999), p. 9; P. Schmitter and T. Karl, 'What democracy is . . . and is not', *Journal of Democracy*, 2: 3 (1991), 75–88; R. Dahl, *Democracy and its Critics* (New Haven: Yale University Press, 1989), pp. 121–30.

4 Schumpeter had his own views on the necessary conditions for successful representative democracy. See *Capitalism, Socialism and Democracy*, pp. 289–96.

5 For example, Dahl, *Democracy and its Critics*; B. Weingast, 'The political foundations of democracy and the rule of law', *American Political Science Review*, 91: 2 (1997), 245–63; M. Levi, *Consent, Dissent and Patriotism* (Cambridge: Cambridge University Press, 1997).

6 See, for example, A. Przeworski (ed.), *Sustainable Democracy* (Cambridge, Cambridge University Press, 1995); J. L. Linz and A. Stepan, *Problems of Democratic Transition and Consolidation: Southern Europe, South America and post-Communist Europe* (Baltimore: Johns Hopkins University Press, 1996); A. Przeworski, S. C. Stokes and B. Manin, 'Introduction' in A. Przeworski, S. C. Stokes and B. Manin (eds), *Democracy, Accountability and Representation* (Cambridge: Cambridge University Press, 1999); F. E. González and D. King, 'The state and democratisation: the United States in comparative perspective', *British Journal of Political Science*, 34: 2 (2004), 193–210.

7 See, for example, Dahl, *Democracy and its Critics*, p. 50.

8 Przeworski, Stokes and Manin, 'Introduction', pp. 1–2.

9 F. Fukuyama, *State Building: Governance and World Order* (London: Profile Books, 2005); S. Chesterman, M. Ignatieff and R. Thakur, *Making States Work: State Failure and the Crisis of Governance* (New York: United Nations Press, 2005). Some go further. Krasner, for example, argues that in some parts of world successful state-building can no longer take place internally, and advocates shared sovereignty with external actors. S. Krasner, 'The case for shared sovereignty', *Journal of Democracy*, 16: 1 (2005), 69–83. In the literature on democratic transitions see Linz and Stepan, *Problems of Democratic Transition and Consolidation*. Also G. O'Donnell, 'On the state, democratisation, and some conceptual problems: a Latin American view with some glances at some post-communist countries', *World Development*, 21: 8 (1993), 1355–69. But contrast Lawrence Whitehead's claim that representative democracy itself can be the agent of state-building: *Democratisation: Theory and Experience* (Oxford: Oxford University Press, 2002).

10 For example, even those like Linz and Stepan who emphasise the importance of the state to democratic success believe that democracies can be consolidated when the possibility of their breaking down in the future 'would not be related to weaknesses or problems specific to the historical process of democratic consolidation per se', which, if establishing the state's power is part of democratic consolidation, could not be a matter of state failure. *Problems of Democratic Transition and Consolidation*, p. 6.

11 See Q. Skinner, *The Foundations of Modern Political Thought, Volume One: the Renaissance* (Cambridge: Cambridge University Press, 1978), part II; J. G. A. Pocock, *The Machiavellian Moment: Florentine Political Thought and the Atlantic Republican Political Tradition* (Princeton: Princeton University Press, 1975); F. Meinecke, *Machiavellism: the Doctrine of Raison d'état and its Place in Modern History*, trans. D. Scott (London: Transaction Publishers, 1998), ch. 1.

12 N. Machiavelli, *The Discourses*, ed. B. Crick and trans. L. J. Walker (Harmondsworth: Penguin, 1984), p. 278.

13 See I. Hont, *Jealousy of Trade: International Competition and the Nation-State in Historical Perspective* (Cambridge, MA: the Belknap Press of Harvard University Press, 2005).

14 See, for example, S. Haggard and R. R. Kaufman, *The Political Economy of Democratic Transitions* (Princeton: Princeton University Press, 1995) and D. Rueschemeyer, E. Huber Stephens and J. D. Stephens, *Capitalist Development and Democracy* (Chicago: Chicago University Press, 1992); L. Diamond and M. F. Plattner (eds), *Economic Reform and Democracy* (Baltimore: Johns Hopkins University Press, 1995); L. C. Bresser Pereira, J. M. Maravall and A. Przeworski, *Economic Reform in New Democracies: a Social Democratic Approach* (Cambridge: Cambridge University Press, 2003); K. Weyland, *The Politics of Market Reform in Fragile Democracies: Argentina, Brazil, Peru and Venezuela* (Princeton: Princeton University Press, 2002).

15 S. Lipset, *Political Man: the Social Bases of Politics* (New York: Doubleday, 1960).

16 See, for example, L. Diamond, *Developing Democracy*; S. Huntington, 'After twenty years: the future of the third wave', *Journal of Democracy*, 8: 4 (1997), 3–12; A. Przeworski et al., 'What makes democracies endure?', *Journal of Democracy*, 7: 1 (1996), 39–55; A. Przeworski, 'Democracy and economic development', in E. D. Mansfield and R. Sissons (eds), *The Evolution of Political Knowledge* (Columbus: Ohio State University Press, 2004).

17 Przeworski et al, 'What makes democracies endure?'.

18 T. L. Friedman, *The Lexus and the Olive Tree* (New York: Farrar Strauss and Giroux, 1999); M. Mandelbaum, *The Ideas that Conquered the World: Peace, Democracy, and Free Markets in the Twenty-First Century* (New York: Public Affairs, 2002); M. Wolf, *Why Globalisation Works* (New Haven: Yale University Press, 2004).

19 M. Weber, 'The nation-state and economic policy', in *Weber: Political Writings* ed. P. Lassman and R. Speirs (Cambridge: Cambridge University Press, 1994).

20 G. M. Luebbert, *Liberalism, Fascism or Social Democracy: Social Classes and the Political Origins of Regimes in Inter-War Europe* (Oxford: Oxford University Press, 1991).

1

The modern democratic nation-state

For Machiavelli and his heirs, reason of state was prudent politics for princes and republics in competition for territory and power at home and abroad using violence. By the time the first aspects of what were to become modern democratic nation-states were emerging during the late eighteenth and nineteenth centuries, the domestic and external conditions in which the authority and power of any state had to be realised were very different. That change began with the gradual emergence of the modern state when several European monarchs sought to establish a monopoly over legitimate violence, and to exclude external legal intrusion in their affairs. In doing so, the most successful created states that claimed to rule as single sovereign entities, large territories inhabited by vast numbers of subjects divided by class, religious faith and mores. Out of the problems this generated, those who led them eventually turned to the idea of representative democracy and nationhood, only to discover that authority grounded in the idea of a national people and letting subjects choose representatives to govern generated a whole new set of difficulties for states.

The modern state

The modern state emerged in contrast to the multiple and fragmented sites of power that had characterised most of Europe after the fall of the western Roman empire. This predominantly Christian world had taken its clearest shape from the late eleventh century after the Papacy started to press a claim to direct political authority, asserting that Christendom was a universal entity in which spiritual and temporal laws were one. The Pope, the Vatican proclaimed, ruled Christendom as an inheritance of St Peter, the Holy Roman Emperor ruled the same territory by delegation from the Pope, and the regional kingdoms of Christendom were ultimately subordinate to a universal legal order sanctioned by God. Within each of the kingdoms of Christendom, the crown shared power with the church, feudal barons and estates and parliaments.[1]

Over the course of three centuries, the English and French crowns attacked this political settlement at home and created a very different kind of rule. In doing so, their apologists used the term 'the state' for the first time specifically to distinguish a legal and constitutional order independent of any particular ruler.[2] During the fifteenth century both the English and French crowns tried to establish the sole authority to use violence. Henry VII destroyed the armies of the feudal barons and enforced new laws against retaining, giving the English crown an effective monopoly of legitimate violence. French monarchs were less immediately successful. Whilst the French king in 1429 advanced the principle that only the king had the right to recruit troops, only, after 1653, when it had put down a second uprising within five years by the provincial aristocracy, did the French crown succeed in stripping the nobles of their armies.

Against the backdrop of the splintering of Christendom by the Reformation, the English and French crowns similarly asserted the distinctiveness of their own legal and political authority against the extra-territorial claims of the Holy Roman Emperor and the Pope. England's claim to be author of its own laws and its rejection of the edicts of others came when, by the 1533 Act of Appeals, the English crown denied any papal or Holy Roman jurisdiction over England, after the Pope refused to grant Henry VIII a divorce from the emperor's aunt. In France, the crown had by the fourteenth century already asserted French sovereignty against the emperor and provoked the Pope to condemn Gallic 'pride', which 'pretended to recognise no higher authority'.[3] Two centuries later, Henri IV's proclamation of the Edict of Nantes, which granted qualified liberty to Protestants, effectively stated the political authority of the French state to be secular and independent of Rome. In sharp contrast to the fiercely Catholic Spanish crown, first Henri IV and then Louis XIII's chief minister, Cardinal Richelieu, defined the interests of the state as French, not Catholic.

The claim of states to external sovereignty against the old regime of the Papacy and the Holy Roman Emperor took its shape most clearly against the backdrop of the Thirty Years War and the Peace of Westphalia. In 1555, after years of violence, the Peace of Augsburg established the principle of religious equality within the empire between Catholics and Lutherans so that each prince could decide on the religion of his own subjects. In 1618, after the Catholic Ferdinand II acceded to the throne of Protestant Bohemia, war broke out within the Habsburg-led empire between the Evangelical Union and the Catholic

League. After Bohemia was crushed and catholicised by the imperial forces, first Denmark and then Sweden intervened to defend the Protestants. In 1635, France joined the anti-imperial forces and declared war on Spain, bringing the Netherlands into the war. By 1648, both the empire and Spain were defeated. The Peace of Westphalia gave assets to treaties worked out at Osnabrück between the empire and Sweden, and at Münster between the empire and France and their respective confederates and allies. Westphalia legally dismissed any idea of the supranational international authority of the Pope, and strengthened the authority of the princes and free cities *within* the empire against the Habsburgs, by granting them the right to sign foreign treaties and re-establishing the principle that the religion of the principalities and free cities was a local affair. But, despite persistent assertion otherwise, it did not propagate a doctrine of external state sovereignty *per se*. To the contrary, it gave Sweden and France the effective right to intervene within the principalities and free cities of the empire to ensure that both the provisions for religious minorities and the privileges of princes and free cities were upheld and maintained.[4] What Westphalia introduced as international convention between states was the sovereignty of the powerful and the right of those states to impose conditions of statehood on defeated and aspiring states. It was this conception of state sovereignty that became the historical norm, upheld at the Congress of Vienna in 1815, the Congress of Berlin in 1878, at Versailles in 1919 and imposed on Japan by economic restrictions after the Meiji restoration.[5]

In asserting their unique authority to command legitimate violence and their sovereignty against external legal agents, the English and French crowns also increasingly claimed the sole right to administer and legislate within their respective kingdoms. Previously in England, Magna Carta in 1215 had established the principle that the crown had to operate within the law and that no free person could be punished except by lawful judgement of his equals or according to the common law of the land. Henry VIII and Thomas Cromwell transformed the Star Chamber into a new judicial court, which was not bound by common law, and used Parliament to make the English Reformation enforceable by law. Henry and Cromwell turned Parliament into an instrument of royal policy and in so doing established the sovereignty of the king in Parliament. In effect, the crown now created the law of the land through Parliament and administered that law through the judiciary. In France, Henri IV simply governed over the will of the estates and the local parlements and brought the duchies and provinces that had maintained a more or less independent political status under the authority of the crown. After the assassination of Henri IV in 1610 threatened more violent conflict, Richelieu centralised power further, and the defeat of the aristocratic rebels by his successor, Mazarin, in 1653 laid the basis for the absolutist rule of Louis XIV. As they centralised authority and power, the English and French crowns replaced indirect administrative rule through feudal relationships with direct bureaucratic rule, imposing uniform laws and administrative arrangements over the whole territory. In doing so, they massively increased the resources available to rulers. By fortifying their coercive power, they enhanced their capacity to tax and fund their own armies.[6]

Those who justified this new kind of state repudiated the rhetoric of Christendom. Given its most forceful theoretical shape by Jean Bodin and Thomas Hobbes, the political language of the modern state centred on the idea of sovereignty as a site of supreme and indivisible authority. For Hobbes, where there was no sovereignty within existing territorial borders, passionate, self-interested and self-righteous individuals would ensure there was no security or peace. Alone in the moral and political pluriverse, individuals could rationally agree to grant each other a natural right to self-preservation even if they chose to forebear their own. A sovereign commanding exclusive power, preferably but not necessarily a monarch, could by fear sustain the security on which any peaceful life depended. The state constructed on this basis was by definition impersonal.[7] As Hobbes put it, the commonwealth was not formed to take 'notice' of '*this* or *that* individual citizen'.[8] No government would, of course, ever think of ruling in this way. But rhetorically, the idea of the impersonal sovereign was a political asset. Since it did not ask subjects to recognise anything of themselves in the state beyond their interest in security, rulers had an argument to justify authority over large territories containing very diverse interests and religious beliefs.

Seen as a whole, the modern state, as Max Weber later explained, became a relationship of rule by human beings over human beings in an explicitly demarcated territory resting on the sovereign application of law and in the final instance on a successful claim to a monopoly of legitimate violence.[9] To maintain the modern state's authority those who led such states needed to accumulate and retain sufficient coercive power to enforce laws and control the arms available to their subjects. To defend the modern state's external sovereignty, leaders needed to defend their state's territory against invasion and any foreign claims to legal jurisdiction. Within these terms, some states were always likely to be more successful than others. But nowhere was such a state established without a bloody political contest. The English and French monarchs could have been defeated at various times in their attempts to establish this kind of state, at home by the aristocratic barons and abroad by the Catholic Habsburg powers still allied to the Papacy, or in some instances, as in the threats to the Tudor regime during Elizabeth I's reign, by a compact between them. Neither, once instituted, could either the internal authority or external sovereignty of such a state be taken for granted. Like all other forms of political order that had preceded it, the modern state had to be defended by deliberate action, alert to domestic rebellion and external intervention.

Nonetheless, compared to monarchs after the demise of imperial Rome, those who commanded the power of modern states had very considerable advantages in maintaining rule. For the monarchs of the Middle Ages, the means of intimidating subjects were, in Macaulay's words, 'very scanty'.[10] Resistance to an established government was therefore very easy. Would-be rebels could quickly raise an army of potentially more men than were available to the crown. And since none could readily command obedience from local barons, every monarch was vulnerable to losing territory to other crowns if domestic rebels allied with foreign enemies. But once monarchs achieved a monopoly of force, their subjects could only hope to mount a military challenge to the state if the crown's standing army joined them in rebellion or they were led by a foreign power. Once subjects were tamed and stripped of the capacity to use their own weapons, the durability of a modern state at home could in good part depend on the effective exercise of violence.

The modern state and the mercantile economy

The primary menace to modern states came from beyond their own borders. A king whose judgement about foreign threats was as wretched as England's Charles I's could as easily throw away his crown and precipitate a revolution as any earlier monarch. But as wealth accumulated and science developed, the external world also spawned new kinds of dangers. By the late seventeenth century, the distinct populations ruled over by modern states were becoming commercially connected. Some, most clearly in the United Provinces, Britain and France, saw that commercial society could be used to increase the power of the state. As mercantilists, they believed that future political and military power had an economic basis and that material resources had to be won in a zero-sum competition for trade and trading routes. If a state lost material resources to others, it would eventually lose military power too, threatening its internal authority. States, therefore, had good reason to encourage exports and discourage imports, to support domestic industries and activities that enhanced military power, to build a strong merchant marine, and to create institutions by which they could borrow money to finance these activities. Those that were most successful in this competition were rewarded with unprecedented levels of state revenue. But, as nowhere previously in a large state, mercantilism turned trade and national prosperity into a reason of state, and tied the stability and durability of monarchical rule to international economic success.[11]

Within this context, the external sovereignty and power of states depended on the ability of governments to structure the economy to the demands of commercial competition with other states as well as the efficacy of military resources and alliances. In competing for resources and power, governments increasingly turned towards large-scale borrowing. To sustain their creditworthiness, governments had to maintain the erratic confidence of those that endlessly bought and sold their debt. If governments failed to make the payments demanded, they risked, in David Hume's words, 'poverty, impotence, and subjection to foreign powers'.[12] Many, like Hume, were horrified at what they took to be this Faustian bargain: for the sake of deferring taxation, the state had handed direct power over its future to those who had no interest in its survival.

Paths to representative democracy

By the last years of the eighteenth century the internal authority and external power of the European modern states were indeed waning. As national debts mounted to unsustainable levels, states desperately tried to extract more revenue in taxes to finance their war machines. But Britain's attempt to tax the American colonies and that of France to tax its own subjects without granting some political representation, induced rebellion. In the subsequent crises either side of the Atlantic different aspects of a new kind of political entity first took their shape. On the western side, the new state that was designed in 1787 was a self-conscious attempt to create a representative republic over a large territory on new federalist principles. On the eastern side, in 1789, came the argument, most forcefully articulated by the Abbé Sieyès, that the entities of political rule should be defined by common membership of a unitary nation and that those who exercised power should be the representatives of that nation. Over the next century, out of the muddled and sometimes contradictory interaction of the practices and rhetoric of a reworked republicanism and a new imaginative notion of nationhood came a form of rule that can be described as the modern democratic nation-state.[13] Within such states in Europe the new rules of rule divided power territorially and between executive and legislatures in different ways, some monarchs retained formal authority and some were eliminated, and the principle of representation held several meanings. But increasingly this form of rule showed several common features: it was founded on the rule of a modern state over a demarcated territory and claimed, whether successfully or not, external sovereignty, it justified the internal authority of that state in the name of a nation, and it gave leadership of that state to those whom the people subject to the state's rule periodically chose in competitive elections. In the conjunction of these practices lay an unprecedented set of political difficulties, not least for the relationship between the state's internal authority and constitutional rules, and its external vulnerability.

The decisive origins of representative democracy as an alternative form of government to monarchy lay in part in despair at the prospects of securing consent to authority at all.[14] In the United States, James Madison and his fellow architects of the American constitution went to Philadelphia in the summer of 1787 driven by the fear that the future of republican government in North America was bleak. They believed that the thirteen state governments established on republican principles in 1776, after the colonies had declared their independence from the British crown, had let loose democratic passions that were inimical to order and the rights of property. The future, Madison and his colleagues feared, was first anarchy and then tyranny.

To save republican government, the founders of the United States rejected the whole tradition of political thought that assumed that large territories could be ruled by only monarchs or emperors. Against all previous assertion, they insisted that a large republic was both possible and desirable. If the disease of republican government was faction, the solution, Madison resolved, was to have a state big enough to disperse divisive interests and passions across it so that they could neutralise each other.[15] Applying the principle of representation to all the three branches of government, the founders extended authority over a territory at least ten times larger than any previous republic. Yet in establishing their large republic, they did not dispense with the existing small ones. Instead they created a federal government, one that on some explicitly stated matters ruled directly over all Americans, but which left sovereignty over all other matters to the thirteen states. Where those who had created modern states had established a single site of sovereignty, one that alone had authority to decide and legislate and the power to coerce, the founders of the American republic trusted that they could territorially divide sovereignty without risking civil war.

Beneath this constitutional structure lay a different kind of understanding of the role of the people in government than had ever taken hold before. Like all their republican predecessors and in contrast to monarchists, the American founders believed that power depended on the consent of the people over whom it was exercised. Unlike older republicans, or indeed many of those who opposed the constitution, they did not infer from this premise the conclusion that the people could or should in any collective capacity govern.[16] The founders gave power to the representatives of the people not because they were like the people or because they shared the same interests but because they were deemed different and better than the people. To realise this essentially aristocratic ambition, the founders allowed the people to choose directly their own federal representatives only in the lower House of Congress. Representation, conceived like this, was a buffer between the people, who could not be trusted to discern the common good, and the state, whose survival still depended on those with power pursuing that good. Madison's hope that representation was the means to secure the old republican end of virtue was on his own terms doomed. In what came to be called representative democracy, those who exercised power were not those best capable of discerning the common good, but those most successful at the arts of electioneering and organising a party machine. The more representatives came to earn a living from these activities, as Joseph Schumpeter later explained, the more they became professionals with their own professional interests derived from the design and circumstances of electoral competition between parties in any particular time and place.

This form of government was at least as potentially precarious as the monarchies of the eighteenth century. Those whose interests were most frequently hurt by its outcomes had good reason to rebel, especially if their nominal representatives transparently inflicted grievous harm, or indeed violence, to court an electoral majority. Meanwhile, those who ran for election needed to try to create political passions and identities for their own immediate purposes whilst containing any counter-passions and identities that might menace the state's authority. During the nineteenth century in Europe, the question of class raised this tension in a particularly acute form, especially when industrialisation created new classes, some of whom were poor and politically self-conscious about that fact. Just as importantly, the survival of representative democracy required restraint by representatives in both the issues in which they engaged in combat, and the exercise of the power bestowed upon them. If collectively they allowed every matter that could be contested to become an electoral weapon, any capacity for prudence and judging reason of state would be destroyed.

Unlike monarchs but as in earlier republics, ministers in representative democracies needed at least in part to disguise their power. Whilst representative democracy excluded the people in any collective sense from government, elections created a language of politics around the 'will of the people'. This language risked disappointment and anger. If these passions were not to be turned against the state, they had to be massaged with material rewards and rhetorical fictions. Representatives had to create and sustain sectional interests and identities and then present them as the manifestation of the 'will of the people'. Those who led the governments of representative democracies had in some sense, therefore, to be moralists in public, whilst privately understanding that they were also demagogues and Machiavellians.

The idea of nationhood

The modern idea of nationhood was born out of the failure of Louis XVI's efforts to use the Estates-General to raise taxes to rescue the French crown from bankruptcy. On 17 June 1789, the Third State of the Estates-General declared itself the 'National Assembly'. Immediately, it decreed the cancellation and then the re-authorisation of all taxes. Henceforth, it proclaimed, sovereignty belonged to the nation, that political body, in the Abbé Sieyès' words, 'of associates living under common laws and represented by the same legislative assembly'.[17] Once the king lost confidence that his troops would put down the ensuing revolt in Paris, the National Assembly's claim to power was vindicated. Over the following months, the members of the Assembly sought to find a means to realise the sovereignty of the French nation within the framework of a constitutional monarchy. For Sieyès, the instigator of the National Assembly and much of its rhetoric, the political logic of nationhood was inescapable: since sovereignty resided in the unity of the nation, it could not be divided, and since the voice of the nation could not be manifested directly in such a large state, it had to be exercised by representatives.[18]

In practice, the constitution presented to Louis XVI in 1791 compromised Sieyès' vision. In granting a form of royal veto to the king, it did divide the sovereignty of the nation over the authority to legislate. But its language was unambiguous: 'The Kingdom is one and indivisible . . . Sovereignty is single indivisible, inalienable and imprescriptible. It belongs to the Nation.'[19] When the radical revolutionaries overthrew the monarchy in September 1792 and established a republic, they employed the same mantra: 'the French republic is one and indivisible'.[20] In their desire to export the republic, the leaders of the new French state passed on to others in Europe – those who wished to overthrow absolute monarchs and replace them with constitutional forms of government and those who aspired to defeat empires and create new modern states – the imaginative idea that the people living in a particular territory could make themselves, by an act of collective will, a unified nation and that the state which ruled them had authority because, and only because, it represented that unity.

In the aftermath of events in France, cultivating the idea of nationhood became the predominant strategy used by those who commanded power to secure consent to the authority of the modern state. Those who chose to use it had to create and sustain collective identifications that would breathe life into the idea of a single people in a vast territory in the face of multiple, divisive and inchoate social identities. Sieyès might have insisted that 'the nation owes its existence to natural law alone',[21] but in reality someone had to create such a body of people by an act of will.[22] Practically, the French revolutionaries and the leaders of the modern states created in the nineteenth century used the power of the modern state to homogenise as far as possible the linguistic and religious sensibilities of their subjects.[23] As Massiomo d'Azeligio famously remarked later, 'we have made Italy, now we must make Italians'. Through membership of the fictitious community of a nation, subjects, their rulers hoped, would accept being represented by a sovereign and, consequently, would through their own volition, rather than the threat to violence, submit to its authority. In an unmistakable echo of ancient *virtù* and the republican patriotism on which Machiavelli had grounded durable sites of power, the security of modern states would become dependent on conjuring and sustaining individual beliefs in a purported community of shared commitments and emotions.

Success in substantiating an idea of nationhood meant that the state could radically increase the demands that it might make on its subjects. Most importantly, effective nationhood created a reason for citizens to pay more taxes to the state and, once again, to fight and die in its wars. Exploiting this opportunity, the French government, after 1792, conscripted an army. Yet citizen armies were also dangerous for modern states. In good part the English and French monarchs had established the modern state precisely because they wanted a monopoly of the means of war. In asking citizens to fight in the name of the nation, the state stirred political passions among its subjects whilst handing arms to them. As Napoleon's seizure of power in 1799 proved, the generals of citizen armies could challenge and destroy authority internally as readily as they could confirm and strengthen the state's power externally. Burnt by the experience during the Napoleonic wars, after 1815, all except the Prussian government reverted to professional armies. Then stunned by Prussia's devastating defeat of France in 1871, most turned back to large-scale conscription. Part of reason of state would thereafter mean working out just what rights governments had to concede in return.[24]

The political language that accompanied the invention of the nation disguised the inherently political nature of rule by the modern state, as did that around representative democracy. Internally, the idea of nationhood precluded explicitly political justifications for authority and power. The state could not explain itself in its own terms because, as the supposed agent of nationhood, the authority and power of the state had to have a purpose beyond itself. Unsurprisingly, the rhetorical language that emerged tended to draw on abstract generalities that denied the diversity of particular interests among a people. Quite obviously, the leaders of some modern states in the nineteenth century had an easier task than others in using their power to mould sensibilities. But the more those who aspired to establish new states successfully utilised the language of nationhood, the more difficult it became for any European government to defend the territorial borders of its state. Once nationhood became the dominant imaginative currency of politics, the leaders of most European states had to confront citizens who in the name of a nationhood offered by another state rejected the authority to which they were subject. Since few leaders wished to cede territory, they were left with a choice: either they could use power more brutally to try to assimilate the rebellious, something which was not easy in representative democracies constrained by constitutional rules, or they had to divide internal authority territorially as the Americans had done and relinquish Sieyès' claim that the sovereignty of the nation was inherently indivisible.

Modern democratic nation-states and the external world

The new states established on either side of the Atlantic in the 1780s were pitched into a hostile external world. In discarding British rule in 1776, the most self-consciously republican of the American revolutionaries believed that they were also rejecting the war-based international politics of the old world and its mercantile economy dominated by Britain. Two months after the war with Britain had begun the Continental Congress had agreed a 'model' treaty to offer France, constructed on the principles of free trade and peace and couched in a language that decried considerations of power. Reality, however, quickly intervened, and in 1778, the American ambassadors concluded a traditional alliance with France that included future territorial conquests, and which eventually secured the victory of the American Confederation.

From the very beginning, the French revolution was also in part a rebellion against the prevailing international politics of Europe. In the seven decades prior to the French revolution, this revolved around the maxim that there was a multiple number of great-power states, none of which could hope to dominate the continent, and that what happened outside Europe was as important as what happened within.[25] States competed for European territory, sought allies within the continent, and organised their economies and military resources to take advantage of commercial opportunities overseas. The new international politics of Europe appeared to leave states with a clearly identifiable set of interests and purposes, understood by their own rulers and predictable to others. The result was almost constant war. Every attempt by a state or an alliance of states to acquire more territory or wealth was generally met by a counter-attack to try to restore the balance of power. These wars, however, were limited in scope: they were fought by small, professional armies, and they did not precipitate continental-wide bloodshed.

As the eighteenth century progressed, Britain and the new states of Russia and Prussia thrived in this world. As Russia and Prussia acquired more European territory, so Britain increasingly dominated the seas and commercial competition. France was the clearest loser. In 1756 it had concluded a treaty with its former foe, Austria, without discernible reward. Defeated in the Seven Years War by Prussia and Britain and deprived of most of its overseas possessions, totally ignored during the partition of its traditional ally Poland in 1772, bankrupted by the American War of Independence, and humbled by Britain over the United Provinces in 1787, the French *ancien régime*, and its opponents, saw balance-of-power politics as national humiliation. Even before the fall of the Bastille, radical pamphlets circulated demanding that France repudiate the Austrian commitment and secure a new alliance system. The most radical revolutionaries wished to transform not only France but Europe too, bringing about a crisis of the sovereign state.[26] As Jacques-Pierre Brissot would later say in the wake of war, 'we cannot be calm until Europe, all Europe, is in flames'.[27]

Beyond its rhetoric, however, the new French regime was for two years generally cautious. Neither, initially, did the other European states seem at all inclined to intervene against it. In the second half of 1791, the internal and external tide of events turned. The Brissotin faction saw in war an opportunity to take power whilst Louis XVI succeeded in winning Austrian and Prussian support for his plight. In April 1792, France declared war on Austria. For the radicals this was the opportunity to use the energy released by the revolution to reverse French humiliation at Austrian hands. In the words of one Brissotien: 'We can see that the

abrogation of this treaty [of Versailles] is a revolution as necessary in
foreign affairs, both for Europe and for France, as the destruction of the
Bastille has been for our internal regeneration'.[28]

After some early setbacks, successive French regimes found in military
republicanism not only a means of defending the French state, but the
practical and imaginative basis of an empire stretching beyond the frontiers of Europe. In conscripting its citizens and mobilising virtually all
seizable national resources, the French state created an enormous,
expansionist military force. By imposing French rule across much of
the continent by annexation and occupation, it sequestered further
material resources, conscripted soldiers and large-scale indemnities
from its defeated enemies. As a result, whilst the *ancien régime* had collapsed under the weight of its debt trying unsuccessfully to check the
demise of French power, Napoleon created an empire without ever
really straining the state's fiscal position.

After France's eventual defeat in 1814–15, the victorious European
states restored the Bourbons to power and returned France to its 1792
borders. But the international and domestic demons let loose by the
ideas of nationhood and democracy were not extinguished. Contrary
to the hopes of liberals, the more states moved towards becoming
both nation-states and representative democracies, the more potential
danger they posed to each other. Although many might have privately
sympathised with Bismarck's adage that 'the foreign policy of a great
empire cannot be placed at the beck and call of a parliamentary majority without being forced into wrong paths',[29] in states in which membership of the nation had in part to be a passion created by politics, the
external world, and war in particular, offered considerable demagogic
opportunities.

Nothing made this clearer than events in France between 1830 and
1871. Louis Philippe, elected by the Chamber of Deputies, believed
that the French state could neither challenge the 1815 settlement nor
become involved in the growing national liberation struggles in southern and central Europe without risking its own security. The French
state, he trusted, had to be a conventional European great power, not
a harbinger of international republicanism at the mercy of excitement-
hungry Parisians. His prudence was put to the test when, in 1840, a
crisis broke in Egypt. Initially Louis Phillipe tried to secure some influence for France independently of the attempt by the great powers to
save Ottoman rule. When the great powers lost patience, they signed a
joint convention without informing him. Tocqueville warned that in
the face of such provocation 'there is not a government . . . that would
not be exposing itself to destruction if it wished to persuade this

country to stand idly by'.[30] Louis Philippe's prime minister, Adolphe Thiers, seemed to agree and threatened to invade the German federation and Austria. But the king secretly told Britain that France would not fight. The alleged humiliation of France provoked large-scale nationalist demonstrations and several attempts to assassinate Louis Phillipe. Tocqueville concluded that under the form of government that was emerging in Europe, prudence in foreign policy was impossible. 'Do you think', he asked in the Chamber of Deputies in November 1840, 'that one can govern free peoples by nullifying and enervating all their passions? For me, there is only one way of taming evil passions, that is oppose them with good passions. . . . But to try to struggle simultaneously against the patriotic spirit and the revolutionary spirit is beyond the strength of any man.'[31] When Louis Napoleon seized power in 1852, he absorbed what he took to be the lesson, and put 'the patriotic spirit' and a bellicose foreign policy at the centre of his Caesarist regime. But his activism was at least as dangerous for the state's internal authority and external power as the king's prudence, blinding him to the intentions of others. When Louis Napoleon decided to invade Prussia in 1870, falling into Bismarck's trap to get him to do just that, he precipitated the demise of his own regime, the loss of French territory and the creation of a large new state on France's eastern borders.

In turning considerations of international politics into a matter of nationhood, the most reckless governments of the nineteenth century moralised justifications for war. Wars sold as part of nationhood could not be openly fought to maintain the balance of power or for commercial interests, but had to serve the passions of patriotism. Such justifications changed the stakes of war. They ensured that states would not easily retreat once committed, and that victorious states had every incentive to destroy their enemies rather than compromise on a peace that could not be justified by the lives, resources and rhetoric sacrificed to it. In 1814 the monarchical powers, after more than twenty years of war against a state bent on imperial expansion, left France armed and unoccupied, with its 1792 borders and without an indemnity. In 1871, after a war that had served its interests, the new German nation-state stripped France of Alsace-Loraine, occupied it and imposed reparations. Modern republics could not escape from the power-politics and *fortuna* in the external world. What war extended to nationhood and what nationhood offered to secure internal authority could exact a ferocious price in external sovereignty that then undermined the language of nationhood itself. Whilst the apparently long peace of the middle of the nineteenth century in Europe disguised the fact, the emergence of the modern democratic nation-state had made international politics that much more dangerous than it had been during the eighteenth century. In doing so it reinforced an older set of difficulties about securing consent to internal authority under conditions of external failure that went beyond the problems generated by the debt-ridden mercantile economy of the eighteenth century. For the most powerful and richest states in Europe, reason of state for the external world of the nineteenth and early twentieth centuries became dominated by international politics, not international economic success, which could comparatively be taken for granted.

European dilemmas

Nowhere in the late nineteenth century, despite the considerable effort poured into nation-building, could those who led these states take justifications for the state's authority for granted. Some worried that rival claims to nationhood might prompt demands for secession. In expanding the franchise in 1884 primarily in rural areas, the British government enfranchised disproportionate numbers of Irish men without redistributing constituencies to take account of the decline of the Irish population over the previous four decades. By doing so, it gave sufficient numbers of votes to a national minority, which neither it nor its successors could ever hope to control for religious reasons, to make or break majorities in Parliament. For their part, the leaders of the new German and Italian states feared Catholics because the Vatican had rejected their existence. Each secularised education and formulated a language of national unity that excluded confessional sentiments. In his first years controlling the German state, Bismarck went further, passing a set of anti-Catholic laws known as the *Kulturkampf.*

By the 1880s, most European governments, having failed either to assimilate or repress Catholics, were also confronted by hostile socialist parties and revolutionary movements. Reflecting on his own government's failures and the pressure they put on the state's authority, the British prime minister, Lord Salisbury, lamented: 'We are in a state of bloodless civil war.'[32] Increasingly from the 1890s, governments dispensed with the idea of nationhood with the most rebellious of their subjects and relied on coercion. In Germany, Bismarck legislated to suppress the socialists, and, in Britain, Salisbury's government passed a Coercion Act to repress violent nationalist activity in Ireland. At times the internal authority of the Italian state appeared to rest almost entirely on force. In 1894 the government dissolved the socialist party, imposed martial law on a recalcitrant Sicily, and secured emergency anti-anarchist legislation.

When rebellion broke out across the country during a general strike in 1898, the government introduced martial law in several big cities.[33]

Judging that coercion could not suffice, Bismarck established state-financed insurance schemes against illness, old age and infirmity in the 1880s. In understanding that the power of the modern state could be used to create an economic dependency among those subjects most inclined to rebel, he made the welfare state a domestic reason of state. Once he did, he made it an external one for other states. When the Boer War revealed just how unprepared British soldiers were for serious military engagement, successive British governments passed a series of education, health and social insurance reforms to try to catch up with Germany.

But neither coercion nor providing new services to its citizens in the name of the nation were sufficient to secure the internal authority of most European states at the turn of the century. Cecil Rhodes was far from alone in assuming that 'who will avoid civil war must be an imperialist'.[34] In Britain, Gladstone triggered the scramble for Africa by sending the navy to Egypt in the face of a domestic political crisis. The Italian government started looking for colonies in the 1880s, believing that imperial expansion was a matter of life and death for the Italian state. This rush to empire brought immense domestic and external risks for the European states. Italian imperialism turned out to be a catastrophic venture. In 1895, the Crispi government plunged into Eritrea, promising to test the country's nationhood in a confrontation with Abyssinia, only to suffer a quick and humiliating defeat at Adowa the following year. Bismarck was always nervous about the prospect of empire, reckoning it to be both costly and disruptive of the balance of power. By contrast, his successor Bülow saw imperialism, backed by the creation of a navy to challenge British seapower, as the only way to rule otherwise ungovernable subjects. As he explained, 'I am putting the main emphasis on foreign policy. Only a successful foreign policy can help to reconcile, pacify, rally and unite'.[35] Imperialism alone, Bülow believed, could stiffen Prussia's position within the Reich by strengthening the constitutional role of the emperor and re-establishing the old alliance of conservative and bourgeois interests against the left. But despite forays in rapid succession into Samoa, Angola, Mozambique, China and Morocco, Bülow ordered a withdrawal in each case when a crisis threatened.[36] As a domestic reason of state to invigorate the idea of nationhood, imperialism ran into all too predictable contradictions. Imperialism proved expensive, requiring new revenue, which bitterly divided parliaments already worn down by the question of taxation. Externally, competitive imperialism reduced the security of all European states. There were now far more disputes that could be turned into international crises, and the balance of power that Bismarck had striven so hard to maintain perished.

In the wake of the politics imperialism generated, the internal authority of the German, British and Italian states lurched towards crisis. By 1910 the German government had become almost totally dependent on foreign policy to maintain the authority of the Reich. Like his predecessor Bülow, Bethmann Hollweg found it difficult to sustain a reliable majority in the Reichstag. In 1911, facing an imminent general election, he sent a gunboat to Agadir, wanting, it would seem, simply to show German strength. He triggered an international crisis, which for the first time made the British government seriously fear German intentions. A year later the social democrats became the largest party in the Reichstag. The German state had reached a constitutional impasse: the radicalism of the social democrats ruled out a liberal-socialist-catholic coalition, but their strength precluded a stable nationalist, conservative alliance. Even though Bethmann Hollweg was well aware that the kind of foreign policy that could have satisfied the nationalists was not a practicable option in the prevailing external world, he had no other idea of how to govern.[37] When Austria-Hungary took Europe towards crisis in 1914, the German state had enemies willing to fight and was militarily led by reckless and unworldly generals. Together they pushed the German state that had been established in 1871 on to a path to complete destruction.

For all its terrible consequences, in one respect Germany's move for war was fortuitous for the British state. In 1914, it was mired in trouble over the failure of either coercion or the idea of British nationhood to secure its rule in Ireland. In 1910, a minority liberal government became dependent on Irish nationalists in Parliament who demanded a united self-governing Ireland as the price for their support. Until 1911 the prospect of a veto by the House of Lords blocked any possibility of an Irish state. But when to secure its domestic programme the government secured the passage of the Parliament Act limiting the Lords' veto, it created an unwelcome opening to legislate on Ireland. It could now not compromise on Ireland without signing its own death warrant. Protestant Ulster, meanwhile, threatened war if it were made subject to Irish rule. Any possibility that state power could be used to face Ulster down vanished when the Conservative leader, Andrew Bonar Law, professed that he could conceive of no lengths to which Ulster might go in its resistance which he would not support. Facing the threat of full-scale violence, and an opposition party willing to arm and organise militias in the province, the government turned to the army to implement Home Rule. Encouraged by Bonar Law, the army resisted. Only by declaring war against Germany after the invasion of Belgium, and winning Irish nationalist support for it, did the Asquith government inadvertently save the British state from a civil war, produced by the lethal interaction of its territorial problems with representative democracy.

For the Italian modern democratic nation-state, the war threatened total disaster. As a site of authority, it was fundamentally weak. It had not secured a monopoly of legitimate violence or the rule of law at home, and it had failed miserably to exercise power abroad. Consequently, successive governments had lacked the means to construct a plausible idea of Italian nationhood. In the wake of these deficiencies, the south of the country remained resistant to legal and administrative control. Few Italian leaders saw past the renewal of a nationalist foreign policy as they attempted to avert disintegration. After the Bosnian crisis of 1908 sealed Austria-Hungary's intervention in the Balkans, Italy's membership of the Triple Alliance turned sour, and right-wing groups began to dream of naval domination in the Adriatic and eastward expansion. Italy's prime minister, Giolitti, correctly saw that Italy was simply too weak to entertain such fantasies. But by 1911, although privately lamenting that war was a matter solely for soldiers and the king's ministers, he decided to use it to mobilise nationalist passions. In 1911–12, he declared war against Turkey, gaining control of Libya but bemoaned afterwards, 'I did not undertake the conquest of Libya out of enthusiasm–quite the contrary'.[38] But even as a desperate defensive act, the acquisition of the new colony only worsened matters, strengthening the hand of Mussolini and the far right nationalist party against Giolitti.

By 1914 the state was losing control, as right and left violently confronted each other. During a general strike, socialists across the country proclaimed republics, disarming government troops and abolishing taxes. Only after ten days of rebellion did the army and police regain control. When other European states turned to war in August 1914, the Italian state, as Giolitti well understood, was not militarily prepared to join battle. Yet if it had stayed neutral it would have forsaken the opportunity to secure new territories on which its imaginative claim to nationhood appeared to rest. In late 1914 Mussolini took over the *fascisti*, previously southern socialist brigades, and threatened civil war and an anti-monarchist coup if Italy did not enter the war on the side of Britain, Russia and France and redeem its national honour. The vast majority of the Italian parliament wished to remain neutral, but, in the middle of 1915, the king and the prime minister secretly negotiated to take Italy into the war in exchange for territory. Then, aided by Mussolini, they whipped up mob support for the war. Italy, they implied, had to choose: civil war or European war. Leading the Italian state under conditions of representative democracy had, it appeared, become incompatible with prudent judgement about the dangers posed to a state by war.

Conclusions

Nothing in the history of the fledging modern democratic nation-states of the nineteenth century suggested an *a priori* truth that the authority of the modern state was simply incompatible with representative democracy, or that the idea of nationhood could not carry the imaginative burden of securing consent to the state's authority. The move to representative democracy had not increased the ease with which subjects could overthrow that authority. It had only perhaps increased the possibility that those with legal violence at their disposal might falter in defending that authority, in Gaetano Mosca's words, 'paralysed by dread of assuming responsibility for repression involving bloodshed'.[39] Contrary to the fears of those who hated it, representative democracy had not destroyed any basis for obedience.

Certainly the history of American democracy in the nineteenth century suggested that even in the most propitious circumstances, that is to say circumstances in which the break with monarchy was most decisive and where governments could expand the territory of the state without serious external risk, securing consent to the authority of a modern democratic nation-state demanded a huge price. For all the triumphalism that the apparent continuity of the American constitution has generated, the world's first representative democracy in its original incarnation failed. The constitution devised at Philadelphia did not establish a sound basis for a modern republic. It had not clearly conferred sovereignty to decide in moments of dispute where authority between the federal government and the states lay, and the differences in economic interests and understanding between the signatories of the terms of the covenant of 1787 were immense. Since the majority of southerners rejected the notion that they had in accepting the constitution in 1787 become part of one nation called 'the American people' and assumed that their membership of the republic was conditional on their consent,[40] and since the federal government lacked the power to substitute manufacturing production for their plantation-based economies or break that self-understanding, this proved lethal. By 1861, once the eleven southern states had decided that they had permanently lost power in Washington, the territorial union of the United States could only be maintained by force. To maintain that union, the federal president Abraham Lincoln ordered a war that killed 600,000 Americans, crushed parts of the constitution, and, eventually, by military occupation destroyed the southern economy. Afterwards, the federal government moved to rework the constitution, stripping the states of any claim to sovereignty, and to formulate a new idea of nationhood premised on the assumption of a singular American people. In doing so, the federal government turned the defeated rebels into reconstructed Americans, voting for American political parties, producing industrialised American goods and abiding by American laws. Conquered, the southerners became quiescent subjects.[41] Federal institutions could damage the sectional interests of the south, as they did during the 1876 presidential election and the agricultural depression of the 1890s, without permanently risking the state's authority. Never again would any of the states respond to electoral defeat with the threat of secession. Just as importantly, the post-civil-war governments had also in the rhetoric of the 'union' and 'freedom' found a language of nationhood that masked the brutality of what had happened, not least the sacrifice of any belief that the rule of republics had to depend on the free consent of their citizens.

Yet for the European governments, Lincoln's solution to the problem of nationhood would have been an extraordinary move. They all were willing to coerce and repress, but none could have contemplated declaring war on the state's own subjects. They could not have dreamt of successfully keeping out other European powers of a civil war. They almost certainly could not have conscripted an army to fight rebels more territorially dispersed than the southern states. And they could not, against the backdrop of Europe's history and traditions of political self-understanding, have concocted such a disingenuous language to turn a bloody struggle over authority and power into a moral crusade to rewrite the mythological origins of the states they led. For each of them, civil war would have meant the total failure of the state's authority. It could not possibly have been a means to reconstruct it.

Nonetheless, the fledgling European modern democratic nation-states were not doomed to failure. Certainly only one or two of them could possibly have used imperialism effectively because expansion was a competitive exercise. For those that came late to statehood, imperialism was from the start a rather reckless gamble. The Italian state needed external success most desperately but for that reason risked most when its leaders sallied abroad. Bismarck, by contrast, never lost sight of the dangers of foreign adventures. The British Liberal government was in an intrinsically stronger external position and was unfortunate in confronting an aspiring Teutonic rival led by Bismarck's successors and in inheriting a state ill-equipped for a quick show of strength as external conditions deteriorated. But domestically it had unnecessarily trapped

itself over Ireland. The frequently short-lived governments of the
French Third Republic took few risks. The Dreyfuss affair during the
1890s revealed bitter, religiously inspired passions that could not be
tamed by law, but between 1905 and 1907 successive governments separated the Catholic church from the state, strengthening the state's grip
on education. Running schools devoted to advancing the patriotic spirit
and having enforced universal conscription since 1889, French governments advanced the idea of the French nation without recourse to dangerous external gambits.[42]

Yet whatever the counter-factual judgement one might want to make
about how things might have turned out differently, in 1914 these fledgling modern democratic nation-states of Europe were at a point of
crisis. Those who had led some of them had failed either to negate rival
claims to nationhood and sovereignty, or to contain sectional interests
and passions around class. Having failed to find stable practical or imaginative foundations for the state's authority, they were confronting
significant numbers of rebellious subjects. In going to war, they were
risking the territorial existence of their states. The war the European
states fought would be unprecedented in the material and human
damage it would inflict. Ironically, but perhaps not surprisingly, in
August 1914, the European governments discovered just the collectivist
identifications in the name of nationhood that most had so surrepti-
tiously failed to find during the previous few decades, allowing them to
mobilise vast citizen armies. But the fates of those citizen armies would
eventually destroy the internal authority of most of the states that participated in the war.

If this outcome would have surprised eighteenth-century liberals, it
probably would not have done Thucydides, the most penetrating com-
mentator of ancient democracies, who had Pericles say of Athens that it
'hath a great name amongst all peoples . . . for the mighty power it yet
hath after the expense of so many lives'.[43] Thucydides went on to show
just how Athenian democracy was destroyed by the fecklessness of the
demos in first deciding to go to Sicily and then removing from
command the one person who could perhaps have won Athens a victory
there. More than two thousand years later, neither the representatives
of the people, who had to compete for votes of frightened electorates
tempted by glory, nor those monarchs trying to hold on to their fading
power against angry democratic passions, appeared any steadier in their
judgement about the external world, or any more cautious in protecting
the internal authority of the state from extraneous hazard than the
Athenian demos had been. Contrary to many of the hopes vested in it,
the modern democratic nation-state in Europe had proved just as

vulnerable to internal instability and external collapse via international politics as ancient democracy and the Renaissance republic.

Notes

1 F. H. Hinsley, *Sovereignty* (London: C. Watts, 1966).
2 Q. Skinner, *The Foundations of Modern Political Thought, Volumes One and Two* (Cambridge: Cambridge University Press, 1978).
3 Quoted in R. C. Van Caenegem, *An Historical Introduction to Western Constitutional Law* (Cambridge: Cambridge University Press, 1995), p. 87.
4 See A. Osiander, 'International relations and the Westphalian myth', *International Organisation*, 55: 2 (2001), 251–87.
5 See S. Krasner, *Sovereignty: Organised Hypocrisy* (Princeton: Princeton University Press).
6 See R. Braun, 'Taxation, socio-political structure and state building: Great Britain and Brandenburg-Prussia', in C. Tilly (ed.), *The Formation of National States in Western Europe* (Princeton: Princeton University Press); G. Ardant, 'Financial policy and economic infrastructure of modern states and nations', in Tilly (ed.), *Formation of National States*; C. Tilly, *Coercion, Capital and European States, AD 990–1990* (Oxford: Blackwell, 1990); T. R. Gurr, 'War, revolution and the growth of the coercive state', *Comparative Political Studies*, 21: 1 (1988), 45–65.
7 T. Hobbes, *Leviathan* (Cambridge: Cambridge University Press, 1996).
8 T. Hobbes, *On the Citizen*, trans. M. Silverthorne (Cambridge: Cambridge University Press, 1998), p. 143.
9 M. Weber, 'Politics as profession and a vocation', in *Political Writings*, ed. P. Lassman and R. Speirs (Cambridge: Cambridge University Press, 1994).
10 Lord Macaulay, 'Hallam's constitutional history', in *Critical and Historical Essays* (London: Longmans, Green and Co., 1877), p. 70.
11 On the consequences of these changes in political thought see I. Hont, *Jealousy of Trade: International Competition and the Nation-State in Historical Perspective* (Cambridge, MA: the Belknap Press of Harvard University Press, 2005).
12 D. Hume, 'Of public credit', in *Political Essays*, ed. K. Haakonssen (Cambridge: Cambridge University Press, 1994), p. 167.
13 I use this term through the remainder of the book. It is an imperfect one because it is a little convoluted, omits any direct reference to the principle of representation on which this form of rule rests, and runs together a real entity and a fictitious assertion. But more shorthand formulations miss something, and this captures both the crucial fact that representative democracy is a form of government of the modern state, and the centrality of the language of nationhood, however futilely deployed in some states, to justifying the authority of modern states.
14 Some modern ideas about representation came out of the French revolution, but because of the trajectory of the revolution and the subsequent

restoration of the monarchy it is hard to say that they had the same impact as the American revolution in producing the form of government that we now think of as representative democracy. The English constitutional settlement of 1689 did produce a form of government in which representation through elections played a part, but, even allowing for the very restricted franchise, it produced few competitive elections because of the pocket and rotten boroughs.

15 J. Madison, A. Hamilton and J. Jay, *The Federalist and the Letters of Brutus* (Cambridge: Cambridge University Press, 2003), no. 10.

16 Madison, Hamilton and Jay, *The Federalist*, no. 63.

17 E. J. Sieyès, *What is the Third Estate?*, trans. M. Blondel and ed. S. E. Finer (London: Pall Mall Press, 1963), p. 58.

18 Sieyès, *What is the Third Estate?*

19 Quoted in J. Godechot, 'The new concept of nation and its diffusion in Europe', in O. Dann and D. Dinwiddy, *Nationalism in the Age of the French Revolution* (London: Hambledon Press, 1988), p. 17.

20 Ibid.

21 Sieyès, *The Third Estate*, p. 126.

22 See B. Anderson, *Imagined Communities: Reflections on the Origin and Spread of Nationalism*, 2nd edn (London: Verso, 1991); J. Breuilly, *Nationalism and the State*, 2nd edn (Manchester: Manchester University Press, 1993); E. Hobsbawm, *Nations and Nationalism since 1780: Programme, Myth, Reality* (Cambridge: Cambridge University Press, 1992).

23 Perhaps most forcefully, the leaders of nation-states strove to impose a single language. By contrast, the French absolutist monarchs had shown little concern for language when they centralised administration. Seventy years after the revolution a quarter of France's population spoke no French. Only in the late nineteenth century did those who led the French state establish French as the national language. E. Weber, *Peasants into Frenchmen: the Modernisation of Rural France, 1870–1914* (London: Chatto & Windus, 1977).

24 Weber concluded that the universal suffrage was the absolute corollary of conscription in modern politics. 'Suffrage and democracy in Germany', in *Political Writings*, pp. 105–6.

25 See D. McKay and H. M. Scott, *The Rise of the Great Powers 1648–1815* (London: Longman, 1983).

26 Hont, *Jealousy of Trade*, ch. 7.

27 Quoted in T. Blanning, *The Origins of the French Revolutionary Wars* (London: Longman, 1986), p. 137.

28 Ibid., 107.

29 Quoted in Meinecke, *Machiavellism*, p. 415.

30 Quoted in R. Tombs, *France 1814–1914* (London: Longman, 1996), p. 365.

31 Ibid., 370.

32 Quoted in M. Bentley, *Politics without Democracy 1815–1914: Perception and Preoccupation in British Government*, 2nd edn (London: Fontana Press, 1996), p. 267.

33 See D. Mack-Smith, *Italy: a Modern History*, rev. edn (Ann Arbor: University of Michigan Press, 1969); C. Seton-Watson, *Italy from Liberalism to Fascism 1870–1925* (London: Meuthen, 1967).

34 Quoted in N. Stone, *Europe Transformed 1878–1919* (Oxford: Blackwell, 1999), p. 89.

35 Quoted in W. Mommsen, *Imperial Germany, 1867–1918: Politics, Culture and Society in an Authoritarian State*, trans. R. Deveson (London: Arnold, 1995), p. 151.

36 See Mommsen, *Imperial Germany*.

37 See F. Stern, 'Bethmann Hollweg and the war: the bounds of responsibility', in *The Failure of Illiberalism: Essays on the Political Culture of Modern Germany* (New York: Columbia University Press, 1992).

38 Quoted in Seton-Watson, *Italy from Liberalism to Fascism*, p. 382.

39 G. Mosca, *The Ruling Class: Elements of the Science of Politics*, ed. A. Livingston, trans. H. D. Kahn (New York: McGraw Hill, 1939), p. 221.

40 See J. Calhoun, *A Disquisition on Government and Selections from the Discourse on the Constitution* (Indianapolis: Hackett, 1995).

41 See R. F. Bensel, *Yankee Leviathan: the Origins of Central State Authority in America, 1859–1877* (Cambridge: Cambridge University Press, 1990); G. Fletcher, *Our Secret Constitution: How Lincoln Redefined American Democracy* (New York: Oxford University Press, 2001); K. Stampp, *The Era of Reconstruction 1865–1877* (New York: Knopf, 1975).

42 For a comparative discussion of the problems facing the different European states see Stone, *Europe Transformed*.

43 *The Peloponnesian War*, trans T. Hobbes (Chicago: University of Chicago Press, 1989), 2.64.

2

The crises of the inter-war years

Nobody in the summer heat of August 1914 had thought that the First World War was about the future of representative democracy or the nation-state. The Allied powers had not entered the war either to impose democracy on Germany and Austria-Hungary, or to break up their empires. Russia was the most monarchical of all the participant states, and so far as the Allies were concerned with the principle of nation-states, it was to defend the independence of those that were small, like Belgium and Serbia, not to create new ones. But in 1914 the war was a European war. Four years of slaughter later, it was coming to an end on the political terms of the American president. Woodrow Wilson's diagnosis of its causes was simple and misleading. Old-style balance-of-power diplomacy and autocratic, imperial government, Wilson deemed, had led to the catastrophe. Only if Europe was reconstructed on the principles of democracy and national self-determination as the expression of the will of the people could it be saved. In January 1918, Wilson let it be known that he would not negotiate a peace treaty with the imperial German state and that he would insist on 'autonomous development for all peoples of Austria-Hungary'. Once the Bolsheviks had made their peace with Germany at Brest-Litovsk and ceded claims to Poland, the Ukraine, Finland and the Baltic states, Wilson went further: the future of Europe had to be based on independent modern democratic nation-states. Wilson's rhetoric about democracy and self-determination presented as morality what was the result of power, including Wilson's own in dictating the terms of Germany's surrender. However, the capacity of democracies to survive would depend not on Wilson's moral light of 'the people' but, as ever, on external success and maintaining internal authority. The problem for European governments was that they were forced to grapple with these imperatives in massively unpropitious circumstances, for which the United States was partly responsible.

The *realpolitik* conditions confronting all European governments in 1919–20 were dangerous and unpredictable. From the west, the United

States had decisively entered the continent's politics, first in the war and then at Versailles, only to withdraw when the Senate refused to support Wilson's peace project.[1] The legacy of the Americans remained in the successor states to the Austro-Hungarian and Ottoman empires and the triumph of democracy in Germany and could not easily be overturned by any of the European states once the Americans left. But when they did depart, the will to resist among those dissatisfied with the peace could fester incessantly. In the east loomed the Soviet Union. Whilst the Bolshevik state was shorn of the territory of the old Russian empire, in 1919 Lenin and his colleagues did not believe that their revolution could survive unless it spread elsewhere in Europe. By the summer of 1920, Lenin's Red Army was advancing rapidly towards Warsaw, with the states in front of it militarily weak, economically crippled and fighting domestic Bolsheviks. Against all the odds, Poland hung on, and Lenin retreated into isolationism, resting his remaining hopes of exporting the revolution on internal sabotage.

The Soviet defeat left the international politics of Europe centred on the ambiguities of power at the heart of the continent. The German government may have felt humiliated by the terms of the Versailles treaty but in the absence of the United States and the Soviet Union, Germany remained potentially the strongest continental power. It still possessed a larger population than France, a far greater iron and steel capacity, and an intact internal communications network. Moreover, it had surrendered when its armies controlled Europe from Belgium to the Ukraine at the mercy of a power that had subsequently retreated. With the demise of the Russian, Austro-Hungarian and Ottoman empires, its neighbouring states were much weaker than at any time since its creation in 1871. If Germany could shake off the worst shackles of a peace treaty that could not easily be enforced, it would be at least as strong as it had been in 1914. But so long as it did not, the internal pressure on those who led the German state to cut free from Versailles would grow.

Nonetheless, the post-war *realpolitik* conditions were understandable to European governments in the political language of the pre-war world. The new external economic conditions were not. Disputes about protectionism notwithstanding, most European governments had not been accustomed to ponder in details the relationship between the internal authority of the modern state and the international economy. In many ways, they had taken the existence of the international economy for granted. Even though it had been constructed and sustained by power and negotiation, those, like the British, with occasion to direct most energy to it had done so from a position of strength. Now the international economy, on which the external power and internal authority of all the European states had in fact depended, was no more, and there was no accumulated knowledge about dealing with the problems it now bequeathed. Europe's international trade had collapsed: the Central powers had been compelled to depend entirely on their own resources, the Allied powers had lost markets to non-European competitors, and the large Russian market was closed by Bolshevik isolationism. Neither could the Allied European states continue to purchase goods from the United States. Having liquidated many foreign assets to finance the war, they no longer had the revenue to cover imports, once American credit dried up after the armistice. But without some measure of success in reconstructing international trade, many European states faced parts of their populations starving and freezing to death.

Just as devastatingly in its consequences, the war had transformed the European states' financial and monetary relationships with the rest of the world. Prices across the continent were massively higher than prior to the war. Whilst the European states, including Britain, had all accumulated huge debts, the United States had become the world's largest creditor, and was the only potential source of capital. Even after its withdrawal from the peace settlement, this left the United States with considerable capacity to exercise power over the European states. As Wilson had noted in July 1917, 'when the war is over, we can force them to our way of thinking, because by that time they will, among other things, be financially in our hands'.[2] For the former Central powers there was no escape. Either they did what was necessary to secure American credit, or they would have to make huge domestic sacrifices to finance reparations. The Allied powers could only hope to escape *de facto* surveillance of their domestic politics if they procured substantial reparations from Germany, which the United States was unwilling to help in abetting either by direct action or offering Germany credit. In 1919, even before the American Senate had jettisoned the League of Nations treaty, there was no way out of these predicaments. When the United States went back on the gold standard in March 1919, no European state could follow suit. The currency volatility produced by floating exchange rates only made international trade more difficult and further exacerbated the debt relationships between states.

In deploying their own particular practical reasoning in these external conditions, European governments faced a competing range of imperatives.[3] For those who led the successor states to the former imperial empires, the first tasks of the peace were to establish a modern state and construct an idea of nationhood. In some instances, the political circumstances were unpromising even leaving aside the chaotic economic conditions. In Poland in 1919, for example, there were five regions with separate administrations, four languages of command in the army, six currencies, three legal codes and two incompatible railway gauges. The state's eastern borders were insecure, and between 1919 and 1921 the Polish government fought six wars over them.

As for creating nationhood, the successor states confronted difficulties of a kind that had troubled earlier governments rather less. Successful nationhood now depended on convincing disparate groups with identities already formed by the struggles of the nineteenth and early twentieth centuries against the imperial empires that they had a distinct national identity and that they should, accordingly, have their own state. When the 1921 unitary constitution of the Kingdom of the Serbs, Croats and the Slovenes pronounced that 'there is only one nationality for all the subjects of the kingdom', Yugoslav state builders were trying to achieve the same thing as those who led the British, French and German states had deemed necessary in previous centuries. But the more not only those who led existing states but those who aspired to create new ones had resorted to nation-building, the more difficult nationhood became for everybody because it could provide the language of resistance to authority as well as obedience. Versailles accentuated the problem for the successor states. It left towards 60 million people as subjects of states where they were national minorities. It also stripped Germany and the successor states of full autonomy in dealing with these groups by imposing treaty commitments on education, language and administration.[4] If they failed to honour these obligations, the League of Nations had the authority to act. Many of these minority subjects were Germans who loathed what they regarded as inferior foreign regimes. If in practice the League of Nations could only act through Britain and France, the same logic left those states closest to Germany in a precarious position once it began to recover.

Where a modern state already existed, or at least was tenuously holding on to its life, the first reason of state was literally a will to act against those who sought to seize power by illegal means. The internal pressure on states across Europe meant governments had to think about the circumstances in which they might have to suspend normal parliamentary procedures to defend democracy against its enemies. Even more pressingly, reason of state dictated that they recognise when it was necessary to use force against the revolutionary left and right. Where the military's support for democracy was at best tepid, this was undeniably difficult. But in practice many elected politicians were unwilling to face what the situation required, mistakenly presuming that democracy could be maintained without a successful claim to a monopoly of legitimate violence.

Beyond direct coercion, European governments had to find a means to contain the tumultuous passions generated by the war. These passions had produced intense, irreconcilable political beliefs of the kind that Hobbes had explained were almost always the root cause of political disorder. Before the First World War, collectivist identifications around nationhood had been most easily conjured by a bellicose foreign policy. Now the inherent dangers of such nationalist adventures had multiplied. Any unilateral effort to reverse the Versailles territorial settlements risked unravelling the whole peace, and any attempt without American support to squeeze more from Germany than it was in the final instance willing to bear was likely to prove self-destructive. But for governments to concentrate on internal action was no less difficult. The war had exposed the hollow transparency of many of the pre-war languages of nationhood. The disappointment that national unity had fractured, the conduct of the war by the respective high commands, and the tedium of peacetime collective life for many veterans could not be readily massaged away with new imaginative fictions.

Perhaps the bitterest passions burnt around the relationship of the war to class. The Russian revolution had already demonstrated just how dangerous to any state's authority these passions could be at a moment of external humiliation. Peasants who had been dragged into a war with states that they sometimes did not know existed, industrial workers unable reliably to feed and heat themselves, and German soldiers who could not understand how their astonishing military effort had translated into defeat had little reason to accept the call for more sacrifice from those who had been most sheltered from both the slaughter and harshness of military production. Yet no European government in 1919 could avoid throwing more oil on to the flames of class passions. However hazardous in the circumstances to the internal authority of the state, politicians needed partisan passions to compete for power, and the more divisive those passions already were, the more incentive politicians had to turn them against the perceived class enemy. In office, they were forced to decide whose interests could be sacrificed to exchange-rate considerations and which citizens would bear the brunt of paying for war debts sometimes owed to other citizens.

The most obvious way for governments to try to contain the passions generated by the war and fend off their electoral competitors was to provide economic services of the kind first envisaged by Bismarck. In some ways, despite the prevailing chaotic economic conditions, they had opportunities on this score unknown to their pre-war predecessors. The old states that had fought the war had amassed extensive economic controls. Once the European governments unpegged exchange rates and eschewed a return to gold convertibility in 1919, they had the power to determine the value of internal money. By printing money they could sustain short-term employment and through the ensuing inflation obliterate the value of their domestic debts.

Nonetheless these opportunities were accompanied by some harsh constraints. Trade union membership had rapidly expanded during the war and governments across Europe had made significant concessions to obtain the unions' support. Once the war was over, many trade unions turned to strikes to improve wages and, on occasion, for revolutionary purposes. With the male industrial working class fully enfranchised, governments struggled to preside over any cuts in nominal wages. By 1920–21, it was clear that wages were, to use Keynes's term, 'sticky'.[5] The conditions that had underpinned some measure of wage flexibility in the nineteenth century were gone. Wages were a palpably political question and any government that tried to impose wage deflation risked the state's authority.

As the war had strengthened the position of labour, so its aftermath transformed the conditions in which the holders of capital made decisions. The immediate post-war years made very clear, as the nineteenth century had not done at least in the most prosperous states, that investment and the ability of the state to retain the external value of money were dependent on confidence. From capital's perspective, the tacit assumptions of the pre-war economy had been destroyed, first by inflation and then by the political fears generated by full-franchise democracy and the Bolshevik revolution. Inflation had killed any possibility of reasonable long-term expectation. Democratic politics sustained a fear that this nightmare would continue indefinitely. The holders of capital in the most prosperous and powerful European states began to consider risks they had not hitherto had cause to entertain.[6] All European governments were now obliged to think quite self-consciously, as a matter pertaining to the future of their states, about the impact of their domestic and external policy choices on the confidence of investors and those holding money in their own currency.

1919–1923: the failures of reconstruction

If for each of the combatant states, the most immediate problems were how to sustain their populations physically and how to convert the wartime mobilisation into peacetime labour, the most obvious answer was to try to reconstruct at least some parts of the international monetary and trading infrastructure that had previously sustained European economic life. More particularly, every government had the incentive to

stabilise their currency and encourage trade where beneficial. But the
European states found co-operation exceedingly difficult. Between 1920
and 1922, the European governments sought a collective international
monetary and financial settlement, which would have included the
United States, but to no avail. The United States would not attend any
conference at which Allied war debts were on the agenda, whilst France
would not attend one to discuss the reparations issue. The British and
French governments were desperate to stabilise their respective currencies at their pre-war parities but both wished other states to accept the
frequently massive depreciation inflicted by the foreign exchange
markets. In 1922, the Lloyd George government wanted to open up the
Soviet Union economically and invited it to the Genoa conference, only
to find that Germany had signed a separate treaty with the Bolsheviks at
Rapallo. In the wake of these failures, most governments, especially the
French, resorted to new tariffs.

Unable to facilitate opportunities in the external economic world,
European governments were thrown back on their domestic political
skill. Unsurprisingly, those who found this most difficult were those who
confronted electorates angry at the terms of the peace. Some found it
impossible. Hungary's fledgling democracy collapsed in the spring of
1919 when its government was unable to defend its provisional borders
with Romania. In the ensuing crisis, the communist Béla Kun seized
power and proclaimed a Soviet republic. When the Allied powers block-
aded Hungary, Romania invaded and deposed Kun, leaving Admiral
Horthy, the commander of the Hungarian army, to assume power and
establish an authoritarian military regime that survived until 1944.[7]

The most spectacular casualty of the immediate post-war crisis was
Italian democracy. Before the war, the Italian modern state was ineffec-
tive, not least because it provided so little internal security over much of
its territory. Meanwhile efforts to create a durable sense of Italian nationhood had been largely unsuccessful. The Catholic church still refused
to accept the state's authority, so far as the south had been pacified it was
by *de facto* military occupation, and the Italian state could not sustain
imperialism. Now, in 1919, those who wielded power confronted a desperate peasantry and a particularly precarious economic position. By
1919, the Italian government could only feed its population by directly
buying and subsidising goods from abroad, whilst tax revenue covered
very little of government expenditure. Nonetheless, in *realpolitik* terms,
the Italian state had on balance gained from the war. Certainly, the terms
of the American entry into the war left it unable to claim all that it had
been promised by Britain and France. But Versailles left the Italian state
without any international obligations to its German and Slav minorities,

and the state's long-standing enemy on its northern frontier was dismantled. Where there had once been an empire with 51 million subjects, there was now Yugoslavia and an Austrian state of 6 million subjects, a circumscribed army and a three-boat navy.

Prudence would have directed post-war Italian governments to prioritise exploiting these favourable circumstances to combat the state's economic weakness. But like their pre-war predecessors, they struggled to avoid the temptation of using foreign policy as an instrument of nation-building and partisan advantage. The first post-war government, headed by Emanuele Orlando, quickly averted its gaze from the crippling economic constraints under which it operated. At Paris, Orlando's government chose to push a fiercely expansionist agenda, insisting on territory that could not be justified on grounds of national self-determination and which Wilson was resolved to give to Yugoslavia, without any accompanying strategy to ameliorate Italy's material dependence on the states that were dominating the peace conference. Orlando's understanding of the reason of state at stake was simple: 'I persist in believing that the most immediate danger . . . capable of overturning Italy would be constituted by a profound patriotic disillusionment'.[8] In order to try to preserve the credibility of the Italian state against charges of servitude, Orlando wanted his government to act like a great power. But by so alienating Italy's former allies, Orlando risked bankrupting the state and mass starvation. In April 1919, Orlando left Paris after President Wilson published a direct manifesto to the Italian people appealing for moderation. The other governments made no attempt to bring Orlando back and altered some of the reparation agreements to Italy's detriment. Finally, Orlando returned and signed the Versailles agreement. Accused of presiding over a national humiliation, his government fell.

In June 1919, Franceso Saveri Nitti succeeded Orlando. Nitti immediately resolved that Italy's foreign policy would be determined by its material dependence on the United States and Britain and not irredentism. But he was at the mercy of events. In September 1919, as the peace conference continued to discuss the Italian-Yugoslav border, the poet Gabriele d'Annunzio and a band of Italian nationalists seized the Adriatic port of Fiume. When Nitti was first told of the coup, he responded: 'we are on the eve of starvation; these events will only hasten it'.[9] Facing a crisis, Nitti found that he could not command the state's military force. The army and navy were unwilling to act against d'Annunzio and some officers deserted and crossed over to Fiume. Nitti played for time, hoping that the Allies would understand his government's impotence and make concessions. None was forthcoming, and Nitti lost power to Giovanni Giolitti.

Towards the end of 1920, the new government finally signed a peace treaty with Yugoslavia and deployed force in Fiume. By this time, the internal authority of the Italian state was in tatters. In the big cities trade unions had set up workers' Soviets in factories, in the countryside peasants had seized land, and everywhere anti-communist war veterans, including Mussolini's fascists, often aided and abetted by local police, had formed armed bands. Successive Italian governments had stood by, seemingly not understanding that in such circumstances the authority of the state depended upon direct action. This was illustrated perfectly when Giolitti forcibly pulled back one of his ministers who protested when a fascist representative drew his revolver in the parliament, rebuking him not to take sides in the developing civil war.[10]

By the summer of 1922, Italian democracy was standing on the precipice, unable to take advantage of external stability or a moderate economic recovery. Giolitti had offered Mussolini an electoral alliance, and those who remained committed to democracy appeared to lack any will to power, leaving the state without a government for several weeks while gang warfare raged across the north of the country. When, in August 1922, the trade unions called a general strike, Mussolini gave the state forty-eight hours 'to show proof of its authority', or otherwise the fascists would 'assume full freedom of action and take the place of the state'.[11] Mussolini acted as he had threatened, breaking not only the strike but also the stranglehold of the left in several cities and towns. Two months later, the king invited Mussolini to form a government and signed the death warrant of post-war Italian democracy.[12]

By contrast, German democracy ultimately survived the immediate post-war crisis. In many ways, those who led the Weimar republic began in even less propitious circumstances. Coming to power in the wake of external surrender, domestic mutiny and attempted revolution, the new German government was forced to fight what Tocqueville had deemed the impossible, both the revolutionary and the patriotic spirit, whilst facing a serious threat of secession from Bavaria. Externally, the terms of Versailles condemned the German state to live under severe constraints and tested the army's support for the new republic. In several respects, the German state now lacked external sovereignty. It had to share authority with the Allied powers over the Saar, and the Rhineland was demilitarised and occupied by the allies for five years. Germany's army was reduced to a volunteer force of 100,000 men, its navy restricted, and its general staff dissolved. It was stripped of all its colonies and compelled to grant duty-free entry to goods from Alsace Lorraine and Most-Favoured-Nation status to France for five years. Given the continuing blockade of the state between the armistice and the signing of

Versailles, the German government could not feed its population without deliveries from the Allied powers. Neither could it secure credit abroad until it had formally satisfied the same powers that it was a secure democracy. And, most lethally, Versailles committed the German government to a yet unspecified reparations bill, and its export-earning capacity, on which its ability to meet such obligations depended, was limited by the treaty. If the German government were indeed to pay the bill, it could only weaken internal support for the Weimar state.

Many citizens considered the new German state illegitimate. For the communist left, the Weimar republic was a botched revolution. For the authoritarian right, including some in the upper command of the army, democracy was simply the price of humiliating external defeat. Throughout 1919–20 revolutionary and counter-revolutionary activity threatened civil war, as both left and right mounted putsches in towns and cities across the country. In the summer of 1920, as Lenin's red army marched westwards with the Communists already holding Saxony, the German state stood on the brink, only in a nice irony of history to be saved by the Polish cavalry.

In these circumstances, the first reasons of state for the social democrat-dominated post-war government was to retain the support of the army and control and disarm those engaged in revolutionary and counter-revolutionary activity. But these two tasks could not be easily reconciled. Disbarred from setting up a conscript army, the government was forced to allow the army's leaders to organise themselves on their own terms. Consequently, when, in January 1919, they mobilised groups of volunteers into a Free Corps to help put down a left-wing uprising in Berlin, the government did not resist. The surrender of the state's claim to a monopoly of legitimate violence created a terrible hostage to fortune. Thirteen months later, Wolfgang Kapp, a prominent member of the nationalist People's Party, and General Luttwitz organised a march of Free Corps' units on the seat of government in Berlin. When the army announced that it was unwilling to fight the Free Corps, the rebels seized power and dissolved the constitution. The government fled to Stuttgart and was only rescued by a general strike. After it was reinstated, it failed to bring any of those responsible for the coup to trial.

Economically, the German government had virtually no room for manoeuvre. Unlike the Allied states, most of its war debt had been borrowed from domestic markets. Once the war was over, the government rapidly monetised much of that debt, and then borrowed more to finance reconstruction, producing inflation. Meanwhile, it faced the most powerful trade union movement in Europe. In 1916, the unions had given their support to the Hindenberg programme to achieve the total mobilisation of the German economy for war on the condition that they could exercise some control over employment. Two years later, the union leader, Carl Liegen, concluded an agreement with the influential industrialist Hugo Stinnes to introduce an eight-hour day and preclude unofficial company unions.[13] In its immediate aftermath, the trade unions secured substantial wage increases, exacerbating inflation further. With internal prices spiralling, the need for new credit unabated, and the trade unions able to resist any cut in nominal wages, no German government in 1919–20 could seriously contemplate any kind of deflationary policy to balance the budget or stabilise the exchange value of the mark. Instead the social democrats concentrated on supplying cheap food to the urban population and securing rapid industrial growth on terms that protected the recent gains of the industrial working class. To both ends, it encouraged corporatist collaboration between employers and trade unions of the kind symbolised by the Stinnes-Legien pact.

By the middle of 1920, after elections to the Reichstag in which the total vote for the constitutional parties was less than 50 per cent, the fate of the Weimar republic stood in the balance. With the revolutionary left less potent than in the immediate aftermath of the war and unemployment very low, the social democrats had become dispensable and left the government. Weimar's future now depended on a confrontation between the state and the anti-democratic right with its 'patriotic spirit' for which those who led the state already appeared to lack the will. The social democrats' economic policy, and especially its inflationary repercussions, had done little to alleviate a sense of injustice among many in the middle classes about the social and material consequences of the war. For their part, many within the agricultural classes felt bitter that they were coerced into cheap production at a time when industrial profits were rising. With Prussia still controlling much of the country's raw materials and industrial resources, secessionist pressure from agricultural Bavaria persisted. And, adulterating all other resentments, there remained the fury created by the terms of Versailles. Once, in April 1921, the Supreme Allied Council finally fixed Germany's reparation bill and demanded a first cash payment for that summer, the viability of the Weimar state was stretched to the limit. Although the German government was allowed to seek a loan from abroad, it still did not have the foreign currency to make a payment without drastic deflation for which it could not hope to secure political acquiescence. In desperation, it simply sold paper marks in the open market. Unsurprisingly, investors took fright and the external value of the mark collapsed. The Allied powers responded by insisting that the Reichstag make the Reichsbank, the central bank, independent of the government. But it made no difference. The Reichsbank was no less determined than the government to print money.

Still retaining *de facto* control over monetary policy and with the American and British governments unwilling to intervene militarily, the German government, whatever its initial intentions, had found in rapid currency depreciation a way to change its external circumstances. It could do so though only at the risk of precipitating a final collapse of its internal authority. In January 1923, the French government took matters into its own hands and occupied the Ruhr to try to grab resources directly. In response, the German government marshalled a campaign of passive resistance in the Ruhr, ending all production. To sustain the Ruhr workers, the government printed massive quantities of money, precipitating hyperinflation, the total collapse of the mark and a swift increase in unemployment. An economic crisis on this scale left the state vulnerable to attack from all sides, and both left- and right-wing groups attempted coups. However, the prospect of the Weimar state collapsing concentrated minds in Washington and London. If, they concluded, Weimar could only be saved by the export of American capital and a substantial reduction in reparations, then the consequences for the French state had to be secondary. Gustav Stresemann, the leader of the People's Party, saw in this judgement the opportunity to recast the Weimar state on a surer external footing. In August 1923, after the resignation of the previous chancellor, he formed a new cabinet that reintroduced the social democrats into the governing coalition. Immediately, he terminated passive resistance in the Ruhr and secured an Enabling Act that allowed him to govern for a short period by decree. Without having to worry about maintaining a parliamentary majority, his government introduced a new currency and balanced the budget. His external reward was the prospect of American credit and the renegotiation of reparations. The internal price, as the nationalists fumed about the betrayal of the Ruhr to 'foreign interests', was a shift to the right. In November 1923, the social democrats left the government and Stresemann gave way as chancellor to Wilhelm Marx of the Centre Party, and took over as foreign minister. One month later, Marx's new government suspended the eight-hour working day. Now the question for those who led Weimar was how far expanding material prosperity could compensate for external dependency. If it could, then they could perhaps dim some of the 'patriotic spirit' that hung over German democracy.[14]

The gold standard and American capital

The Ruhr crisis pushed Europe towards another abyss. If the Weimar state bound in by Versailles failed, then so would the peace. The Dawes plan of 1924, which set out a new schedule for reparations and allowed Germany to secure a foreign loan, and the Locarno treaty of 1925, by which Britain and Italy guaranteed the Franco-German border, were an attempt by the American and British governments to secure the European peace on the basis of a more moderate policy towards Germany and a more open international economy. In their wake, as American credit began to flood into Europe, governments across the continent managed to stabilise currencies, restore some form of gold convertibility, and therefore establish very different international economic conditions than they had lived with for the first five years of the post-war era.

For all the opportunity it presented, the renewed gold standard came at a considerable external and internal price, especially for those already restricted by Versailles. All the central and eastern European states received loans endorsed by the League of Nations on the condition that they permanently balanced their budgets and established an independent central bank. Germany faced particularly stringent conditions. The Allied powers appointed a trusteeship to oversee German payments and finances and placed the German railway under international control to privatise it. Even more drastically, the Dawes plan effectively stripped the Reichsbank of its monetary autonomy. A new Reichsbank law, passed in August 1924, created a general council consisting of seven German and seven foreign members to choose its executive. It further stipulated that 40 per cent of the note issue be covered by gold and foreign exchange reserves, and it forbade the central bank from ever financing government budget deficits. Interpretation of the law was subject to international control through the executive council of the Bank of International Settlement in Basle. Under these terms, German monetary policy could never be used for inflationary purposes to wreck reparation payments.

Under the revived gold standard all states found themselves with less domestic economic room for manoeuvre. The gold standard made currencies once again convertible into gold at a fixed price and removed most restrictions on the flow of capital and gold. With most currencies once more pegged against gold, it created a new fixed exchange rate system in which balance-of-payments deficits and surpluses were settled by gold movements between states. At the centre of the new gold standard lay the United States, which, in 1926, possessed around 45 per cent of the monetary gold in the world.[15] Gold ruled out the kind of discretionary macro-economic policies that most governments had pursued after 1918 because monetary and fiscal policy now had to be directed to maintaining confidence in a state's gold parity. It meant that elected politicians lost some of the autonomy and power which they had previously enjoyed, leaving them reliant on central bankers who did not necessarily share their concerns about high growth and employment. Most troublesomely, they had to adjust to the anti-inflationary monetary policy pursued by the American Federal Reserve Board at the same time as the American government heavily discriminated against imports. For the gold standard to work several things were necessary, all of which had a deflationary bias. Governments had to keep their economies sufficiently open for gold to move without restriction, to make the balance of payments a higher priority than domestic production, to encourage the internal adjustment of domestic prices and wages to the exchange rate, and to maintain a balanced budget. And their commitment to these things had to be credible to investors. In the pre-war world, governments had largely taken credibility for granted. In the political conditions of the 1920s, they could not.[16] Whilst there had been plenty of financial crises in the pre-war gold standard, they had not generally been induced by political fears. Now, liquid asset-holders reacted quickly against any sign of political instability or any discussion of policies deemed redistributive or inflationary. Governments of the centre-left, those not expected to survive long in office, those that controlled monetary policy themselves, and those that faced high levels of industrial action were particularly vulnerable to capital flight. Once capital had taken fright, governments could only prove their 'sound' credentials by reversing ever more of their policies.[17]

Between the move to international economic stability in 1924 and the renewed economic crisis of 1929, five democracies – the Albanian, Lithuanian, Polish, Portuguese and Yugoslav – collapsed. By the middle of the 1920s, the Polish government had succeeded in creating the apparatus of a modern state, including an effective administrative and legal system. Nonetheless, parliamentary politics took place against a persistent backdrop of violence, leaving the army sceptical about the capacity of elected representatives to rule effectively. After several years of hyperinflation, the Polish government took its opportunity in 1924 to reconstruct the domestic economy, stabilising the exchange rate and issuing a new currency. Two years later, it had balanced its budget and secured itself international credit. Paradoxically, however, Europe's general revival after 1924 left the Polish government more externally exposed. International trade did not flourish because Poland's largely agricultural producers were unable to find new export markets to replace the Russian market. More fatally, the states that had signed the Locarno treaty had pointedly failed to guarantee Poland's frontiers with Germany. In May 1926, Marshall Jozef Pildsuki, the former head of the army, seized power in a coup, dismayed at the implications of the treaty and what he saw as the corruption and incompetence of the elected politicians.[18]

In Yugoslavia, officially until 1929 the Kingdom of the Serbs, Croats and Slovenes, politicians were less successful in creating even the rudiments of a modern state and confronted an enormously difficult task in trying to fashion any sense of nationhood. Again, the particular terms of the reconstruction of Europe in 1924–25 gave the Yugoslav government little freedom of action. Although it did succeed in stabilising its currency in 1926, its inability to settle Serbia's war debt to Britain and France meant that it had to do so without the kind of loan from the League of Nations that most central and eastern European states enjoyed. The cost was particularly severe deflation, and a persistent budget deficit that made commercial borrowing difficult. Meanwhile, from 1927, Mussolini turned his attention towards eastwards expansion, signing alliances with Albania and Bulgaria, pointedly directed against Yugoslavia. As its external security deteriorated, so Yugoslavia's internal nationalist tensions, particularly between Serbs and Croats, intensified. The Serbs saw Italian penetration of the Balkans as a direct threat to Yugoslavia's existence, but the Croats partly welcomed it as an opportunity to push for greater autonomy from Belgrade. Both turned increasingly violent. In June 1928 a Serb parliamentary representative killed the leader of the largest Croat party. From his deathbed, the Croat denounced the constitution and threatened that Croatia and Bosnia would withhold further payments on the state's international debts. In January 1929, the king suspended the constitution and disbanded parliament, proclaiming that 'blind political passions have started to abuse parliamentary democracy . . . to such a degree that it has obstructed all future endeavour in this state'.[19]

By contrast, French governments were able to reconstruct their domestic economy on the back of the new international settlement without too many external worries. After the Ruhr crisis, they had been forced to accept that their dependence on international capital markets meant that they could not pursue an independent foreign policy. But as Germany posed no direct security threat, French governments could concentrate on enhancing material prosperity and developing a welfare state. Given the hopes of earlier French governments, Poincaré's successful stabilisation of the franc well below the pre-war parity might have seemed another defeat, but in the circumstances it gave French producers a considerable competitive advantage, especially compared to their British counterparts. As a result, France's industrial production grew rapidly. The government had little difficulty maintaining budget surpluses, allowing it to finance a national system of employment insurance.[20]

Less decisively in their political outcomes, the British and German governments laboured with some difficulty under their respective external constraints. The British modern democratic nation-state, now rid of its troublesome territorial problem by Ireland's secession in 1921, was probably the most secure of any in Europe. But of all the industrial economies, the British benefited least from the general growth of the 1920s and suffered most from the deflationary bias imposed by the gold standard. In 1925, the then Conservative government had returned sterling to gold at the pre-war parity of $4.86 without restoring the relationship between British and American prices. This presented considerable difficulties for producers in those sectors that were exposed to international competition, especially where, as in the coal industry, exporters were already struggling to retain their old markets. Consequently, the parity lacked any hard-core credibility. To stave off speculative pressure, the Bank of England had to maintain a tight monetary policy, which, after the austerity in the first half of decade required to steer sterling back to $4.86, strangled growth and kept unemployment persistently high. First Conservative and then Labour ministers became increasingly frustrated with the Bank, protesting that it was insufficiently sensitive to political considerations. Yet the Bank's policy simply reflected the reality of economic power under the reconstructed gold standard: the British state was now monetarily subordinate to the American Federal Reserve Board. Meanwhile, many industrial producers reacted to the problems of competitiveness by trying to cut wages, provoking fierce resistance from the trade unions. In 1926, the National Union of Mineworkers asked the Trade Union Congress (TUC) to support its industrial action against wage cuts with a general strike. For nine days, the unions brought all major industries to a halt. Although the government won the confrontation with the TUC, by using the army to maintain food supplies, and the miners subsequently returned to work on lower wages, the Conservative government refused to contemplate any kind of systematic wage policy to put some solid domestic ground under its commitment to the sterling parity. Instead, from 1929 to 1931 it, and its Labour successor, chose to drift, but in the absence of the kind of radical opposition groups present in other European states, they ran fewer risks than others did in doing so.

The international settlement of the middle of the decade certainly gave the German state the opportunity glimpsed by Stresemann. In February 1924, the German president revoked the state of emergency and the Bavarian state government abandoned its claims to independence. By the end of the year, the German government had balanced its budget and returned to the gold standard. Once reintegrated into the European economy, German agriculture flourished. Between 1924 and 1929, the German economy received over 50 per cent of the gross flow of investment into Europe. Whilst the Reichsbank was forbidden to finance budget deficits, many private investors were prepared to do just that, allowing the government to expand the welfare state. By 1929, the German state, once more, provided the most generous welfare provision in the world at the same time as wages were rising. For all its additional demands, the 1924–25 settlement also re-secured a measure of external sovereignty for the German state. By the end of 1926, France had evacuated its troops from the Ruhr, Germany had joined the League of Nations, and the Allies had lifted the restrictions imposed at Versailles on German commercial policy. The settlement also offered the hope that domestic economic and political success would eventually yield long-term American investment of a kind that would give American presidents a very direct material interest in German prosperity, and persuade the Allies further to reduce reparations.

Yet although electoral support for anti-democratic parties, including the Nazis, unsurprisingly fell away between 1924 and 1929, various shadows still lurked around the Weimar republic. Despite undoubted material prosperity relative to the first part of the decade, the German economy did not grow as quickly as the French. Most significantly, it was plagued during these years by high structural unemployment. This increasingly put Germany's welfare state, which included generous unemployment insurance, under strain. When a new social democrat-dominated coalition took office in June 1928 under the chancellorship of Hermann Müller, the government's overall budget and the insurance fund were both in deficit and unemployment was rising. Even before the American stock-market crash of October 1929, American investors had placed a handbrake on the flow of capital into Germany. Müller's government was left to finance the respective deficits domestically when virtually all savings had been wiped out earlier in the decade by hyperinflation. At the same time, the capital flight of early 1929 reopened the question of just how much Germany could pay in reparations without external assistance. The Young plan, negotiated between the Allied powers and Germany, reduced immediate payments and withdrew some of the international controls over the railways and the Reichsbank, temporarily saving Müller's government. But clearly if the economy were indeed heading towards a full-scale crisis, 'the patriotic spirit' that had bedevilled German governments between 1918 and 1923 would resurface, putting the future of the Weimar state at risk again.[21]

The international economic crash and the rise of Nazi Germany

The reconstruction of the terms of the European peace and the international economy in 1924–25 had given European governments certain kinds of opportunities, albeit more difficult to take advantage of in some instances than others, underwritten by American credit and a measure of diplomatic goodwill. The American stock-market crash in October 1929 transformed that whole external environment in which Europe's democracies had been precariously constructed. Immediately, all existing American loans to Europe were suspended. After 1930 no new credit from anywhere was available. Once much of the world economy slumped into depression, governments found it difficult to maintain the gold standard. First in Latin America and then in Europe, they withdrew their currencies, until by 1933 only France, Italy, Belgium, the Netherlands, Switzerland, Poland and Romania retained gold parities, and by the end of the decade, even these states had given up on gold. Most states, when they left the gold standard, proceeded to impose some form of capital and exchange controls. All adopted tariffs, and most international trade collapsed. What remained were competing currency and trade blocs, which gave considerable political power to the dominant state within each.[22]

In a depression, which saw unemployment rising inexorably across the continent, European governments faced immense problems in trying to maintain democratic states. Falling living standards exacerbated the political tensions that were already apparent in the 1920s, and gave hope to those who were determined to destroy democracy and replace it with one form or another of an authoritarian state. Even when democracy survived, elected governments assumed emergency powers to govern by decree. In Germany in 1933, Austria in 1934 and Romania in 1937, democracy fell from within, to its authoritarian enemies.

The failure of the German state was, of course, the most consequential. Internal support for the Weimar state depended above all on some revision to Versailles and a measure of economic prosperity from which all classes could accrue some benefit. Externally, this required new capital, access to trade markets and a willingness of the Allies to negotiate. The economic crisis killed the first and the second almost immediately. Agricultural markets and prices, on which one-third of the working population depended, collapsed. Germany's conspicuous borrowing in the boom years made investors particularly unwilling to extend new credit. And France, by virtue of its gold reserves the one European government that could have helped, would only do so on terms too humiliating for any German minister to accept. As the Reichsbank could neither print nor lend the government money, the German state could not take credit-creation into its own hands. But since the demand for unemployment relief was accelerating rapidly and support for the Nazis was rising, neither could the government easily cut public expenditure.

In March 1930, Müller's government fell when the social democrats found it impossible to reach an agreement with their coalition partners over unemployment insurance, and the president, Paul von Hindenburg, refused Müller emergency powers. Hindenburg then gave the powers he had denied Müller to the more conservative Heinrich Brüning, who formed a government without a parliamentary majority. From the beginning, Brüning had an acute sense of the external constraints under which the German state had to operate. Making full use of his authority to issue decrees, Brüning prioritised deflation and reparations, believing that the first was the best means to secure the second, and substantially cut expenditure. But Brüning's political position remained precarious as unemployment continued to rise. In June 1930, after the Reichstag voted to abrogate his emergency powers, Brüning called new elections two years before they were required, and lost a substantial number of seats to the Nazis.

In the middle of 1931, the collapse of the largest Austrian bank precipitated a full-scale banking crisis. With the banks starved of credit, the Reichsbank haemorrhaging gold, and the Reichsmark under massive downward pressure, Brüning's government abandoned the gold parity and introduced exchange controls. By the end of the year, industrial production had halved since 1929 and unemployment had reached 6 million. Brüning issued more and more authoritarian decrees, culminating in December 1931 in an edict that reduced all existing collective wage agreements to their 1927 level and reduced many prices. Since such radical deflation angered his own constituency of industrialists and large landowners, Brüning could only survive if it yielded a quick reward on reparations.

When none was forthcoming, Brüning resigned in May 1932, having terminally lost the confidence of Hindenburg, only for the Allied powers to agree two months later to end reparations. Brüning's successor, Franz von Papen, backed by a group of conservatives imbued with anti-democratic sentiments, turned towards macro-economic expansionism to try to resurrect growth and reduce unemployment. His economic programme enjoyed a measure of success. But, fatally, he was far less concerned than Brüning had been to defend what remained of the authority of the Weimar state, using an emergency decree to remove the social democrat Prussian state government, courting the Nazis in the Reichstag and rescinding Brüning's action against their armed bands. Ironically, he pushed the republic to the brink just at the moment when unemployment was starting to fall and Hitler was losing support. In the election of November 1932, the Nazis' share of the vote and number of seats fell sharply, and Hindenburg replaced von Papen with General Kurt von Schleicher. But Von Papen was desperate to return to power and believed that the Nazis, still the largest party in the Reichstag, were his opportunity. In January 1933, under the illusion he was using the Nazis for his own ends, he persuaded Hindenburg to accept a new government headed by Hitler. The Weimar state was dead because nobody with authority had the will to defend it even as external and internal other circumstances were turning in its favour.[23]

The Swedish modern democratic nation-state was probably the most successful in the 1930s. In many ways Swedish governments from the late 1920s faced just the same internal and external problems as other European states. Although production levels survived relatively unscathed in 1929 and 1930, once the international economy collapsed in 1931, Sweden's export-oriented economy was precipitated into depression too. Once it was unable to sustain material prosperity, the Swedish state, like others, risked an anti-democratic rebellion. But in one important respect those who led the Swedish state had a crucial advantage in dealing with the crisis: its geographical position and neutrality in European affairs since 1814 meant that they could reasonably hope to remain detached in any renewed confrontation between Germany and the Allied powers. Although Swedish governments in the 1920s had placed some hope in the League of Nations, their successors increasingly disengaged from the League and from 1936 reiterated Sweden's neutrality, and therefore avoided the need to direct substantial amounts of financial and productive resources to rearmament.

But beyond the question of security, the Swedish governments in the 1930s succeeded because they developed a coherent strategy to govern effectively in the face of the international economic crisis. The social democratic government that came to power in 1932 saw that the collapse of the gold standard offered an opportunity for states to realise some domestic autonomy in both macro-economic policy and the organisation of production. If credibility in international capital and foreign exchange markets was unnecessary, and if producers were not seriously competing with others for markets, then non-orthodox domestic economic policies became plausible. Between 1919 and 1923, the price of such discretion had ultimately been prohibitive, but the extreme deflationary pressure after 1929 mitigated any serious inflationary or exchange-rate risk. To this end, the social democratic government began by securing an alliance with the Agrarian party. Reversing long-standing hostility towards agricultural producers, it accepted the party's demand for government regulation of domestic prices and tariffs on foodstuffs. In return, the Agrarian party provided the parliamentary support necessary to secure an expansionary monetary and fiscal policy, including counter-cyclical borrowing, to try to resurrect growth and employment. How far the social democrats' policies were actually responsible for the recovery of the Swedish economy is open to some serious doubt, but the strategy indisputably succeeded in retaining the loyalty of the vast majority of Swedish subjects to representative democracy.[24]

The success of Swedish democracy, however, mattered far less than the failure of German. The rise of the Nazis soon transformed the international politics of Europe and with it external conditions for democracies across the continent, not least in Spain. At the beginning of the 1930s, the future of the Spanish state appeared to depend almost entirely on its internal politics. Having remained neutral during the First World War, it was exempt from the complicated territorial politics of post-war Europe. The Spanish economy, meanwhile, was relatively isolated from international trade and capital flows and Spain's military dictator, General Primo de Rivera, had never restored the Spanish currency to the gold standard. When in 1931 a democracy was instigated for the first time since 1870, no other European government was particularly interested in the turn of events.

But whatever had happened externally, Spanish democracy stood on weak internal foundations. Few Spanish subjects were actually prepared to let the ballot box determine who exercised power. Many in the higher echelons of the army were opposed to the new republic, as were the conservative oligarchs who had supported the constitutional monarchy after the First World War. Whilst the republic had been brought about by the strength of the left, the well-organised anarcho-syndicalist Confederación Nacional del Trabaji (CNT) and the Communist party were hostile from its inception. Even many of those who formally supported the republic among the political class were far from unequivocally committed to electoral politics. Significant factions of the Socialist party (PSOE), which became the largest party in Parliament after elections in June 1931, were committed to revolution. For its part, the electoral confederation of Catholic parties (CEDA), which won the most seats in the subsequent general election of November 1933, had links to fascist paramilitaries and rebel monarchists.

Although the Spanish crown had incorporated all of Spanish territory under its rule by 1512, the Spanish state was weak, and neither the nineteenth- and early twentieth-century monarchs nor de Rivera had created an effective idea of Spanish nationhood.[25] But even if the state had been stronger, the opportunities for those who led it to advance a new idea of nationhood were limited. No government could hope to exploit a nationalist foreign policy for this purpose since in 1921 Spain had lost its final colony in a military disaster in Morocco and it had long been isolated from Europe's diplomatic politics. Materially, over half of the country's land belonged to 1 per cent of the population, leaving the large mass of peasants living on tiny holdings and meagre wages. These economic divisions were complicated by Catholic and anti-clerical passions. Whilst the Catholic church's position as a major landowner and its attachment to the monarchical cause encouraged the left to see secularising measures and land reform as complementary sides of the project to create a modern version of Spanish nationhood, in promoting this approach the left effectively excluded many peasants who remained loyal to the Catholic faith. For its part, the right refused to separate the question of religious tolerance from the issues of property rights and the abuse of land by absentee owners. Language presented further difficulties. Both Catalonia and the Basque country were home to linguistic minorities keen on autonomy. In 1930 the Catalan nationalists had secured a promise from their socialist and republican allies for a measure of sovereignty when the republic was realised. This guarantee inflamed both Basque nationalists, who, as Catholics and conservatives, were of little interest to the leftist republicans, and many on the right who believed that the unity of Spain had become a pawn in the internal politics of the left.

These problems were compounded by the inability of those aspiring to power in Madrid to agree on any constitutional rules. When finally ratified in December 1931, the constitution included a clause declaring that all wealth would be subordinate to the nation. Most lethally, it tried to enshrine anti-clericalism in the constitutional foundations of the republic. But no democracy where divisions between citizens ran so deep could afford a constitution that demanded substantive agreement about values and excluded parties representing a potential electoral majority from constitutional politics.

Over the next five years, the constitution was virtually useless in exercising any restraint over those who participated in politics, including the

army. Left and right saw holding power via the ballot box as an opportunity to repress opponents whom they regarded as illegitimate regardless of the outcomes of electoral competition, and each regarded
opposition as a licence for rebellion. In August 1932, fuelled by the
progress through Parliament of a statute for Catalan autonomy, the
army's most popular general led a rebellion in Seville before he was captured. When, after a general election in November 1933 in which the
conservative Radical party formed a new government that included
members of CEDA, the PSOE incited an uprising in Asturias and a
general strike in Madrid, whilst Catalan nationalists declared independence. After quelling the attempted revolution, the new government,
backed by the army, arrested thousands of socialists, severely restricted
the left-wing press, drove the CNT underground, and suspended the
statute guaranteeing Catalan autonomy. In January 1936, a newly organised coalition of the left-wing parties, the Popular Front, narrowly won
the republic's third general election, prompting intense plotting by the
army and various right-wing paramilitaries and politicians. Seven
months later, the army, led by General Franco, rose in almost every city
in the country to try to seize power. After some of Franco's officers
hesitated, the republican government acted to arm the CNT and other
trade-union organisations and organise large-scale resistance to defend
democracy.[26]

As Spanish democracy headed towards its definitive crisis, Hitler's
objectives were becoming increasingly expansionist. In March of that
year, he had ordered German troops into the demilitarised zone of the
Rhineland. Discovering that the French and British governments had
little will to resist him, he now had a basis from which to attack France
and to fortify Germany's western frontier. Once Germany was safe in the
Rhineland, Hitler could turn his attention eastwards, giving a worried
Stalin every reason to deepen his recent re-engagement with European
affairs. In transforming the balance of power on the continent, Hitler
precipitated the Spanish republic into a radically different external
world than the one in which it had been born with such indifference.
Now what happened in Spain could determine the balance of power in
Europe.

Consequently, whilst the war to defend Spanish democracy was caused
entirely by internal politics, its outcome was largely determined by the
ways in which other states responded to the conflict. From the beginning of the war, Franco's rebel forces enjoyed a significant advantage.
During the first week of fighting, Franco asked Hitler and Mussolini for
help, and by August the rebels were receiving German and Italian air
support. By the beginning of 1937, the two dictators had sent troops as

well as regular supplies. By contrast, neither London nor Paris were willing to support the Spanish government, and, with Roosevelt's agreement, proposed that all the European states should agree a pact of non-intervention, which the fascist powers were flouting as it was being agreed. Even when, three months into the war, Stalin began to supply the republican forces, and a 50,000-strong brigade of international volunteers arrived, this support simply allowed the government to prolong its resistance rather than swing the military balance of power against the rebels. Since Stalin's interest was not in a republican victory but in buying time to defend the Soviet Union from Germany, this impasse initially suited him. When, in late 1938, he effectively withdrew Soviet support, the Spanish government was doomed, and in March 1939, Franco's forces captured Madrid.[27]

By contrast, the Czechoslovak modern democratic nation-state had been in an externally precarious position from its inception. Internally, Czechoslovakia's leading politicians, both Czechs and Slovaks, co-operated to maintain a succession of centrist coalition governments and keep the anti-democratic parties away from power. But since the Czechoslovak state was surrounded by three states – Austria, Hungary and Germany – which had been truncated by its sheer existence, and another, Poland, that had lost to Czechoslovak demands at Versailles, and since it contained national minorities from each of these states not least the 3.5 million Germans who lived in the Sudetenland, it desperately needed external support. Throughout the inter-war years, those who led the Czechoslovak state had an acute understanding of their predicament. From the onset of the peace they had looked to make alliances to maintain the status quo in eastern and central Europe and agreed to the Little Entente with Yugoslavia and Romania. In 1925, the Czechoslovak government secured a guarantee from France in the event of attack from Germany. Hitler's rise to power, however, made external support that much more urgent, especially when he moved to launch a Nazi party in the Sudetenland. Although in 1935 the Soviet Union agreed to protect Czechoslovakia on the condition that France fulfilled its obligations, once Germany asserted its power in the Balkans and prised Yugoslavia away from the Little Entente, the state's security prospects radically deteriorated.

By 1938, the future of the Czechoslovak state depended on the intentions of the British government led by Neville Chamberlain. Only if he were prepared to act to defend Czechoslovak integrity could France and the Soviet Union be trusted to act as they had promised. Chamberlain, however, saw only fantastical horror in going to war for a 'quarrel in a faraway country between people of whom we know nothing'.[28] After three meetings with Hitler, culminating in the Munich agreement, he demanded that the Czechoslovak president hand away his state's sovereignty not only over the Sudetenland but to territory claimed by Poland and Hungary too, costing the Czech state a third of its population, its entire defence fortification, its most significant armaments factories and its richest raw materials. Once a medium-sized European state with an effective army and military strategy, it was left defenceless against German invasion, and fell in March 1939.[29]

French democracy also fell to Germany but only after it had survived a protracted internal battle for survival. Between 1929 and 1931, it had withstood the economic crisis remarkably well, protected by its undervalued currency. Whilst most other European governments were forced back into deflation and retrenchment, the French government embarked on a programme of expensive defensive fortification and social and economic reform without seriously jeopardising the franc. But in 1932–3, as other economies began tentatively to emerge from the worst of the depression, the French began to collapse. Thereafter, a succession of centre-right and right-wing governments turned to severe deflation to try to salvage the gold parity. As living standards deteriorated, the long-standing divisions between the French left and right intensified to the point where they once again threatened the future of the republic.

After the Popular Front, a broad electoral alliance of left-wing parties and organisations, won the elections in 1936, the socialist Léon Blum formed a new government committed to nationalisation, a reduction in the working week and a substantial expansion of the welfare state. But Blum soon found that external conditions gave him little room for manoeuvre. With the franc bedevilled by speculation and capital flight, Blum was soon forced to abandon much of his economic programme. By the end of 1936, the spectre of civil war loomed.[30] The communists, having refused to enter Blum's government, were more concerned to jockey for long-term influence within the fratricidal struggles of the left than they were to defend the republic. Many on the right began to flirt with alternatives to democracy, some of which certainly raised a question about whether they were committed to an independent French state at all. For its part, Blum's government lacked the political resources to stamp the authority of the state on the situation. Whilst it was able to disband various fascist bands, it could never persuade the French Senate to give it decree powers as routine parliamentary procedures broke down.

The internal weakness of the French state in 1936 only exacerbated its external difficulties. Ever since the armistice, French governments had had good reasons to fret about the state's security. At Versailles, Clemenceau had not procured a permanent occupation of the Rhineland, and the American Senate had not ratified the Anglo-American guarantee. Consequently, the French state maintained a large army throughout the inter-war years. In 1921, it made a defence agreement with the Little Entente states. Eight years later, the government began to construct in the Maginot Line a military fortress across the state's eastern frontier, despite having secured a partial guarantee from Britain in the Locarno treaty, and in 1935, it struck an alliance with the Soviet Union. Nonetheless by the end of 1936, Blum's government had every reason to be anxious. To the east, Germany had reoccupied the Rhineland, leaving the Little Entente states isolated. To the south, Italy and Germany had entered the Spanish civil war, depriving the French state of one possible ally in Italy, significantly expanding Germany's access to mineral wealth for rearmament, and turning the Pyrenees into a potentially hostile border. And, to the north-east, Belgium had withdrawn from the Franco-Belgian pact into neutrality, leaving an unfortified frontier north of the Maginot Line. Whilst Blum had initially wanted to aid the Spanish republican government to try to counter German and Italian expansion, he reversed course once he concluded that if he did, the French state would disintegrate into civil war.

In March 1938, Blum's second Popular Front government collapsed and Eduoard Daladier assumed office at the head of a centre-right coalition government with the authority to rule almost permanently by decree. But for all the faith the French high command placed in the Maginot Line, the French state could no longer be saved by strong executive government. It could only survive if some combination of Britain, the United States and the Soviet Union were willing to defend it, and until the moment had passed they were not. The British government was mired in the delusions driving its policy of appeasement, the Roosevelt administration was unable to secure congressional support to reverse isolationism, and Stalin was unwilling to help states who, as he saw it, had all too readily sacrificed east-European interests to Germany. Forced back on to its own resources, and its accompanying Maginot illusion, the French state was simply defenceless when Hitler turned German power against it in May 1940.[31]

Of the European modern democratic nation-states that had to cope with the economic crisis and fight for their survival against Germany, only the British endured. For British governments, however, the matter at stake was never simply the independence of its home islands or preserving its democracy, but the future of its empire. If the empire could not survive, then, the history of the demise of previous imperial powers suggested, they would have to confront the possibility that the internal authority and constitutional rules of the state would collapse too. In the 1920s successive British governments had exposed democracy to a mire of domestic and external contradictions. But, whilst the terms of Britain's membership of the gold standard, and its monetary dependence on and continuing war debts to the United States, restricted successive governments' freedom of manoeuvre in economic and foreign policy, the actual political price paid for these tensions was not particularly high. Despite persistent high unemployment, and the failure of the Labour prime minister, Ramsay MacDonald, to hold his cabinet together over public expenditure in August 1931 to save the sterling parity, few British citizens turned towards authoritarianism or fascism. And despite growing nationalist resistance to imperial rule, British governments were able in the 1930s to slash defence expenditure.

At least in its immediate aftermath, sterling's departure from the gold standard in September 1931 liberated the National government formed by Ramsay MacDonald after the Labour government collapsed. It freed monetary policy from direct constraint, lessened the grip of American monetary and financial power over the economy, and, abetted by the worldwide collapse of agricultural prices, paved the way to imperial protectionism, something that British governments had always eschewed. During 1932 the National government turned the empire and white dominions into a trading and currency bloc on the basis of restrictive tariffs and internal sterling convertibility. Britain's sterling area did create its own constraints. In order to encourage the dominions to hold their assets in sterling, the National government had to balance the budget, necessitating a significant cut in welfare provision. Nonetheless, the immediate political rewards were sizeable. Whilst international economic conditions during the second half of the 1920s had left British governments at the mercy of the United States, their successors could act more autonomously. Seizing the opportunity, the National government took control of monetary policy from the Bank of England and pushed interest rates down, stimulating a partial economic recovery and averting any substantial appreciation in sterling against the dollar. Even though the government's fiscal retrenchment left unemployment rampant, its geographical distribution, and the impotence of the Labour party after the events of the second half of 1931, meant that the issue never caused the National government serious difficulty.

But, if amidst dissent and rebellion elsewhere in Europe, the internal authority of the British modern democratic nation-state remained robust, it paid the price in external security. British governments could neither rearm nor direct industrial reconstruction whilst maintaining fiscal discipline. By 1933, Britain was exposed in Europe and the Pacific. Germany was in the hands of a man who was determined to undo Versailles, and, in invading Manchuria, Japan had already proved its unwillingness to abide by the agreements on China it had signed a decade earlier. The external threats posed by Germany and Japan slowly pushed the National governments, led from 1935 by a Conservative prime minister, into an increasingly dependent relationship with the United States. They could not act against Japan without the United States nor could they afford to go to war in Europe without American material support. After the National government defaulted on its war debt in 1933, and Congress forbade private loans to any country with outstanding obligations, Britain could not hope to receive any such support without the American president exacting a formidable price. Once the Roosevelt administration concluded that American interests lay in more open trading markets, the shape of that price became clearer: if the British state had once more to be rescued financially by the Americans, it could not expect to keep its commercial empire.

Constrained domestically by its own economic policies and externally by American isolationism, the National government had few options as the international crisis worsened. It did spend money on a moderate programme of rearmament. But since another war would in good part be fought in the air, any region of Europe from which bombing raids could be launched was now vital to British security. Stretched in too many different directions, the government placed its hopes on appeasement, offering commercial concessions to Japan and Germany and turning its gaze away when the one invaded Manchuria and the other strolled into the Rhineland. But by the end of 1936, Italy's invasion of Abyssinia and its axis with Germany left Britain exposed in the Mediterranean too. Unless the British government was prepared either to change course domestically, or to contemplate a withdrawal from empire, it was trapped. When the Munich settlement reinforced the risk of war, it finally accepted large-scale rearmament and the material dependency on the United States that followed with all the ensuing consequences for its economic empire. Even then it took Germany's invasion of Czechoslovakia finally to destroy the illusion that Hitler could be contained by diplomacy and commercial concessions, and to prompt the government to offer military guarantees to its dwindling European allies.[32]

After the fall of France in June 1940, the choice facing the British government could not have been clearer. It could fight for the independence of the British state, bankrupt it and allow the Americans, in Keynes's words, 'to pick out the eyes of the British empire',[33] or it could make a peace with Germany on Hitler's terms and hope that this time he would keep his word. When Winston Churchill and his ministers chose to fight, they first and foremost had to find a way to persuade the American Congress to supply goods that they had no means to pay for even after selling substantial imperial assets. During the latter stages of the war, Churchill tried desperately hard to convince the rest of the world that the security and democracy of the British state could still be made one with its independence and empire. But the reality was otherwise. Its entire future had become dependent on the quality of the Americans' mercy.

Conclusions

In 1918, Wilson had held that the future of democracy and international peace lay with setting 'the people' free from the power of autocrats and the calculations of *realpolitik*. Wilson got most things the wrong way round about the relationship between internal and external politics and public opinion and power. The 'will of the people' would not have saved Europe in 1914 and democracies were neither a sufficient condition for peace nor immune from the kind of territorial worries that could help destroy constitutional authority, as they did first in Hungary and then in Poland. 'Enlightened' public opinion could not stop Germany and Italy expanding once fascists ruled them. And because the United States withdrew from European politics and, consequently, there was no balance of power in Europe, no state, single-handedly, could prevent German and Italian expansion either. Since the British and French governments in the 1930s were suspicious of each other and unwilling to entertain an alliance with the Soviet Union, and since Stalin had no conceivable interest in acting as a guarantor of democracy, nor did the states that could have thwarted Hitler co-operate. In the wake of that fact, the Spanish, Czechoslovak and French democracies all fell to one form or another of German intervention.

Internally, what transpired after 1914 reinforced the truth that as a form of government representative democracy depended on an effective state and those leading that state successfully defining a singular people through an idea of nationhood. Most democracies that collapsed from within during the inter-war years, not least the German and Italian, failed in at least one of these respects. Many who held elected office did not understand that for any state to survive, those who commanded power had to defend its internal authority against those who wished to destroy it. Far from being exempt from this particular reason of state, democracy proved particularly dependent on it because competitive elections and the organisational and demagogic skills that they rewarded offered a relatively easy route to power for parties like the Nazis. Instead, elected politicians in different countries gave away the state's right to self-defence, either assuming that the enemies of democracy had to be tolerated in the name of democracy, or because they were shackled by Versailles.

The difficulties of creating and sustaining a belief in nationhood were, unsurprisingly, most acute in the successor states in eastern Europe and the Balkans, especially for the hugely ambitious Yugoslav state. As these states had liberal constitutions, powerful neighbours prepared to manipulate the politics of their national minorities, and were restricted by treaty obligations, they could not readily resort to the level of coercion that the leaders of older states had deployed to create an idea of nationhood. But the most intractable difficulties were more general. Without economic prosperity and high levels of employment, elected politicians struggled to present to the citizens of democracies a convincing picture of a single people directed in the name of a single national purpose. The war and a full franchise had generated material expectations and incited class passions that leaders ignored at their peril. Yet in the circumstances of the inter-war years, economic success that offered something to the industrial working classes and agricultural producers required a depth of political control over economic life that appeared more readily achieved in a totalitarian state like the Nazi one, and which only Swedish politicians in the 1930s worked out how to realise within the constraints of democracy. Where the political judgements had to be attuned to a more complicated range of circumstances, as in France in the 1930s, or where, as during the Weimar republic, those who commanded the power of the state were fearful of revolution and bereft of monetary sovereignty, governments were, by contrast, operating in an international economy that demanded a fierce domestic discipline and introduced a dangerous degree of *fortuna*. Vulnerability to these kinds of external forces not only had terrible practical consequences for those democracies that had survived until 1929, most catastrophically the German, it also undermined the imaginative hold of the state as an independent agent directed to a collective purpose on which the whole idea of nationhood had to rest. If the British modern democratic nation-state alone survived such vulnerability intact, its politicians owed it to an empire that they could not hope to sustain once a new peace was in place. In one sense Wilson had been right, although not in the way he had intended: representative democracy did require a safer and more predictable external world but primarily economically.

Notes

1 See F. Ninkovich, *The Wilsonian Century: US Foreign Policy Since 1900* (Chicago: University of Chicago Press, 1999); T. J. Knock, *To End All Wars: Woodrow Wilson and the Quest for a New World Order* (Oxford: Oxford University Press, 1992); J. A. Thompson, *Woodrow Wilson* (London: Longman, 2002).

2 Quoted in A. Mayer, *Political Origins of the New Diplomacy*, 2nd edn (New York: Meridan Books, 1964), p. 322.

3 For comparative discussions of the experiences of different European states see F. Stern, 'The new democracies in crisis in inter-war Europe', in A. Hadenius (ed.), *Democracy's Victory and Crisis in Inter-War Europe* (Cambridge: Cambridge University Press, 1997); M. Mazower, *Dark Continent: Europe's Twentieth Century* (London: Allen Lane, 1998), chs 1–4; K. J. Newman, *European Democracy between the Wars*, trans. K. Morgan (London: Allen and Unwin, 1970); J. Linz and A. Stepan (eds), *The Breakdown of Democratic Regimes* (Baltimore: Johns Hopkins University Press, 1975).

4 On states and national minorities and the League of Nations during the inter-war years see C. A. Macartney, *National States and National Minorities* (London: Oxford University Press, 1934); I. L. Claude, *National Minorities: an International Problem* (Cambridge, MA: Harvard University Press, 1935).

5 K. D. Moggridge (ed.), *The Collected Writings of John Maynard Keynes, Volume VII: the General Theory of Employment, Interest and Money* (London: Macmillan, 1973), ch. 2.

6 See R. Nurske, *International Currency Experience: Lessons of the Inter-War Period* (Geneva: League of Nations, 1944).

7 See H. Seton-Watson, *Eastern Europe between the Wars* (Cambridge: Cambridge University Press, 1962).

8 Quoted in C. S. Maier, *Recasting Bourgeois Europe: Stabilization in France, Germany, and Italy in the Decade after World War I* (Princeton: Princeton University Press, 1988), p. 115.

9 C. Seton-Watson, *Italy from Liberalism to Fascism 1870–1925* (London: Meuthen, 1967), p. 541.

10 D. Mack-Smith, *Italy: a Modern History* (Ann Arbor: University of Michigan Press, 1969), p. 347.

11 Quoted in Seton-Watson, *Italy from Liberalism to Fascism*, p. 609.

12 On the failure of Italian representative democracy after 1919 see Mack-Smith, *Italy*; Seton-Watson, *Italy from Liberalism to Fascism*.

13 See C. S. Maier, *Recasting Bourgeois Europe: Stabilization in France, Germany, Italy in the Decade after World War I* (Princeton: Princeton University Press, 1988).

14 See C. S. Maier, 'The vulnerabilities of inter-war Germany', *Journal of Modern History*, 56: 1 (1984), 89–99; H. Heiber, *The Weimar Republic*, trans. W. E. Yuill (Oxford: Blackwell, 1993).

15 B. Eichengreen, *Globalising Capital: a History of the International Monetary System* (Princeton: Princeton University Press, 1998), pp. 63–7.

16 See Eichengreen, *Globalising Capital.*

17 B. Simmons, *Who Adjusts?: Domestic Sources of Foreign Economic Policy during the Interwar Years* (Princeton: Princeton University Press, 1994), ch. 3.

18 See J. Rothschild, *East-Central Europe between the Two World Wars* (Seattle: University of Washington Press, 1974); N. Davies, *Heart of Europe: a Short History of Poland* (Oxford: Oxford University Press, 1984), ch. 3.

19 Quoted in M. Glenny, *The Balkans: Nationalism, War and the Great Powers* (London: Granta Books, 1999), p. 412. On the Yugoslav state in the 1920s see J. R. Lampe, *Yugoslavia as History: Twice there was a Country* (Cambridge: Cambridge University Press, 1996), ch. 5.

20 See K. Mouré, *Managing the Franc Poincaré: Economic Understanding and Political Constraint in French Monetary Policy, 1928–1936* (Cambridge: Cambridge University Press, 1991).

21 See Heiber, *The Weimar Republic.*

22 See C. Kindleberger, *The World in Depression 1929–1939* (Berkeley: University of California Press, 1973); B. Eichengreen, *Golden Fetters: the Gold Standard and the Great Depression, 1919–1939* (Oxford: Oxford University Press, 1992).

23 See I. Kershaw, *The Nazi Dictatorship: Problems and Perspectives* (London: Edward Arnold, 1985).

24 See T. Notermans, *Money, Markets, and the State: Social Democratic Economic Policies since 1918* (Cambridge: Cambridge University Press, 2000); A. Lindbeck, *Swedish Economic Policy* (Berkeley: University of California Press, 1974).

25 J. L. Linz, 'Early state building and late peripheral nationalisms against the state: the case of Spain', in S. N. Eisenstadt and S. Rokkan (eds), *Building States and Nations: Analysis and Data Across Three Worlds* (Beverly Hills: Sage, 1973).

26 See R. Carr, *Spain 1809–1939* (Oxford: Clarendon Press, 1966); G. Brenan, *The Spanish Labyrinth: an Account of the Social and Political Background of the Civil War* (Cambridge: Cambridge University Press, 1943); J. Linz, 'From great hopes to civil war: the breakdown of democracy in Spain', in J. Linz and A. Stepan, *The Breakdown of Democratic Regimes: Europe* (Baltimore: Johns Hopkins University Press, 1978).

27 See R. Carr, *The Civil War in Spain* (London: Weidenfeld and Nicolson, 1986); H. Thomas, *The Spanish Civil War*, 3rd edn (Harmondsworth: Penguin, 1977); M. Alpert, *A New International History of the Spanish Civil War* (Basingstoke: Macmillan, 1994).

28 Cited in C. Thorne, *The Approach of War* (London: Macmillan, 1982), p. 91.

29 See Seton-Watson, *Eastern Europe between the Wars.*

30 See M. Wolfe, *The French Franc between the Wars, 1919–1939* (New York: Columbia University Press, 1951).

31 See A. Adamthwaite, *France and the Coming of the Second World War* (Cambridge: Cambridge University Press, 1977); J. Joll (ed.), *The Decline of the Third Republic* (London: Chatto and Windus, 1959).

32 See P. Kennedy, *The Realities Behind Diplomacy: Background Influences on British External Policy, 1865–1980* (London: Fontana Press, 1985), part III; M. Cowling, *The Impact of Hitler: British Politics and British Policy 1933–1940* (Cambridge: Cambridge University Press, 1975).

33 Quoted in R. Skidelsky, *John Maynard Keynes: Volume Three, Fighting for Britain 1937–1946* (London: Macmillan, 2000), p. 98.

3

The Bretton Woods rescue

The end of the Second World War left the United States as the most powerful state in the world with only the Soviet Union as a conceivable competitor. Economically, it had an extraordinary advantage even compared to the one it had enjoyed during the 1920s. Whilst all of the other significant powers were substantially poorer in 1945 than they had been in 1939, the United States was richer. It now accounted for more than half of the world's manufacturing production, supplied more than a third of the world's exports, and possessed two-thirds of the world's gold reserves. Militarily, the United States controlled the seas, commanded the air and enjoyed a monopoly of nuclear weapons. In allying with Britain and the Soviet Union to defeat Germany, and then single-handedly clinching victory against Japan with a brutal demonstration of atomic supremacy, Franklin Roosevelt and Harry Truman had turned the United States into a state capable of projecting power to any region in the world accessible by sea.

Yet as the war came to an end, just what American presidents would do with this power, and how American predominance would shape the fate of other states, was far from clear. Roosevelt had taken the United States into the Second World War without seriously considering the specifics of the peace he hoped would follow. He had led the war without aims beyond the unconditional surrender of Germany and Japan and had refused to discuss with Stalin and Churchill any details of a future geo-political and territorial settlement. He did not wish, however, the burden of keeping the peace to fall on the United States. Consequently he neither wanted American troops to stay in Europe once the war was won, nor to have to reconstruct Europe economically. Instead, albeit in the most general terms, he hoped for a peace policed collectively by the United States, the Soviet Union, Britain and China in the name of the universal values for which he had proclaimed the United States' return to the international stage in 1941.

In many ways, the language Roosevelt had used to persuade a sceptical

American Congress to enter the war was the same as that Wilson had evoked more than twenty years earlier. As Wilson had tried to turn the First World War into crusade for democracy, Roosevelt had promised in the Atlantic Charter in the summer of 1941 to seek a 'better' world in which the right of all peoples to choose their form of government would be respected and which renounced the use of force as an instrument of diplomacy. But Roosevelt meant the 'world' far more literally than Wilson had done. Whereas Wilson had confined his vision to Europe, Roosevelt was looking eastwards and southwards. If the new world was to be based on the principle of self-determination, the European states had to dismantle their empires and accept the separate sovereignty of all peoples. Deploying this universal rhetoric, the Roosevelt administration led its war allies, most of the exiled governments of Europe, and the Free French to sign a joint declaration as an entity of 'united nations' endorsing the Atlantic Charter. One year later, it persuaded these governments to work to establish a permanent international organisation, the United Nations (UN), as an agent of collective peace and a guarantor of democracy, freedom and human rights to the peoples of every hemisphere.

Roosevelt's ambitions for a collective peace were as doomed as Wilson's. The UN's security council could not possibly act as a collective policeman since the British and French states ended the war bankrupt and militarily weakened, the Chinese government was in the throes of a civil war, and Stalin had no intention of acting according to American mantras. Indeed in settling that each of the permanent members of the security council had a veto, Roosevelt revealed that he did not trust his own creation, and ensured that the United States could only respond to acts of aggression by one of the major powers independently of the UN.

Even on his own terms, Roosevelt was committed to rather less than his rhetoric suggested. For all his grandiose cant, he and his closest advisors understood that American economic interests, and the likely unwillingness of crucial sections of the electorate to tolerate further military intervention in Europe, would not sit easily with his liberal presumptions. Whilst the administration wanted the Europeans to abandon their colonies, it wished to ensure that the governments of the independent successor-states would be friendly towards the United States, especially where there were crucial raw materials. Most transparently, the administration wished to protect a cheap supply of oil from the Middle East, regardless of what form of government was practised by the regimes willing to guarantee it. Somewhat less willingly, Roosevelt accepted that the post-war world would include a communist Soviet Union expanded well beyond its 1939 borders, commanding a sphere of influence that, at a minimum, would include Poland, Romania, Bulgaria and northern China. Put differently, Roosevelt wanted a world of democracies that resembled his language of American political virtue except where to insist on it would risk American prosperity and lives.

The Roosevelt administration was far clearer about the specific shape it wanted to give to the post-war international economy than it was about the geo-political peace. Roosevelt's advisors believed that American policy-makers after 1918 had misunderstood the United States' own economic and security interests in the fate of other states. They understood that during the inter-war years the internal authority and external sovereignty of the European modern democratic nation-states had proved as vulnerable to events in the international economy as the threat of invasion. Whilst large numbers of citizens had come to believe that the state should act to advance their economic welfare, most states had proved disastrously unable to meet these expectations. In good part, they had failed because they had been unable to find a robust way of financing trade with the United States; or to manage exchange rates and share markets under conditions of proliferating short-term capital flows that were drawn to New York; or to absorb the consequences of the United States' monetary demands or interest rates set by the Federal Reserve Board. Since the Second World War had excited citizens' expectations further, and since the United States was now even stronger financially, if the Roosevelt administration wanted to protect those American interests which rested on democracies surviving abroad, it would have to establish a different kind of international economy.

Just one week after the United States entered the war in December 1941, Roosevelt's treasury secretary, Henry Morgenthau, and the treasury's director of monetary research, Harry Dexter White, began to think about the specifics of the post-war international economy. Morgenthau and White judged that the United States should establish a multilateral trading order with firm rules about capital flows, controlled formally by international institutions based in the United States, and from which Germany and Japan would be excluded. On this basis, they believed, Washington could force Britain to dismantle its imperial trading and currency bloc, and maintain co-operative relations with the Soviet Union. In militarily neutering Germany and Japan through enforced de-industrialisation, constructing a feasible basis for European trade, and guaranteeing American access to foreign markets, they hoped, lay the foundations of an international peace.[1] To these ends, between 1943 and 1944, White developed technical plans to create two institutions to stabilise monetary and exchange-rate relations in the post-war world and a parallel institution to facilitate international trade.

Only the British government was in a position to challenge the nuances of White's planning if not the strategy that lay behind it. In 1941, John Maynard Keynes had begun his own work sketching a postwar international monetary and trading order. Like White, he believed that future prosperity and peace would depend on the resurrection of international trade. However, he was more anxious than White about the domestic political consequences of any new international monetary arrangements and the likely difficulties of the transition from a war to a peacetime economy. Keynes hoped to persuade the Americans that what they wanted to achieve would be lost unless they distinguished between trade and capital flows and provided plentiful credit to states struggling with balance-of-payments deficits.

After a series of bilateral negotiations between the American and British governments, forty-four allied states met at Bretton Woods to discuss post-war monetary and exchange-rate matters, leaving international trade to a future conference. The agreement that they reached contained three central provisions. First, it created two international financial institutions. The International Monetary Fund (IMF) would provide temporary credit to states suffering from balance-of-payments difficulties against specifically allocated drawing rights. The Fund could also sanction governments, including states running payments surpluses deemed responsible for destabilising international monetary relations. The World Bank, by contrast, would concentrate on granting long-term loans for reconstruction and development. Second, Bretton Woods established a system of fixed, but adjustable, exchange rates whereby member states would act to maintain the value of their currencies within 1 per cent of the formal parity unless the IMF agreed to a devaluation or revaluation. Third, and perhaps most radically, the settlement gave states the right to use permanent capital controls, which would stop money for purposes other than trade entering and leaving a country, and for at least three years on current accounts too.[2]

For Keynes, at least, capital controls were now a reason of state. Without them, he suspected, democracies other than the United States would crumble. They would be once more open to currency speculation and capital flight, especially when led by parties of the left. They would be constrained by the same kind of deflationary bias that had plagued European governments under open capital flows after 1924. And they would be unable to use monetary policy to achieve full employment. The consequences, Keynes feared, would be as fatal as they had been during the inter-war years. Without stable exchange rates, trade would collapse and states would revert to trade and currency protectionism, and without a belief that citizens could choose their own representatives free from the preferences of markets, the idea of democracy would lose credibility. And without something approaching full employment, no government could hope to survive in office.[3]

Keynes knew that the political utility of capital controls depended, as did everything else designed to sustain an expansionary bias in macro-economic policy, on attitudes in Washington. Unless the Americans co-operated in implementing capital controls and persuaded the New York bankers to refuse illegal capital outflows from Europe, governments would not enjoy monetary autonomy. Without American agreement, currencies could not be devalued. Only if the American president could persuade a reluctant Congress to release more funds for temporary credit and open American markets to European exports, could European governments contemplate managing the balance of payments with equanimity.

In the first nine months after Franklin Roosevelt's death, the Truman administration offered the European governments far less than what they deemed necessary. Most dramatically, in July 1945, three months after it had done the same to the Soviet Union, the administration terminated its lend-lease agreement with Britain. Wishing the post-war world to be multilateral as soon as possible, the loan that Truman offered as recompense came with fierce conditions, not least to restore sterling convertibility by July 1947. However, by the middle of 1947, events had forced the Truman administration to abandon its multilateral project and the security policy that underpinned it. Quite simply, everything that Roosevelt had wanted in 1944 could not be made to go together. In December 1945, after Stalin indicated that the Soviet Union would not participate in Bretton Woods, the administration had to accept that unless it was willing to return to war, eastern Europe would be a Soviet sphere of influence isolated from the international economy. Meanwhile, the financial position of the west European governments was far worse than Truman had supposed. Cut off from eastern European markets, they needed to find far more dollars to pay for essential imports than they could conceivably earn from exports. The IMF struggled to provide sufficient credit to alleviate the ensuing balance-of-payments problems, and most governments, despite the use of capital controls, were suffering from persistent capital flight. In August 1947, the British government abandoned sterling convertibility just six weeks after introducing it. American-imposed restrictions on German industrial production made matters even worse. Morgenthau might have been right in arguing that a de-industrialised Germany could not start another world war but that still left the problem of how the other west European economies could recover and prosper without access to German coal, manufactured goods and import markets, especially in conditions that prohibited large-scale imports from the United States.

By the end of 1947, the Truman administration had a new foreign policy with a rather different set of political implications for the rest of the world than those entailed in the Bretton Woods settlement. Territorially, it redefined the scope of the international economy. Although Truman offered the Soviet Union financial aid in 1947, he was unconvinced that he could use material temptation to break the Soviet sphere of influence. Instead he turned American attention to the two states that Roosevelt and Morgenthau had determined should have no place in an open multilateral trading system. To ensure their own economic recovery and that of the surrounding economies, he wanted to reconstruct Japan and the western zones of Germany as rapidly as possible to save them from the Soviet Union. Financially and institutionally, the administration switched its emphasis from multilateralism and the international financial institutions established in 1944 to bilateralism and regional organisations. In 1947, the administration announced the Marshall plan which would depend on bilateral American grants. Truman also accepted that the west European governments could retain trade restrictions and currency inconvertibility indefinitely in return for ridding their ministerial ranks of communists and controlling inflation.

After 1949, the Truman administration made further adjustments to the international economy, convinced that the cumulative effect of the Chinese communists' success, the Soviet Union testing an atomic bomb, recession in western Europe, and North Korea's invasion of South Korea had significantly disadvantaged the United States. Monetarily and financially, the administration further compromised its multilateral ambitions. In the second half of 1949, the west European governments faced another acute shortage of dollars, after demand for European exports fell. In September 1949, the British government succumbed to a devaluation and others followed suit. Thereafter, the administration tacitly encouraged the west European governments to discriminate against the rest of the world. In 1950, it sponsored the creation of a European Payments Union (EPU), which allowed its members to trade with each other on preferential terms at American expense. The EPU diminished still further the possibility of early currency convertibility and excluded the IMF from any significant role in European financial recovery.[4] Not until 1958 did the west European governments liberalise their current accounts. Even then, Bretton Woods still did not function as its architects had planned, and keeping exchange rates stable became dependent on central bank governors co-operating on a daily basis to stop runs on weak currencies.[5]

In the productive sphere, the Truman administration welcomed the plan advanced in May 1950 by the French foreign minister, Robert Schuman, to create a European Coal and Steel Community (ECSC). Although many in the administration had reservations about the prospect of prolonged discrimination against American exports, Truman put a far higher premium on France accepting the rehabilitation of West Germany than economic multilateralism. But in supporting a regional economic bloc in western Europe he demanded more action against the communist left, and asked the governments to control left-wing trade unions.

After 1947, the Truman administration also reversed its approach in east Asia. Even before the outbreak of the Korean War in June 1950, it was trying to revitalise the old industrial centres of the Japanese economy. When the war began, it turned the speedy rehabilitation of Japan as the dominant economic power in the region into an explicit strategic imperative, regardless of the terms on which the rest of the world could enter Japanese markets. Since Japan's reconstruction depended on risk-free access to raw materials, the administration endeavoured to tie the oil- and mineral-rich south-east Asian economies to its economic orbit.

For Washington, international economic questions had become first and foremost questions of military security, and by the late 1940s, Truman wanted to translate the American economic sphere of influence into a set of security blocs across the world. In western Europe, Truman established the North Atlantic Treaty Organisation (NATO), as the United States' first ever peacetime military alliance, and by 1955, his successor, Dwight Eisenhower, had rearmed NATO's members, established an integrated military organisation under American command and, despite considerable French anxiety, incorporated West Germany into the alliance. In Asia, Truman imposed a security pact on Japan that effectively established a permanent American military base there, and Eisenhower sponsored the South East Asia Treaty Organisation (SEATO), which included France and Britain in an agreement of mutual, if unspecified, support. In the Middle East, Eisenhower pushed the British government into a commitment to the Baghdad pact.[6] In Latin America, Truman brokered an agreement, the Rio pact, which deemed an attack on any American state, from inside or outside the western hemisphere, an attack on all requiring collective action, and between 1952 and 1954, he and Eisenhower signed bilateral mutual defence pacts with ten states on the continent.

Prospects for representative democracy in the post-war world

The political and economic world that the Americans created during the course of the 1940s was simultaneously kind to and inauspicious for representative democracies in Europe, Asia and Latin America. The rise to dominance of the United States meant that there would soon be many more democracies than there had been ever before. The European powers that forsook their imperial possessions granted independence to distinct territorial entities, the leaders of which rarely conceived of any other form of authority. Only within the Soviet sphere of influence and the Middle East would a different form of rule endure. Within the rest of Europe, as sites of authoritative rule backed by coercion, the post-war states enjoyed some advantages compared to their immediate predecessors. Germany's eastern frontier excepted, the west European states were territorially defined much as they were in 1919, and no state was in a diplomatic or military position to contest them. Meanwhile, during the war governments had radically expanded the administrative scope and tax-raising capacity of modern states. Yet the very nature of the United States' supremacy, and the terms on which it had established the international financial institutions, funded reconstruction and developed regional security blocs meant that even the most powerful states could not hope to retain or acquire absolute external sovereignty. Where the political classes and subjects were accustomed to a very different experience of statehood, securing domestic consent to the authority of states would in part have to turn on obtaining acquiescence to that fact.

In nurturing the language of nationhood, the governments of almost all states faced considerable difficulties. The inter-war experience in Europe had suggested that the internal authority of modern states did indeed depend on governments succeeding at this activity. Yet the devastation wrought by the war, the dominance of the United States, and the unwillingness of many colonial subjects to tolerate continuing foreign rule, all made it virtually impossible for European governments to look to an expansionist or imperial foreign policy to advance the notion of a singular nation bound by common purpose. Elsewhere, as American presidents came to exempt no part of the developing world from their conception of the credibility of national power, none of the new states could hope to acquire military power quickly enough to adopt an aggressive foreign policy. Since the external world offered few opportunities for cultivating nationhood, its burden would fall on providing economic services. At least in Europe, the experience of the inter-war years suggested that governments would succeed at this if they could use the power of the state to ensure high levels of employment, provide unemployment relief and sustain agricultural incomes relative to those in the industrial sector. To achieve these ends, governments had to find a means of redistributing money between citizens without fatally alienating those from whom disproportionate sacrifices were demanded. As one obvious way of appeasing high taxpayers would be to make them the beneficiaries of state expenditure too, the scope for expanding the state's activities in the name of the nation was enormous.

The prospects for democracy were in some ways better after the Second World War than they had been after the First. Fascism's cult of communal energy and military-style leadership had proved self-destructive, and in defeating Germany, the United States and Britain had shown that the Nazis were wrong in claiming that democracy was militarily useless. Nonetheless, communism had been strengthened by the war in Europe. Not only had the Soviet Union established an empire in eastern Europe, but communists in other parts of the continent had constituted a significant part of the anti-fascist resistance. If the industrial working classes across Europe did not quickly find their standards of living rising once reconstruction began, then governments could reasonably expect communist parties, with or without encouragement from Moscow, to encourage rebellion. In Asia, meanwhile, the Chinese communists had effectively adapted Marx's and Lenin's language to the particular circumstances of the local peasantry and were, by the end of the war, edging their way to power. Further south, the harder national liberation movements had to fight militarily to end European rule, the more radical and authoritarian the governments that finally secured independence were likely to be.

Within this general set of predicaments confronting democracies, there was a range of more particular difficulties. In losing the war, Germany and Japan had effectively lost their statehood. They were occupied by other states, they were stripped of their empires, and Germany had lost a substantial part of its territory. They would be reconstructed as states by those powers that had defeated them in war. In both places, the ideas of nationhood that had previously helped to sustain the state's internal authority had been utterly discredited and were unusable for future governments. Indeed, the occupying powers were determined to destroy systematically whatever remained of older nationalist sentiments. Since foreign adventures as acts of nation-building were inconceivable, the West German and Japanese governments, beyond all others, had to succeed in providing material services, yet they presided over ruined economies subject to international restriction. Constitutionally, the Allies imposed democracy on both states, despite the fact that democracy had already failed in Germany after being imposed by the same coalition of powers; and despite its being totally alien to traditional customs of oligarchy among the political class in Japan.

Those democracies that were allied with the United States at the war's end confronted a different set of political difficulties. Whilst the British and French states had not lost external sovereignty territorially, their impoverished governments could no longer afford to act, as they had done for centuries, as independent great powers. They had to face the consequences of withdrawing from empires in the knowledge that there was no historical precedent for a state retreating from its imperial possessions without precipitating a crisis of internal authority. In the case of the French state, the war had another legacy too. It had been rescued by the intervention of other states, leaving the apparatus of a state that needed to be purged of those who had collaborated with the Nazis and whose loyalty to democracy was suspect.

In confronting this array of difficulties, the governments of these postwar democracies operated in external conditions in which the United States was offering considerable economic opportunities. Those who read international economic markets intelligently could protect politically significant sectors from competition and sustain rapid export-led growth. Although capital controls were not as effective as they would have been if the Americans had co-operated over inflows into the New York banks, they did give these governments the opportunity to decide monetary policy according to domestic political criteria. Governments could direct interest rates towards realising higher growth and full employment, and, if they so chose, control the whole organisation of credit for their own political purposes. Capital controls and the need to maintain a fixed exchange-rate parity meant that they could also maintain the high tax regimes constructed during the war,[7] allowing them to extend the state's powers. Where governments embraced the opportunity, states could be made to do internally what those who led them said they were there to do. Nonetheless, these opportunities were dependent at least in part on understanding that the constraints of fixed exchange rates produced an imperative to ensure anti-inflationary wage discipline either through centralised bargaining or some form of incomes policy.[8] Without such discipline, governments could not pursue export-led growth, or hope to avoid the kind of balance-of-payments problems that would provoke American demands for deflation.

American economic benevolence, however, came at a high price. American presidents would not allow those states that took American money and protection to decide for themselves the parameters of their internal politics, or their security policies. For the West German and

Japanese governments, this reduction in external sovereignty did have internal uses because they could rely on American troops to help quell any anti-democratic rebellion. Similarly, in insisting on the exclusion of communists, the Americans also helped several governments keep the authoritarian left away from power whatever its electoral performance. And under the Americans' watchful eyes, few leaders could fail to see, as some had done during the inter-war years, that when necessary they had to exercise power to defend the state's internal authority. Nonetheless, where, as in Britain and France, the idea of nationhood had become deeply tied to the imaginative language of great-power status, governments had to ask whether the loss of external sovereignty was really worth the material compensations.

By contrast, the Latin American states, outside the Caribbean, all enjoyed territorial sovereignty, were free from the problems of empire, and had not been coerced into accepting democracy. They had been economically devastated by the Depression but they were not carrying financial burdens from the war. Internally, however, most of the Latin American states were rather decrepit. Few had succeeded in establishing a monopoly of legitimate violence, and nowhere had the notion of impersonal sovereign authority taken hold within the political class. In pushing industrialisation through import-substitution in the 1930s and trying to co-opt various groups into the administrative apparatus of the state, military-backed governments in Brazil and Argentina had compounded what had become a habitual elision of public authority and sectional material and political interest. Constitutionally, those who had power in 1945 were inclined to use competitive elections to try to sustain it, but they were generally unwilling, as were their opponents, to abide by democratic rules. Among the citizens, fascism still had some resonance for those wanting to preserve what they thought of as traditional Catholic order, whilst the radical left attracted those angered by poverty and a corrupt, oligarchic politics.

The external world that the Roosevelt and Truman administrations created offered the Latin American states very little. Neither thought of Latin America as an area requiring development because it had done rather well out of the Second World War. They did not advance financial aid, and Truman was quite willing to see Latin American producers lose markets to those west European and Asian economies he deemed strategic assets. Certainly no American president would be indifferent to foreign intervention on the continent but in the 1940s there was no threat of it. When the Truman administration tied the Latin American states into a military pact, it did to so to procure help in policing other parts of the world. Only after the Cuban revolution in 1959 did

American presidents become frightened about the consequences of under-development on the continent. Nonetheless, Latin American governments could not rely on American indifference to their internal politics, even before Fidel Castro came to power. Formally, the Truman administration had sponsored the creation of the Organisation of American States (OAS), which enshrined the principle of non-intervention in the internal affairs of the member states. But given the constancy of the Monroe doctrine assumption that Latin America was the United States' backyard, no American president was likely to regard it as a serious constraint, and no elected government in Latin America could embark on a radical economic policy that would hurt the interests of American investors without putting democracy at risk.

For those in Asia who aspired to their own modern democratic nation-state, the task ahead was the most enormous. They had to create modern states where there had hitherto been none. Whilst the departing European powers bequeathed sites of rule and structures of administration, these were in various conditions of disrepair. The indigenous political classes had to agree constitutions, reconfigure institutions and secure a monopoly of legitimate violence for the army and police whilst ensuring their own political control of that coercive power. Having reinvented political authority, they had to use it to advance an idea of nationhood that could encourage obedience from its subjects whilst dampening the rebellious passions generated during the struggle for independence. In trying to do so, they had to carry the intense expectations about just what a modern nation-state should do generated by the bid for self-rule under conditions of economic impoverishment.

Where the political classes were also wishing to establish democracy, the problems multiplied. Where modern states had successfully taken root, very few of those who had inaugurated them had simultaneously introduced competitive elections on a full franchise to determine who should rule. When, in the nineteenth century, the Latin American political classes had founded independent states on republican principles, they had created a tiny electorate. The leaders of the successor states to the Austro-Hungarian and Ottoman empires had from the beginning created modern states whilst establishing representative democracy on a full franchise, but only the Czechoslovaks did so successfully before their state fell to external invasion. Most of those who had successfully created modern states had used violence to do so. Even in the United States, where there appeared to be a precedent for successfully coupling new-found independence with a representative form of republican politics, establishing a site of sovereign rule had required a bloody civil war and the systematic destruction of competing claims to authority.

Contrary to Madison's faith in size, the larger the state the more acute the problems in trying to realise such a project were likely to be. Territories like the Indian and Indonesian, stretching over disparate peoples speaking different languages and practising many different religious faiths, were not obviously conducive to experiments that depended for their success on strong sites of central authority, unifying collectivist identifications and granting the power of the modern state to representatives chosen by numerical majorities.

The external world looked rather different to those who aspired to establish modern democratic nation-states in Asia than it did in the capitals of western Europe and Japan. In comparison, the first post-war American presidents offered comparatively few opportunities. Morgenthau and Dexter White had envisaged that the World Bank would guarantee loans by private banks and investors rather than grant credit for development, and the Bank, anyway, was soon dwarfed by the Marshall plan. GATT, meanwhile, contained no provisions for liberalising trade in agricultural goods or the commodities on which many developing countries would depend unless and until they could industrialise. So far as the Truman administration was concerned about the trade of developing countries, it wished only to connect those rich in raw materials to the western economic bloc. During the 1950s, new opportunities in the external world did arise. Once authoritative rule was established in a particular territory, other states treated a state's jurisdiction as permanent and saw any attack on it as a threat to regional stability.[9] In Asia, the former imperial powers offered support to the new states once the terms of their exit were settled, and, in time, Washington offered some governments substantial aid for military purposes. Once, from 1954, the Soviet Union began to give economic aid to non-communist states, some states succeeded in playing off the two superpowers against each other and extracted aid from both. By the early 1960s, the World Bank had sponsored regional development banks and created an International Development Association (IDA), allowing it to make soft loans.[10] Beyond the need for capital, some governments of developing countries enjoyed more autonomy in foreign policy than their developed-country counterparts because they were not bound into American security alliances.

But, unsurprisingly, from the start it was the constraints of the external world that were decisive. Whilst American detachment yielded sovereignty in security matters, in doing so it left the militaries of the new states as independent political actors. Indeed, where an American president claimed that the communists were a serious threat, there was always the risk that Washington would at least tacitly side with the military in overthrowing an elected government. Economically, those who came to lead the new states could lay claim to some of the same power enjoyed by their older counterparts. They could protect significant sections of their economy from international competition and use control over some central aspects of production to direct material rewards to their political clients. But without a far steadier inward flow of capital, they could not hope to achieve high levels of growth through rapid industrialisation unless they had the domestic political strength to reduce immediate consumption and accumulate domestic savings. Without more open access to rich states' agricultural markets and so long as the price of commodities remained low, they could not realise high growth via non-industrial production. Without high growth, the burden of inventing nationhood could not be carried by providing economic services and would be pushed further towards an idea of national liberation from external forces. In its most radical form, this idea demanded that a nation-state be totally free from external economic control and any semblance of oppression derived from the imperial past.[11] Yet whatever its attractions as an instrument of nation-building, any attempt to withdraw substantially from the international economy would almost certainly provoke foreign governments and the international financial institutions to withdraw aid and credit, and expose the state to possible direct or indirect American intervention.

West Germany

In May 1949, the Allies established the state of West Germany on a truncated piece of the territory that had once held the Weimar republic. Few Germans regarded it as an acceptable German state. The Soviet Union controlled what had been Prussia, West Berlin was isolated deep within what would become East German territory, and, even if reunification could one day be secured, the Allies had insisted that the state's eastern frontier ran along the Oder and Neisse rivers, which conceded territory to Poland and the Soviet Union. In crucial respects, the new West German state also lacked external sovereignty. It was not allowed an army, it could not determine its own foreign or trade policy, and the Allies regulated its industrial production. Militarily, it was utterly dependent on American support but it was excluded from the United States' security alliance in western Europe. Any West German government was, consequently, in a precarious position since their domestic opponents could all too easily charge that they were accepting subordination to the Allies and acting too slowly to secure reunification – without which, in the medium to long term, the state's authority was politically suspect.[12]

Constitutionally, the Allies had reconstructed the West German state on federalist and parliamentary principles. The constitution separated power between the federal government and ten Länder and Berlin, giving the Länder specified formal powers within their own territories and through the Bundesrat, the second parliamentary chamber, a veto on any legislation directly affecting their competences. These powers were protected by a constitutional court with the right of judicial review and a constitution that forbade much amendment. The West German state was not, however, as weak as most federal counterparts. It had considerable fiscal powers and, with the exception of Bavaria, none of the Länder had a strong historical claim to autonomy. Unlike the Weimar constitution, West Germany's Basic Law, in dispensing with anything more than a symbolic president, did create a single source of leadership in the office of the chancellor. Where there were no restrictions on sovereignty, the West German state could be led.

As for nationhood, West German governments confronted a particular dilemma. The burden of nationhood had to fall on the provision of economic services and perhaps a constitutional patriotism. In one sense, the expulsion of large numbers of Germans out of the post-war territories of Poland, Czechoslovakia and the Soviet Union made this easier. Leaving aside the East Germans, virtually all those claiming German nationality were living in territory formally recognised as German, and the Holocaust meant that there were no internal national minorities except for a small Danish population in Schleswig Holstein. East Germany, however, did present an acute problem. Those who led West Germany wanted to reconstruct a German, not West German, nationhood that would in the future provide the basis for support for a reunified German state. But that German nationhood had in the circumstances to be primarily defined through the actions of a West German state within its own territory, and if successful, it would effectively undermine the imaginative idea of the Germans as a single people both for those who benefited from its rule and those who didn't.[13]

Securing support for democracy was similarly problematic. Once more an alliance of other states had imposed it on a German state. Nonetheless, the limitations on external sovereignty encouraged the West German political class to see far more clearly than their Weimar predecessors had done that for democracy to survive those with power had to defend it against its enemies. Former high-level Nazis were purged from public life and until 1953 stripped of the franchise. The Communist party was banned and known communists discriminated against in the public sector. Only those who accepted that the question of who exercised power should be settled by elections were constitutionally allowed to run for office, and the electoral system gave representation in the Bundestag solely to those who received 5 per cent of the national vote. For all the potential problems it faced, the West German state was unlikely to fail because of the absence among democrats of any will to, or understanding of, power.[14]

In the first elections of the Federal Republic, the Christian Democratic party (CDU) scraped a narrow victory. From the outset, Chancellor Konrad Adenauer was convinced that his government had to commit itself unequivocally to the United States. The pursuit of reunification had indeed to be a reason of state but it could only be securely realised, Adenauer believed, within the framework of the Atlantic alliance. Anybody who dissented from that, and that included the Social Democratic party (SPD), had no place within a West German government. Aware that this strategy offered the SPD the chance to present itself as the party of German nationalism against his own kow-towing to Washington, he worked to get as much external sovereignty as possible restored quickly. First and foremost, he pushed for European and Atlantic multi-state associations that West Germany could join. In giving French governments and officials a say over aspects of West German economic and political life, Adenauer asked for restrictions to be lifted. This required him to deploy the language of Europe, presenting institutions and policies that served West German self-interest as a necessary and general European good.[15]

Adenauer received his first rewards in May 1950 when the creation of the ECSC secured the dissolution of the International Ruhr Authority, and the outbreak of the Korean War led Truman to decide to rearm Germany. French governments procrastinated about the auspices under which rearmament should take place, but Washington would not accept anything less. By 1955, the Eisenhower administration had ensured the demise of the occupation statutes, admitted the rearmed West German to NATO, and freed it of all industrial restrictions. Nonetheless sovereignty was still incomplete. The Allies retained prerogatives in Berlin, over a peace treaty and in settling reunification. Forbidden an independent nuclear deterrent, the West German state was dependent for defence on American and British forces sited in its territory.[16]

By the late 1940s, the economy was beginning to recover from the devastation, food shortages and inflation of the immediate post-war years on the back of American financial support. Unlike many other European governments, Adenauer's finance minister, Ludwig Erhard, wanted to recreate a reasonably liberal economy. The state, he judged, could not be an effective direct agent of industrial development even under the conditions of the Bretton Woods settlement. Instead, he believed the state could best serve growth by protecting market competition between firms and supporting those willing to produce export-competitive goods. After 1949, the West German government proceeded to liberalise more rapidly than any other large west European state and did nothing to discourage a flood of imports even when the balance of trade moved into significant deficit, forcing the independent central bank, the Bundesbank, to tighten monetary conditions. But when, during the Korean War, the Americans demanded an end to a policy in practice biased against the kind of industrial production necessary for rearmament, Erhard had to fight extremely hard to save the government's liberal approach because the Americans wanted raw materials allocated to areas of the economy they deemed vital for security interests, and Adenauer wanted to make concessions to win more sovereignty.[17]

By 1955, Erhard's approach, often referred to as 'the social market', was yielding clear rewards. The West German economy had become the locomotive of west European growth. Its exports were growing faster than its imports, and much faster than its GDP. The profits generated provided the basis for ever-growing levels of investment. Throughout the 1950s, Erhard and Adenauer were able to exploit American anxiety about the future of the state to keep the Deutschmark at an undervalued rate even as annual trade surpluses accumulated. Abetted by the Bundesbank's statutory responsibility to direct monetary policy towards price stability, they also used fiscal policy and informal negotiations with trade unions and business groups to maintain a tight anti-inflationary discipline. Without ever tempting a balance-of-payments crisis, by the end of the 1950s, the West German government had realised both full employment and some capital account convertibility.[18] Such economic success made the SPD's opposition to Erhard's social market politics, and with it the Atlantic commitment on which they in one way or another depended, increasingly difficult, and in 1959 the SPD repudiated reformist Marxism.

The CDU government could not, however, turn its economic success into a platform to reassert the West German state as a European power equal to Britain and France. During the negotiations to create the European Atomic Energy Community (EURATOM) and the European Economic Community (EEC), it was at a clear disadvantage to the French government. EURATOM offered the West German government little because it was prohibited from nuclear development. Given the economy's export success, the EEC would also have served it better as a west European free trade area rather than a customs union that invited retaliation from those against whom its external tariff was directed. But the price for pressing this case, as Erhard wished to, was high. Without giving the French what they wanted on trade, there would be no new west European multi-state association, and membership of all such associations, as Adenauer understood, was a necessary condition of securing reunification when the opportunity came. So long as the West German state was divided and others could claim to fear it, it had to remain subordinate to Paris on the terms and direction of western Europe's multi-state associations.[19]

Even more seriously, by the end of the 1950s events were exposing the full extent of West Germany's dependence on the United States. In November 1958, the Soviet premier, Nikita Khrushchev, issued an ultimatum that if West Berlin were not transformed into a demilitarised neutral city within six months, he would hand it over to the East German government, something that Adenauer would not tolerate. But it soon became clear that the Americans were nowhere near as concerned about such a development as Adenauer and, if Khrushchev were serious, might even contemplate a neutral Germany before taking any substantial risk to protect the territorial status quo. When, in August 1961, the East Germans erected the Berlin Wall, the Kennedy administration was unwilling to act militarily. Locked so far into East German territory, West Berlin could only be defended by a nuclear war that the Americans weren't prepared to fight. Adenauer claimed not to want such a war, but he reacted angrily to what he saw as the American betrayal.

By the end of 1962, events had secured Soviet acceptance of West Berlin as West German territory. Nonetheless, after the Cuban missile crisis Kennedy concluded that the United States had to find some kind of accommodation with the Soviet Union. Redrawing the territorial boundaries within Europe to suit the West German government could not be part of any such détente. The Americans had never pushed the issue of Germany reunification. But for more than a decade they had done nothing publicly to suggest that their rhetorical commitment to it was insincere. Now, their priorities were transparent, and the mythical elision of West German and American interests in Adenauer's external political strategy was exposed.

Adenauer turned towards Paris, and accepted de Gaulle's unconditional support for West Germany's territorial integrity throughout the Berlin crisis. In January 1963, the two governments signed a Franco-German friendship treaty which provided for permanent consultation 'prior to any decision, on all important questions of foreign policy, and in the first place on questions of common interest, with a view to arriving, insofar as possible, at a similar position'.[20] But Adenauer comprehended perfectly clearly that an alliance with France that appeared to restore a diplomatic parity between the two states did constitute a security policy. That still depended on the United States, and Kennedy wished to entice West Germany away from de Gaulle. In the summer of 1963, Kennedy offered membership of a fleet of nuclear missiles under NATO command. He had, however, though lost faith in Adenauer and his officials made their warmest overtures to Erhard, a known sceptic regarding the Franco-German treaty. In October 1963, knowing that he had lost the Americans' loyalty, Adenauer resigned.[21]

Under Erhard's chancellorship, the economy continued to thrive but the government struggled to keep some of the conditions on which that success rested out of its relationship with the United States. Erhard saw no reason to challenge the United States' monetary dominance. But once confidence in the dollar ebbed during the Vietnam War, his government had to fight to defend the undervalued Deutschmark. It also had to find reasons to justify why, given its prosperity, it could not finance its own security. In the autumn of 1966, at a moment when the economy had entered recession, Johnson asked the West German government for full 'offset' payments for the maintenance of the 200,000 American troops in the country. When Erhard failed to get Johnson to soften the terms, his government fell. Its successor, a grand coalition between the CDU and the SPD, paid what the Americans demanded.[22] Economic success had achieved much, but sustaining nationhood appeared to demand action towards full sovereignty and autonomy, the viability of which had proved illusory.

Japan

The Truman administration and the Supreme Commander for the Allied Powers (SCAP) that assumed authority in Tokyo in 1945 were convinced that the Japanese state had to be tamed and turned into a democracy. They resolved to demilitarise and reconstruct the existing state, and to transform the economic and social lives of the citizens subject to it. In this spirit, SCAP imposed a new constitution that reduced the emperor to a 'symbol of state', subordinated the bureaucracy to an executive dependent on a parliamentary majority, and renounced the possession of armed force. In so doing, the Americans appeared convinced that the necessary condition of Japanese democracy was a democratic society, one in which all remnants of feudalism and concentrations of economic power were eradicated and organised labour could participate. If democracy were to thrive, SCAP judged, the powers of the Japanese modern state had to be weak and the claims of citizens against it strong.[23]

By 1952, when SCAP handed power to a Japanese government, the Truman administration was operating from a rather different set of assumptions as to what was at stake in securing the success of the Japanese state. Above all, it now wanted to preserve Japan from the Soviet and Chinese spheres of influence, and this demanded that the Japanese state had more power than SCAP had envisaged. Economically, the Americans allowed the Japanese cabinet to cultivate close relations with the revitalised *zaibatsu*, which concentrated industrial and financial power in interconnected oligopolies, and to retain considerable controls on foreign exchange, trade and prices. Legally, the state was given the authority to arrest communists, forbid strikes and control trade unions. Militarily, it could command physical force, initially in the form of a 75,000-strong police reserve corps, which, by 1955, had become a self-defence force of 200,000 men.[24]

Nonetheless, the new Japanese state, like its West German counterpart, did not enjoy full external sovereignty. The United States forbade trade with China, Japanese producers' most obvious foreign market. By the terms of a security treaty signed at the same time as the peace treaty, the US retained control over Okinawa and the Ryukyus and Bonin islands whilst having the right to station troops in Japan. The Japanese government received no guarantee that the Americans would defend Japan, whilst having to accept that they could be used to put down any internal rebellion. In the words of John Foster Dulles, the treaty 'amounted to a voluntary continuance of the occupation'.[25]

As in West Germany, the absence of full external sovereignty left the party of government, the conservative Liberal Democratic Party (LDP), vulnerable to attack from nationalists. The left, centred on the Japanese Socialist party (JSP), saw in the issue a path to power, convinced that the state could not simultaneously maintain its anti-war constitution and serve as the linchpin of American security commitments in Asia. Nonetheless, the circumstances out of which the security treaty was born offered significant opportunities to the LDP government. Truman wanted an unrestricted American military presence in Japan because he considered that the United States had vital security interests in east Asia. The first military consequence of this judgement was Truman's decision in 1950 to fight in Korea, which the then Japanese prime minister, Shigeru Yoshida, described as a 'gift from the gods'.[26] Very quickly, Washington established Japan as its multi-purpose base for the war, and the economy began to boom. Industrial producers who could meet American defence demands thrived, and since the Americans paid for the goods in dollars, the Bank of Japan (BoJ) accumulated foreign exchange reserves. By the time the security treaty came into effect in

1952, there was a basis for export production and a promise from the Truman administration to protect Japanese trading interests.[27]

The LDP government gambled in 1952 that it could make enough of these economic opportunities to contain the dangers created by the security treaty. The post-war Japanese state would survive if those who ruled it could convince sufficient numbers of its subjects that economic success, not external sovereignty, should be the first reason of state whatever the ensuing humiliations. From the beginning, Yoshida's government understood that an effective trade policy was the necessary condition of growth. Without any raw materials, Japan had to import them. Unable to sell to China or the Soviet Union, the state had to exploit whatever export markets the US was willing to open. It was imperative, therefore, the government judged, to import only what was absolutely necessary whilst ensuring that these purchases could be paid for with export earnings that were neither subject to significant cyclical variation, nor likely to be undercut by lower-cost competitors.

To the first end, the government set out systematic import controls, deploying low tariffs on raw materials and the kinds of capital goods that could be used to develop domestic industries whilst slapping high duties on almost all finished goods and consumer products. To the second, the government sought to construct an export capacity in capital- and technology-intensive sectors, oriented towards western markets, and an integrated shipping infrastructure to support that trade.[28] To realise both ends, the government retained fierce capital and exchange controls. Only those whose capital was directed towards raw material extraction were allowed to invest abroad, and only foreign capital offered in the form of official loans, such as from the World Bank, was allowed to enter Japan.[29] This kind of strategy required that the state possess a range of powers and within it a site of authoritative economic judgement, insulated from the dynamics of electoral politics.[30] The Ministry of International Trade and Industry (MITI) gave 'administrative guidance' to firms and worked through the Bank of Japan to direct credit to its chosen patrons.[31] It encouraged the *zaibatsu* to regroup around a bank and hold each other's shares, allowing these firms to build up high levels of long-term debt without coming under any kind of market pressure.[32]

By any standards, the LDP governments were successful. By the early 1960s, Yoshida's successor, Kishi, was presiding over average growth rates of 10 per cent. With Japanese consumers saving a significant proportion of their income in government-sponsored post-office accounts, the state had also built up a considerable pool of capital, allowing it to repudiate foreign investors. Obviously, with resources concentrated in export sectors and those on whom the LDP depended, some lost from the government's approach, and a large wage differential emerged between those firms that directly benefited from the state's resources and those that did not. Japanese consumers, meanwhile, were forced to pay high prices for domestically produced food and consumer goods, and the trade unions were excluded from any political influence. And, unlike, their counterparts in Europe, the LDP governments did not look to protect the relatively poor with transfer payments. But in the face of what the government could so easily present as *national* prosperity, nobody in the opposition wished to challenge it on this political territory.

The question for the LDP governments was whether they had gambled correctly in attaching primacy to the economy. During the first half of the 1950s they had little reason to doubt that they were right, but during the second half of the decade the relationship with Washington tested their judgement. Externally, Japan's economic success strengthened the Eisenhower administration's belief that it should contribute more to its own defence. Internally, some within the LDP were becoming uneasy about the price of Japanese security. In 1958, Kishi formally asked Washington for negotiations to revise the security treaty, but Eisenhower saw no reason to move when the US was wading further into the quagmire of Vietnam. Only when Kishi convinced Eisenhower that the LDP could actually lose power to those who wanted a neutral external strategy did he extract a promise to negotiate.

But in pushing the issue, the government gave the anti-militarist and neutralist opposition the opportunity to rally. In March 1959, the left established a new organisation to mobilise dissent, and won a preliminary court victory declaring the treaty unconstitutional. In this context, any concessions Washington offered would never be enough to turn the negotiations to Kishi's advantage. When, in January 1960, the two governments signed a new ten-year treaty that gave an explicit guarantee in event of attack, the opposition responded with large-scale strikes and demonstrations. The government struggled to ratify the treaty. In an increasingly tense atmosphere, it used the police to eject members of the JSP from the Diet and cancelled a planned visit from Eisenhower because it could not guarantee his safety.[33]

Although the government survived the crisis of 1960 with the treaty intact, nobody within the LDP could any longer seriously doubt that it had to protect its flank on sovereignty. In such a spirit, Kishi's successor, Hayato Ikeda, pressed for the return of Okinawa. But the external conditions supporting the LDP's rule were deteriorating. From the outset, the LDP government's economic strategy had been shaped by American willingness to sacrifice its short- to medium-term trading interests for the sake of security. If Japanese producers were to continue to export easily into American markets and to enjoy protection at home, the government could not afford to miscalculate where the limits of American tolerance lay. The more the Japanese current account surplus grew, the greater the risk became. To press too hard over Okinawa could only strengthen the will in the White House to restrict Japanese exports or to demand a revaluation of the yen. Nonetheless, the LDP government still believed in 1968 that the Americans were sufficiently anxious about the state's survival to do everything they could to protect its hold on power, especially after they returned the Bonin islands to Japanese administration. But that expectation was subject to Washington maintaining a strategic commitment in Asia that was causing it mounting problems. If that expectation were dashed, there were good reasons to suppose that the LDP's whole strategy for securing consent to the Japanese democratic state would be in some jeopardy.

Britain

If the post-war West German and Japanese governments had no choice but to absorb the domestic political consequences of a substantial loss of external sovereignty, the implications for the British and French democracy of the United States' rise to global dominance were rather less certain. During the last years of the war Churchill had tried to persuade Roosevelt that when peace came Britain must remain a first-rank great power. Of course, Churchill accepted, the war had cost the economy dearly, but, he asserted, it had also demonstrated the British state's moral right to stride the world stage the equal of any. Nobody could reasonably expect a British government to forsake the rewards of six years of suffering, or expose itself, once competitive electoral politics resumed, to the charge that it had lost the peace.

In this spirit, at Bretton Woods the British government established sterling as a reserve currency whilst retaining a sterling area that would allow Britain to retain dollar-earnings from its colonies, and the inconvertibility of the current and capital accounts. Churchill's military and diplomatic intentions were no less ambitious. Britain would relinquish those territories where rule had become impracticable, including India and Palestine, but the empire in Africa and the Middle East would remain and be defended on the waters of the Mediterranean. In December 1944, Churchill ordered the British troops that had landed in Greece to end the Nazi occupation into a war against Greek resistance. Later, Churchill extended a security guarantee to Turkey too.[34]

Yet whatever premium most of the British political class attached to external status, the ambitions of post-war governments were financially

hostage to Washington. By the end of the war, exports had fallen precipitously, the economy's need for imports was still accelerating, and the
British state was the most indebted in the world. Securing American aid
was an essential reason of state. In 1945 the new Labour prime minister,
Clement Attlee, and his chancellor knew that they could only resist
Washington by plunging the economy into a far worse crisis. By the end
of 1946, the American demand for sterling convertibility by July 1947
forced the government to confront the reality that it could not afford
both the Mediterranean commitment and an expanding welfare state.
If it stirred demand at home, sucking in American imports, and spent
dollars abroad, it could not conceivably realise convertibility. In
February 1947, Attlee told Truman that he was terminating all aid to the
Greek and Turkish governments.[35] For a moment in the second half of
1947, Attlee's foreign secretary, Ernest Bevin, convinced himself that
Marshall aid presented an opportunity to resurrect British power. Saved
from immediate balance-of-payments doom, he fantasised, Britain now
had the opportunity to ally with France to develop western Europe with
an African hinterland as a third force. But such an economic bloc could
not enhance British security. As Bevin understood perfectly well, a
balance of power in Europe depended on the United States. Facing this
truth in 1948–49, Bevin worked harder than anyone to push the Truman
administration towards NATO.

The internal authority of the British state proved remarkably robust
in the face of these developments. The Labour government had withdrawn from the state's prize possession abroad, humiliatingly abandoned other imperial commitments because of currency problems and
made the security of the British state dependent on membership of a
regional security alliance commanded by a foreign power. But the political fallout was minimal. Few rebelled within the Labour party, the
Conservatives were unable to turn events into an opportunity to recapture power, and no new nationalist movement emerged. When
Churchill returned to office in 1951, he continued to cultivate the
grandiose rhetoric of the imperial state and protested that his foreign
secretary was too willing to accommodate himself to the lifeless task of
matching commitments to scare resources, but he did not reverse
course.

Nothing more demonstrated the resilience of the British state to the
merciless decline of its external power in a world dominated by the
United States than the Suez affair in 1956 and its aftermath. In 1875,
Britain had bought nearly half the shares of the Suez Canal Company
when Egypt was placed under an Anglo-French protectorate, and still
had its troops in Egypt seventy years later. In 1954, after three years of

guerrilla attacks, the Conservative government agreed to a two-year timetable for withdrawing British troops from Egypt, leaving a base at Suez for use in the event of future emergencies. When, in July 1956, the Egyptian president, Colonel Nasser, nationalised the Suez Canal Company, Eden wanted to act decisively to reverse what he deemed an unacceptable attack on legitimate British interests in Egypt, since a quarter of British imports and 60,000 British troops passed through the canal a year. He looked to Eisenhower for support. When none was forthcoming, he turned to France and Israel. Without informing most of his cabinet, the responsible civil servants or Eisenhower, he concocted a plan in which British and French troops would seize the Canal after Israel had first attacked and given Eden and the French premier a pretext to issue Nasser an ultimatum that they knew he could not possibly accept. When British and French forces began their attack Eisenhower was furious. Militarily, Eisenhower was presented with a *fait accompli*. But like all its post-war predecessors, Eden's government was operating under severe financial constraints. After six days of speculation in the currency markets, during which the Bank of England lost 15 per cent of its dollar and gold reserves, Eisenhower indicated that he would not support an IMF loan to salvage sterling. With half an eye on the premiership, the chancellor, Harold Macmillan, told Eden that he would have to resign if the war did not cease. Without consulting the chiefs of staff, Eden ordered British troops to withdraw.[36]

Virtually everything about the Suez affair was disastrous for Eden. He had divided his ministers, he was humiliated by Eisenhower, he was caught lying to the House of Commons, he had left the relationship with France in tatters, he had become the first leader in British history to end a war he was winning at the behest of another state, and, in January 1957, in failing health and dissembling feebly about what had happened, he resigned. Yet beyond Eden's demise, the Suez affair brought remarkably little political fallout. Eisenhower's brutal demonstration of the realities of the post-war world was certainly an existential thunderbolt for the British political class, most of whom, despite the events of 1947, appear never to have contemplated the possibility that the exercise of British military force could be curtailed either by the tedious problem of managing an exchange rate, or by American derision. Yet for the future of the British democracy, the Suez affair was significant not for what did happen but what did not. The military neither disobeyed orders, nor charged the politicians with betrayal. Without fuss, the Conservative party picked Macmillan, the man who had effectively taken the decision to terminate the war, to succeed Eden, and were comfortably re-elected two years later. Those within the electorate who reacted most angrily to events were not those stunned by Eisenhower's disloyalty, but by Eden's mendacity and disregard for the UN. And in none of Britain's remaining colonies did nationalists seize the opportunity to press their advantage, ensuring that future governments could withdraw from the remains of the empire at their own speed.[37]

In the wake of Suez, Macmillan ordered a full-scale review of Britain's external commitments. Just months after he had taken office, his defence secretary announced a 50 per cent reduction in the size of the army, the end of conscription and the withdrawal of troops from various imperial outposts. So far as Britain would remain a power on the world stage, the government explained, it would be as an independent nuclear power. Since Britain's nuclear forces relied entirely on a single weapons platform, this necessitated the development of a new delivery system. Yet within three years, the government had abandoned its nuclear programme and persuaded the Eisenhower administration to sell it air-to-surface missiles for its existing bombers. However, Kennedy's defence secretary, Robert MacNamara, was not keen for Britain to hold nuclear weapons, and cancelled the air-to-surface project. Only after Macmillan had made a bid for membership of the EEC at Kennedy's behest was he able to convince the president to grant him submarine-launched missiles as a replacement. The weapons could only be used with American consent, giving lie to any claim that Britain possessed an independent nuclear deterrent. In pursuing his cause, Macmillan antagonised the French president, Charles de Gaulle, who responded by vetoing British membership of the Community.[38]

Yet as the last semblance of independent power slipped through Macmillan's hands, few wanted to blame anybody and nobody saw an opportunity for radical political change. The potentially lethal undercurrent to the Suez affair was not the failure of foreign policy but the weakness of sterling. In keeping sterling as a reserve currency and encouraging creditors in the Commonwealth to keep their money in London after the war, successive governments had exposed the currency to the ebbs and flows of movements in financial markets, despite the protection that capital controls afforded to a fixed exchange rate. Throughout the 1950s, large-scale expenditure on overseas military commitments had put the balance of payments under persistent pressure and stretched confidence in sterling. Successive governments had responded by modestly deflating the economy. With British exports sluggish in the face of an overvalued exchange rate, and domestic consumption stuck in a stop-go cycle, British growth was lower than that of any other developed country.

If there were to be any threat to the internal authority of the British over the next decade, it would come from economic failure. After 1961, governments of both parties had tried to use the state's powers to modernise infrastructure and direct producers. But, albeit less dramatically, they were as constrained by sterling's weakness in economic policy as Eden had been over Suez. If exports did not improve rapidly, they could only escape the deflationary bias created by sterling by antagonising Washington, either by devaluing or by pulling out of Malaya, where British troops were fighting communists, as the United States sank further into the quagmire of Indo-China. In the wake of what Macmillan and his successors took to be the lesson of Suez, none wished to do either. By the middle of the 1960s, the continuing drain of resources abroad and an ongoing balance-of-payments deficit had put sterling under immense pressure, requiring a steady stream of credit from the Johnson administration to save a parity that Washington's demand for assistance in Asia was undermining. But when, in the summer of 1966, the Labour government led by Harold Wilson was forced to choose between its domestic ambitions for growth and the Atlantic relationship, Wilson opted for the second and deflated the economy for the sake of the sterling parity.[39]

He could only, however, delay the inevitable. In 1967 the Wilson government succumbed to a devaluation, and a year later it announced a permanent retreat from all commitments east of Suez. As a result, the British modern democratic nation-state was left without effective external support. Without a British presence in south-east Asia, Washington no longer had a geo-political rationale to support sterling, but no British government could make a serious bid for EEC membership as long as de Gaulle remained French president. Yet, having come so late, neither devaluation nor reducing overseas expenditure were panaceas for the economy. By the time the Wilson government had minimised the external pressure on the balance of payments, wage inflation at home was stoking it. Rising wage increases had proved immune to the voluntary incomes policy of the Conservative government and the statutory approach adopted since 1966 by Labour. In 1969, Wilson tried another tack, proposing legal reforms to the trade unions to make strike action more difficult, only to be defeated by a rebellion from his own cabinet. Over the course of a decade, governments had been first unwilling and then unable to impose the state's authority over recalcitrant trade unions and employers. Yet if British governments continued to be impotent in the face of accelerating wage increases, the balance of payments would soon put sterling under renewed strain, recreating a severe deflationary bias in economic policy for which Johnson's successor had little incentive to assume responsibility. In these circumstances, the government could not expect to maintain its expenditure on the welfare state, or sufficient demand to ensure full employment. Without either one the idea of British nationhood as governments had articulated it since 1945 would look rather threadbare. The authority of the British modern democratic nation-state had proved exceptionally robust through a succession of difficulties since 1918. But even it was likely to be put to test by such an outcome.[40]

France

The internal authority of the French state and French democracy proved far less pliable to American power than the British. In the ignominy of dependency on the United States one constitutional republic failed and another was established to revert it. For Charles de Gaulle, the architect of the second post-war French republic, the durability of the state could not possibly depend solely on economic success or providing welfare services. Unlike any other post-war European leader, de Gaulle acted on the belief that the state could only secure obedience from its citizens and survive in a hostile world if the imaginative conception of external sovereignty endured.

After the defeat of the Third Republic in 1940 and of Vichy in 1944, a new state had to be inaugurated on French territory. For most of those who aspired to lead that state, simply securing rule over French territory was insufficient. They wanted a state commanding authority over the left bank of the Rhine and the Saar and the whole of the pre-war empire. The immediate external weakness of the French state made the first ambition difficult to realise. France only had occupation rights in Germany because Churchill had insisted upon them. Financially, like everybody else, the provisional French government was at the Americans' mercy. Territorially, the southwards reach of the French state was less immediately vulnerable. But if French governments were unwilling to relinquish any colonial territory, even in the face of effective independence movements, they would have to commit massive amounts of resources to the enterprise. Without a substantial hike in taxation, this would leave them dependent either on American aid when the Truman administration's purposes in Africa and south-east Asia were unclear, or on domestic debt that would allow the Americans to use the rules of Bretton Woods against them. It would also leave them requiring the day-to-day support of an army entrenched outside metropolitan France.

Internally, the new French state was dependent on elected politicians refashioning some belief in a singular French people and winning support for the compromises of democratic politics. During the 1930s, the governments of the Third Republic had struggled to do either. The external humiliation of 1940 and the events of the war had done nothing to dim the divisive passions of that decade. For most of the left, the collaborationists of Vichy had betrayed their country for private gain. For the right, the Resistance was too infested with communists to be trusted. In the face of bitterer passions than existed in Britain, French governments had rather better reason to presume that external success and glory were a necessary condition of conjuring a usable fiction of nationhood back into life. Meanwhile, support for democracy among the political class was equivocal. The Communist party (PCF), which was the largest party in the constituent assembly elected in October 1945, was led by a Stalinist. De Gaulle, who served as premier from October 1944 and was elected provisional president in November 1945, disliked the whole notion of competition between parties. In January 1946, de Gaulle resigned. After his departure, the other anti-Vichy parties found it easier to agree constitutional rules for the Fourth Republic. In a referendum in May 1946, the electorate accepted a constitution that gave decisive power to the lower house of the legislature rather than the executive, and established a single French political union extending over metropolitan France and the overseas departments and territories.

Until 1946, the provisional government tried to consolidate the state's internal authority and external security on its own autonomous terms through swift economic reconstruction and by subjugating Germany. The Monnet plan, announced in January 1946, served both these ends. The plan set out a five-year timetable to develop production and trade through extensive industrialisation, administrative planning and massive investment. It assumed that internal political stability would depend on growth and prosperity on recovering from the war before its Rhineland neighbour.[41] As matters of both territorial security and economic necessity, therefore, French ministers were determined to claim the Ruhr's natural resources as reparations, press for international ownership of the region, and enforce long-term limits on German industrial production even as the post-Morgenthau American predilection for rehabilitating and reconstructing Germany was gathering pace.

Before the Fourth Republic had even formally begun, events were forcing unwelcome choices on the provisional government and exposing the weak foundations of the new French state. In December 1946, the nationalist Viet Minh attacked a French garrison, and the prime minister, Léon Blum, reluctantly ordered the army to respond, and in doing so began a war for Vietnam. Within metropolitan France, the deterioration of economic conditions during the winter of 1946–47 prompted waves of strikes that strengthened the PCF's claim to the premiership, something which no senior figure in the centre parties or the Truman administration would tolerate. In May 1947, the socialist prime minister, Paul Ramadier, evicted the communists from the government and was rewarded with a World Bank loan of $250 million. But in accepting tutelage, Ramadier made the French state vulnerable to attack from the Gaullists as well as the communists on the issue of external sovereignty. That autumn, more than 3 million workers went on strike, calling for pay rises and protesting against the 'American party'. Ramadier's government fell. Convinced that France stood on the brink of civil war, its centrist successor incorporated eighty thousand reservists into the army to put down what it deemed an insurrection.

As elsewhere, the Atlantic relationship was not without its economic opportunities. Marshall aid propelled a successful Monnet plan. Through controlling the allocation of the fund's credits and import licences, a planning commission, insulated from the vagaries of electoral politics, assumed the authority to modernise appreciable sectors of the economy. Although the commission's influence waned after Marshall aid ended, its planning powers passed into the routine administrative apparatus of the French state, allowing bureaucrats, working with the Bank of France, to channel investment into long-term industrial development. Aided by a substantial devaluation of the franc in 1949 and generous tax support, French exports thrived. By 1958, the economy was growing at an annual rate of nearly 5 per cent.[42]

Diplomatically, successive French governments were able to extract payment from the Americans for acquiescing to a largely sovereign West German state. If the Americans wanted West Germany bound into multi-state associations in western Europe and wished the French to take the initiative in forming them, then French politicians came to realise that these associations could be designed first and foremost to serve French purposes. Just as the ECSC gave France a share in directing German coal and steel production, the proposals for the EEC and EURATOM, finalised in the Treaty of Rome in 1957, offered the French state substantially more than the other five members. EURATOM, in opening up Belgium uranium, procured a path to a nuclear deterrent. The EEC, meanwhile, bound the other member states into an economic commitment to the French empire, which was to be treated as part of the common market, and to French farmers through the promised Common Agricultural Policy (CAP). Most significantly perhaps, the EEC focused the diplomatic politics of western Europe, NATO aside, on a Franco-German alliance that France dominated. Whatever the fate of the empire, French governments had a stage on which they could strut as great power.

Nonetheless, the weight of American power eventually proved too heavy for the Fourth Republic to bear. In trying to finance industrial growth, a welfare state and wars in Vietnam and Algeria, successive governments took inflationary risks and ran significant budget deficits, ensuring persistent balance-of-payments problems and swelling illegal capital flight. By 1957, the state's finances were in crisis as ministers struggled to agree a budget with the Assembly whilst currency reserves were exhausted. In January 1958, the government, led by Félix Gaillard, procured a new American loan. The next month, French bombers destroyed a Tunisian village, convinced it was a base of the Algerian National Liberation Front. Immediately, Eisenhower threatened to withdraw the loan unless the government accepted American 'good offices' to negotiate Algerian independence. Gaillard succumbed but the Assembly would not back him, and in April his cabinet fell. Since governments of the Fourth Republic were notoriously short, Gaillard's exit was unexceptional, but this time the president, François Coty, could not find a successor. Of the parties in the Assembly, only the communists were willing to grant independence to Algeria and thus accept the American loan conditions, but the whole nature of the Atlantic relationship precluded such a government.[43]

In the political vacuum, sections of the army in Algeria and the European settlers determined that the future of the territory should be decided by all-out war, regardless of the will of those with constitutional authority in Paris. On 5 May, a desperate Coty asked de Gaulle to form a government. He refused. Three days later, Coty finally persuaded the centrist Pierre Pflimlin, who had come to accept a negotiated ceasefire, to take office. When the supreme commander in Algeria, General Raoul Salan, informed the president that the army would rebel if Pflimlin were invested, Coty declared a state of siege and assumed emergency powers. Salan threatened an invasion of metropolitan France, and waited for Pflimlin to resign and de Gaulle to assume office. Sensing that the country stood on the brink of civil war, Coty acquiesced. The next month, the Assembly gave de Gaulle six months' plenary powers to write a new constitution.

The Fourth Republic had failed because those in the army on whose coercive power it depended in the final instance had been unwilling either to pay the price Eisenhower demanded for financial support, or accept the authority of elected politicians to control that power.[44] Well aware of this truth, de Gaulle was far more concerned to reconstruct the internal authority of the state by establishing a clearer site of sovereignty within it, and to reclaim the autonomy it had lost to the United States, than he was to keep Algeria. In devising a new constitution he relocated

the political power of the French state in a president, chosen by an electoral college, and holding the authority to dissolve the Assembly, call ref-
erenda, appoint a prime minister and assume emergency powers. In a
referendum in September 1958, the electorate accepted the constitution by an overwhelming majority. Legislative elections, two months
later, secured de Gaulle a majority in the assembly, and a vote in the electoral college the following month gave him the presidency. The overwhelming test for the revamped French state was whether the army in
Algeria would accept its authority, especially since de Gaulle was ready,
once peace had been restored, to accept Algerian independence. When,
first in January 1960 and then again in April 1961, the army rebelled, De
Gaulle simply demanded their obedience on national television, and the
rebels yielded.

Only for one moment afterwards did the internal authority of the
French state appear at immediate risk. In the spring of 1968 thousands
of students in Nanterre and Paris took to the streets and occupied university buildings, demanding reform. When, in May 1968, millions of
workers joined forces with the students and went on strike, de Gaulle
persuaded the army to support him in exchange for an amnesty for
those charged with sedition over Algeria and threatened military action,
prompting the students and workers to capitulate.

Externally, de Gaulle wanted to restore the independence of the
French state in the hope that collectivist sentiments around the idea of
the French nation could carry some of the burden of securing consent
to the state's authority. On the EEC, he declared that he would not countenance any move to more supra-national authority. Most radically, he
wished to reassert the French state's authority over its own security whatever the financial cost. For de Gaulle, the governments of the Fourth
Republic in subordinating French decision-making to Washington had
abdicated responsibility over what should have been the first reason of
state. When NATO's chief commander refused to tell him where
American nuclear devices were on French territory, he raged: 'General,
this is the last time, I am telling you, that a French leader will hear such
an answer'.[45] Gradually, de Gaulle pushed the French state towards self-
defence, withdrawing the French Mediterranean fleet from NATO
command in 1959, ordering atomic testing in 1960, taking the French
Atlantic fleet out of NATO in 1963, and finally, in 1966, taking France
out of NATO and closing all American bases on French soil.

Whilst de Gaulle viewed the Atlantic military relationship as an urgent
liability, on economic issues he was initially more circumspect. Far from
banishing American investment capital, de Gaulle initially wished to use
it to stabilise the balance of payments. But once the balance of payments

had swung into surplus, he started to push against the post-war international economic order too. In 1963, after the American firm Chrysler had purchased a controlling interest in France's third-largest automobile manufacturer, de Gaulle's prime minister, Giscard d'Estaing, insisted that American investment capital was not welcome in France. Two years later, de Gaulle began to demand gold for dollars and publicly berate Johnson for expecting the rest of the world to hold inflated dollars to finance an unwinnable war in Indo-China. But in this confrontation with Washington, de Gaulle had fewer options. Certainly he had ended the financial dependency that had destroyed the Fourth Republic. But to change the terms of the post-war international economic order de Gaulle required allies and none was forthcoming, and de Gaulle's stance simply pushed capital that might have gone to France elsewhere. Neither would any other government support de Gaulle in trying to discipline the United States by turning Bretton Woods into a gold standard. So long as other states absorbed dollars, France's refusal to hold them could not precipitate a full-scale convertibility crisis.[46]

In part de Gaulle had been proved right in his judgement that the internal authority of the French state depended on more than economic success. In creating a constitutional basis for leadership and then using it to reclaim French sovereignty over security, he made the Fifth Republic internally stronger than probably any of its predecessors. But when, in April 1969, de Gaulle resigned after losing a referendum on constitutional issues, he bequeathed a set of economic problems that had potentially lethal consequences. As confidence had faltered during May 1968, so French currency reserves had drained away and de Gaulle was forced to accept a devaluation of the franc. The wage increases granted to stop the strikes soon produced a rise in inflation portending to more currency problems ahead. As in Britain, this would eventually impair the ability of governments to deliver the economic services to which citizens had become accustomed. But for the French state this would have other consequences. French presidents could not hope to maintain France's position vis-à-vis West Germany, on which the imaginative narrative of the grand-power state partly depended, if they had to accept the liability of a soft currency relative to the Deutschmark.

Italy

For Italian governments the price of American services proved rather easier to absorb, in good part because of the internal weakness of the Italian state. To succeed they had to secure an effective central site of authority and power, reconfigure a conception of Italian nationhood

without any imperialist connotations, and, in dire economic circumstances, safeguard support for democracy from the threat posed to it by
the most radical communists and the authoritarian wing of the Catholic
church. By 1945, almost all Italy's old trading markets had vanished. The
empire in Africa was gone, and Germany and Britain were in no position
to export raw materials on the scale they had done before the war. GNP
stood at the level it had done in 1911 whilst real wages were down a
quarter of their value in 1913. Strikes swelled across the country, peasants occupied land in the south, and the supply of labour was increasing
whilst employment opportunities diminished. Without external help,
thousands of Italians were likely to starve to death.

Initially, the anti-fascist political parties showed no special interest in
courting anything other than material support from Washington. In
June 1945, a new Italian government was formed under the leadership
of the deputy commander of Resistance forces. Five months later, the
Christian Democratic party (DC) leader, Alcide De Gasperi, replaced
him. From the outset, De Gasperi wished to build the post-war state on
Italian foundations. Within the governing coalition, he wanted to
defend the DC's credentials as a democratic Catholic party against the
Vatican's monarchical leanings, and to use the Socialist (PSI) and
Communist (PCI) parties' membership of the coalition to try to contain
the urban and agricultural rebellions that were spreading across the
country. Institutionally, he wanted to reclaim the powers of the old
fascist state for the new regime, including the semi-autonomous special
agencies Mussolini had sponsored.

For a short time, De Gasperi's judgement was vindicated. In June
1946, the electorate gave the DC the largest number of parliamentary
seats and voted to end the monarchy, strengthening the DC's grip on
power without sacrificing De Gasperi's tactical alliance with the left. But
internal and external circumstances quickly turned against him. In the
second half of 1946, the economy sank into an abyss of inflation, dollar
shortage and capital flight. That November, the DC performed disastrously in local elections. As relations between the United States and the
Soviet Union deteriorated, the DC and the PCI struggled to find compromises whilst the Vatican charged that the DC was undermining
Catholic values. When, in February 1947, the government was forced to
accept a peace treaty that required it to pay substantial reparations and
put Trieste under international supervision, De Gasperi's need to
protect the DC's right flank became overwhelming.

The events of the early Cold War and the problems of the economy
pushed De Gasperi towards a radically different strategy. He could not
deflate the economy without prompting the left to leave the coalition,

and he could not secure Marshall aid to offset deflation without meeting Truman's demand that he expel the PSI and PCI from the government. For a moment, in May 1947, events once again conspired against him. Just as he was finalising his move to form a new government of the centre-right, the Mafia shot dead eleven Sicilian peasants celebrating Labour Day. The initiative was passed back to the communists, and in the political fallout, De Gasperi resigned. But after his leftist successor failed to win a parliamentary majority, De Gasperi re-emerged to form a new DC government from which he excluded the left. Henceforth, the Italian state would be externally supported from Washington on terms that severely circumscribed who could command the power of that state regardless of the electorate's preferences.

The opportunities that American alliance offered the DC government were considerable. Most immediately, Marshall aid gave it a means to absorb the consequences of reducing inflation, without which it could not hope to win the confidence of the business classes who were illegally sending their capital abroad. It could now pursue both deflation and reconstruction without also having to worry so much about the consequences of the former or the cost of the latter. So long as the strength of the PCI appeared to leave the Italian state at permanent risk, the DC government had a trump card in asking Washington for more money. Where economic aid came, military protection followed. As control of the Mediterranean had become an essential component of the United States' strategic position in Europe, the Italian government was relieved of what would otherwise have been a considerable defence burden. By the early 1950s, Italy was a member of NATO, the recipient of a substantial amount of American arms, and the site of significant American bases. Nobody within an Italian government bearing these commitments was in a position to entertain the illusions about the inappropriateness of exercising power in a democracy that had sometimes afflicted Giolitti.

Domestically, the American alliance offered the DC government sufficient economic resources to try to enervate the radical left, and to regain the support of the Vatican and those Catholics hitherto tempted by a more authoritarian politics. In this way, the alliance tied the future of the Italian state to the success or failure of one political party. The DC's first crucial test was the parliamentary election of April 1948. The Americans spared little effort in helping their client. If the communists won, the US warned, all American aid would cease. One month prior to the election, the US restored Trieste to Italian rule. Against the fear of economic collapse, the electorate rewarded the DC with an absolute parliamentary majority.

The PCI was far from spent as an electoral force. But after failed insurrections in northern cities in the summer of 1948, the moment for revolution appeared to have passed. Thereafter, the party struggled to maintain any semblance of unity within the trade-union movement. Not having to fear well-organised resistance from the industrial working class, De Gasperi's government was free to chase growth through a low-wage economy. Having categorically excluded and weakened the left, the DC government was protected on its authoritarian flank. It could assure the church and its believers that the language of Italian nationhood was an indivisible Catholicism and anti-communism. The opponents of the church, the government promised, were also the political enemies of the Italian state. The very Catholic bent of the Italian language of anti-communism gave it a nationalist tone that perhaps more subtly than elsewhere disguised the power relations on which the Atlantic Alliance rested. In the past, many governments had tried to use the external world to advance a broad idea of Italian nationhood by conquest. Under the Atlantic Alliance, the DC used the support of a superior power to enforce the state's rule and exclude a substantial number of subjects from rhetorical membership of the Italian nation.[47]

De Gasperi was convinced that if he were to take full advantage of the American opportunity, he had to exploit whatever external economic resources were on offer. The economy needed a stable supply of raw materials and fuel, and export earnings to pay for them. Italian producers' advantage within the western European export competition lay in low wages and, compared to the franc and sterling, an undervalued exchange rate. If, the DC government calculated, large manufacturing producers in the north concentrated significant resources on exports, the economy could absorb unemployed agricultural labour from the south and grow without reigniting inflation. To increase investment in the export sectors, the government encouraged an external flow of capital and relaxed controls on investment abroad. To consolidate Italian producers' access to raw materials and other West European markets, the government joined first the ECSC and then the EEC. By the end of the 1950s, the government was rewarded with a rate of export growth faster even than the West German one.[48]

As well as searching for external capital and markets, the DC government sought to export abroad what it feared was the economy's excess labour. In 1955, the government struck an agreement that gave Italian workers special privileges in the West Germany labour market. In the Treaty of Rome, it won the inclusion of labour markets in the general commitment to trade liberalisation, which in procuring access to other states' labour markets saved the Italian economy from high unemployment.[49]

As it did elsewhere, this kind of external economic strategy depended on the state assuming certain powers. Since inflationary wage increases would have undermined the export drive, the DC government maintained a system of national collective bargaining. Industrially, the state took direct control of some commercial enterprises, and used the semi-autonomous agencies resuscitated by De Gasperi to reorganise production. Where companies were free from direct state involvement, ministers and bureaucrats forged close links, mediated through the Bank of Italy, with the large businesses and banks deemed most vital to prosperity. Successive DC leaders used these powers as direct instruments of patronage to reward their clients and shut out their opponents.

In securing the DC as the party of the government, De Gasperi and his successors uncovered a new strategy for turning the south into a quiescent territory. They began with land reform. By 1950, the government had expropriated sections of the large estates and redistributed them among the peasants. Through a collateral peasant organisation and local boards that distributed the land, the government tied the reform to its own patronage machine. Having begun to change the economic landscape of the south, the government then endowed a new agency, the *Cassa per il Mezzogiono*, to develop the south's infrastructure and also tied it through patronage to the DC. In creating a new class of peasants and dependent local bosses, the government had engineered a constituency in the south whose interests were for the first time tied to the political status quo. The alienated former landowners, meanwhile, were in no position to construct a broad coalition that could threaten the DC whilst the peasant organisations responsible for the post-war agitations were broken by the reforms that benefited most directly those who kept their distance from radical dissent.

The general strategy embarked upon by De Gasperi in 1947 was eventually undermined by its very success. During the years 1958 to 1963, the Italian economy grew at an annual average of 6 per cent, and investment and industrial production more than doubled. Several problems ensued. Territorially the rewards were uneven. The industrial north flourished but, even with an injection of resources, the still predominantly rural south could generate nowhere near the same level of average incomes. High growth, emigration to other EEC states, and migration from the south to the north created nearly full employment, but, as incomes rose, the onus on anti-inflationary discipline in wage bargaining intensified. Without it, or a devaluation of the lira that Washington would probably not have tolerated, Italian export producers competing on costs would be undercut. But, unlike its West German counterpart, the DC government could not easily entice the majority of trade unions towards restraint because they had deemed those allied to the PSI and PCI enemies of state.

The predicament divided the party. Some concluded that it had to court the non-communist left. Others distrusted any compromise, especially one that might antagonise Washington. In March 1960, the right-leaning Fernando Tambroni formed a new government without coalition partners but reliant on parliamentary support from the neo-fascist Movimento Sociale Italiano (MSI) and the monarchists. But after the police shot unarmed demonstrators in Genoa, citing the prime minister's authority to do so, those Christian Democrats led by party secretary Aldo Moro who had always doubted that supping with neo-fascists was viable, forced Tambroni to resign and put in place a new government allied to the republican and social democratic parties.

The DC had now reached an internal impasse. The right had been defeated but Mori could not win support for an alliance with the socialists against the communists, despite the PSI's embrace of NATO membership. They were saved by a new American president. Over the State Department's doubts, Kennedy signalled that he would support an opening to the socialists in order to rebind Italy into the Atlantic alliance at a moment when France was moving towards confrontation. In March 1962, the DC formed a new government that enjoyed the tacit parliamentary support of the PSI. Twenty-one months later, the PSI entered the government under Moro's leadership. But by the time Moro had secured the opening to the left, the economy was rapidly deteriorating. In 1962–63, wages increased by more than 40 per cent, spending on imports imploded, the balance of payments slid into deficit and capital flew abroad. Reform required expansion but the circumstances demanded deflationary measures to restore confidence and encourage acceptance of wage restraint, and the PSI found it increasingly necessary to protect its left flank.

Once the DC government had contained the communists in 1948, it paid little price for embracing the United States. Unlike the early postwar French governments, the DC did not have to defend the republic from rightists committed to external sovereignty. But in adopting the political strategy they had adopted, the DC governments had created economic problems that exposed fragility of a different kind in the Italian state. During the autumn of 1969, nearly 1.5 million workers were at one time or another on strike. Only after employers made substantial concessions did the government succeed in reimposing order. But the inflationary cost was less easily absorbed. Whatever help Washington offered, a fixed exchange rate did constrain economic policy, especially where governments were pursuing export-led growth. Only if the government could solve this problem in a way that the American president could accept could those who led the Italian modern democratic nation-state save it on the terms envisaged by Moro.

India

American presidents offered less to the democracies of Asia and Latin America, and such offers as were forthcoming were made less immediately. Where and when such help didn't materialise, the issue of sovereignty in relation to the United States was of little consequence. But it left the governments of these new states to find their own solutions to problems that were difficult even for governments of richer countries that could tap American resources more readily. Where Washington did eventually extend assistance, few governments were in a position to contemplate the cost in external sovereignty as readily as the Italian government did, however desperate their need for foreign capital to improve living standards.

One of the few democracies to survive the experience was India. In some ways, the prospects for an Indian modern democratic nation-state were inauspicious. Prior to the British entry into the sub-continent, nobody had established unified rule over the domain that now constituted India, and the partition of the territory that the British had administered as a single realm left the new state with jurisdiction over land, primarily in Kashmir, claimed by Pakistan. Even if sovereign rule could be secured, the task of winning more willing consent to authority through the idea of nationhood appeared Herculean. India contained fourteen major linguistic groupings, three thousand caste groups, and a Muslim minority constituting one-sixth of the population. The religiously inspired violence that accompanied partition cost half a million lives. Out of this, those with power had to conjure, in Sunil Khilnani's words, 'an idea of India' on a scale beyond anything needed by those who had established states in the European world.[50] They also had to win support for democracy from the masses of the rural poor, some of whom in other parts of Asia were turning towards communism, and from high-caste Hindus whose hierarchical religion offered a strong argument against the whole notion of one-person one-vote.

The Congress government, led by Jawaharlal Nehru, that assumed power in August 1947 had to deal with these difficulties in forbidding economic conditions. Britain's wartime expenditure had triggered severe inflation, and partition had created food-supply problems. By

1949, Indian price levels for food and primary produce were considerably higher than elsewhere on the continent. Without a substantial reduction in prices, and all the ensuing deflationary consequences, governments would struggle to export, and the balance of payments and exchange reserves would become constant constraints on economic policy.[51]

Nonetheless, Nehru and his colleagues inherited an effective imperial state, laying claim to a well-trained central bureaucracy and a disciplined army. Since the British had devolved power to Congress at the provincial level in 1937, Nehru's government was also already educated in some of the complexities of democratic politics. Unlike some in interwar Europe, it understood that the state had to be defended against its enemies by power and banned the nationalist Hindu Mahasabha after the assassination of Gandhi in 1948, whilst encouraging several state governments to declare the Communist party illegal. Meanwhile, although caste sustained deep differences between Indian citizens, it also restrained aspiration and ambition and helped leave the majority of the rural poor illiterate and lacking in political consciousness beyond local circumstances.[52]

Just as the British had used regional diversity for their own purposes and so reduced the need for coercive rule from the centre, so Nehru wanted federalism to act as a buffer between the state and the potentially explosive passions of religion and language. The national government would neither seek to impose homogeneity, legal or otherwise, on the regions, allowing them to define themselves by their own governments in their own terms, nor allow itself to be captured by those demanding community rights to defend particular religious and linguistic identities. English, therefore, not any vernacular tongue, became the Indian language of state. Certainly the national government enjoyed a considerable array of powers. The president had the authority to proclaim a state of emergency and suspend the prerogatives of the state governments. Unlike in some federal constitutions, the fiscal powers of the Indian state were largely concentrated at the centre whilst national government could impose controls on the economy and direct material rewards to its regional supporters. But Nehru and his Congress colleagues conceded virtually all authority over agriculture, including its taxation, to the state governments in exchange for the large rural landlords agreeing to deliver the local vote for Congress.

If the Indian state could not be the vehicle of transforming Indian citizens into a more homogenous people, then the idea of India, Nehru concluded, had to be secular, accepting of religious plurality and opposed to Hindu nationalism.[53] Once the practical burden of conjuring nationhood could not lie with grafting particular symbols of identity onto the state's veneer, it had to be realised through economic success, including moderate redistribution. Constructed in this way, the imaginative terms of nationhood shaped a set of *de facto* rules for the electoral competition for power that worked hugely to Congress's advantage. Politicians at the centre did not directly appeal to sectional interests, passions or beliefs. Instead, they provided economic services mediated by regional and local barons who used non-political social identities to mobilise votes.[54] Consequently, any party that tried to represent particular social groups directly, Congress could deem an enemy of state.

Even if Washington had been more interested, Nehru was determined to lead the Indian state as an independent power in the external world. He believed that the size of India, the moral dignity of its struggle for self-determination, and the pluralism inherent to the idea of Indian nationhood, allowed the state to stay above the immediate fray of the Cold War. Despite Beijing's territorial claims on parts of the Himalayas under Indian rule, Nehru wanted an alliance with China, not the United States or the Soviet Union, and in 1951 obtained a non-aggression and non-intervention treaty. Although his government did take foreign aid to finance a large shipment of food grain and subsequently an American loan, Nehru was determined to stay militarily neutral.[55]

Economically, Nehru also wished to go it alone, using an import-substitution strategy to industrialise. In 1950, he established a planning commission directly under his authority and autonomous from the cabinet and Parliament. Under a succession of five-year plans, the first of which was published in December 1952, the commission placed certain spheres of production under state control and imposed tight rules on external access to the Indian economy. It shut out foreign investment, and through strict foreign-exchange rationing allowed imports only of the capital goods absolutely necessary to sustain domestic manufacturing, whilst keeping them cheap with an overvalued exchange rate. Recognising that its project would run into a balance-of-payments constraint without self-sufficiency in food production and exporting at least some surplus abroad, the government simultaneously set out to increase agricultural productivity through new co-operative farming ventures.[56]

By the end of the first plan in 1956, Nehru's internal and external strategies were in some difficulty, the one in part undermining the other. At home, under pressure from Congress's regional barons, Nehru had reluctantly accepted new boundaries for the state governments, except in the Punjab, on the basis of language, whilst the grip of the state governments over agriculture made structural reform to increase productivity impossible. Unable to finance its import bill from its diminishing supply of foreign exchange reserves, it saw its balance-of-payments deficit steadily worsen. Nehru responded by accepting short-term American credit and loosening controls on foreign investment whilst backing a second five-year plan to produce some capital goods domestically. Militarily and diplomatically the state's independence proved difficult to sustain. When, in 1962, China invaded Indian territory and inflicted a humiliating defeat, Nehru turned to Washington for help. Fortunately for him, Kennedy wished to improve relations and offered military aid. In accepting this help, Nehru made the Indian state partially dependent on a power that had for nearly a decade been allied to Pakistan. The third five-year plan, for 1961–66, meanwhile, promised virtual industrial self-sufficiency within ten years. In reality, this was impossible. To procure sufficient capital to proceed, the government succumbed to another American loan under the auspices of the World Bank, leaving it at the mercy of an external coalition intent on radical changes to export and import control, agricultural organisation and foreign investment.[57]

Nehru died in 1964, and his successor, Lal Bahadur Shastri, was willing to accommodate Washington and the World Bank on agriculture but ruled out devaluing the rupee or cutting tariffs. Shastri's own successor, Indira Gandhi, was even more determined to hold firm against external adjustment but events weakened her hand. The failure of two successive monsoons in 1965–66 made food imports essential to prevent starvation at a time when half of the country's imports were already being paid for by foreign aid, worsening the balance of payments and undermining the rupee parity. When, in September 1965, Pakistan invaded, locking the two states in military combat for four months, Johnson responded by cutting off aid to both of them. Finally, in the summer of 1966, Mrs Gandhi relented, devaluing the rupee by more than half, liberalising some tariffs and reducing export subsidies in return for new aid.

Seen to have wilted under external pressure, the government's credibility was badly damaged. It had promised that India would be an independent player in world politics and control its own economic destiny but it was trapped in the power-politics of the Cold War and the post-war international economic order. Victim of an attack from Pakistan made possible by American-supplied equipment, it had to turn to the Soviet Union for arms, but it could only survive economically by taking help from the American-dominated international financial institutions on whatever terms were available. With an impending election in 1967 and facing a charge of having betrayed national sovereignty to neo-imperialists, Mrs Gandhi tried to reconstruct the Indian state's autonomy. The summer after the devaluation, she used a trip to the Soviet Union to attack American policy in Vietnam as immoral. In retaliation, Johnson put the Indian government on a 'short leash', refusing to commit food aid more than one month in advance, and making its shipment dependent on Mrs Gandhi's 'good behaviour'. By the end of the year, Johnson had suspended all aid.

The imaginative language of national independence brought Mrs Gandhi limited reward, and when the elections came, Congress lost ground both nationally and regionally. Neither could the government do without external financial and military support and Mrs Gandhi now had little alternative but to turn to the Soviet Union for help. But having gambled on the possibility of autonomy from the Americans, Mrs Gandhi found her opportunity once agricultural production recovered. Despite the loss of American and World Bank aid and a fall in industrial investment in the late 1960s, her government stabilised the balance of payments by ditching radical import-substitution for financial prudence. Since Moscow demanded far less than Washington, Mrs Gandhi had freed the state's economic development from external pressure at the price of sluggish growth. To maintain this external stance, she had to exercise a tight domestic grip, both to contain demands from the poor for more rapid rises in incomes, and to control the state's expenditure. Increasingly obsessed with her own leadership, Mrs Gandhi seized the chance to justify a more personal form of rule. After the 1967 election, she bypassed the regional Congress bosses and tried to govern exclusively from the centre. Two years later, she split the Congress party into two, severing the channels of patronage that had connected the national government to the swathes of rural voters. She used the language of socialism, but she showed little interest in the kind of constitutional changes on agriculture that any genuinely redistributive politics required. Rather she was trying to contain radical passions by co-opting them rhetorically. In creating expectations that she had no intention of meeting and cultivating the cult of her own personality as a substitute for a structure of regional support, Mrs Gandhi was taking another political risk. But after directly appealing to voters in 1971 with the pledge that she would 'abolish poverty', she won a landslide election victory. The practical impossibility of the promise seemed irrelevant. So long as the government appeared the agent of radical politics and independent from the United States, it could protect the Indian modern democratic nation-state from pressure for land reform and faster industrialisation which would have been likely in their consequences to threaten the state's internal authority and democratic constitutional rules.

Indonesia

If Indian democracy succeeded without American support, Indonesian democracy collapsed quickly in the absence of any such support. In many ways, Indonesian democracy owed its existence to American power. For four years after the end of hostilities in the Pacific, Holland had fought a war to deny the rule of the republican government proclaimed by Indonesian nationalists as the Japanese left. In 1949, the Truman administration threatened to cut Marshall aid to the Dutch if they did not retreat, and the imperial power conceded independence over the territory except, at least for twelve months, to Irian Jaya, the western half of the island of New Guinea. But thereafter the Truman administration saw little reason to expend more energy on Indonesia although the country had strategic raw materials. When, in 1950, Acheson defined the American 'defensive perimeter' in the Pacific, he and his colleagues were convinced that Indonesia was securely within the American sphere of influence. The Americans would supply economic aid and military assistance, but they did not think concessions, such as settling Indonesian sovereignty over Irian Jaya, were necessary to secure an alliance.[58]

Internally, the Indonesian state faced the same handicaps as the Indian state without any of its advantages. Like India, Indonesia had never been ruled as a single territory before the arrival of its European conquerors. Unlike its Indian counterpart, the government that took office in 1949 was inexperienced in peacetime decision-making, and inherited an imperial state weakened by war. It confronted a decentralised army that regarded itself as superior to civilian leadership, having carried the struggle for independence single-handedly after the Dutch had captured the cabinet of the republican government. The subjects of the new Indonesian state were massively heterogeneous. Although the Japanese had made Indonesian the national language across the archipelago, the country contained more than 350 self-conscious ethnic groups, including a substantial Chinese population, and many of these groups were complicated by religion. The war for independence had deeply politicised significant numbers of citizens, and spawned protracted and sometimes violent conflict between the army, the republican government, traditional Islamic groups and the Communist party (PKI). The secular language of Indonesian nationhood that the republican government under the leadership of the radically minded Sukarno had cultivated centred on revolution and alienated much of the Islamic political class. It was also at least as likely to excite some to rebel against routinised authority, as to convince them to see the representation of a singular people in the new state.

In sharp contrast to India, scepticism about democracy was rife within the Indonesian political class and parts of the army. The first post-independence government was a coalition between the moderate Islamic party, Masyumi, and Sukarno's Indonesian National Party (PNI) under the leadership of Hatta Mohammad, Sukarno's more conservative former vice-president. Although the constitution unveiled in 1950 relegated Sukarno to a ceremonial presidency except in constitutional matters, and gave the new ministers at least formal control over the military, Sukarno and the most belligerent officers in the army had in Irian Jaya a clear issue around which to mobilise support. Elsewhere, significant opponents of democracy had already emerged during the war for independence. In the province of Aceh on Sumatra, local Islamic leaders had seized control after 1945 and established an Islamic regime. In 1948, the PKI had attempted a coup on Java against the republican government. In these circumstances, the fate of democracy would turn on whether those in office could outmanoeuvre enemies brooding within the state, and disarm those Indonesian subjects already directly challenging the state's authority.

The economic conditions that Hatta's government confronted were appalling. The war had badly damaged the country's infrastructure, and exhausted foreign exchange reserves. A black economy was beyond the control of the state. In the final year of the independence struggle, the republican government had collected tax receipts amounting to only two-thirds of its gross expenditure. The cumulative result was rampant inflation. Three months into office, Hatta's government announced a monetary purge, cutting large notes in half and sequestering sizeable bank deposits as compulsory loans. But when, as a result, liquidity and production plummeted, the government backtracked and passed emergency legislation to issue a new currency.

If federalism was a possible strategy to secure the state's internal authority in the circumstances, Sukarno moved to deny Hatta's government the option. To accept federalism, Sukarno believed, would be to betray the claim to an Indonesian revolution. The terms of the independence agreement had established a complicated federal constitutional structure, dividing the territory into a large Republic of Indonesia and fifteen smaller states under the auspices of a United States of Indonesia. In August 1950, Sukarno simply proclaimed that Indonesia would henceforth be a unitary state and announced elections for a constituent assembly. But actually securing territorial unity was deeply problematic. The governments of some of the smaller states were determined to maintain federalism. The East Indonesian government declared itself independent, prompting Hatta's successor to despatch the army to re-establish Indonesian sovereignty. But resorting to coercive force in the face of direct resistance could never be a sufficient condition for securing the state's internal authority. Without radically restructuring the economy, any government of the centre had to pursue a trade policy that palpably served only one or other of the interests of the net-importing Java or the net-exporting outer islands. Confronted with this dilemma, the instinct of successive governments in Jakarta was to protect the Javanese economy with a high exchange rate, thus hurting producers across the rest of Indonesia and gifting the secessionists a rallying cause for rebellion.

Labouring under this tense territorial politics, the first two governments formed under the new constitution, led by Natsir Mohammad and Sukiman Wirosandjojo respectively, concentrated on trying to dampen expectations of revolution. Domestically, these governments, especially Sukiman's, tried to suppress the PKI. Externally, despite a formal position of neutrality, they looked to court western support. They decided against confronting the Dutch over investment, and bided their time over Irian Jaya. Although Natsir's government rejected the military aid offered by the Truman administration in October 1950, it did take an American loan under the auspices of the Export and Import Bank, and also welcomed American and British investment capital. For much of the Korean War such caution was rewarded with substantial growth. As the demand for raw materials in the West and Japan intensified, the price of Indonesian exports, especially rubber, rose. Off the boom in trade, these governments balanced the budget, stabilised the balance of payments and built up a supply of reserves. Once solvent, they devoted resources to development projects, financing numerous new private firms, run by Indonesians, and an array of state companies in the hope that growing prosperity would quell the excitement of revolution and sustain routinised authority.

But by the middle of 1952, the external foundations of what development had taken place were being eroded. As the Korean War wore on, the Americans began to press harder for concessions on security in exchange for their dollars. In January 1952, Sukiman secretly accepted new aid under the terms of the Mutual Security Act. Once the deal became public, his government fell, accused of betraying Indonesian sovereignty. His successor, Wilipo, inherited a full-scale financial crisis. From February 1951 to September 1952, the price of rubber fell massively, making it impossible for the government to finance imports of manufacturing products from the West and Japan, the balance of payments fell back into deficit, absorbing most of the state's foreign exchange reserves and discouraging foreign investors, and growth stalled.

Wilipo's government responded by imposing import restrictions and a range of austerity measures. The burden of deflation fell heavily on the Indonesian firms that the Natsir and Sukiman governments had sponsored and on expenditure on the army. Unwilling to accept that government ministers had the authority to act against military interests, the army's leaders organised demonstrations, and tried to intimidate Sukarno into dissolving Parliament. Whilst the army failed in its immediate objective, it had indicated in harsh terms the limits of its support. In June 1953, Wilipo's cabinet fell. He was replaced as prime minister by Ali Sastroamidjojo of the PNI, who formed a cabinet without any Masyumi ministers. Within months Ali was left even more dependent on the army than his predecessors when radical Islamic groups established a rebel government in Aceh. Ali ordered the army to quell the insurrection but a military stalemate ensued and the rebellion spread. By 1954, the army was entrenched not only in Aceh but in West Java and South Selawesi too.

Notwithstanding the precarious economic and territorial circumstances with which his government struggled, Ali reversed the political strategy followed by the first three post-independence governments. Where they had been cautious, seeking practical rewards from pragmatic policies, Ali's cabinet wished to reanimate the idea of revolution and restored the PKI's legal status. Where they had opened markets to external competition, it discouraged foreign capital and pressed for overtly Indonesian control over the economy. Where they had not pressed hard on Irian Jaya, it ordered a series of infiltrations. Where, within certain limits, they had courted American support, Ali, in alliance with Nehru, sponsored the first conference of non-aligned states. But privileging the imaginative over the practical required more political cover than Ali's government enjoyed. Externally, it alarmed the Americans and foreign investors without enticing alternative sources of diplomatic and economic support. Domestically, whilst it pleased some within the army over Irian Jaya, it also antagonised other high-ranking officers, especially over the PKI. When, in June 1955, the cabinet tried to appoint a commander against its will, the army united to oust Ali from power and replace him with a prime minster from Masyumi.

The first general election held in 1955 pushed the Indonesian democracy further towards a definitive crisis. The long campaign let loose intense communal passions, and the votes produced a stalemate between the PNI, the PKI, Masyumi and the latter's breakaway Islamic counterpart, Nadhlatul Ulama (NU). No party could govern without the support of others, but the coalition between the PNI and the two Islamic parties, on which a successful democracy had to rest, was straining to breaking point. The idea of Indonesian nationhood had failed, and the divisions between the islands were now showing within the internal command of the army. After Ali returned to office in March 1956, one faction of the army began to plot to seize power. For his part, Sukarno had become visibly impatient with electoral politics. Opening parliament in March 1956, he urged it to act on the basis of 'real Indonesian democracy' and not the fallacious principle that '50 per cent plus one are always right'.[59]

Increasingly bereft of options, Ali turned once more to external confrontation, this time repudiating a substantial amount of debt to the Dutch. But as Hatta, who until November 1956 was once again Sukarno's vice-president, saw, constantly invoking the revolution was destroying representative democracy.[60] The idea of revolution, however necessary to the imaginative idea of Indonesian nationhood, was no substitute for power, and those who, like Hatta, understood this did not have power, and did not have another state willing to help them impose their will on the army, Sukarno or local rebels.

Ali's government was now at the mercy of a struggle between those to whom it lost power. In a speech in October 1956, Sukarno once again attacked representative democracy as inappropriate for Indonesian development. What Indonesia needed, he argued, was 'guided democracy' through which proper attention could be devoted to the problem of Irian Jaya. Fearing that Sukarno was ushering the PKI towards power, regional military commanders seized control in West Sumatra, and the chief of command for East Indonesia proclaimed martial law over the region. Sukarno responded by forcing Ali's resignation, declaring martial law over the whole of the country and announcing his personal rule. By 1960, with the support of radicals within the army, he had banned Masyumi and the Socialist party, cancelled elections, reimposed the 1945 republican constitution, and given the army seats in a non-elected parliament. Only in Acech was he unable to re-establish the Indonesian state's rule, granting the province partial autonomy in 1959.[61]

No Indonesian government had been able to take real advantage of such opportunities as there were for developing countries in the post-war international economy. These demanded an effective modern state and a pragmatic approach towards international trade and investment, not one that turned these questions into matters of sovereignty and nationhood. Unable to establish authoritative rule over Indonesian territory and handicapped by a ramshackle bureaucracy, the first post-independence governments were structurally unable to direct the economy towards either export-led growth or import substitution. Without the necessary foundations to use the economy politically, governments invested more energy in the imaginative politics of nationhood. Yet, important as that was to the state's internal authority, the more Indonesian governments reached for the revolutionary spirit, the more acute their problems became because they lost the will to take authoritative decisions as the agents of a sovereign state.

Nonetheless, as Sukarno discovered, when in 1965 he was overthrown in a military coup led by General Suharto, the circumstances made it difficult for any regime to secure and retain power. A significant number of Indonesian subjects did not accept the state's authority over the territory in which they lived, and the kind of coercion that dealing with secessionist threats entailed, gave the army more power than was prudent. Yet the Americans had offered those who had tried to establish democracy few opportunities to alleviate these problems. Above all, neither Truman nor Eisenhower had been willing to back Indonesian democracy directly. Even when the PKI regained strength in the mid-1950s, the Americans assumed that they could take Indonesia's place within their sphere of influence for granted. They offered little on Irian Jaya and accepted Japanese intransigence over developing south-east Asia as a trading bloc. Of course, the fate of Sukiman's government and the rhetorical commitment to revolution in much of the language of Indonesian nationhood strongly suggest that more direct American support would have ignited bitter controversy over sovereignty and been a gift to the PKI. But without an external guarantee, successive governments had few means to discipline the enemies of representative democracy lurking within the state, and, therefore, virtually no chance of success.

Brazil

Post-war Brazilian democracy was similarly terminated by internal enemies, but with the tacit encouragement of the United States. Understanding that in entering the Second World War the Brazilian state's future was tied to the judgement of American presidents, the army established democracy in 1945 by deposing the populist dictator, Getulio Vargas, who had ruled the country since 1930. From the outset, the future of the new democracy was bleak because there was only the semblance of a Brazilian modern state. Nobody who had ruled Brazil since the departure of the Portuguese had succeeded in establishing a robust site of central authority, or convincing large numbers of those nominally subject to that authority to consent to the exercise of power from the centre without inciting violence. The post-independence monarchy had governed by patrimony. The republic created after the army had toppled the emperor in 1889 had rested on the local rule of army colonels and large landowners, and had granted massive autonomy to the regional states, especially to São Paulo. Vargas and his supporters had attempted to centralise authority but had been only partially successful. Although they had suppressed an armed revolt from São Paulo in 1932 and consolidated the federal army, they never succeeded in disarming the state militias and securing a monopoly of legitimate violence. Neither had they sought to create the kind of impersonal administrative apparatus through which they could translate their own will into a binding legal order independently of the material demands of particular political groups. Instead they had incorporated a number of such sectional interests, including private industrial investors and trade unions, directly into the bureaucracy, allowing the regime to contain those groups politically but turning personal relationships into the basis of all claims to authority. So far as the Vargas regime did succeed in expanding the state's power, it did so without any imaginative project around Brazilian nationhood to accompany it. It promised industrial development but the primary beneficiaries of this transformation were all too visibly Vargas's direct political clients. In these circumstances, the state's authority was purely contingent on the regime's success. Vargas himself was dependent on the army, and those who controlled the regional states saw no reason to accept that they had terminally lost the war to exercise political power.[62]

The constitution promulgated in 1946 did nothing to strengthen the Brazilian state. Territorially, it left the centre weak, limiting presidents to one term in office and giving the states specific authorities, representation in the federal Senate and the right to a significant proportion of the revenue raised by the federal government. Parties that competed for power at the centre had little alternative but to court the support of political bosses within the states, who were then able to demand material reward in exchange for their electoral favours. Electorally, the constitution established a set of rules that invited dissent and promised future conflict. Although nominally based on universal suffrage, the constitution restricted the franchise to only half of the adult population by depriving illiterates and men enlisted in the armed forces of the vote. For those who enjoyed the power of, and the wealth engendered by, the post-war Brazilian state, the possibility of enfranchising the rural poor became something to fear and resist; for those excluded from either, something to advance; and for both, something through which to contest the legitimacy of any authoritative act that they didn't like.

Without an effective site of sovereign authority backed by power, Brazilian democracy was more than usually exposed to the will of its political class to maintain it. That political class was dominated from the outset by the upper hierarchy of the army. Notwithstanding its actions in 1945, the army's partisan allegiances were apparent. It had feared Vargas's attempt to mobilise the urban working class and wanted to defend the propertied classes against redistributive politics. No president could afford to forfeit the army's support and since the command of violence appeared to be the final arbiter of authority and direct access to arms was relatively easy, political groups representing the propertied classes, particularly those allied to the conservative National Democratic Union (UDN), had little incentive to accept that defeat at the ballot box should preclude their claim to power.

The first post-war presidential election resulted in victory for the candidate backed by the army and the United States, General Eurico Gaspar Dutra of the UDN. Dutra's government began life in what were in some respects propitious economic circumstances. The steep fall during the 1930s in the price of coffee, Brazil's primary export, had drastically reduced the capacity to buy imports. Whilst this had slowed down the country's industrial development, which was very much dependent on a foreign supply of machinery and equipment, it had also allowed the government to conserve large amounts of foreign exchange reserves. Since, by 1946, the price of coffee was on an upward trajectory, Brazil could now both increase export earnings and begin to import substantial quantities of raw materials and capital goods. But what was not on offer to Dutra's government was either American economic support or forbearance. Contrary to its Cold War mindset about Europe and east Asia, the administration's instinct was to encourage Dutra to pursue economic openness.

For two years, Dutra and his ministers tried to stabilise their own internal position against the left – banning the Brazilian Communist party (PCB) in 1947 – whilst pursuing a liberal economic policy that scrapped heavy tariffs, capital restrictions and internal controls over domestic markets. They quickly precipitated an external financial crisis, as Brazil's foreign-exchange reserves were absorbed by a binge of consumer imports, and, by the end of 1947, they were forced to retreat. Through the Bank of Brazil, Dutra's government imposed exchange controls and a system of import licences that prioritised machinery and raw materials at the expense of consumer goods, and it fixed the exchange rate at a level that gave few but coffee producers any incentive to export. The Brazilian economy was simply too weak for the UDN to sustain power through luxury consumption for its own clients whilst relying on coercion to contain the nascent industrial working class.

Having first ascertained that the army would accept him, Vargas returned to power in 1950 after winning the presidential election as the candidate of the Social Democratic party (PSD) and the Brazilian Labour party (PTB). To do so, he had mobilised a populist coalition around the aspiring industrial bourgeoisie, urban workers and the old state party machines, all of whom he promised would benefit from accelerated development through intensified import substitution.[63] But the space for Vargas to act remained slight. Externally, the Americans offered diminishing returns. Although Vargas negotiated a set of military accords with Washington, only to leave them unratified, no direct economic aid arrived. And whilst the Truman administration sponsored a commission to provide technical assistance and long-term loans, Eisenhower and his advisors terminated the project, insisting that private investment was the medicine Brazil needed. Domestically, Vargas's government had to maintain the broad coalition supporting it before the promised land of development was reached. The easiest way to do that was to use the supply of administrative jobs and revenue it controlled to buy off critics with the state's resources. The more, however, that the government spent on the public sector and subsidies, the more it created inflation. The more that inflation rose, the more Brazilian exporters struggled. And the more they suffered, the less foreign exchange the government had to finance the massive imports of capital goods required for development.[64]

Just over two years into office, during the first months of 1953, Vargas and his ministers tried to put import substitution on a surer domestic and external footing. Determined to reduce inflation and increase export earnings, they introduced strict credit controls and multiple exchange rates to create divergent price values for exports and imports in different sectors of the economy. Nonetheless, precisely because Vargas's domestic strategy required inflation, stabilisation was a significant political risk, and by the middle of the year, Vargas had replaced his cabinet with one that leant further to the left. Vargas's rhetoric about the country's external relations switched to confrontation, promising that the Brazilian state would seize control of its own economic destiny from international and colonial forces. Even when, in early 1954, a further upturn in the price of coffee presented the government with an opportunity to consolidate its external finances, Vargas and his new ministers demurred, insisting on maintaining a minimum price, prompting a boycott of Brazilian coffee in the American market and so worsening the balance of payments.

Yet whatever premium Vargas imagined lay in the language of economic nationalism, especially when tied to an apparent attempt to redistribute wealth to the urban poor, it could not but incite the kind of partisan conflict that a prudent president would have tried to avoid. Too many conservative interests were bound up with the presence of foreign capital and stood to lose from continuing inflation. For the army, the government's overt anti-Americanism and incompetence in the face of external constraints was sheer provocation. In an increasingly tense atmosphere, Vargas's palace guard tried to murder the influential conservative Carlos Lacerda. Botching the job, they killed an air-force officer. When, in August 1954, a group of senior generals told Vargas they would no longer support him, he returned to his office and shot himself, leaving a final message that 'the underground campaign of international groups [had] joined that of the national groups which were working against the policy of full employment'.[65]

Having exercised its coercive muscles over Vargas, the army proceeded to determine the terms in which any successor could govern. The winner of the presidential election in 1955, the PDS candidate, Juscelino Kubitschek, was only installed in office in January 1956 when the war minister staged a coup against the acting president, who appeared to be plotting to prevent him assuming power. Kubitschek was subsequently far more assiduous than Vargas in trying to keep the senior generals on his side. But he inherited economic problems that left him with the same dilemmas. Inflation was rising, and the price of coffee was falling. Unless non-essential imports could be squeezed further or export earnings in non-commodity sectors increased, the government would have to access new external credit to finance its balance-of-payments deficit and with it invite foreign pressure for anti-inflationary reform.

For most of his term in office, Kubitschek believed that more foreign capital and more investment in infrastructure were the most likely means to achieve quick growth without another financial crisis. Where Vargas had eventually adopted a nationalist stance towards trade and capital, Kubitschek wanted to use external investment to make more rapid gains from import substitution, and offered exchange, tariff and credit incentives to foreign companies to locate heavy industrial production in Brazil. His government was rewarded with high growth and the revenue to finance the building of a new capital, Brasilia. For a while the bounty was sufficient to sustain the PDS–PTB coalition without

demanding that Kubitschek choose between the different interests that
constituted it. Yet the internal politics that high growth appeared to
make possible also worked to undermine it. The government spent
more on its political clients than could be sustained without borrowing
and the wage increases that the government conceded swelled inflation.
Even with the inflow of foreign capital, by the end of 1957 the balance
of payments was plunged back into a substantial deficit. Kubitschek was
forced to turn to the IMF for help, leaving him at the mercy of Brazil's
creditors' demands for anti-inflationary action, whilst his whole domestic strategy for rule necessitated accommodating inflation. After preliminary discussions with the IMF to secure a large loan conditional on
various deflationary measures, Kubitschek terminated negotiations and
resorted to the kind of nationalist rhetoric that had characterised the
last year of Vargas's presidency.

As Kubitschek struggled to maintain his cross-class political coalition
within the constraints of the post-war international economy, events
elsewhere transformed the external and domestic political landscape in
which the Brazilian state had to survive. Castro's success focused the
Cold War gaze of an American president on Latin America for the first
time. In part, the fear that the Cuban revolution induced in Washington
was an opportunity for the Brazilian government. Once an American
president had deemed Latin America a security risk, the region's
economic development assumed an importance for Washington.
The Kennedy administration committed large sums of money in the
'Alliance for Progress', in the hope that economic growth and social
reform would strengthen democracies across Latin America. In terms of
aid at least, the Brazilian state now had an external sponsor. But such
support came, as it did elsewhere, at a price. The Americans would not
finance an inflationary boom and, allied with the IMF, they expected the
Brazilian government to stabilise the balance of payments. Domestically,
in the face of Cuba's example, *de facto* membership of the American bloc
splintered the coalition between the PSD and PTB that had brought
Vargas and Kubitschek to office, dividing the middle from the urban
working classes. Moreover, the generals could now charge any president
whose actions offended their sensibilities with communist sympathies
and expect the argument to resonate domestically and in Washington.
The grounds for an array of groups to contest the, always precarious,
authority of the presidency had become enormous.

Although he managed to complete his term in office, Kubitschek was
unable to pass power to someone from either the PSD or PTB. Whilst
his successor, Jânio Quadros, the candidate of the UDN opposition, was
expected by his conservative supporters to seize the opportunity of the

American alliance to secure anti-inflationary domestic reform, he tried instead to create a new political space in which the right could govern without sacrificing the imaginative idea of Brazilian independence. Taking office in January 1961, his government cut subsidies, increased incentives to export, and imposed a credit and wage squeeze. Most drastically, it substantially devalued the currency and reduced the multiple exchange rates, militating against the bias in favour of capital goods imports that had driven exchange-rate policy since 1947. Quadros's reward, in May 1961, was more than $2 billion of credit. But on foreign policy, Quadros courted confrontation. He took American capital without accepting that this bound Brazil into the American security bloc, re-establishing diplomatic relations with the Soviet Union. Unsurprisingly, Quadros's room to find his own way was less than he imagined. Whatever the Kennedy administration was willing for a time to tolerate, the army was not. Faced with its anger over Guevara, Quadros gambled that he was still a far more palatable alternative than his PTB vice-President, João Goulart, and resigned only eight months into his tenure.

The army's senior officers, however, now wanted more overt parameters to Brazilian democracy. They did allow Goulart to take over from Quadros but only after they had curtailed the authority and power of the presidency, leaving Goulart dependent on a prime minister and Congress. Goulart had to govern on the army's terms or face the same fate as Vargas. Deteriorating economic conditions intensified the constraints further. The IMF and the Kennedy administration demanded cuts in state expenditure and borrowing before they would release new credit, but Goulart, constrained constitutionally, had little to offer his supporters without spending more money and distributing more government jobs. He either had to accept the political game that the army had constructed, which required an external discipline that would wreck the PTB's base, or he had to try to mobilise a new coalition from those hitherto excluded from both the franchise and the post-war industrial economy and see if he could use it to break the political grip of the army. In June 1962, Goulart turned towards direct confrontation. After his first prime minister resigned, he appointed a radical PTB successor. When Congress refused to accept the nomination, he successfully appealed for a general strike. Six months later, he won a plebiscite to restore full powers to the presidency, and concluded that he had won the chance to pursue the kind of reforms that would turn the peasants into a significant political constituency.

But if Goulart hoped he could rewrite the rules of Brazilian democracy, he was paying insufficient attention to external realities. The more radically he played the domestic game, the more he troubled the IMF and Washington. In March 1963, his finance minister secured an agreement for new loans and aid, but their full release was contingent on reforms monitored by the IMF. Unconvinced that he could sell the deal at home, Goulart removed his minister, repudiated the IMF's conditions and turned against foreign investors. Without American aid, Goulart's position vis-à-vis the army deteriorated. After Johnson had succeeded Kennedy in the White House, Goulart's opponents within the army, already covertly backed by the CIA, believed they would enjoy American support for a coup. In March 1964, Goulart presented them with their opportunity when he announced that he had signed a land-reform decree, nationalised all remaining private oil refineries and would soon enfranchise illiterates and legalise the Communist party. If Congress resisted, he threatened, he would call another general strike and a plebiscite with an enlarged electorate. After Goulart refused an ultimatum by a senior army general to abandon his most radical political allies or leave office, the army deposed Goulart with American help and forced a purged Congress to elect Marshal Humberto Castello Branco as president.[66]

Whatever the relative economic success of import substitution during the 1950s, its enduring capacity to secure the development on which democracy depended was hampered by domestic political conditions.[67] The opportunities for growth by import substitution obliged governments to control inflation if economies were not to overheat from domestic demand. Yet the need to use patronage to sustain virtually any coalition, and the risk that imposing the burden of deflationary policies on any particular sectional interest beyond the rural poor would precipitate a crisis of the state's internal authority, led Brazilian governments to accommodate inflation even when they saw the imperative to act differently. Even the opportunity offered by the Kennedy administration still depended on authoritative action to reduce inflation. Whilst the army made its own contribution to the problem, standing guard against any attempt to impose the price of domestic adjustment on the propertied classes, the ensuing economic muddle only strengthened its claim that elected politicians were unfit to lead the state. Eventually, Goulart had been trapped for reasons beyond his own inadequacies. He could only try to strengthen the sites of elected authority at the expense of the army and its conservative supporters in the states by pushing the American president to a position where he had little reason to attach much premium to the survival of Brazilian democracy. In doing so, he granted the generals the external licence they sought for a coup to destroy it.[68]

The end of Bretton Woods and détente

From the early 1960s, the consequences of American foreign policy began to strain the post-war world that the Roosevelt and Truman administrations had made. The trading opportunities that the Americans were granting to other states were always dependent on American presidents diffusing criticism from domestic producers of a policy that sacrificed them to security politics. Once West Germany and Japan began to accumulate substantial trade surpluses and the United States slipped into a trade deficit, they could not easily ignore protectionist sentiments. After the Kennedy round of GATT was completed in 1967, Congress refused to ratify two parts of the agreement. By 1970, textile, iron, car and steel producers had joined forces with organised labour in an effective congressional protectionist lobby to demand a retreat from open industrial markets.[69]

Meanwhile, maintaining the dollar as the anchor currency of Bretton Woods came at a rising price. By the end of 1960, American foreign monetary liabilities had exceeded American gold reserves, destroying the principle of gold convertibility on which the credibility of the dollar theoretically rested, and the market price of gold had risen above $35. To avoid a rush to convert dollars to gold, presidents thereafter had to fashion a macro-economic policy that inspired confidence in the dollar as a stellar currency. Johnson was unwilling to do so. Fearing the domestic consequences of a tax rise, he decided to pay for the war in Vietnam, his Great Society welfare programme and the race to the moon by borrowing and printing money. Although American inflation remained low by historical standards, it began to creep above that of most other industrialised economies, creating mistrust amongst those holding dollars abroad.

As the 1960s progressed, Bretton Woods required ever more salvage operations on a scale way beyond the means of the IMF. In November 1961, the EEC, British and Swiss governments established a gold pool with the United States under which the Europeans pledged to retain dollars and sell gold. In 1962–63, the Federal Reserve negotiated for other central banks to lend it currencies. Beginning in July 1963, the American administration began to impose some controls on the movement of capital out of the country, culminating in 1968 in a mandatory ban on lending abroad by financial institutions.[70] In one way or another these tactics were demanding. Any American president could avoid a choice between ending Bretton Woods or sacrificing domestic commitments and the Vietnam War only for as long as the west European and Japanese governments were able to accommodate the domestic consequences of holding inflated dollars, as well as angry passions about the American presence in Indochina. Always appalled by inequalities in the Atlantic relationship, de Gaulle withdrew France from the gold pool in June 1967, forcing Johnson to increase the American contribution. After sterling was devalued, five months later, prompting a huge exit into gold, the arrangement became untenable and was formally terminated the following spring. In the aftermath of its demise, the private market price of gold advanced to more than $40 an ounce, $5 above the official rate, creating a strong incentive for central banks to exchange their dollars for gold from the Federal Reserve Board and then sell on the private market. The more the Federal Reserve Board was compelled to exchange dollars for gold, the less tenable dollar–gold convertibility became.

Whilst capital controls bought the Johnson administration some time, they also came at a price. Defeated by Morgenthau and White back in 1944 over European controls, the American banks were even more recalcitrant over restrictions on their own immediate activities. To appease them, the administration granted access to the emerging, unregulated Euro-dollar market in London. Their presence transformed what since the late 1950s had been a short-term money market into a full-scale international capital market. Such a market had advantages for a government that needed to persuade foreigners to supply a regular flow of revenue, but in allowing so much money to swirl around beyond the law of any state, it also increased currency speculation and made the pegged exchange rates of Bretton Woods that much harder to defend.

Just as confidence in the dollar diminished during the 1960s, so did the credibility of American power. Whilst Johnson had sent troops to Vietnam primarily to defend that credibility, the war soon began undoing it, since the Americans couldn't impose their will on a militarily massively underpowered enemy. By the end of January 1968, the plausibility of the Truman doctrine was in tatters. The war seemed unwinnable by conventional means and the nuclear option was unthinkable. Increasing numbers of the American electorate were turning against the war and the human, material and ethical sacrifices it entailed. The United States could not fight communist intrusion anywhere in its proclaimed sphere of influence because its armed forces were ill prepared to fight guerrilla wars, and its electorate was not equipped by the country's own historical experience to understand what such a foreign policy demanded.

Johnson's failure either to win in Vietnam or to maintain majority support for a protracted war destroyed his presidency. When his successor, Richard Nixon, took office in January 1969, he did so with a very different set of purposes and assumptions in relation to the rest of world than those that had guided either Johnson over Vietnam or Roosevelt and Truman in making the post-war world. He and his national security advisor, Henry Kissinger, did not presume, even as a theoretical starting point, that economic interdependence, democracy and military security all served each other. In that presumption, they believed, had lain the folly of investing the credibility of American power indiscriminately across the world without duly considering the internal consequences or whether this actually served American national interests vis-à-vis the Soviet Union. Instead they prioritised the balance of power, convinced that the United States could best secure a stable international order by pursuing its own interests, prudently and predictably, whilst recognising the legitimacy of its enemies' interests as power-states.

Within two years Nixon and Kissinger had shaped a very different foreign policy than that bequeathed by their predecessors. In November 1969, the president unveiled what he termed the Nixon doctrine. It promised its allies that Washington would maintain the nuclear umbrella, but told them that in the event of a conventional attack, they would have to assume the primary responsibility for their own defence. In July 1971, Nixon announced that he wished to normalise relations with China, and in February 1972 he travelled to Beijing to meet Mao and signed what was effectively an alliance to block any attempt at Soviet expansion in Asia. The United States, Nixon and Kissinger hoped, could now preserve its position in south-east Asia without having to offer more bilateral commitments to individual states.

The reversal of policy had huge implications for the remaining democracies within the American sphere of influence. In Asian states not in a formal alliance with the United States, politicians could no longer assume that Washington could be enticed into offering aid by anti-communist rhetoric unless they had influence over something that mattered in balance-of-power terms. Since Nixon and Kissinger had used the Pakistani government as a secret conduit to Beijing in securing the opening to China, the Indian government was particularly exposed by this fact. When war ensued with Pakistan over the attempted secession of East Bengal, the Nixon administration unequivocally backed Islamabad, and cancelled the licence for what remained of Indian arms purchasing in the United States.

For the west European and Japanese governments, the departure of some American troops meant greater expenditure on defence at a moment in time when most were already struggling to finance their existing fiscal commitments. It multiplied the price of security for each state without returning external sovereignty where it had been lost. In West

Germany, Nixon and Kissinger's retreat from the extravagant Cold War rhetoric of the previous two-and-a-half decades finally destroyed the delusions about reunification on which successive Christian Democratic chancellors had acted. After the grand coalition between the CDU and the SPD broke down in 1969, the SPD fought and won the subsequent election on a commitment to work to eventual reunification through a rapprochement with the East. Forming a coalition government with the Free Democrats under Willy Brandt's leadership, they pushed what Brandt termed '*ostpolitik*', recognising East Germany, accepting the Oder-Neisse border with Poland, and enhancing diplomatic and trading relations with the Soviet Union in exchange for a guarantee over West Berlin. For the Japanese government, Nixon's actions rewrote the whole external context in which it had to operate. When Nixon announced his opening to China, the Japanese government was given an hour's notice, and was dismissed by Kissinger as 'those petty book-keepers in Tokyo'.[71] It was now left to work out an economic and political relationship with its most powerful neighbouring state and most natural trading partner, after having organised the state's economy and diplomatic relations on the premise that such a relationship was prohibited. The crisis plunged the government into a bout of intra-factional fighting which toppled Sato as prime minister. His successor, Kakuei Tanaka, normalised Japanese relations with China in September 1972, creating trading opportunities. No Japanese government could now have reason to trust that Nixon would trumpet its interests over China's if and when the two clashed.

Nixon's approach to the international economy turned out to be no less radical, if sometimes rather less deliberately fashioned. Domestically, Nixon had courted protectionist sentiments among textile producers in the south, where he was trying to establish a new constituency of Republican voters from Democrats disillusioned with their party over civil rights and the anti-war movement. Once in office, he pressed the Japanese government to sign a multi-fibre agreement restricting Japanese textile exports, and insisted that any movement on Okinawa would be dependent on substantial concessions. On Bretton Woods, Nixon was as unwilling as Johnson to readjust American macroeconomic policy. By 1971, American gold reserves covered just 22 per cent of liabilities to foreign central banks. That spring, with massive quantities of dollars flowing out into Deutschmarks, the West German government and the Bundesbank tried to force the administration's hand by halting intervention. But Nixon was now prepared to contemplate the end of Bretton Woods. On 15 August, his treasury secretary announced an end to dollar–gold convertibility and a 10 percent surcharge on imports of goods. In ending dollar–gold convertibility the

Nixon administration unilaterally ripped apart the foundations of the Bretton Woods exchange-rate system. Henceforth all confidence in the anchor currency of the system was conditional on the day-to-day willingness of any American administration to defend the dollar's value. In acting without consulting any other members of Bretton Woods or the IMF, the Nixon administration had graphically demonstrated that it saw the dollar as primarily a matter for domestic economic management rather than multilateral, international economic agreement. In December 1971, at the Smithsonian conference, the other states agreed to an 8 per cent devaluation of the dollar without a restoration of gold convertibility, a revaluation *inter alia* of the yen and the Deutschmark, and a margin of fluctuation vis-à-vis the dollar of 2.25 per cent, in exchange for the abolition of the import surcharge.[72]

The consequences were immense. The creeping protectionism and the revaluations imposed on several states reduced the efficacy of trade policies that relied on selling large quantities of goods into the American market. Given the size of the American economy and its relative insulation from the usual inflationary consequences of currency depreciation, other states were left vulnerable to further rounds of dollar devaluation. Their governments were left choosing between buying dollars and risking inflating the domestic money supply to try to stabilise the new pegged rates, or finding some political means of responding to the exporting interests that suffered as a result of currency appreciation. At worse, unless capital controls proved robust, the continuing risk of exchange-rate instability threatened to re-internationalise monetary policy, leaving decisions about interest rates once again dependent on short-term capital flows and the decisions of the Federal Reserve Board.

For the EC states, the fallout of the events of August 1971 was particularly momentous. The Smithsonian agreement effectively created a 9 percent possible fluctuation margin between any two Community currencies, but both the expansion of intra-EC trade and the Common Agricultural Policy had been premised on stable exchange rates. The Nixon administration's actions revealed all too clearly that it saw no interest of its own in protecting and advancing the EC's unity as a trade bloc. Indeed, Nixon and Kissinger were increasingly opposed to the whole idea of further integration, believing that it reduced their ability to influence west European decision-making. Any attempt to find an alternative to Bretton Woods that safeguarded a shared exchange-rate framework would have to be made by the EC states themselves.

The French modern democratic nation-state was the most exposed. The EC had financially protected its farmers and its commercial interests in Africa, and had given it an international stage to dominate in great-power style. Already, *ostpolitik* had curtailed the old incentive for West German governments to use the EC to advance reunification, so diminishing what any French government could extract in return. Now, the French government needed to find a way of countering the emergence of the Deutschmark as the premier European currency, and so protect its leadership of the EC. Whilst de Gaulle would have seen any transfer of sovereignty over monetary and exchange-rate policy as worsening the French predicament, his successor, Georges Pompidou, came to think differently. In 1970 he secured Brandt's support for a plan to achieve monetary union within the EC by 1980. The detail, however, proved impossible because the West Germans would not assent to anything that compromised the principle of central bank independence. In the aftermath of the Smithsonian settlement, the EC governments agreed to peg their currencies against each other with 2.25 per cent bands, halving the possible fluctuation between them. But the Deutschmark's strength turned the so-called 'Snake' into a Deutschmark standard which committed the French to trying to match West German anti-inflationary discipline without an independent central bank. What was soon to become West Germany's monetary dominance over the EC states restored the issue of German power as a political problem for states across the continent, including the West German.

Conclusions

Successive administrations in Washington had set the limits of democracy in the post-war world. Everywhere, they had determined the terms on which states in external financial difficulties had received credit. In Western Europe and Asia, they had assumed responsibility for security and extracted their price in external sovereignty. And in Latin America, they had given tacit support to anti-democratic coups against left-wing and populist governments. These limits did sometimes yield pragmatic advantages for these states, and where they were absent, as in Indonesia, democracy was fatally weak. But they also challenged the whole imaginative conception of nationhood as absolute external sovereignty on which the internal authority of modern democratic nation-states had hitherto, in light of European experiences, appeared to depend. After all, what kind of state accustomed to being a great power allowed another state to station military force within it or retreated from empire and reformed its domestic economy at the financial behest of another power? This may historically have been the fate of those defeated in wars but no serious British, French, German or Italian politician before 1945 would have considered it compatible with a viable conception of nationhood and the internal authority of the state.

It was because de Gaulle believed that this truth still held that he acted as he did. But only those governments which maintained a stable balance of payments while acquiring independent nuclear weapons, as de Gaulle's did, or striking a military deal with the Soviet Union, as Mrs Gandhi's did, could practically decide and act for themselves in ways that gave any force to the imaginative language of the independent and autonomous nation-state. Where, as in Brazil and Indonesia, governments tried to cultivate a conception of nationhood through the language of sovereignty without fulfilling these conditions, they simply created internal and external problems. Whilst resistance to foreign capital and the international financial institutions could yield political capital regardless of the deleterious economic consequences, by apparently trumpeting incompetence it could also court resistance from those opposed to democracy and expose the state's internal authority to ridicule.

Yet in other respects, the post-war experience suggested otherwise. The reduction of external sovereignty, the end of imperialism and the imaginative sacrifice of the idea of an independent nation-state proved perfectly compatible with the success of representative democracy. Economic success based on trade not conquest could be made to matter by using the power and resources of the state at home to serve the material interests of a large number of citizens. A modern democratic nation-state's imaginative claim to authority could be judged almost exclusively by economic growth and the domestic standard of living and well-being that it made possible. Whether without the crisis of 1929 Weimar could have endured solely through economic success must remain an open question, but the West German democratic state had survived when the illusion around reunification was shattered.

Such economic success appeared to depend on low inflation and an external strategy that procured a surplus or some equilibrium in the balance of payments. To maintain a long-term anti-inflationary discipline, governments had to have the capacity and will to impose adjustment on particular groups of citizens to the benefit of others and to contain the domestic consequences of doing so. To secure the balance of payments, governments had to sustain comparative trading advantages and to minimise external commitments that had to be paid for in dollars. Success came easiest on the front line of the Cold War and where those in power early in the post-war years established themselves as the dominant party of government, leaving them equipped either to use the Atlantic relationship to contain dissent, or to force the burden of adjustment on the constituencies of their opponents. The Japanese government achieved this most spectacularly. Whilst the constitution forbade rearmament and external adventures, the LDP's dominance diffused the grievances of trade unions and any aspiration to greater consumption, and made it possible for elected politicians and bureaucrats to ally in taking long-term economic decisions. West German governments were not far behind. There, virtually the whole political class agreed to keep monetary policy out of electoral politics, whilst successive governments offered sufficient inducements to persuade the trade unions of the long-term benefits of wage restraint.

Where the state's internal authority was weak, low inflation proved politically impossible and democracy tended to fail. Brazilian and Indonesian ministers could not trust that the economic losers from anti-inflationary policies would accept their defeat without recourse to violence, and they spent money they could not afford to appease awkward political interests. In each case, inflation exposed the inability of the political class to agree on constitutional rules and the unwillingness of the military and significant numbers of citizens to accept authority when their immediate interests were threatened.[73] Whilst economic development theoretically offered a means of cultivating nationhood, it presupposed the very authority of the state that was wanting.

The Nixon administration's actions in 1971 did nothing to accommodate political difficulties with either inflation or the balance of payments. Indeed for governments of those developed countries, like the British and Italian, which were by the end of the 1960s faring least well in containing inflationary pressure, the imperative to do better was becoming more acute. With rising inflation already undermining their economies' price competitiveness, they faced the prospect of an appreciation of their currency against the dollar. Those who then lost out were likely to expect looser domestic monetary conditions to compensate, stoking inflation further and thus creating a vicious cycle in which external exchange rate and financial difficulties and rising domestic prices reinforced each other. Far enough down this path, the deflationary action necessary to reverse it would threaten recession, and would therefore diminish the capacity of politicians to continue to deliver the standards of living and economic services on which these states had rested their internal authority since the Second World War.

Notes

1 See S. Krasner, 'United States' commercial and monetary policy: unraveling the paradox of external strength and internal weakness', in P. Katzenstein

(ed.), *Between Power and Plenty: Foreign Economic Policies of Advanced Industrial States* (Madison: Wisconsin University Press, 1978); C. S. Maier, 'The politics of productivity: foundations of American international economic policy after World War II', in Katzenstein, *Between Power and Plenty*; C. Hull, *The Memoirs of Cordell Hull* (New York: Macmillan, 1948); J. Morton Blum (ed.), *From the Morgenthau Diaries Vol. III: Years of Achievement 1941–1945* (Boston: Houghton Mifflin, 1967).

2 See E. Helleiner, *States and the Re-emergence of Global Finance: from Bretton Woods to the 1990s* (Ithaca: Cornell University Press, 1994), part I; R. Gardner, *Sterling-Dollar Diplomacy in Current Perspective: the Origins and Prospects of our International Order* (New York: Columbia University Press, 1980); W. M. Scammell, *International Monetary Policy: Bretton Woods and After* (London: Macmillan, 1975); F. Block, *The Origins of International Economic Disorder* (Berkeley: University of California Press, 1977).

3 D. Moggridge (ed.), *The Collected Writings of John Maynard Keynes, Vol. XXV, Activities 1940–1944, Shaping the Post-War World: the Clearing Union* (London: Macmillan, 1980), p. 149.

4 See J. Kaplan and G. Schleiminger, *The European Payments Union: Financial Diplomacy in the 1950s* (Oxford: Clarendon Press, 1989).

5 See B. Eichengreen, *Globalising Capital: a History of the International Monetary System* (Princeton: Princeton University Press, 1998), ch. 4.

6 See M. Leffler, *A Preponderance of Power: National Security, the Truman Administration and the Cold War* (Stanford: Stanford University Press, 1992); S. Ambrose, *Eisenhower, Vol. II: the President* (New York: Simon & Schuster, 1984).

7 On post-war taxation see S. Steinmo, *Taxation and Democracy: Swedish, British and American Approaches to Financing the Modern State* (London: Yale University Press, 1993).

8 See T. Notermans, *Money, Markets, and the State: Social Democratic Economic Policies since 1918* (Cambridge: Cambridge University Press, 2000).

9 R. H. Jackson, *Quasi-States: Sovereignty, International Relations and the Third World* (Cambridge: Cambridge University Press, 1990).

10 See R. Wood, *From Marshall Plan to Debt Crisis: Foreign Aid and Development Choices in the World Economy* (Berkeley: University of California Press, 1986), chs. 1–2.

11 See S. N. Macfarlane, *Superpower Rivalry and Third World Radicalism: the Idea of National Liberation* (London: Croom Helm, 1985), ch. 4.

12 See C. W. Eisenberg, *Drawing the Line: the American Decision to Divide Germany, 1944–49* (Cambridge: Cambridge University Press, 1996); M. P. Leffler, *The Struggle for Germany and the Origins of the Cold War* (Washington, DC: German Historical Institute, 1996).

13 See P. Krüger, 'The Federal Republic as a nation-state', in J. S. Brady, B. Crawford and S. E. Wiliarty (eds), *The Post-War Transformation of German Democracy, Prosperity and Nationhood* (Ann Arbor: University of Michigan Press, 1999).

14 On West Germany's democratic politics see G. Smith, *Democracy in West Germany: Parties and Politics in the Federal Republic*, 3rd edn (Aldershot: Dartmouth, 1990).

15 J. Joffe, 'The foreign policy of the German Federal Republic', in Roy C. Macridis (ed.), *Foreign Policy in World Politics* (Englewood Cliffs, NJ: Prentice-Hall, 1989).

16 See ibid.

17 See A. Nicholls, *Freedom with Responsibility: the Social Market in Germany 1918–1963* (Oxford: Oxford University Press, 1994).

18 See M. Kreile, 'West Germany: the dynamics of expansion', in Katzenstein (ed.), *Between Power and Plenty*.

19 See S. Kocs, *Autonomy or Power?: The Franco-German Relationship and Europe's Strategic Choices, 1955–1995* (Westport, CT: Praeger, 1995).

20 'The Common Declaration and the Treaty Between the French Republic and the Federal Republic of Germany', 22 Jan. 1963. Quoted in H. Kissinger, *Diplomacy* (London: Touchstone, 1994), p. 615.

21 See F. Mayer, *Adenauer and Kennedy: a Study in German-American Relations, 1961–63* (London: Macmillan, 1996).

22 See P. Windsor, *Germany and the Management of Detente* (London: Chatto and Windus, 1971); G. F. Treverton, *The Dollar Drain and American Forces in Germany: Managing the Political Economies of Alliance* (Athens, OH: Ohio University Press, 1978).

23 See J. Dower, 'Occupied Japan and the Cold War in Asia', in *Japan in War and Peace: Essays on History, Race and Culture* (London: Harper Collins, 1995); M. Schaller, *The American Occupation of Japan: the Origins of the Cold War in Asia* (New York: Oxford University Press, 1985).

24 See Leffler, *A Preponderance of Power*.

25 Quoted in R. Buckley, *US–Japan Alliance Diplomacy 1945–1990* (Cambridge: Cambridge University Press, 1992), p. 78. On the political implications of the problem of sovereignty see J. Dower, 'Peace and democracy in two systems', in A. Gordon (ed.), *Post-War Japan as History* (Berkeley: University of California Press, 1993).

26 Quoted in Buckley, *US–Japan Alliance Diplomacy*, p. 55.

27 See W. S. Borden, *The Pacific Alliance: the United States' Foreign Economic Policy and Japanese Trade Recovery, 1947–1954* (Madison: University of Wisconsin Press, 1984).

28 See T. J. Pempel, 'Japanese foreign economic policy: the domestic bases for international behaviour', in Katzenstein (ed.), *Between Power and Plenty*.

29 R. Ozaki, *The Control of Imports and Foreign Capital in Japan* (New York: Praeger, 1972).

30 See C. Johnson, *Japan, Who Governs? The Rise of the Developmental State* (New York: Norton, 1995).

31 See C. Johnson, *MITI and the Japanese Miracle: the Growth of Industrial Policy, 1925–1975* (Stanford, CA: Stanford University Press, 1982).

32 See K. E. Calder, *Strategic Capitalism: Public Policy and Private Purpose in Japanese Industrial Finance* (Princeton: Princeton University Press, 1993); S. Tsuru, *Japan's Capitalism: Creative Defeat and Beyond* (Cambridge: Cambridge University Press, 1993).
33 See Buckley, *US–Japan Alliance*, ch. 4.
34 See T. Sfikas, *The British Labour Government and the Greek Civil War, 1945– 1949: the Imperialism of Non-Intervention* (Keele: Keele University Press, 1994); J. Kent, *British Imperial Strategy and the Origins of the Cold War* (Leicester: Leicester University Press, 1994).
35 See J. Tomlinson, *Democratic Socialism and Economic Policy: the Attlee Years 1945–1951* (Cambridge: Cambridge University Press, 1997), chs. 3–4.
36 See H. Thomas, *The Suez Affair*, 3rd edn (London: Weidenfeld and Nicolson, 1986).
37 See L. Epstein, *British Politics in the Suez Crisis* (London: Pall Mall Press, 1961).
38 See W. Kaiser, *Using Europe, Abusing the Europeans: Britain and European Integration 1945–1963* (London: Macmillan, 1996).
39 See S. Blank, 'Britain: the politics of foreign economic policy, the domestic economy and the problem of pluralistic stagnation', in Katzenstein (ed.), *Between Power and Plenty*.
40 On the failure of attempts to reform the British economy during the 1960s see D. Marquand, *The Unprincipled Society: New Demands and Old Politics* (London: Jonathan Cape, 1988).
41 See F. B. M. Lynch, 'Resolving the paradox of the Monnet Plan: national and international planning in French reconstruction', *Economic History Review* 37: 2 (1984), 229–43.
42 See J. Zysman, 'The French state in the international economy', in Katzenstein (ed.), *Between Power and Plenty*.
43 On France's relations with the United States during the Fourth Republic see R. Kuisel, *Seducing the French* (Berkeley: University of California Press, 1993), ch. 3; F. Costigilio, *France and the United States: the Cold Alliance since World War II* (New York: Twayne, 1992), chs. 2–3.
44 See C. S. Maier and D. S. White, *The Thirteenth of May: the Advent of de Gaulle's Republic* (New York: 1968). On the Fourth Republic see J.-P. Rioux, *The Fourth Republic 1944–1958*, trans. G. Rogers (Cambridge: Cambridge University Press, 1987).
45 Quoted in J. Lacouture, *De Gaulle, Volume II; the Ruler*, trans. A. Sheridan (London: Harvill, 1991), p. 421.
46 On de Gaulle's relations with the United States see F. Costigilio, *France and the United States: the Cold Alliance since World War II* (New York: Twayne, 1992), ch. 4; R. O. Paxton and W. Nicholas (eds), *De Gaulle and the United States* (Oxford: Berg, 1994).
47 See J. L. Harper, *America and the Reconstruction of Italy, 1945–1948* (Cambridge: Cambridge University Press, 1986); P. Vannicelli, *Italy, NATO, and the European Community* (Cambridge, MA: Harvard University Centre for

International Affairs, 1971); F. R. Willis, *Italy Chooses Europe* (Oxford: Oxford University Press, 1971); P. Ginsborg, *A History of Contemporary Italy: Society and Politics 1943–1988* (London: Penguin, 1990), chs. 1–9; D. Sassoon, *Contemporary Italy: Economics, Society, and Politics since 1945*, 2nd edn (London: Longman, 1997), chs. 1–3; P. A. Allum, *Italy – Republic Without Government* (London: Weidenfeld and Nicolson, 1973).

48 See A. Prosner, 'Italy: dependence and political fragmentation', in Katzenstein (ed.), *Between Power and Plenty*.

49 See F. Romero, 'Migration as an issue in European interdependence and integration: the case of Italy', in A. S. Milward, F. M. B. Lynch, F. Romero, R. Ranieria and V. Sörensen, *The Frontier of National Sovereignty: History and Theory 1945–1992* (London: Routledge, 1993).

50 S. Khilnani, *The Idea of India* (London: Hamish Hamilton, 1997).

51 See B. R. Tomlinson, *The Economy of Modern India: the New Cambridge History of India* (Cambridge: Cambridge University Press, 1993), ch. 34.

52 See J. Manor, 'How and why liberal representative politics emerged in India', *Political Studies*, 38: 1 (1990), 20–38.

53 J. Nehru, *The Discovery of India* (Oxford: Oxford University Press, 1946); S. Khilnani, *The Idea of India* (London: Hamish Hamilton, 1997), ch. 4; S. Kaviraj, 'Crisis of the nation-state in India', *Political Studies*, 42: special issue (1994), 115–229.

54 See A. Kohli, *India's Democracy: an Analysis of Changing State–Society Relations* (Princeton: Princeton University Press, 1988), pp. 89–107.

55 On the implications of India's domestic politics for its foreign policy see Maya Chadda, *Ethnicity, Security and Separatism in India* (New York: Columbia University Press, 1997). On relations with the United States see Norman D. Palmer, *The United States and India: the Dimensions of Influence* (New York: Praeger, 1984).

56 See F. Frankel, *India's Political Economy 1947–77: the Gradual Revolution* (Princeton: Princeton University Press, 1978); A. Gupta, 'The political economy of post-independence India: a review article', *Journal of Asian Studies*, 48: 4 (1989), 787–97; A. R. Hanson, *The Process of Planning: a Study of India's Five Year Plans, 1950–1964* (London: Oxford University Press, 1966).

57 See V. Joshi and I. M. D. Little, *India: Macro-Economics and Political Economy 1964–1991* (Washington, DC: The World Bank, 1994).

58 See G. R. Hess, *The United States' Emergence as a Southeast Asian Power* (New York: Columbia University Press, 1987).

59 H. Feith, *The Decline of Constitutional Democracy in Indonesia* (Ithaca: Cornell University Press, 1968), p. 515.

60 Quoted in Feith, *The Decline of Constitutional Democracy*, p. 608.

61 On the failure of Indonesia's post-war democracy see Feith, *The Decline of Constitutional Democracy*; M. C. Rickliefs, *A History of Modern Indonesia* (London: Macmillan, 1981); U. Sundhaussen, *The Road to Power: Indonesian Military Politics 1945–1967* (Kuala Lumpur: Oxford University Press).

62 Riordon Roett, *Politics in a Patrimonial Society*, 3rd edn (New York: Praeger, 1978), ch. 2.
63 For an overview of import substitution in Latin America see A. O. Hirschman, *A Bias for Hope: Essays on Development in Latin America* (New Haven: Yale University Press, 1971); R. Thorp, 'A reappraisal of the origins of import-substituting industrialisation 1930–1950', *Journal of Latin American Studies*, 24: supplement (1992), 181–95.
64 See R. Kahil, *Inflation and Economic Development in Brazil* (Oxford: Clarendon Press, 1973).
65 Quoted in P. Flynn, *Brazil: a Political Analysis* (London: Benn, 1978), p. 170.
66 See A. Stepan, 'Political leadership and regime breakdown: Brazil', in J. J. Linz and A. Stepan (eds), *The Breakdown of Democratic Regimes in Latin America* (Baltimore: Johns Hopkins University Press, 1978); A. Stepan, *The Military in Politics: Changing Patterns in Brazil* (Princeton: Princeton University Press, 1971), pp. 122–3; J.K.Black, *The United States' Penetration of Brazil* (Philadelphia: Philadelphia University Press, 1977).
67 For a general discussion of Brazil's development projects see S. A. Hewlett, *The Cruel Dilemmas of Development: Twentieth Century Brazil* (New York: Basic Books, 1980); A. Fishlow, 'Brazilian economic development in long-term perspective', *American Economic Review*, 70: 2 (1980), 102–8; L. B. Pereira, *Development and Crisis Within Brazil, 1930–1983* (Boulder, CO: Westview Press, 1984).
68 For general histories of post-war Brazilian politics see P. Flynn, *Brazil: A Political Analysis* (London: Benn, 1978); T. E. Skidmore, *Politics in Brazil 1930–1964: an Experiment in Democracy* (New York: Oxford University Press, 1967).
69 On the development of American trade policy in the 1960s see T. W. Zeiler, *American Trade and Power in the 1960s* (New York: Columbia University Press, 1992).
70 See J. Conybeare, *US Foreign Economic Policy and the International Capital Markets: the Case of Capital Export Controls, 1963–74* (New York: Garland, 1988).
71 Cited in G. Hawthorn, *The Future of Asia and the Pacific* (London: Phoenix, 1998), p. 11.
72 See S. Strange, 'International monetary relations', in A. Shonfield (ed.), *International Monetary Relations of the Western World 1959–1971* (London: Oxford University Press, 1976); J. Gowa, *Closing the Gold Window: Domestic Politics and the End of Bretton Woods* (Ithaca: Cornell University Press, 1983).
73 On this problem across Latin America see G. W. Wynia, *The Politics of Latin American Development*, 3rd edn (Cambridge: Cambridge University Press, 1990), ch. 2; P. Mcdonough, *Power and Ideology in Brazil* (Princeton: Princeton University Press, 1981).

4

Crises and non-crises: financial liberalisation and the end of the Cold War

By 1973, the class of democracies was smaller than during the first two decades after the Second World War. Whilst communist rule was entrenched in the Soviet Union, eastern Europe, China, North Korea, North Vietnam and Cuba, in most post-colonial states, both those created after 1945 and those dating back to the nineteenth century, democracy had collapsed, leaving only Colombia and Venezuela in Latin America, Botswana in Africa, and India and Sri Lanka in Asia with this form of government.

The histories of Europe and the United States might have predicted that politicians in post-colonial, developing countries would struggle to establish a modern state whilst simultaneously introducing competitive elections on a full franchise. The failures of state-building across most of these countries were immense. As in Brazil, most governments had not settled a monopoly of legitimate violence for the state or an institutional apparatus of rule at the centre. Whilst bearing the outward appearance of being states, sites of rule in these countries were frequently personal, where governments distributed the resources they commanded to those with a material stake in their survival. Where there was little or no impersonal authority representative democracy did not survive. By contrast, Indian democracy had endured the first thirty years of independence relatively unscathed in part because Congress had inherited the apparatus of an effective modern state from the departing colonial power. Where state-building failed, the political classes also struggled to agree constitutional rules. Many democracies in post-colonial countries began with constitutions that presumed the same non-existent concurrence over values and substantive policies that had proved so disastrous in Spain during the 1930s, and ignored procedural questions about how to resolve disagreements authoritatively. In Latin America, the two surviving democracies, Columbia and Venezuela, were different from the other states because the leading parties made pacts with each other promising to guarantee what each deemed its vital interests whilst denying those of anyone else.[1]

Without an effective modern state, conjuring an idea of nationhood was extremely difficult. When the governments of the post-colonial states took power, they inherited a ready-made language of nationhood created by the battles for independence, but no leaders could create the notion of a singular people simply out of opposition to imperial rule. Since the post-colonial states were largely poor and dependent on an international economy over which they had little influence, they could not readily underwrite prosperity or deliver universal material benefits. Where, as in Africa, the territorial boundaries of the state were transparently artificial, the problems of constructing an effective idea of nationhood were even more intense. Here, when governments, frequently constituted only by particular sections of the electorate, proclaimed a universal 'we' to define 'the people' ruled by the state, they tended to stoke divisive ethnic passions, and these divisions provided opportunities for other states to intervene.

In the wake of these failures, democracies in post-colonial countries proved vulnerable to military coups, because most governments lacked the power to impose their will on rebellious subjects at just the moment at which the external pressures to do so, from the United States or the Soviet Union, were exceptionally great. Governments like the Indonesian and Brazilian that had not established clear lines of political command over the army were left at its mercy. As the exercise of power unconstrained by institutional rules lacked authority, those who wished to could grab it relatively easily. In many states coups had become the conventional form of political succession; amongst those states assuming independence after 1945, the first one in which an opposition party peacefully took power after winning an election was Jamaica, in 1972.

By contrast, the LDP in Japan had under American tutelage made representative democracy work and in western Europe it appeared more secure by the early 1970s than it had been either in the immediate post-war period or during the inter-war years. Of the European democracies only the Greek had fallen to a coup. No significant anti-democratic right-wing parties had emerged in any European state, and where, as in Italy, the Communist party was strong, it had flourished at the ballot box, not through violence. Where, as in Britain, the state had endured through the war; or where, as in France, there was some historical basis for centralised authority; or where, as in West Germany and Japan, the United States had imposed sites of power, democracy had not fallen victim to the problem of state-building. Democracy had also succeeded in Europe because, despite the imaginative cost of the loss of some external sovereignty, governments had used economic prosperity to construct a load-bearing idea of nationhood.

By the mid-1970s, the external conditions that had underpinned that success were being undermined. In abandoning dollar–gold convertibility and imposing a surcharge to force other states to revalue at the same time as it was pursuing détente, the Nixon administration separated the post-war international economy from American security policy and coupled it to the vagaries of American electoral politics. In doing so, it left its allies on their own domestically. The United States would still provide for their security, albeit in the expectation that they would pay for it, but American presidents would no longer decide economic issues with regard for the material well-being of other states' citizens. Either America's allies were economically strong enough to maintain themselves as democracies without further sacrifice of American interests, Nixon and his advisors had concluded, or their form of government was not especially important to their future within the American bloc. American foreign economic policy over the next decades would hold some opportunities for politicians in democracies, but they were no longer the result of a belief in Washington that the United States' own security interests demanded such openings.

In the months after the Smithsonian agreement, the Nixon administration paid lip service to the mantra of international monetary co-operation. It agreed to discussions from the autumn of 1972 until June 1974 through the auspices of the IMF in the Committee of 20 (C-20). Throughout the C-20, the West European and Japanese governments pressed the Americans to accept responsibility for the exchange-rate consequences of their macro-economic policies and to agree to new parities backed by a set of rules in which the United States had symmetrical obligations to others. But the Nixon administration would not contemplate any arrangement that could bind American monetary and fiscal decisions to external considerations and insisted that the problem of exchange-rate instability had been generated by the Japanese and West German trade surpluses.[2] When the dollar came under fierce downwards pressure in the spring of 1973 and Nixon refused to respond, the West German government and the Bundesbank, worried that further reserve intervention would trigger inflation, decided to float the Deutschmark and, consequently, the other EC currencies pegged to it.

The more unstable foreign exchange markets became, the more those governments that wished to maintain some measure of currency stability had to rely on capital controls. After August 1971, the French government, in particular, pushed for more co-operation in making controls effective. Nixon and his economic advisors, however, had a far more radical agenda. Since American capital controls had been introduced in the 1960s to try to maintain the dollar–gold parity, such restrictions had served their purpose. At the same time, liberalisation could encourage a flow of capital into the United States to finance the current account and budget deficits. In February 1973, the administration announced that it would disband all American controls by the end of 1974, and within eleven months, it had done so. In June 1974, it successfully demanded that the IMF be given the authority to discourage states from using capital controls to manipulate their balance of payments. Two years later, the Ford administration secured an amendment to the IMF's articles of agreements to include the exchange of capital as an essential purpose of the international monetary system.[3]

The most conspicuous eruption of American domestic politics into the post-Bretton Woods international economy came via issues of trade. By the beginning of 1973, the devaluations of the dollar had virtually eliminated the American current-account deficit. Nonetheless, the Nixon administration wanted to use a new round of GATT talks to limit regional trading arrangements and to secure better access for American agricultural producers to West European and Japanese markets. For Congress, GATT was insufficient. It subjected the United States to multilateral rules and offered no effective means of punishing those who broke agreements. In 1974, the Democrat-controlled Congress passed a new Trade Act which increased Congress's influence in trade policy and gave the executive branch, under Section 301, the right to impose unilateral sanctions against a state whose trading practices a president deemed unfair regardless of GATT's jurisdiction.

The immediate impact of these shifts in American policy was compounded by the oil shock of October 1973, precipitated by OPEC's wish to punish the United States for supporting Israel during the Arab-Israeli war. With OPEC increasing the price of oil by around 400 per cent in three months and the available supply falling, all oil-importing states experienced a rise in inflation and a serious deterioration in the terms of trade. Both the United States and its allies had come to take access to cheap oil for granted. During the Bretton Woods years, Washington's willingness to guarantee the flow of oil from the Middle East was a significant reason for the West European and east Asian states to continue to accept American support once their economies had recovered from the Second World War. But the United States could now no longer exercise the same influence over the Middle East. Although Iran and Saudi Arabia were American allies, they were not sufficiently dependent for Washington to control via financial pressure. Arab nationalism, the withdrawal of Britain from the Persian Gulf, and the growing capacity of the Soviet Union to command military power in the region, all, meanwhile, ruled out direct intervention.[4]

The oil shock detached the United States from its allies because it alone could partially substitute its own domestic oil production. The richest, like West Germany, sought to protect supply by paying high free-market prices for imports. Others looked to secure preferential agreements either, like Japan, by distancing themselves from Israel and the United States, or, as in the cases of France and Britain, by putting pressure on their own oil companies. And as the price continued to rise into 1974, many European governments came to suspect that the Nixon administration was rather less disgruntled at the turn of events than its public proclamations suggested. Even though the United States had to scramble for its share of the diminished supply and the price increase did feed into inflation, the American balance of payments relative to all its major competitors improved. The United States imported less oil than other states and since oil was priced in dollars, it did not have to earn more foreign exchange to pay the increased bill. Just at a moment when it had become clear that West German and Japanese economies could successfully compete with the United States, and Washington had rewritten the rules of the international economy to reposition the American economy, events gave the United States the chance to exploit its remaining economic advantages.

This opportunity was reinforced by the financial and monetary implications of the crisis. The OPEC states had procured far more dollar earnings than they could absorb in the productive sectors of their economies. From the outset, the Nixon administration was adamant that the recycling of these petro-dollars would advance American interests and worked to keep the international financial institutions away from the money. As early as December 1973, the US treasury offered the Saudi government inducements to secure first call on petro-dollars, and, in 1974, it reached a secret agreement with the Saudi central bank to buy government securities outside the normal auction. As a result, the OPEC states placed large accumulations of dollars in the big New York banks and the Federal Reserve Bank, providing new capital for the United States on a scale that easily dwarfed that available to any other state in the world.

This claim on petro-dollars significantly altered the balance of economic power between the United States and its allies. Since the spare capital generated by OPEC was denominated in dollars and so much of it was deposited in American banks, the United States could reliably borrow in its own currency and then reduce the value of its debt by depreciating its own exchange rate. Whilst other states had good reason to be prudent in macro-economic policy to prevent increases in inflation and in the value of foreign debt through substantial currency depreciation, the United States was under no such constraint. Moreover, Washington did not have to provide capital to other states to alleviate the problems caused by inflation and poor growth because petro-dollars provided an alternative source of credit. It could dispense with the IMF, where its voting rights were falling, and still be the predominant power in international monetary matters because of the reserve role of the dollar and its unrivalled ability to borrow. When American presidents wanted to bind others into policies that suited their own purposes, they could increasingly rely on bilateral relationships and American influence within the Group of Five (G-5) forum of finance ministers that had emerged out of the discussions to realign currencies after the end of dollar–gold convertibility.

After the American current account returned to deficit in 1977, the Carter administration made the most of these monetary opportunities. It talked down the dollar and, during the first seven months of 1978, persuaded the West German and Japanese governments to stimulate their economies to increase demand for American exporters. American autonomy, however, was not limitless. By the second half of 1978, the depreciation of the dollar had turned into a crisis of confidence in the international reserve currency. Whilst the American economy could absorb the inflationary consequences of a weak dollar, America's Saudi creditors were not enamoured at the depreciation of their dollar assets. When Saudi Arabia began to sell its dollar reserves and warned of a further increase in the price of oil if the dollar's depreciation continued, Carter was forced to accept that America's dependence on foreign capital did impose some constraints. In November 1978, he announced an anti-inflationary programme that included public expenditure cuts. The Federal Reserve Board responded with an increase in interest rates.[5]

Bretton Woods had constrained American economic choices, and had been rescued in 1947–48 out of a conviction that the United States had to sponsor the material prosperity of those it had chosen as its allies. Now, Carter and his successors could choose their economic purposes according to a range of criteria. Once the advantages of a weak dollar had been exhausted, the opportunities offered by a strong dollar could be exploited. As American presidents had a surplus of alternatives from which to choose, the international economy had simply become a far less predictable site on which those who led other states had to deploy their political judgement, and it would become much more difficult for them to sustain any particular political strategy since so many external economic circumstances could rapidly change. Governments now had to adapt to the movements of the dollar, and expect direct pressure from Washington about the level of domestic demand their response created.

The deleterious consequences of this reality and the oil shock were reinforced by Nixon's decision to abolish capital controls and the proliferation of petro-dollars. The opening up of capital markets and easy access to credit did offer opportunities. As growth stalled and tax revenues diminished, short-term borrowing could finance high levels of public expenditure and inflated oil bills. But over the medium term any influx of capital came at price. It increased the risk of exchange-rate crisis because the rapid accumulation of debt was liable to make investors nervous. Just as potently, increased capital mobility threatened to reinternationalise fiscal and monetary policy, so killing Keynes's hope that each state could set interest rates without reference to those prevailing elsewhere. Only if states' capital controls remained effective help, and if states succeeded in containing the proliferation of financial markets, could they hope to ignore the macro-economic stance of competing states in decision-making. If, to the contrary, macro-economic policy was reinternationalised, the experience of the inter-war years suggested that a strong deflationary bias would emerge, especially for left-wing and centre-left governments that wished to pursue expansionary policies. For those who had relied on a welfare state to contain the grievances of those who had been least well served by the post-war economies, borrowing was likely to offer only a temporary respite from the pressure to increase taxes and cut expenditure. For those who had built a domestic electoral coalition by controlling credit to the benefit of their chosen political clients, the likely internationalisation of monetary policy would expose the allocation of capital to external market forces. Meanwhile, lost export markets, rising inflation and unemployment risked revealing serious divisions of economic interests between different sections of the electorate and exposing the fiction of languages of nationhood based on citizenship as a shared fate of 'the people'.

Viewed historically, something potentially significant had happened. European governments during the inter-war years had struggled to sustain democracy under conditions of open capital flows and the monetary dominance of the United States, and because they had, Keynes had wanted capital controls to be permanent. The new external world that the Nixon administration had fashioned implicitly reopened the question of just why democracy had failed during the inter-war years. Did the demise of so many representative democracies in this period reveal some general truth about the three-way relationship between this form of government and an open international economy and the unconstrained dominance of a single monetary power, or something more circumstantial? If this kind of external economic world were indeed to damage prevailing conceptions of nationhood, would governments this time find means to deal with its problems that would not tempt the losers to rebel against the state's authority and the constitutional rules of democracy? A range of alternative developments, some not mutually exclusive, appeared possible. First, governments could adjust to the new international economy in ways that enabled them to reinvent their economic success by different means. Given the experience of the inter-war years, such a strategy might well turn out to depend on shifting the locus of economic decision-making to insulate it from electoral pressures, and might require a new political language about economic welfare to justify the state's authority in a democracy. Second, governments could offer non-economic reasons for subjects to accept the state's authority, which might entail a return to using foreign policy to stir collectivist identifications. Third, governments could try to use the power of the state to defeat decisively those who lost from the new international economy. Fourth, governments could fail at all of these and precipitate a crisis of the authority of the state and the constitutional rules of democracy that might conceivably threaten the external sovereignty of states too.

Chronologically, the discussion in this chapter is divided into four periods. The first part, 1973–78, covers the early consequences of the demise of Bretton Woods and American financial liberalisation; the second, 1979–84, examines the fallout of the rise of the dollar after the second oil-price shock and the United States' military build-up under Reagan; the third details the problems posed by exchange rates once the Reagan administration ended its strong-dollar policy; and the fourth surveys the repercussions of the United States' economic and military power after the end of the Cold War. The cases in this chapter are deployed, sometimes in pairs, to bring out the most significant constraints and opportunities for states created by each of these changes. Where one of the cases is left out for a particular period because it is not particularly revealing for these years, the subsequent discussion of that case brings the analysis up to date.

1973–1978: Japan and West Germany

Those who responded to the new constraints of the international economy most effectively were those who led the West German and Japanese states. Since each had exploited an undervalued exchange rate to drive export-led growth, they had most to lose from the dollar's devaluation, and bore the brunt of American protectionist resentments. They now either had to find alternative means to sustain exports, or risk inflation by increasing domestic demand. Each also had received a harsh lesson in their external subordination to the United States. Given the importance the United States attached to its military presence in each state and the legacy of their inter-war past, neither state could realistically use foreign policy to compensate for economic failure. Consequently, the premium on reinventing economic success appeared enormous.

The LDP government in Japan had fiercely resisted yen appreciation, but at the Smithsonian conference had agreed to a revaluation of around 17 per cent. By the time the yen was floated in the spring of 1973, it had risen against the dollar nearly as much again. The political consequences of the yen's appreciation were immediate, and in the general election in 1972, the LDP lost seats to the communists. Meanwhile, the humiliation of the manner of Nixon's opening to China was an opportunity for the left to press its argument about sovereignty. If, in the circumstances, material prosperity were in jeopardy, the LDP would accordingly find it harder to justify subordination to the United States.

The LDP government's first instinct was to expand domestic demand to compensate for the loss of exports. With inflation already rising towards more than 10 per cent, the oil-price shock hit the Japanese economy particularly hard. Japan relied on oil for 70 per cent of its energy needs, was dependent on imports for 99 per cent of its oil, and received about 80 per cent of its oil imports from the Middle East. Inflation for 1974 rose above 20 per cent as wage earners pressed demands for compensation. Confronted by an appreciating currency and increasing domestic costs, Japanese exporters were in no position to earn the additional foreign exchange necessary to pay for oil imports.

By the middle of the 1970s, the LDP government had worked out a more deliberate strategy to create an economy that was less dependent on heavy industry and consumed less energy. On trade, the government sought to restructure exports and control its import dependency. It financially backed export-oriented firms to move into higher valued-added production. For the first time, it allowed capital to move abroad and encouraged Japanese firms to invest in raw-material extraction and labour-intensive manufacturing in south-east Asia. Such investment turned the south-east Asian economies into component suppliers and sub-contractors for Japan. At home, meanwhile, Sato's successor, Kakuei Tanaka, introduced a range of social security programmes to try to broaden the political base of the LDP and appeal materially to those tempted by the JSP's stance on security. To enhance welfare provision without igniting inflation, the government tightened monetary policy and negotiated a *de facto* incomes policy in which private-sector labour agreed to moderate future wage demands in exchange for guarantees of job security. But the strategy did leave LDP governments even more vulnerable to what happened in the international economy because they had to control the value of the yen with greater capital flows, and preserve access to foreign markets whilst hoping that demand in them was kept at a higher level than their own.[6]

In almost every respect the LDP government reaped political reward from its approach. The Japanese economy recovered quickly from the recession of 1973–74 and returned to growth rates unmatched by any other developed country. By the late 1970s, Japan's GNP was as large as those of Britain and France combined. Even when the yen appreciated during the bout of dollar selling in 1977–78, the balance of payments remained in surplus. In the wake of this economic success, the left was unable to exploit anti-American sentiments and the communists lost votes in the 1976 election. When, in the same year, the Soviet Union began a military build-up in the Pacific, the arguments of the left against the security treaty lost much of their force. With the LDP's dominance once again secure, the government could tread more carefully on welfare issues, not needing to risk inflation by further expenditure programmes and borrowing. In its relations with the United States, the LDP government absorbed the opening to China, establishing its own relations with Beijing, and fended off demands from both the Ford and Carter administrations to increase defence expenditure without igniting a confrontation over trade.

Like the Japanese, those who led the West German state wanted to contain the consequences of the currency appreciation imposed by the United States, and also encouraged foreign direct investment to alleviate pressure on the Deutschmark. But unlike the LDP, the coalition Social Democratic (SPD) and Free Democratic (FDP) government, led by Willy Brandt, could not contemplate an inflationary solution to the predicament. When the Brandt government allowed the Deutschmark to float upwards in March 1973, the Bundesbank responded to its new freedom by tightening monetary policy. Brandt's successor as chancellor, Helmut Schmidt, welcomed the opportunity to enforce anti-inflationary discipline to try to maintain export competitiveness. In 1974, Schmidt announced that the government and the Bundesbank had agreed to set money supply targets as a framework for wage bargaining. Having failed to control the demands of one of the public-sector trade unions earlier that year, Schmidt wished to use the Bundesbank to punish inflationary wage expectations: if, he insinuated, the targets were not met, then the Bundesbank would continue to raise interest rates and with them unemployment. When, in 1975, a recession came, the government did borrow heavily but Schmidt returned to fiscal prudence once signs of recovery appeared. The pay-off for the SPD-FDP government of keeping domestic demand cool was higher growth and lower unemployment than any of the other west European economies for the best part of the decade.[7]

Once the SPD had accepted that the United States would not sponsor reunification, Brandt and Schmidt recast détente into an opportunity. In December 1972, Brandt formalised *de facto* recognition of the East German state, and turned towards rapprochement with the Soviet Union. If Washington would not help recover East Germany, then, Brandt hoped, the road to eventual German unity went through Moscow. Free from Adenauer's illusion, Schmidt informed Ford in June 1975 that he would not sign a new offset agreement to pay for American troops in Europe. Meanwhile, West German firms quickly exploited the new markets and investment opportunities in eastern Europe and the Soviet Union. Regardless of American intentions, Brandt and Schmidt had created a distinctive West German interest in maintaining détente.[8]

Yet if the West German state had escaped the predicaments in which its limited external sovereignty had hitherto trapped it, the success of the government's economic strategy after 1973 created a new set of external problems. When, in 1978, the Carter administration wanted to stabilise the dollar, it put the Schmidt government under intense pressure to bear some of the burden by reflating the West German economy. Whilst Schmidt agreed to a modest fiscal stimulus, the Bundesbank soon undermined the policy by raising interest rates. Within the EC, the Bundesbank's anti-inflationary discipline and the consequent strength of the Deutschmark were changing the balance of power between West Germany and other states. If other states could not maintain their currencies at a parity with the Deutschmark, they had to accept the inflationary consequences of depreciation, which made any attempt to restore parity without a loss of competitiveness extremely difficult. In January 1974, the French government left the European Snake system and floated, only to rejoin in 1975 and leave again the next year. Even when the government headed by Raymond Barre tracked West German interest rates to try to reduce inflation and stabilise the franc, the foreign-exchange markets continued to view the French currency as less credible than the Deutschmark.[9] Since the whole *raison d'être* of the EC for French governments was that it was a platform from which to assert French power from within western Europe on to the world stage, West Germany's monetary and exchange-rate supremacy was a huge problem.

In sheer economic terms, no West German government could welcome the difficulty that the other EC states had in maintaining exchange-rate stability. It kept upward pressure on the Deutschmark and always risked pushing West German exporters further than they could go in compensating for that appreciation by other means. Between 1972 and 1976, the SPD-FDP government offered financial support to the French, Italian and British governments to stay in the Snake. The bout of dollar depreciation in 1978 triggered a further fall in the other EC currencies against the Deutschmark, and Schmidt became increasingly aware that West German strength was unpalatable to others. Any attempt to deal with the problem required a European appearance. In the words of the author of one SPD strategy document from 1977:

> [the Federal Republic has become] in the eyes of the world *de facto* economically the second world power of the West. [It is] necessary for us, so far as possible, to operate . . . in the framework of the EC and the Alliance. *This attempt to cover our actions multilaterally will only partly succeed* because we will (necessarily and against our own will) become a leadership factor in both systems. (italics in original)[10]

In this spirit, in April 1978 Schmidt began secret discussions with the French president, Valéry Giscard d'Estaing, that culminated in a joint proposal to create a European Monetary System (EMS). The centrepiece of the EMS would be an Exchange Rate Mechanism (ERM), pegging currencies in bands against each other that would allow them to fluctuate 2.25 per cent either side of a central parity denominated against a basket of EC currencies called the ecu. All members of the ERM would be obliged to intervene to support the currency bands, including when strong currencies threatened to break through their limits. Where it was not possible to maintain bands, the ERM would allow for an orderly realignment agreed by all members. In July 1978, the EC states agreed in principle to establish the EMS. Five months later, they resolved to launch the system in March 1979, all but the British government agreeing to immediate membership of the ERM. Schmidt hoped that within an institutional structure, especially if he could ensure that the Bundesbank met its intervention obligations, other states could maintain some measure of currency stability against the Deutschmark. If, nonetheless, they were unable to maintain the ecu-based parity, he had guaranteed the West German state a say in the scale of the devaluation that ensued. Schmidt also hoped that in making the Bundesbank partially responsible for defending weak currencies and pegging currencies against the ecu rather than the Deutschmark, he had conceded enough, and the French government to disguise the real distribution of monetary power within the EC.[11]

1973–1978: Britain and Italy

By contrast, the Italian and British governments failed economically, and, as the external consequences of those failures mounted by the end of the 1970s, they were nervously turning towards confrontation with the sections of the electorate that had most to lose from states accommodating the new international economy. In the first half of 1973, the Christian Democratic (DC)-led government was already in serious inflationary trouble, and took the lira out of the Snake. When the oil-price shock came, only the Japanese and Danish economies among the industrial countries were hit harder than Italy. To pay the fuel-import bill and to increase welfare expenditure and the state-holding sector, the government borrowed furiously. By early 1975, it was presiding over a large foreign debt. In accumulating that debt, it had, in part, borrowed directly from other governments, including the West German, with whom it had agreed as collateral some of the central bank's gold reserves. With an effective national guarantee in the *scala mobile* that price rises would be compensated for by wage increases, Italian inflation was running more than 10 per cent higher than West German. The more the DC government made itself dependent on creditors, the more problematic this became since both Bonn and the IMF expected the government to implement an austerity programme as a condition of financial assistance.[12] Not for the first time, the problems of the Italian state at a moment of economic crisis were exacerbated by growing violence, as a self-styled autonomous workers' organisation, the Red Brigades, took to arms against the state and the business class.

In dealing with the crisis, the DC regime enjoyed some domestic fortune. In October 1973, the Communist party (PCI) leader, Enrico Berlinguer, offered to compromise with the DC and their then coalition partners, the socialists (PSI), to rescue the economy. Some leading Christian Democrats, led by Aldo Moro, the author of the party's rapprochement with the PSI ten years previously, were keen to find some way to do so, believing that the presence of the PCI in office would protect the government from a serious left-wing offensive, and help persuade the working class to accept some measure of wage restraint. Without a move to accommodate the communists, Moro feared, the only alternative strategy was an open confrontation with industrial labour, with uncertain consequences for the internal authority of the state in a political climate in which violence was becoming commonplace.

But for the Italian state's creditors, such a strategy was unacceptable. If Italy wanted further credit, Bonn and Washington insisted, the PCI could not be in government even though the party was now committed to the Atlantic alliance. What would have allowed the DC government to act economically as its creditors were demanding was ruled out by the political conditions of that credit. During 1974, the DC's internal problems intensified when the PSI left the government. The next year, confidence in the lira evaporated amidst a severe recession, and the PCI and PSI polled 47 per cent of the vote in local and regional elections. For the first time since 1948, the DC regime faced serious competition.

When the general election came a year early in June 1976, the DC just survived. But the question of how to secure material concessions from those who supported the left without upsetting the state's creditors remained. The new DC premier, Giulio Andreotti, found a temporary solution by asking the PCI and PSI to support the government in parliament in return for consultation on all legislative proposals. Reassured that there was no danger of PCI members in the cabinet, the West German government agreed to roll over Italy's loan, the interest payments on which Andreotti's government was in no position to meet without further borrowing. In October 1977, Andreotti tested the external limits of the state's solvency further by seating the PCI in the government's area in the parliament.

In the room he found for manoeuvre, Andreotti reaped some rewards. Inflation fell to 12 per cent in 1978 from its peak of 19 per cent in 1973 and exports increased. Andreotti's approach was, nonetheless, more tactical improvisation than a serious attempt to find a surer external and domestic footing for either the DC regime or the Italian state. Domestically, the republic's long-standing problems remained as acute as ever. Unemployment in the south was twice that in the north, and significant political groups remained wed to violence. In spring 1978, the Red Brigades kidnapped and murdered Moro. Externally, the weakness of the lira was a liability. The EMS initiative left the DC government having to respond to something that it could have no interest in either supporting or opposing. It could not hope to maintain a pegged exchange rate against the Deutschmark when Italian inflation was so much higher than in West Germany, and it could not afford to stay outside a development within the Community without reducing the effectiveness of the EC as a site of external support for the Italian state. Once it became clear that the EMS would happen, Andreotti and his DC cabinet colleagues decided to try to secure membership on the most generous terms, asking both for wide bands of 6 per cent for the lira and renewed financial support. The PCI and PSI leaders disagreed, believing that the deflationary pressure would be too much for their increasingly restive electoral bases. After Andreotti agreed in late 1978 that the lira would enter the ERM without securing much new money, the PCI and PSI voted 'no' when the matter came before the Chamber of Deputies, and brought the government down.[13]

In some ways the DC's accommodation with the PCI had run its course by the end of 1978 even without the EMS question. President Carter had become increasingly agitated about the influence of the PCI, and after Moro's death, the strongest internal voice for further compromise with the left was gone. But in placing the lira in the EMS Andreotti's government went down a path towards confrontation with the industrial working class. Unless Italian inflation came down to something approaching the EC average, the lira and the government's capacity to borrow would be at the permanent mercy of the foreign-exchange markets, the West German government and the Bundesbank. And unless the DC government found a means to curb wage expectations and squeeze demand, no such thing would happen. If the DC failed in the confrontation, it could not hope to maintain the support of the West German government.

Independently of the changes in American policy wrought by Nixon, British governments in the 1970s confronted a rather different external world than their post-war predecessors, since as Britain no longer held a position east of Suez they could not claim privileges in Washington. Edward Heath, who was prime minister when dollar–gold convertibility ended, believed that British governments after the Second World War had sacrificed too much in relations with the EC states and economic growth to the Atlantic relationship. After de Gaulle had departed office, Heath secured an agreement in principle from the French and German governments for Britain's entry to the EC. But the British government was turning towards the Community at a moment when the material gains were few. Since Britain had a small agricultural sector, it could only benefit from EC expenditure under a proposed new fund for regional development. Otherwise, as a large economy and the most significant importer of food from outside the common market, Britain would be a large net contributor to the EC budget, despite having one of the lowest GDPs per capita among the member states. With the risk that membership could become a financial liability, the Heath government had to use rebel Labour votes to ratify the treaty of accession. Even inside the Community, no British government could take domestic support for membership for granted, especially since the West German government baulked at funding regional aid for other member states. Almost immediately EC membership had become a serious predicament for British governments. Long-term, it offered trade markets and an alternative to the Atlantic relationship and could only be abandoned with a painful loss of credibility; but the apparent inequities of the budget, the conjunction of accession with the downturn in the international economy, and the resonance of the language of sovereignty to an electorate accustomed to the rhetoric of great-power autonomy constituted a gift to any opposition party.[14]

Initially, Heath and his chancellor, Anthony Barber, viewed the end of fixed exchange rates as an opportunity. Although they agreed to put sterling in the Snake in May 1972, Heath abandoned the policy six weeks later. Worried about rising unemployment, Heath and Barber wanted immediate growth. They embarked on an expansionary boom financed by short-term borrowing and tried to control the inflationary consequences with an incomes policy. As a Conservative prime minister, and one who in his first two years in office had pushed through legal restrictions on trade unions, Heath did not have the political capital to secure voluntary co-operation over wages and had to rely on coercion. For around a year, the government succeeded in holding to its policy. The oil-price shock, however, proved a fatal blow. Inflation immediately spiralled, and it gave the mineworkers' trade union the chance to break the incomes policy. Confronted by a miners' strike through the winter of 1973 and early 1974, Heath was forced to put the economy on a three-day week. That February the Conservatives lost their parliamentary majority, after Heath had called a general election to ask voters to decide whether the government or the miners governed.[15]

On most fronts, the new Labour government was in immediate trouble because it had no clear sense of how to reconcile the conflicting imperatives of domestic politics and external realities. On the EC the government was very divided. To try to avoid derailing the government before it had really begun, Wilson promised to renegotiate the terms of Britain's accession to the EC and then put Britain's continuing membership to a referendum, in which members of the cabinet would be free to choose sides. On the economy, Wilson and his chancellor, Dennis Healey, hoped that they could make expansionary policies work through their relationship with the trade unions. Brandishing a promise from the trade unions to practise wage restraint in exchange for a commitment by the government to restore full employment, Wilson and Healey returned to the international capital markets to finance large increases in public expenditure. Wage increases, however, continued to rise, sending inflation in 1974 to

24 per cent. The balance-of-payments deficit ballooned, producing a serious crisis of confidence in sterling. In the summer of 1975, Wilson and Healey were forced to accept that they could not be indifferent to the exchange rate and that borrowing had to be controlled. But market confidence in the Labour government was not easy to restore. As soon as Healey showed some signs in March 1976 that he wished to steer sterling gently downwards, the markets sold sterling massively, and Wilson suddenly resigned.

Facing the prospect that foreign-exchange reserves would soon not cover imports, the new prime minister, James Callaghan, requested assistance from the IMF and foreign central banks and received credit with few demands attached. But sterling remained under pressure. When, in the autumn, Callaghan and Healey asked for further help, things became far more difficult. Neither the American nor West German governments were prepared to contribute more money without large cuts in public expenditure and borrowing. The IMF's terms bitterly divided Callaghan's cabinet, with some members wishing to reject the credit and withdraw from the international economy. Able to alarm Washington that worse might be to come, Callaghan and Healey persuaded the IMF to reduce its demands on public expenditure and finally got the loan through the cabinet.

Something momentous had happened. As Callaghan explained bluntly to the Labour party conference in 1976, in making these expenditure cuts the state could no longer take responsibility for maintaining full employment at the expense of inflation. And, as he passed by rather more quickly, if governments could not maintain the confidence of financial markets by their anti-inflationary resolve and they did not raise more in taxation, the state could not continue to maintain existing levels of welfare entitlements. For all its honesty that circumstances had changed, as an account of thirty years of British economic policy Callaghan's speech was either a muddle or disingenuous. British governments had spent four years, not thirty, using deficit financing to spend their way out of recession, and during the Bretton Woods years, British governments had frequently resorted to modest deflation in the light of external constraints. But whatever the causal simplifications, Callaghan was rhetorically repudiating the expectations of the state that had been crucial to the language of nationhood articulated by British politicians since the Second World War.

For two years after securing the IMF loan, the Callaghan government kept fiscal and monetary policy relatively tight and introduced a staged, compulsory incomes policy. Inflation fell, growth was restored, the balance of payments improved, and sterling was relatively stable. But the 1976 crisis had taken its toll. In 1977, the government lost its majority and became reliant on the Liberal party for parliamentary support. When the Liberals withdrew from the pact the following year, Labour was left as a minority government. In this context, as for the Andreotti government, the Franco-German EMS initiative was a serious blow. Outside the EMS, sterling would appear to be a weak currency. But precisely because sterling was a weak currency, Callaghan and Healey worried that it would not be able to withstand the restrictive discipline membership would entail, and they could not see how they could persuade the cabinet and the parliamentary Labour party to accept more deflationary policies. After some procrastination, they agreed that sterling would not join the ERM.

Yet even in retaining an independent exchange-rate policy, the need to maintain wage restraint remained the government's most immediate weakness. In the autumn of 1978, the Callaghan government embarked on the final stage of its incomes policy. This time it met fierce resistance from public-sector workers and the government lacked the legal means to take authoritative action against sympathy strikes. The ensuing chaos as essential services were disrupted wrecked what support remained for Labour. After he lost a vote of confidence in the House of Commons, Callaghan was forced to hold an election that he could not win, and in May 1979 the Conservatives, under Margaret Thatcher's leadership, returned to office.[16]

In failing in their confrontations with the trade unions over wage restraint, both the Conservative and Labour parties had destroyed their reputations for economic competence and left the economy vulnerable to external crises of confidence. Certainly there was little evidence in the spring of 1979 that what had been a decade of economic crisis had damaged support for democracy. The territorial fallout of the crisis was also limited. When offered the opportunity in 1978 to devolve power from London to Edinburgh and Cardiff respectively, both the Scottish and Welsh electorates rejected it. Nonetheless, there appeared no plausible way in the circumstances in which the new government could advance non-inflationary growth. Without it, unemployment was likely to rise to levels that British politicians had assumed since 1945 were incompatible with any party staying in office, and the pressure to curtail welfare expenditure would intensify. If the state's internal authority were to endure, history suggested that the Thatcher government would either have to redefine British nationhood, or it would have to risk using the full force of the power of the British state against the economic losers of radical reform.

1979–1984: the second Cold War and the rise of the dollar

By the end of 1979, the United States was once more rewriting its security policies in ways that let loose more difficulties for other democracies. In 1978, Carter promised a 3 per cent real increase in defence expenditure, and in January 1979 he agreed within NATO to deploy American Pershing and Cruise missiles in western Europe unless the Soviet Union agreed to reduce its SS-20s. The same month, the United States' client regime in Iran fell and the Islamic fundamentalists who seized power took American hostages. In December, the Soviet Union invaded Afghanistan. Carter responded by withdrawing the second treaty on strategic arms limitations from the Senate, cancelling grain sales to Moscow and asking Congress for further increases in defence expenditure.

The events of 1979 also led the Carter administration to another change in dollar policy with huge consequences. The Iranian revolution precipitated a further two-fold rise in the price of oil, and a further rise in inflation. In August 1979, Carter appointed an anti-inflationary hawk, Paul Volker, as chairman of the Federal Reserve Board. Three months later, Volker announced a serious rise in American interest rates, which soon reversed the dollar's weakness.

The Reagan administration accentuated Carter's policy, determined to resuscitate the reality and appearance of American power. To this end, it massively increased defence spending, insisted that the deployment of intermediate nuclear missiles in western Europe would go ahead in 1983, and announced that the United States would develop a defensive nuclear shield. To try to curtail Soviet influence in the developing world, it directly financed and armed anti-communist guerrillas in Afghanistan, southern Africa and central America. This military build-up had to be financed. Since Reagan wanted to cut taxes and American domestic savings were low, his only option was to borrow from abroad. To sustain a budget deficit of around 5 per cent of GDP, Volker was forced to raise interest rates further and the dollar soared. With imports sucked in by the fiscal expansion and exports struggling under the weight of the dollar, the current-account deficit quadrupled between 1980 and 1984. Through the twin deficits the United States moved from the world's largest creditor to, in absolute terms, its largest debtor.

For the United States' NATO allies, the end of détente wrecked the autonomy that they had enjoyed in relation to eastern Europe and the Soviet Union.[17] When they continued to collaborate with Moscow to build a gas pipeline through Siberia, the administration imposed sanctions. Whilst the Reagan administration eventually rescinded these sanctions, the limits of its tolerance for western European autonomy were clear, and whatever reassurance intermediate nuclear missiles had once promised, they would in the circumstances inevitably reopen the awkward question of sovereignty over defence.

Meanwhile, the American response to the second oil-price shock reinforced all the problems that the Nixon administration had let loose earlier in the decade. States whose balance of payments moved back into serious deficit needed to import capital and were thus less able to resist at least some financial liberalisation. The reinternationalisation of monetary policy left those wanting a stable currency obliged to try to match American monetary policy. And, the harder containing the dollar's appreciation became, the more governments were forced to tighten their fiscal policy to impress the foreign-exchange markets with their anti-inflationary will. Most fatally, high interest rates dramatically increased the cost of servicing debt.

In August 1982, the Mexican finance minister announced that Mexico would be unable to meet its upcoming interest obligations to foreign banks.[18] Fearing that the default of a single major debtor could trigger an international financial collapse, the Reagan administration assembled a bail-out package that included credit from banks, governments and the IMF, first for Mexico and then for other states. But the new credit came at a ferocious price. Each state that rescheduled its debt agreed a structural adjustment programme that demanded reforms and radical cuts in public expenditure. Although the Reagan administration had come into office contemptuous of the international financial institutions, it pushed the burden of disciplining the debtor states on to them.[19] Since no state could reschedule its debt or secure new credit without the IMF's blessing, debtor states either had to submit, or default and withdraw from the international economy with all the ensuing consequences for growth, access to raw materials and food, and securing consent to the state's authority.

By borrowing as it had, at a time when American interest rates were already high and balance-of-payments problems rampant, the Reagan administration had transformed the post-Bretton Woods international economy. Since it had created such a demand for foreign capital in the United States, states in developed countries would now struggle to maintain capital controls as states in developing countries would to service their debt. Whether in order to preserve exchange rates, or to comply with structural adjustment programmes, governments could only adapt to the conditions either by raising more revenue at a time when economies were already an electoral liability for most of them, or by confronting the material expectations that citizens had of the modern democratic nation-state even where governments had continued to meet them after the end of Bretton Woods.

1979–1984: Japan

For the Japanese government, the immediate consequences of the changes in American policy were the least threatening. The economy certainly suffered from the second oil-price shock, and, by the end of 1979, the balance of payments showed a large deficit. Nevertheless, Japanese investment in south-east Asia diversified Japan's energy supply. The move into higher value-added production had reduced industrial energy consumption whilst the comparative advantages that Japanese firms had established in high-technology sectors had expanded the base for export earnings. Once the dollar began to rise, the LDP government saw the opportunity to export its way out of potential trouble. Curtailing domestic demand to control inflation, the government did nothing to try to stabilise the yen, producing a surge in exports. Alone among the G-7 states, the Japanese government contained the inflationary pressure of 1979–80 without triggering a recession.

The government's success, however, came at a price. Predictably, export-led growth provoked American anger. Arguing that capital controls were shutting American financial institutions out of Japanese markets and keeping the yen artificially low, the Carter administration demanded that Japan free capital flows. Yielding to the pressure, the government moved in 1980 to allow more foreign money to enter the country. Some within the LDP and the ministry of finance began to push for further liberalisation, believing that Japanese firms could take the political pressure off the balance of payments by investing abroad, and that the Japanese financial sector could establish some comparative advantages in international banking.

Trade and security questions proved more intractable. The economy could only benefit from liberalising more imports as a *quid pro quo* if there was threat either to Japan's export markets or to its energy supply. But whilst Carter had tolerated cosmetic changes, Reagan's advisors wanted a rapid reduction in Japan's trade surplus and for the LDP government to contribute far more to defending the international order on which Japan's prosperity was dependent. In April 1981, the LDP government reluctantly agreed to restrict the volume of car exports. The following month, the prime minister, Tadakatsu Suzuki, promised Reagan during a summit that Japan would take more responsibility for defence and agreed a joint communiqué to that effect. But when Suzuki spoke to the Japanese press after the summit, he disowned his vow, prompting his foreign minister to resign.

Domestically, the growth of public expenditure after 1973 to fund welfare expansion had taken a heavy fiscal toll and the government was still in the early 1980s running a persistent budget deficit. In 1981 the Suzuki government established a commission on administrative reform to make proposals for reducing expenditure by rationalising the state's bureaucracy. But when the commission published its first report calling for an immediate cut in subsidies, the government failed to respond. If the government were to curtail ministries' ability to direct resources to the party's clients, then the LDP would have to revise its whole electoral strategy. Neither could the government hope to curtail expenditure without inciting tensions within the party, as to which factions, with their different ties to particular ministries, should bear the brunt of retrenchment. After rejecting another recommendation from the commission in the summer of 1982, Suzuki lost credibility and was soon replaced by Yasuhiro Nakasone.[20]

Nakasone was the most radical leader the LDP could have chosen. He believed that his predecessors had taken too many risks in the relationship with the United States. Nobody could sensibly presume, he held, that the Japanese state could permanently free ride on Washington. Japanese prosperity depended on American support, and unless the economy was opened to foreign goods, capital and technological knowhow, and unless the political class ended its self-indulgence on security matters, that support would eventually vanish. He aimed, he proclaimed, to turn Japan's economic strength into economic dominance by accelerating the push towards high-technology sectors, and to transform Japan from 'a follower state' to an 'international state', or, put differently, from a state whose external status rested on the denunciation of military power to one constructed according to more conventional reason of state.[21]

Courting American support for this project was easy, but he struggled to find domestic allies either in the LDP or the economic ministries. Nakasone's preferred tactic became to invite American pressure. With its need for foreign capital growing massively, the Reagan administration readily obliged over capital flows, and in May 1984 the two governments unveiled a 'yen–dollar' agreement that committed Japan to full financial liberalisation and capital-market deregulation, and thus freed large sums of Japanese savings for American use. The consequences of this agreement were immense. Immediately, a massive amount of capital headed abroad, into both foreign direct investment and the American bond markets. Just as significantly, full financial liberalisation transformed significant aspects of the domestic economy. Henceforth, no government could hope to exercise the kind of control over credit by which LDP governments had hitherto directed economic development and serviced their political clients. Now, financial institutions could lend abroad and companies that were shut out of patronage networks had an alternative source of capital. As for containing the pressure for yen appreciation, governments now had to rely on macro-economic policy and reserve intervention. Nakasone had wanted to convert Japan from a 'follower' state to an 'international state', but these were not the antitheses he had presumed. In trying to turn Tokyo into an international financial centre, in encouraging investment overseas, and in internationalising the yen, Nakasone's government had created considerable incentives to follow developments abroad in setting economic policy. Whether Nakasone realised it or not, high growth in Japan, on which consent to the authority of the Japanese state appeared to depend, would now require aligning the Japanese economic cycle with that of the United States, and creating some commonality of macro-economic interest between the two states.[22]

1979–1984: West Germany and France

Within the developed world, the West German and French modern democratic nation-states for different reasons bore the immediate brunt of the Reagan administration's policies. For the West German, the primary problem came from the end of détente. Having transformed détente from a disaster to an opportunity and refashioned a growth strategy, the SPD-FDP government in Bonn had every reason to resent the return of the Cold War because it reminded West German citizens of their fealty to the United States. Not wishing to see their country dependent on American decisions in matters of life and death, around 40 per cent of the West German electorate, and many within the SPD, now appeared to prefer neutrality to the Atlantic alliance. From the autumn of 1981 through to the summer of 1982, hundreds of thousands of West Germans demonstrated against the missile project. Convinced that West Germany could not abandon NATO without jeopardising its security, Schmidt sought to broker a deal with Brezhnev to eliminate the Soviet SS-20s and with them the case for the American deployment. When he could not, he became increasingly isolated within his own party. To make matters worse, he lacked European allies on the issue. The Thatcher government in Britain had welcomed the return to the Cold War, and the French president, François Mitterrand, was first and foremost worried about just what the West German anti-nuclear movement revealed about Bonn's commitment to the western alliance.[23]

American dollar policy from 1979 also had very awkward implications. Once the Bundesbank became alarmed at the likely inflationary consequences of allowing a substantial depreciation of the Deutschmark, it aligned its monetary policy with that of the Federal Reserve Board without being able to re-establish the currency's value. To try to revitalise the Deutschmark in 1981, the government lifted German capital controls, most of which had been deployed over the previous few decades to keep capital out. Worried about employment, the Schmidt government then loosened fiscal policy, which sucked in imports, exacerbated the downward pressure on the Deustchmark, and induced the Bundesbank to tighten monetary policy further, causing a recession.[24]

By the beginning of 1982, the two difficulties caused by Washington were reinforcing each other and Schmidt was terribly caught. He wanted to persist with fiscal expansion as an inducement to the SPD to accept the arrival of the missiles. But the more he pushed for a further stimulus, the more he tempted the Bundesbank to raise interest rates and alienated his FDP partners, who were convinced that fiscal laxity was the primary cause of the problem. By the autumn of 1982 Schmidt had exhausted his space for manoeuvre. After the FDP demanded public expenditure cuts that the SPD ministers would not accept, the FDP abandoned Schmidt to form a new government with the Christian Democrats (CDU) led by Helmut Kohl. In the general election that followed in March 1983, the SPD fought on a platform promising West German neutrality against the CDU-FDP coalition which endorsed the missile deployment. The coalition won more than 50 per cent of the vote and condemned the SPD to their worst performance since 1961. Contrary to what appeared the case just a year earlier, there remained sufficient support for a West German state bound to Washington, at whatever the cost to hopes of advancing the cause of German unity through accommodation with Moscow.

The problems generated by the first Reagan administration for the French modern democratic nation-state were first and foremost economic. For France, sovereignty in military matters was secure. After he was elected president in May 1981, Mitterrand became a loud supporter of other states taking American missiles. Since French military independence depended upon the presence of American and West German troops to France's east and the American nuclear guarantee, anything that changed the balance of power in the centre of the continent was detrimental to French security. Reason of state, Mitterrand understood, demanded that West Germany take the missiles and eschew neutrality.[25]

Economically, French governments were much weaker. Giscard had hoped that the EMS would bind West Germany to his objective of rescuing the franc from its post-Bretton Woods problems. After the second oil-price shock and the increase in American interest rates, the EMS offered rather less. French governments now had to worry about capital flight to the United States, and, once the Bundesbank responded to Volker, to accept a far greater deflationary bias, if they were to maintain any measure of exchange-rate stability against the Deutschmark. Mitterrand assumed the presidency in 1981 and resolved to break through these constraints and if necessary to rethink the relationship with Bonn and the place of the EC in French foreign policy. He wanted as his first priority, he promised the electorate, to restore full employment and redistribute wealth. After his Socialist party won a majority in the National Assembly in May 1981, Mitterrand appointed four communists to his government, led by Pierre Mauroy, and embarked upon a policy of macro-economic expansion, welfare expenditure and cuts to the working week. Immediately, the franc came under heavy speculation. By autumn 1981, a huge amount of French capital was moving abroad, inflation was escalating and the balance of payments had plunged into a massive deficit. With the franc's ERM parity under unsustainable pressure, the government was forced to devalue. The devaluation neither spurred growth nor alleviated the pressure on the franc, and, in June 1982, a renewed bout of speculation wrecked the new parity, leaving Mitterrand and his ministers without any effective external support. When they asked the other EC governments to consider Community-wide capital controls, they were rebuffed, and neither the West German nor the American government would offer credit without an end to the expansion.

Once, in early 1983, the government had exhausted loans from a consortium of international banks and Saudi Arabia, it was forced to choose. Either it could continue to expand the economy behind a barrage of tariffs and capital controls and leave the EMS, or it could accept retrenchment and an end to redistribution. Mauroy's cabinet was divided, but after local elections in which the communists performed poorly, Mitterrand finally decided to save France's EMS membership, and agreed to devalue the franc again and implement an austerity package in exchange for a large loan. Henceforth, the economic policy of Mitterrand's governments would have a single purpose: at all cost, they would maintain a *franc fort*. They would seek to drive French inflation down towards West German levels by matching the Bundesbank interest-rate change for interest-rate change and orientating their fiscal and wage policies to the franc–Deustschmark parity. Their economic reward, they hoped, would be the kind of credibility in the foreign-exchange markets that under conditions of open capital flows appeared a necessary condition of sustainable economic growth. Their political gain would be to stop the West German government turning its monetary dominance into uncontested leadership of the EC.

The implications of Mitterrand's U-turn for the language of French nationhood cultivated during the Fifth Republic were severe. Since French governments could neither reverse American financial liberal-isation, nor penetrate the Bundesbank, French exceptionalism in eco-nomic policy had proved impossible. To continue to talk as though it were attainable could only invite a level of capital flight likely to pre-cipitate problems of a kind that no government in a democracy could sanely contemplate. Henceforth, French governments would have to acknowledge in their public utterances that in macro-economic matters they were subordinate to West Germany. Whether this would restore growth was an open question. But it did require a different lan-guage of French nationhood than that cultivated by de Gaulle, one which substituted the rhetoric of Europe for that of national external sovereignty.

1979–1984: Italy and Britain

Paradoxically, the consequences of the second oil-price shock and the foreign and economic policies of the Reagan administration were more rather more beneficial for the British and Italian modern democratic nation-states where the immediate political stakes of inflationary failure appeared highest. In Italy, the return of the Cold War suited the Christian Democrats because it was part of the post-war language of Italian nationhood, and it fortified all the external arguments against the PCI as a party of government; but the second oil price shock and the upward trajectory of American and German interest rates were severe blows. Given that Italy was importing as much oil as in 1973, Italian infla-tion rose faster than West German and put pressure on the lira, and the *scale mobile* made matters worse as it adjusted wages to prices. Yet if the government used high interest rates to stabilise the lira, it risked resist-ance from the trade unions and pushing unemployment towards what there was every reason to expect would be politically dangerous levels. Trapped, the government resolved to reform the economy, announcing in 1979 a three-year plan to reduce the proportion of GDP as public expenditure, freeze the real rate of wage increases and encourage labour mobility. To reject these changes, the government paper warned, was tantamount to 'giving up staying in Europe'.[26]

To succeed, the government had to confront the trade unions over the *scala mobile*. For all the proclaimed urgency, however, DC ministers were initially nervous. Their big-business allies were less circumspect. In October 1980, Fiat announced large-scale redundancies, prompting a strike by the unions at the company, which the PCI leapt to support. But after counter-demonstrations by other Fiat workers, the unions capitulated, leaving them and the PCI substantially weaker. This episode suggested that in conditions of rising unemployment, trade unions could not easily maintain the kind of solidarity on which their capacity to resist reform had to depend. In the aftermath of Fiat's victory, other large companies moved towards confrontation. By 1984, the DC-PSI government had amassed the confidence to issue a decree unilaterally revising the scale of protection the *scale mobile* offered against price increases. Some of the unions tried to resist, but when the decree was put to a referendum, the government comfortably won.

Cutting public expenditure proved far more difficult. Here, to succeed, the Christian Democrats had to attack some of their own clients and rethink their approach to the state's resources. Some pushed for the party to reinvent itself. Others, led by Andreotti, were more cautious. In the fallout, the DC lost 6 per cent of its vote in the 1983 general election and had to concede the premiership to the socialist Bettino Craxi. Craxi talked the language of modernisation, but he wanted to use the state's resources to turn the PSI into a client-based party, well removed from any alliance with the PCI. As the DC-PSI coalition became closer through an increasingly shared network of patronage, it increased public expenditure via new borrowing. Nonetheless, a fall in inflation to around 10 per cent convinced the foreign-exchange markets that Italian governments were not much more likely to devalue than their fellow ERM members. And as market confidence in the ERM grew, so did the macro-economic rewards of membership. In following the Bundesbank in monetary policy, the Italian government purchased some of West Germany's anti-inflationary credibility, bringing down real interest rates for any given rate of inflation, and with them the cost of servicing Italy's debt.

The apparent price of the DC's determination to pursue ERM membership was a rise in unemployment to more than 10 per cent. Christian Democrat leaders in the 1970s might have wondered whether the Italian modern democratic nation-state could have survived such an outcome. Yet, by the middle of the 1980s, the state's internal authority appeared more secure than 10 years previously. The Red Brigades were largely under control, the PCI was a spent political force, and a socialist prime minister had imposed his will on the unions over the *scala mobile*. To those on the left who charged that the reduction in inflation had been bought at the expense of employment and social justice, the DC-PSI regime could retort that the international economy left governments of medium-size states with no realistic alternative: either the electorate could live with this level of unemployment, or it would have to contemplate far worse. Whatever had been true when de Gasperi was trying to re-establish Italian democracy, full employment no longer seemed to be a reason of state in this representative democracy.

In Britain, the Thatcher government came to power in May 1979 confronting the same problem of wage-driven inflation. Both its predecessors had lost elections because having turned to confrontation against a section of the electorate, they had met resistance that they had been unable to break. Thatcher and her ministers' clearest aim was to avert the same fate. To succeed, they wished to strengthen the state as a site of authoritative rule in economic policy by reducing inflation and deploying coercive power when necessary. In attacking the trade unions in this spirit the Thatcher government was decisive, imposing a new set of legal restrictions whilst developing serious contingency plans in the event of a miners' strike. But on inflation, it plunged into immediate difficulties. Certain that another incomes policy could only spell trouble and wanting to cut income tax, Thatcher and her chancellor of the exchequer, Geoffrey Howe, leapt at the monetarist argument that inflation could be cured solely by controlling the money supply through interest rates. Under this illusion, the government set money-supply targets, raised interest rates, cut income tax, increased indirect taxes on consumer goods, and conceded public-sector workers a large pay increase.

The result was another surge in inflation peaking at more than 20 per cent by the middle of 1980. Backtracking somewhat, the government unveiled a Medium Term Financial Strategy (MTFS) in March 1980 to reduce inflation by reducing public expenditure and borrowing as well as tightening interest rates. But inflation was now far from the government's only problem. In tying interest rates to the domestic money supply, Thatcher and Howe had ignored the external constraints on monetary policy wrought by American financial liberalisation. The higher British interest rates compared to those elsewhere, the more sterling rose. Any possibility that the government could control this appreciation had disappeared when, in October 1979, Thatcher and Howe abolished all British exchange and capital controls. By early 1980, sterling had risen by more than a third against the dollar and almost as much against the major European currencies, destroying the price competitiveness of large numbers of British exporters. With high interest rates also squeezing domestic demand once the MTFS had cooled fiscal policy, the economy descended into a severe recession that wiped out around a quarter of manufacturing production and sent unemployment towards the levels of the inter-war years.

For much of 1980, Thatcher and Howe blamed sterling's appreciation on its newly acquired status as a petro-currency. But once new advisors had persuaded them that it was their own high-interest-rate policy that was doing the damage and that to continue with money-supply targets was electoral suicide, they reversed course. In March 1981, they abandoned the MTFS and reduced interest rates until sterling had been driven down to a more competitive rate, whilst increasing taxes and cutting public expenditure to combat inflation. Henceforth, they directed monetary policy at the exchange rate. Although they were not prepared to admit it, Thatcher and Howe discovered, like Mitterrand and Mauroy, that under conditions of increasingly open capital flows a European state could not operate a macro-economic policy at odds with those of the United States and West Germany.[27]

The U-turn of March 1981 brought the government little immediate reward. Through the summer of 1981, riots flared across most large cities and the Conservatives haemorrhaged support. Yet the Thatcher government had advantages in the face of its economic failures that neither of its immediate predecessors had enjoyed. However unpopular the Conservatives were, there was no government in waiting. In opposition, the Labour party had lurched to the left, prompting the defection in 1981 of some of its MPs to a new Social Democratic party (SDP). The SDP struck an alliance with the Liberal party and together the two parties won a succession of spectacular by-elections, but the Alliance's support was geographically diffuse and it could not win many seats under a first-past-the-post electoral system.

The Thatcher government also looked to the language of aggressive nationalism to compensate for its economic problems. As the relationship between the United States and the Soviet Union deteriorated, Thatcher seized the chance to move closer to Washington. Resurrecting the language of Britain as a great power committed to protecting liberty, she increased defence expenditure and attacked détente. She had also turned her nationalist rhetoric against the EC, demanding that Britain be given a new budgetary settlement. Before long, the Thatcher government was reaping rewards from foreign policy. Abroad, she had persuaded Ronald Reagan that Britain was indeed the United States' premier NATO ally. At home, the Labour party had embraced neutrality, unilateral nuclear disarmament and a withdrawal from the EC, allowing her to attack it as unfit for office.[28] Then, in April 1982, Argentina invaded the Falklands and Thatcher decided to go to war to recover the territory. Committed to a sea battle several thousand miles from Britain without adequate air protection, her government risked ignominy. But once Thatcher had persuaded Reagan to provide some military help, the war became a clear opportunity. After British troops recaptured the islands, the government proclaimed a more general political victory. Just as the government had shown proper resolve over the economy, so Thatcher professed, it had done the same in the south Atlantic.

Even though unemployment continued to rise, the government was returned with a landslide majority in June 1983. As the Christian Democrats and socialists had proved in Italy, unemployment no longer had to be the serious political liability that most politicians in western Europe had supposed since the 1940s. The Conservatives had been virtually annihilated where unemployment was highest, but they had sufficient seats elsewhere for that not to matter so long as the electoral system penalised a divided opposition. Nine months after the election, the National Union of Miners (NUM) called the strike that the government had long anticipated. Now relishing the battle, it deployed the full array of the state's powers to divide the miners and break the strike. After a year of sometimes bloody confrontation, the NUM capitulated, demoralising the entire trade union movement, and Thatcher pronounced another 'British' victory over 'the enemy within'.[29]

On virtually every score, the Conservative government had inadvertently rewritten the post-war assumptions of British politics. In liberalising capital flows, Thatcher and her ministers had made it that much more difficult for any future Labour government to contemplate a unilateral macro-economic expansion in the name of employment. In politically absorbing unemployment, they had made it easier for Conservative governments to use fiscal and monetary policy to squeeze demand, and to rely on insecurity about employment to suppress wage demands. In creating a rhetoric that tied into a single narrative the boasts that the British state had been reborn as a great power abroad and triumphed over the threat of 'socialism' at home, they had found a language of nationhood that did not rely on the state as the guarantor of material entitlements. And in revelling in that language, they had raised the possibility that fear could perhaps replace interests or identity as the reason why those who were the political losers of economic decisions might accept the authority of the British modern democratic nation-state.

1973–1988: Brazil and India

Most states in the developing world, whatever their form of government, proved far less robust in the face of American monetary policy after the second oil-price shock. Brazil suffered as much as any other state. Since 1974 the moderates in the military regime had won the upper hand over the hardliners and had cautiously begun to liberalise its rule. In 1978, the newly appointed president, General João Batista Figueiredo, had resolved to restore democracy gradually. One year later, he secured a law permitting new parties to form.[30] As the state's debts became increasingly difficult to service and the economy slipped towards crisis, he found himself ever more dependent on the old political classes in the states to govern.[31] Recognising this reality, Figueiredo allowed competitive elections in 1982 for the state governorships. Thereafter, the military's grip on power declined. After Figueiredo had reached an agreement with the IMF in December 1982 to implement an austerity programme, the economy sank into recession, hurting many of those middle-class and business interests that had previously supported the regime. Wishing to reinstate civilian rule when his tenure ended in 1985, Figueiredo found he lost control of events. Having resisted opposition demands for a direct election for the presidency, he reworked the rules of the electoral college to try to ensure that the military's party would retain a majority. But with the army splintering, Tancredo Neves, the leader of the main opposition party, the Party of the Brazilian Democratic Movement (PMDB), succeeded in co-opting various members of the military's party to his cause and won the election. In a final twist of fortune, Neves died before he could be inaugurated, leaving the presidency to his military-supporting vice-presidential candidate, José Sarney.[32]

Institutionally, any new government would have struggled. The law on parties was permissive and had produced a plethora of frequently fleeting associations. The electoral law left individual candidates from the same party competing for votes in each constituency. Consequently, parties were weak. Free from party obligations, the representatives concentrated on delivering patronage to their supporters. Under these conditions, no president could hope to sustain a majority in Congress. For Sarney the problem was particularly acute since the Congress elected in 1986 was controlled by the PMDB. For virtually every piece of legislation he had to mobilise a coalition using patronage, which put the budget under permanent pressure.[33]

The new government inherited massive economic problems. After 1979, the military regime had accumulated huge new debts to cope with the hike in interest rates and frequently devalued the currency, producing inflation for 1984 of more than 200 per cent. From the summer of 1982, foreign investment dried up and the state was shut out of private capital markets. Forced that December to turn to the IMF, the

Figueiredo government had strained to meet the Fund's ensuing demands, and had signed seven different letters of intent for a three-year loan. Worried that the new government would be subject to populist pressures, the IMF had wanted Neves to endorse the adjustment programme agreed with Figueiredo. But Neves was caught, as Sarney would be too. Only if they stuck to fiscal austerity could they hope to bring back foreign capital to finance development that had now stalled for more than a decade and on which the long-term future of the internal authority of any Brazilian state probably rested; but if they did so, they could not possibly meet the material expectations wrought by the restoration of democracy.

During the first months of 1985, Neves failed to convince the IMF to release the credit for the third year of the existing loan. Sarney reopened discussions, but offered no fiscal assurances, leaving his government unable to reschedule official and private debts. Its subsequent move was a radical one. Setting itself against the formulas of the IMF, it announced in February 1986 a programme that sought to break the inflationary psychology without using fiscal or monetary policy to do so. The plan created a new currency and fixed the currency against the dollar. It froze all prices, and eliminated all automatic indexing to inflation practices for a year. To protect workers, it increased wages by 15 per cent before freezing them with safeguards for a year. For a short while, these measures succeeded and inflation fell rapidly. But the plan did not impress the official creditors and commercial banks, which continued to insist that an IMF agreement was a pre-condition of any restructuring of loans. During the summer and autumn, the economy deteriorated. The rise in wages was swelling demand, and Sarney increased public expenditure for the Congress. The result was a further rise in inflation. After the election, won by the PMDB, Sarney and his finance minister, Dilson Domingos Funaro, tried to dampen demand again and abandoned the fixed peg against the dollar. The trade unions and the opposition parties reacted angrily, calling a general strike and organising large demonstrations, which provoked a violent reaction from the army. Under mounting pressure, the government agreed to negotiate about wages, but the talks quickly broke down.

By the beginning of 1987, output and employment were falling, the current account was in deficit, and foreign-exchange reserves had fallen by around 50 per cent from their level a year earlier. Funaro did, in January 1987, persuade the Paris Club to reschedule some debts without a new IMF agreement, something that no other state had succeeded in doing since the debt crisis began. But the deal gave little immediate relief, and just one month later, Funaro announced that Brazil was suspending medium- and long-term interest payments to foreign banks, and threatened a total default.

With the banks unyielding and the pressure to spend immense, inflation hit 400 per cent during the first quarter of the year. In April 1987, having exhausted the possibilities of heterodoxy at home and confrontation abroad, Sarney replaced Funaro with the more conservative Luiz Carlos Bresser Pereira. The new finance minister was no more inclined than his predecessor to acquiesce to the IMF, but he did wish to stabilise the economy sufficiently to persuade the commercial banks to deal with Brazil independently. Two months after taking office, he announced another anti-inflationary programme. Like its predecessor, the Bresser plan froze prices and wages, this time for three months, but it also tightened monetary policy and promised cuts in public expenditure. Sarney, however, was nervous about the domestic consequences of any fiscal squeeze, and ambushed the proposed cuts, prompting Bresser Pereira to resign.

But Sarney did not have an alternative strategy. Without an agreement with either the IMF or foreign banks, his government could now only spend money by having the central bank print it with all the ensuing inflationary consequences. Faced with this reality, the government resumed interest payments in January 1988. Six months later, it agreed a new loan from the IMF, allowing it to reschedule debts both with the Paris Club and commercial banks on the understanding that it would adopt a shock therapy programme.

But any serious hopes that the government had of stabilising the economy through debt relief were dashed when, in October 1988, a new constitution was finally agreed. The two houses of Congress elected in November 1986 had sat as a Constituent Assembly, and worked on the document for the previous two years. Whilst the army had concentrated authority and resources at the centre, the new constitution re-established a federal state, leaving to the states all powers not explicitly granted to the federal government, and making the municipalities full members of the federation. It gave states enormous fiscal resources. It bestowed around one-fifth of income tax and VAT directly on the states, more on the municipalities, and a further 3 per cent to regional financial institutions without concurrent spending obligations. It simultaneously authorised state governments to borrow from state commercial banks and made the federal central bank responsible for covering any ensuing deficits, thereby giving state governors a free licence to spend and making the federal government liable for the resulting fecklessness.

Whilst the new constitution left the federal government beholden to the states, it did not do so equally between the states. Each state had three senators, and whilst the principle of representing populations was applied in the Chamber of Deputies, there were lower and upper limits for each state's delegation, over-representing the northern states at the expense of the south-eastern, including the largest and richest state, São Paulo. Similarly, the transfer of tax revenue to the states entailed taking money from São Paulo and giving it to the poorer states. Whilst the constitution thus tried to address the large inequalities between its constituent states that were likely to have consequences for democracy, it did so by creating strong incentives for tax avoidance in the most populous state in the federation.[34]

If the territorial rules of the new constitution were detrimental to the authority of the federal government in fiscal matters, the determination of the Constituent Assembly to fix narrow substantive parameters within which any president could govern left it potentially impotent. Rather than concentrating on establishing institutions and the relations between them, the Constituent Assembly prescribed policy commitments. *Inter alia*, it granted workers a vast array of labour and pension rights regardless of financial cost, prohibited the entry of foreign capital into various sectors of the economy, set an upper limit on real interest rates of 12 per cent, nationalised various industries and protected land ownership. Effectively, the constitution turned over economic policy to the realm of judicial politics, and tried to deny the reasonableness of conflict about it. Any president who wished to govern differently would have to secure majorities of 60 per cent of each house of Congress and revise the constitution.

Since the federal government could exercise so little control over expenditure and borrowing, it could not possibly meet the fiscal targets set by the IMF. In January 1989, with inflation around 1,000 per cent, the Sarney government made one last-ditch attempt to retain external credit. The Summer plan established another currency, froze prices again, once more terminated wage indexing, tightened monetary policy and promised fiscal retrenchment. But Sarney's new finance minister had even less political means than Bresser Pereira to deliver fiscal austerity. In the wake of his failure, inflation rose towards 1,800 per cent, the IMF refused to release scheduled credit, and the government once again suspended payments to foreign banks. The constitutional rules of the Brazilian state were simply incompatible with any government exercising the kind of fiscal discipline that reducing inflation and access to foreign capital required.

By contrast, the Indian modern democratic nation-state was well protected from much of the fallout of American monetary policy. By the time the Nixon administration had dismantled the Bretton Woods settlement, Mrs Gandhi had already moved the Indian state beyond the direct reach of American power, and turned to a military and economic alliance with the Soviet Union. When the oil-price shock hit, the Indian economy staved off an immediate crisis thanks to the reserves the government had accumulated since the 1966 devaluation. Most strikingly, Mrs Gandhi's government had reacted more cautiously than almost any government in the developed or developing world to the opportunities offered by the recycling of petro-dollars. Having to fund oil imports at a far higher price, her government had the same incentive as any other to borrow commercially. It also, like the governments of many other developing countries, had the opportunity to escape from the strictures of the international financial institutions. Yet Mrs Gandhi and her advisors had eschewed private borrowing abroad, apparently convinced that if the state were to incur debt of this kind its authority would eventually be jeopardised. In rejecting this option despite being desperate for credit, Mrs Gandhi put her government back at the mercy of Washington through the IMF.

Mrs Gandhi's fiscal prudence during the 1970s saved the Indian state from the debt crisis that devoured the external autonomy of Brazil. By 1977, her government had secured a balance-of-payments surplus and accumulated sufficient foreign exchange to avoid the IMF. Nonetheless, the second oil-price shock hit the Indian economy harder than the first in part because it coincided with a disastrous harvest. In January 1977, Mrs Gandhi had submitted what since 1975 had become her personal rule under a state of emergency to an election and lost. After the oil shock, the new Janata government, a right-wing coalition of Hindus and farmers led by Morarji Desai, radically increased domestic borrowing, printed money and transferred more of the federal government's revenues to the states. These moves ultimately broke the Janata coalition and a general election in 1979 returned Congress to power.

The inflationary consequences of the Janata government's fiscal laxity turned the exchange rate into a serious difficulty for Mrs Gandhi's new government. Since Indian inflation was rising more quickly than in the countries to whose currency the rupee was pegged, the real exchange rate appreciated after 1979. As a result, exports stagnated and the current-account deficit slumped by 1981. Fearing a repetition of the fallout of the 1966 devaluation, Mrs Gandhi ruled out any depreciation of the rupee to try to improve the balance of payments. This left her government struggling to finance imports and unable to contemplate expansion and new investment without enormous risk. Still unwilling to borrow any sizeable amount commercially, Mrs Gandhi turned back to the IMF. Having already drawn small amounts of credit in the first part of 1980, the government in the autumn began negotiations for a large loan. The Reagan administration insisted that any loan had to include strict terms to liberalise the public sector and India's trade policy. To try to demonstrate its macro-economic credentials in the face of American scepticism, Mrs Gandhi's government radically tightened fiscal policy, and in November 1981 the IMF voted, over an American abstention, to grant India a large loan on conditions rather less restrictive than those it would soon demand of the states caught in the debt crisis.

In practice, Mrs Gandhi's government implemented little of what the IMF expected. Yet the loan incited considerable domestic opposition and, with the exchange rate continuing to rise in real terms, the current-account deficit remained precarious. By 1983, the economic strategy that had driven Mrs Gandhi's rule since 1966 was nearing exhaustion. Having done her best to minimise the external financial pressures on the Indian state and Congress's rule, her government was now trapped in an uncertain relationship with the IMF whilst growth was insufficient to allow the federal government to meet the increasingly feverish expectations placed on it. With an election impending the following year, Mrs Gandhi and her advisors concluded that the Indian state needed to spend more and to do so more freely, and turned to international capital markets to finance a fiscal expansion.[35]

Beyond the economy, the Indian state's authority was weakening in some parts of the country. Since she had returned to office, Mrs Gandhi had tried, once again, to curtail the power of the state governments. In Assam and, in particular, the Punjab, her efforts had provoked a violent response. The Punjab had been divided by partition in 1947 and contained a Sikh majority. A regional Sikh party, Akali Dal, had participated in the Janata coalition. Mrs Gandhi deposed it from power in the Punjab, and encouraged an alternative Sikh leader, Jarnail Singh Bhindranwale, who soon established an armed secessionist movement. Akali Dal responded by launching its own crusade for independence. In 1984, Mrs Gandhi imposed presidential rule on the Punjab and ordered the Indian army to assault the Golden Temple in Amritsar where Bhindranwale had an operational base. In October, in revenge for the attack, two of Mrs Gandhi's Sikh bodyguards assassinated her. In the aftermath, members of Congress organised and directed violence against Sikhs and two thousand Indians died.

Indian democracy had survived during two decades in which failure to deal with the difficulties generated by the external world had destroyed democracies across many states in Asia, Latin America and Africa. In part, it had done so because although those who had controlled that state had failed to raise standards of living as rapidly as others, in exercising fiscal restraint and observing the consequences of the current account for foreign-exchange reserves, they had protected the external sovereignty and autonomy of the Indian state from the kind of ferocious pressure that had elsewhere provoked constitutional crises, weakened the internal authority of states and prompted coups. Yet the aftermath of Mrs Gandhi assassination revealed just how far those who led the Indian state had come to rely on power to maintain their rule and the state's authority over various minorities. Nehru had hoped that federalism, allied to a secular and pluralist idea of Indian nationhood, would minimise the need for such overt coercion. That strategy for rule now appeared to have broken down irretrievably in the Punjab, which could only be kept under the Indian state by effective military occupation. Since Congress was willing to collude in the murder of those it deemed its political enemies, any idea of the state as an impersonal agent of a collective Indian people was untenable. When the same dominant party encouraged its own supporters to articulate their material interests in the language of communal identity as Mrs Gandhi had begun to, they invited religious minorities to reject the Indian state's authority. Meanwhile, among the Hindu population, caste was becoming more contested and in Bihar local politicians and landowners were being allowed to organise caste-based private armies. Unable to win consent to its authority from some subjects, and unwilling to ensure the state's monopoly of legitimate violence, those who led the Indian modern democratic nation-state had placed its internal authority in some jeopardy for reasons which had virtually nothing do with either economic failure or a faltering claim to external sovereignty.[36]

1985–1988: the falling dollar and American trade

By the middle of the 1980s, Reagan's dollar and borrowing policies were having significant domestic consequences that his advisors wished other states to absorb. The accumulating current-account deficit precipitated by the strength of the dollar had ignited fierce protectionist demands from some manufacturing sectors and agriculture. Since 1948 American presidents had generally accepted the limitations of GATT as an instrument to advance the interests of American producers and consumers. They had eschewed bilateral and regional arrangements outside GATT's multilateral framework, tolerated Japan's persistent disregard for many of its rules, and acquiesced to the EC's recalcitrance over agriculture. From 1985 Reagan's economic advisors moved to escape from these constraints. They brokered a free-trade agreement with Israel, and adopted unfair trade proceedings against Japan, the EC, South Korea and Brazil. In 1986, they persuaded the EC and Japan to begin a new session of GATT talks, named the Uruguay round, to cover agriculture, financial and service sectors, intellectual property rights and tougher enforcement measures, all issues on which the United States would benefit most directly from reform.

Meanwhile, the administration calculated that without anti-inflationary action to depress domestic demand in which it could have no interest, it could only alleviate the current-account deficit if its allies expanded their own macro-economic policies and absorbed more American exports. When neither the West German nor Japanese governments were obliging, Reagan's treasury secretary, James Baker, tried to force an adjustment upon them through dollar depreciation. From the administration's point of view, a weaker dollar and the lower interest rates that would have to accompany it represented far less of a risk than they would have earlier in the decade because the yen–dollar agreement of 1984 had secured a steady supply of capital into the American bond market.

In September 1985, at a meeting of G5 finance ministers in the Plaza Hotel in New York, Baker brokered an agreement with the Japanese, French, West German and British governments to depreciate the dollar through massive joint reserve intervention. In his next state of the union address, Reagan called for 'target zones' for the major currencies, and automatic and binding rules to force states with balance-of-payments surpluses to adjust their economic policy to restore equilibrium. Whilst neither the Japanese nor West German governments were willing to agree to rules so clearly contrary to their interests, they were not immune to more direct American pressure to accommodate a cheaper dollar policy. When the Federal Reserve Board loosened monetary policy, the Bank of Japan and the Bundesbank followed suit. In September 1986, the Japanese government agreed to an expansionary supplementary budget, after being assured by Washington that there would be a limit to the appreciation of the yen precipitated by the Plaza agreement.

The administration's interest in dollar depreciation was not limitless. Plaza did not lead to any significant reduction in the American current-account deficit, and, given the extent of federal borrowing, any permanent decline in the inflow of foreign capital was unsustainable. In early 1987, Baker concluded that the dollar was now in danger of falling too far and needed to be stabilised. Again, he wanted to achieve that outcome without adjusting American macro-economic policy. In

February, he brokered another international agreement, this time including the Italian and Canadian governments, to stabilise exchange rates. Unlike Plaza, the Louvre accord explicitly committed its signatories to co-ordinate their macro-economic policies. In practice, Baker had no intention that the Americans would do any such thing. The burden of the agreement fell on the Japanese government, whom he cajoled into a substantial monetary and fiscal stimulus. Market sentiment about the dollar, however, was more difficult to reverse. In October 1987 stock markets across the world crashed and the dollar soon plummeted to the level at which it had begun the year. Without currency stability, the pressure on other states to absorb the administration's unwillingness to deflate the American economy by adjusting their own monetary and fiscal policies remained unabated.[37]

Yet neither did the dollar's depreciation do anything to dampen the protectionist passions raging in Congress. After the Democrats took control of both houses in January 1987, they steered into law a new trade act. In addition to giving the president fast-track authority to pursue the Uruguay round until at least May 1991, this act expanded section 301 of the 1974 Trade Act to a new provision, Super 301, which allowed action against states designated as 'unfair' traders. The Reagan administration wanted a new multilateral trade settlement that could be better enforced than the rules of GATT, but, in signing the 1988 Trade Act, it had accepted Congress's demand that the United States should exercise unilateral power when American producers lost out, regardless of whether or not they did so according to international rules.[38]

1985–1988: Japan

Japan bore the brunt of the Reagan administration's second term. In the immediate aftermath of Plaza, Nakasone believed that he could use an appreciation of the yen to advance Japan's status abroad and secure more liberalisation at home. By the spring of 1986, however, the yen was rising more rapidly than even Nakasone could sanely contemplate. Fearing that small- and medium-sized exporters would collapse under the pressure, MITI announced a large package of low-interest loans. But the help immediately ignited wrath in Washington, and MITI was forced to administer the credit solely to restructure the production of the smaller exporters into the domestic market. Having sustained much of the structure of the domestic economy since the onset of floating exchange rates, the LDP government was now trapped: to sustain economic success either it had to find an international strategy to contain dollar weakness, or it had to restructure the economy.

In practice, any international strategy would rely on the kind of external support that the Japanese government could no longer command.
Despite strenuous personal effort, Nakasone could find allies neither
within the American State Department nor the National Security
Council to counter Baker's control of the issue from the Treasury.
Neither was the West German government sympathetic. Although it was
also frustrated at American dollar policy, it was quite willing to accept
Washington's line that Japan's particular problems with the yen were the
direct result of Japanese trade policy. In these circumstances, the only
plausible option was radical structural reform. In April 1986, an advisory
group set up by the government published a report that recommended,
amongst other things, that those industries suffering most under the
appreciation of the yen should move more production to north-east and
south-east Asia. If Japanese firms invested overseas, they could reduce
the trade surplus by replacing exports from Japan with local production
whilst increasing imports from the same source. In theory, at least, the
Japanese economy would be in a position to cope with the swings of the
dollar. In conditions of a rising dollar and falling yen, Japanese firms
could produce from their domestic base. In conditions of a falling dollar
and a rising yen, they could produce from their regional bases, where
the local currencies were pegged to the dollar. To secure their acquiescence to the strategy, the LDP government offered its neighbour states
foreign aid, commercial loans, technology and preferential access to the
Japanese markets. Japanese firms responded between 1986 and 1990 by
investing nearly $30 billion in north-east and south-east Asia.[39]

Yet whatever the likely medium- to long-term pay-off of the turn
towards the rest of Asia, it could not provide Nakasone with immediate
cover from the charge that he had sacrificed Japanese interests to the
American alliance at Plaza for little if anything in return. Although
the LDP won an easy victory in the general election of 1986, the
more the yen appreciated, and the more, in the months preceding
Louvre, the Reagan administration pressurised the government to
loosen monetary policy and reform the domestic economy, the more
precarious Nakasone's position became. When his government agreed
in September 1986 to the American Treasury's demand for a cut in interest rates and a supplementary budget with tax reforms, several prominent interest groups that had traditionally supported the LDP deserted
him. Despite Louvre, the yen's appreciation persisted into 1987, forcing
unemployment up, albeit to a level that would still have delighted
most west European governments. Ironically, domestic pressure for
expansion now began exactly to reinforce the demands coming from
Washington. Yet since Japanese interest rates were already down to

2.5 per cent over the previous thirteen months, the scope for further monetary stimulus was relatively small. In May 1987, the Nakasone government did concede a large fiscal expansion, which to please various LDP clients included a large-scale urban development project that stimulated a rapid rise in land prices and an increase in the stock prices of the companies that owned land. The bias of the Japanese domestic economy was now set to boom without any safeguards against inflation or constraints to stop Japanese banks from borrowing abroad and feeding that boom with easy credit.

1985–1988: West Germany and the ERM

The troubles of the Japanese government under the constraints created by Plaza and Louvre reflected in the extreme the price that all governments of developed countries paid for managing exchange rates according to the dynamics of the foreign-exchange markets and the demands of Washington. For most of the ERM states, the exchange rate created an additional set of problems. The need to turn policy in the direction set by the prudence of the Bundesbank produced dependence on decisions made by central bankers in Frankfurt. It also resulted in what many believed were lower rates of growth and higher levels of unemployment than most governments could comfortably accept, notwithstanding the possibility suggested by the early 1980s experiences of the Italian and British governments that democracies could now withstand high levels of unemployment.

The French government's dissatisfaction with this state of affairs was most acute. Mitterrand and his supporters had not conceived the *franc fort* either as an anti-inflationary end in itself or as a permanent recognition of West Germany's monetary superiority. By the second half of 1987, Mitterrand was hoping for a return that showed no sign of coming. French growth was sluggish, unemployment persisted at the level created by the recession of the early 1980s, French interest rates remained higher than West German because the financial markets still believed that the Deutschmark was a more credible currency than the franc, and even the Americans had been unable to procure any relaxation of West German monetary and fiscal rectitude. For both Mitterrand and his Gaullist prime minister, Jacques Chirac, the status quo had become intolerable. Against all probability, Chirac's government successfully negotiated a draft treaty with the Kohl government to create a Franco-German council to co-ordinate economic policy and to bind each state's central bank to common objectives determined by the council. This appeared to be just the opportunity to negate the power of West German monetary policy for which French governments had looked since the collapse of Bretton Woods. But French cheer was short-lived. When the Bundesbank discovered the terms of the draft treaty, it denounced the plan as illegal and persuaded Chancellor Kohl to drop those provisions that threatened its independence.

Defeated again, the French government now turned towards a far more radical solution, which in looking to abolish the franc and the Deutschmark would eventually put to the test how far European governments could compromise prevailing languages of nationhood and perhaps the whole conception of representative democracy. As a question of exchange-rate management, French reasoning was easy to follow. If there were no way around the credibility of the Deutschmark and the power of the Bundesbank, then why not, the French reckoned, replace them with a single European currency and a single European central bank? In this spirit, in January 1988, the French finance minister, Edouard Balladur, submitted a memo to his EC colleagues, denouncing the ERM and proposing monetary union.[40]

The French argument fell on the welcoming ears of those governments who also resented the burden of West German monetary and fiscal policy. But on these terms the West German government had no more reason to accept French prescription than it had had to take on the Bundesbank. Only if there were to be some compensation in another sphere could Kohl contemplate supplanting the Bundesbank with some form of European monetary authority. Within a few of months of Balladur's memo, Kohl's foreign minister, Hans Dietrich Genscher, had decided that such an opportunity did exist. If Bonn agreed to move towards monetary union on sufficiently anti-inflationary terms to quell a rebellion from the Bundesbank, it could, Genscher judged, ask France to support more supra-national decision-making. With somewhat less enthusiasm and to a rather different end, Kohl's finance minister, Gerhard Stoltenberg, agreed. If, Stoltenberg reckoned, the government obliged on monetary union, it would have the bargaining means to keep all of the EC states to the timetable for full financial liberalisation set in the Single European Act of 1986, and the Deutschmark would be saved from the risk of appreciation against other European currencies at moments of currency turbulence.[41]

In May 1988, the EC governments agreed to establish a committee of central bankers, chaired by the Commission president, Jacques Delors, to consider the means necessary to realise monetary union. When published in April 1989, the Delors report recommended the creation of a single currency backed by an independent European central bank and a three-stage plan to achieve it. Two months later, at the Madrid summit, the EC heads of government accepted the Delors report and agreed to convene an inter-governmental conference, which culminated two and a half years later in a final treaty at a summit in Maastricht. Only the British government was reluctant. Within the British government the ERM had become a divisive issue, dividing Thatcher from both her chancellor and her foreign secretary. For her part, Thatcher could not see why having escaped from the strictures of the Bundesbank, a British government should bind itself to a project conceived of completely independently from British interests. But even cabinet ministers who would readily have submitted to the discipline of the ERM were sceptical as to just how a British government could absorb the spectacle of formally handing over authority in monetary policy from the British Parliament to a European central bank.

In turning to monetary union, the EU states were taking a considerable political risk. Whatever the problems of the ERM, the case for monetary union was in part that against democracy in macro-economic decision-making. National politicians could not be trusted to take decisions about interest rates, this argument presumed, because they were too likely to sacrifice the long-term common good to short-term sectional interests. But in the circumstances monetary union could only work if two things were true. First, that in the member-states without a historical memory of hyperinflation most of the political class and the electorate had become persuaded that price stability was an indivisible and politically incontestable public good. Second, that there could be an enduring conviction amongst national electorates in the EC that the consequences of a *European* monetary policy did not in the long term favour any particular set of interests over any other. In other words, for monetary union to succeed, voters in different parts of the EC would need to accept that they could be short-term political losers without fearing that they would always be so. There would have to be in place something that would prevent any desire to secede from the project when decisions made by the central bank damaged the interests of particular groups within the Community. By implication, the EC governments were gambling that there existed, or if not that they could create, some form of belief in a common European people sharing collective interests and purposes, which could act as the kind of fiction nationhood had been in sustaining authority.

1989–2001: American power after the Cold War

The most difficult problems the external world created for democracies in the late 1980s were economic, the consequences of which were far from played out. But since the Cold War had defined so much of the external world the United States had shaped after 1945, its end necessarily had profound consequences of a wider kind. The fall of the Soviet Union defeated the only alternative form of government to representative democracy left in Europe, and it precipitated the introduction of competitive elections in eastern Europe, some of the former Soviet republics, and less directly Yugoslavia and Albania too. Democracy was also becoming the dominant form of government again in much of the rest of the world. The debt crisis in Latin America had weakened military regimes on the continent and by 1990 democracy prevailed in every South American state. In Asia, the Philippines held competitive elections in 1986 and South Korea and Pakistan in 1987, whilst by the early 1990s, moves towards democracy were in place in South Africa and some central American and Caribbean states.[42]

The opportunity offered to the United States by the end of the Cold War to shape the external world in which other democracies had to survive was massive. Militarily, it had no rivals. Economically, the demise of the Soviet bloc opened up parts of the world that had been closed to American goods and capital for more than forty years, and left the new governments there looking for financial assistance in return for which concessions could be extracted. Rhetorically, any American government could proclaim the victory of the supposed American values of free markets and liberal democracy over anything that smacked of socialism or authoritarianism and in so doing justify external intervention against states where representative democracy faltered. Nonetheless, not for the first time in the twentieth century in the wake of victory in a major geopolitical conflict, the American president and Congress had a choice as to whether exercise the new power the United States had acquired.[43] Having defeated one of the two states that could attack the United States with intercontinental ballistic missiles, enjoying vast nuclear superiority over the other, and having discredited radical economic and political alternatives, the immediate American interest in continuing an activist foreign policy was probably limited to maintaining access to a reliable supply of oil and opening protected markets where American producers and investors had clear comparative advantages. Unless a president could persuasively articulate a coherent conception of where national interests were threatened in a world that the United States could dominate virtually at will, then Congress was likely to check the president's supremacy in foreign policy.

George Bush senior never considered a retreat from the world that his predecessors had shaped. Bush's decisive opportunity to give renewed purpose to American power came when, in the summer of 1990, Iraq invaded Kuwait. At home, Bush struggled to convince Congress that military action was needed, winning a war mandate from the Senate by only five votes. Abroad, he obtained support from the UN for collective action against Iraq under American command. When the UN forces won an easy victory, Bush proclaimed the onset of a 'new world order' run by an 'international community'.

The rhetorical fiction of an international community embodied in the UN gave the Bush administration the instrument to exercise American power on an unprecedented scale. Successive American presidents had regularly ordered interventions in the domestic affairs of other states. Formally, however, article two of the UN charter prohibited such action. In his last month in office, Bush persuaded the UN to license intervention in Somalia for what he and his advisors deemed 'humanitarian' purposes. Under this guise what was invariably the unilateral exercise of American power no longer had to be at odds with the universal language deployed within the UN. Beneath this rhetoric lay an aspiration to permanent dominance. As the Pentagon articulated it, 'strategy must now refocus on precluding the emergence of any future global competitor by convincing potential competitors that they need not aspire to a greater role'.[44]

In its approach to the international economy, the Bush administration was more circumspect. The national debt that its predecessor had accumulated in winning the Cold War ruled out offering the kind of financial support to the states of the former Soviet Union and eastern Europe that would have made their governments structurally dependent on the United States. Hoping that the EC would provide the capital for reconstruction, Bush and his economic advisors relied on the IMF to enforce the argument that there was only one way to organise a state's economy and politics. In other parts of the world, the United States was similarly confined. Before the Cold War had ended, the Bush senior administration had under the Brady plan offered debt-reduction agreements through the IMF and the World Bank to developing countries that restructured outstanding sovereign loans into liquid-debt instruments. The price for the indebted states was further restrictions on their autonomy, and from 1989, the international financial institutions demanded that they meet new political conditions on governance, accountability and transparency.

On trade, the end of the Cold War reinforced what was already becoming a more protectionist stance in American trade policy. In December 1990, with only three months left of the president's fast-track authority, Bush coupled a request to Congress for authority to resurrect the GATT negotiations with one to begin discussions with Mexico about creating a North Atlantic Free Trade Area (NAFTA). The prospect of free trade with a low-wage economy like Mexico's incited a new round of protectionist fervour, this time emanating from organised labour and environmental groups. Although Bush won fast-track authority for both negotiations, he had to promise labour and environmental concessions from Mexico as part of any agreement. With a new protectionist coalition having emerged, a majority in Congress pressed for renewal of Super 301. When the Republicans lost a Senate seat to the Democrats on the slogan that Americans should take care of their own, Bush turned to the old language of Japan-bashing.[45] When the American economy slipped into recession, the Democrats charged that Bush had sacrificed national economic interests to establishing his 'new world order', helping Bill Clinton to victory in 1992.

As he had promised in the election, Clinton's first priorities were the domestic economy and improving American trade competitiveness. His administration would, he warned, find new markets for American exports, and close foreign producers out of American markets if they were damaging domestic workers or compromising environmental and labour standards. Unsurprisingly, the burden of the Clinton administration's economic ambitions fell on East Asia. For eighteen months after entering office, it allowed the dollar to fall precipitously against the yen. In July 1993, it forced the Japanese government into a framework agreement for negotiating structural reforms to several sectors of the Japanese economy so as to increase American access, and nine months later it issued a Super 301 order against Tokyo. Four months later, Clinton went to an Asia Pacific Economic Co-operation (APEC) summit meeting, and declared that the region, including China, should dismantle all protectionist practices. Within a year, his officials had persuaded the developed-country members to complete a free trade and investment area by 2010 and developing countries by 2020. In Latin America, the administration was just as ambitious. Despite pressure from Congressional Democrats to abort the project, Clinton persisted with the NAFTA negotiations and secured two side-agreements on environmental and labour standards that protected American producers. Within a year, he was pressing to extend NAFTA across the continent to establish a Free Trade Area of Americas (FTAA).[46]

In pressing for regional agreements that the United States could dominate, Clinton did not wish to abandon the multilateral trading order. Indeed, in steering the Uruguay round to a final conclusion in December 1993, he wanted to strengthen it. For over two years, the participating governments had been discussing a Canadian proposal to institutionalise GATT by creating a World Trade Organisation (WTO). Fearing any member-based international organisation in which the United States enjoyed only the same formal voting rights as any other state, the administration was nervous. But on the final day of the round it accepted the proposal, judging that a WTO that included robust dispute-settlement procedures offered the United States a means to enforce the rules of the multilateral trading regime in a manner which had not hitherto existed.[47] Beyond the EC's recalcitrance over agriculture, the Uruguay round gave much else to Washington. It produced significant cuts in tariffs in manufactured goods and included for the first time an agreement on services, where many American producers enjoyed comparative advantages. It tied the states of developing countries to rules that had never in practice applied to them under GATT, and it subjected them to standards on intellectual property rights that established fierce protection for American patents. Since the round created rules for the WTO to uphold that were generally far more advantageous to developed than developing economies, the United States had far more to gain than to lose from accepting adjudication from the new international institution. Even if the WTO allowed another state to retaliate, the size and diversity of the American economy would allow it easily to absorb punitive sanctions without having to take correction action.[48]

Nonetheless, Clinton could not establish a pro-trade coalition in Congress. In 1993, he had to rely on Republican votes to get NAFTA ratified by Congress. In ratifying that Uruguay treaty in 1994, Congress gave itself the right to a vote every five years on whether to continue WTO membership. The same year it denied Clinton any new fast-track authority for the FTAA, as it did again in 1997 and 1998. Without fast-track, no other government could have any interest in serious negotiations. In 1995, Clinton pushed the OECD states to begin talks on a multilateral investment agreement to establish common rules on foreign direct investment, only to abandon the discussions in the face of fierce opposition at home. Soon other governments were able to exploit Clinton's weakness. At the first ministerial meeting of the WTO in 1996, the administration pressed to put labour standards under the organisation's authority, but was easily rebuffed. When at the next summit, in Seattle in December 1999, Clinton proclaimed that states that violated labour rights should be subject to trade sanctions, the meeting acrimoniously collapsed.[49]

On financial and monetary matters, the Clinton administration rewrote the international economy to American advantage. Having allowed the dollar to depreciate substantially during its first two and a half years in office, it reversed course in mid-1995 and navigated the dollar upwards. Meanwhile the administration moved to push more states, especially in east and south-east Asia, towards financial liberalisation.[50] Most consequentially, in 1996, it secured South Korea's agreement to a staggered timetable for liberalisation. An unprecedented credit boom across most of the region ensued, as unsupervised financial institutions borrowed abroad and lent the money on to domestic firms, frequently those that were the political clients of the ruling parties. By the middle of 1997, the ensuing explosion of foreign capital was turning to bust. Massive speculation against first the Thai and then other Asian currencies precipitated a crisis. The Thai, South Korean and Indonesian governments all turned to the IMF for new credit as foreign-exchange reserves dwindled, presenting the Clinton administration with a clear opportunity to impose its will. Involving themselves directly in the IMF's negotiations with South Korea, Clinton's Treasury officials, Robert Rubin and Lawrence Summers, demanded massive structural reform as the condition of any financial package and took the IMF into a whole new area of conditionality.[51] Succumbing, the South Korean government agreed to allow more foreign ownership, external access to domestic banks, a reconstituted central bank, western practices of accounting in the financial sector, reforms of the country's largest companies and new labour laws. It also agreed that nobody should run for the impending presidential elections who did not support the IMF loan. In the aftermath of the crisis, the east Asian economies were seriously penetrated for the first time by American capital.

Having shown little interest in using American power directly in most parts of the world during its first years in office, the Clinton administration gradually moved towards a different strategic judgement about foreign policy with significant consequences for other states. In eastern Europe, it edged towards enlarging NATO, using Russia's dependency on credit from the IMF to secure its acquiescence to the entry into the alliance in 1999 of the Czech Republic, Hungary and Poland. In the Middle East, it invested heavily in the Israeli-Palestinian peace talks. In central America, it led a UN operation in Haiti to restore democracy after the incoming president was deposed in a coup. In Africa, it used humanitarian arguments to justify UN interventions in Angola, Liberia, Mozambique and Rwanda. In east Asia, it abandoned its earlier hostile plans to reduce troops, secured a 'framework agreement' with North Korea to curtail Pyongyang's nuclear programme, and reversed its stance towards China, encouraging the communist leadership towards market reforms and eventual WTO membership. Perhaps most consequentially, it turned its attention to the Balkans, first bombing the Bosnian Serbs and then organising the Croatian government's march to recapture the Krajina region and expel the local Serb population.

Thereafter, the settlement of the Yugoslav wars of succession had to be on American terms.[52]

Nothing revealed more about the world that the Clinton administration was creating through American military power than the war it embarked on in 1999 against Serbia. Slobodan Milosevic's continuing presence in power irritated many in the administration. In the second half of 1998, Clinton decided to confront Milosevic about Kosovo, as the war waging between the Serb forces and the rebel Kosovo Liberation Army (KLA) intensified. In October, the administration persuaded Milosevic to reduce the Serbian military and police presence in the province to pre-war levels and to accept a ceasefire without making demands on the KLA. When the ceasefire unsurprisingly broke, and the killings on both sides continued, the administration pressed for an international summit. The Rambouillet conference was billed as the last opportunity for peace, but representatives of the Clinton administration went to it in search of a war. Determined to engineer an agreement that would be acceptable only to the Kosovar Albanians, the administration presented Serbia with a demand to allow NATO troops into the whole of Yugoslavia. When Milosevic refused, it led NATO to war without seeking UN authorisation.[53]

The United States' final victory in the Balkans demonstrated much about US dominance of the post-Cold War world. The administration had successfully usurped the language of universal values to justify a military intervention in the internal affairs of a sovereign state. It had asserted that the United States and not the UN was the vehicle of the 'international community', but it was nonetheless able to use the UN to run Kosovo as a protectorate once the war was won. It had acted unilaterally in deciding to use force prior to Rambouillet and stopped trusting NATO militarily in the middle of the war, but it had kept an expanded NATO together. It had brought an initially hostile Russian government into the diplomatic negotiations by procuring the release for Moscow of suspended IMF credit. And in doing these things, the United States had successfully expanded the practical and imaginative basis on which it could now exercise military power.

The end of the Cold War and the growing assertion of American military and economic power through the 1990s had profound consequences for the United States' allies in Europe and Asia. Those governing parties that had used the Cold War and the language of the Soviet threat either to demonise the opposition as unfit for rule or as part of the language of nationhood had lost important external capital. Militarily, governments could commit fewer resources to defence, but Washington was still invested in their security arrangements. In the early

1990s, the west European states remained the subordinate members of a military alliance the purpose of which was not entirely clear, and Japan was bound to a bilateral security pact for which Washington extracted a growing material price. By the end of the 1990s, the west European members of NATO were liable for contributions to ventures that appeared to be conceived first and foremost as an assertion of American power. Only if the EU and Japanese governments had the will to develop independent military power could they think about reclaiming their external sovereignty in defence.

Economically, the end of the Cold War created some new constraints for governments in western Europe and east Asia. The restoration of a balanced budget in the United States lessened American dependency on foreign capital and made it easier for Washington to manage the dollar and, therefore, even more difficult for other states to navigate their way through the consequences of American macro-economic decisions. Meanwhile, an increasing number of investors in a more stable political world took their capital abroad in search of the highest returns, looking for low-cost production sites and access to free trade areas. The more willing investors became to shift manufacturing production away from traditional sites in Europe and North America, the more low-skill producers there lost their comparative advantages. The more external barriers to investment were reduced, the more internal economic organisation and the state's distribution of revenue and resources became a significant part of international competition for capital. In one sense, of course, the surge in foreign direct investment offered the beneficiaries better growth prospects. But it did have awkward implications for governments that since the end of Bretton Woods had succeeded in shielding some aspects of the national economy from international markets and procured political stability by doing so. If economic success could not be reinvented in another set of international circumstances, the Japanese and German governments, in particular, would either have to engage in radical reform and confront the losers, or watch the existing economic foundations of consent to the authority of their modern democratic nation-state unravel.

For democracies in developing countries, the consequences of the United States' post-Cold War policies were even more serious. The international economy of the 1990s did offer opportunities to link consent to the state's authority to the material well-being of its subjects. The growth of foreign direct investment through the first three-quarters of the decade opened up a massive source of capital, and the Brady plan enabled those governments that could satisfy the IMF to return to private credit markets. But if they allowed portfolio investment, and opened up domestic financial markets, these governments took substantial risks. Few had banking systems that could supervise financial institutions absorbing large inflows, and any government that ran into difficulty servicing its debt became highly vulnerable to capital flight and speculation. If governments were hit by currency crises, the value of their debt could rise enormously, leaving them even more at the mercy of the IMF. The expansion of international trade likewise was an opportunity at a clear price. The Uruguay agreement reduced some tariffs on agricultural goods and more sharply on textiles, but it imposed commitments on intellectual property rights that offered no benefits and were costly to implement. Although the WTO's dispute-settlement procedure could in principle end arbitrary discrimination, the governments of poor countries could not expect to retaliate against rich states that broke the rules without damaging their own economies. Beyond the framework for multi-trade, at least some governments could hope to strike trade agreements that would open large markets to their producers, but their acute economic needs always put them at negotiating disadvantage. Whilst, as a majority of the WTO membership, the governments of developing countries could rebuff American demands to include labour and environmental standards, they found it far harder to resist such covert protectionism in any bilateral or regional agreement with Washington. So long as they remained dependent via the IMF on the states with whom they were negotiating trade agreements, they could not hope to advance their trading interests more effectively, or easily rebut the charge that they were giving more to foreigners than they were securing for their own citizens.[54]

Given what had happened to some democracies in post-colonial, developing countries during the confrontation between the superpowers, the external world was now in some other respects conducive to their survival. So long as American presidents wished to conduct their foreign policy in the name of 'the international community', they could ill afford to be seen backing military coups to overthrow democracies. Without the prospect of support from Washington, the armies in the states of developing countries were weakened as domestic political actors. Nonetheless, the external sovereignty of modern democratic nation-states across the developing world in the 1990s was acutely vulnerable. Militarily, most were weak, having operated during the Cold War through their ability to secure the support of one of the superpowers. Financially, most remained bound to the IMF. As a result, those governments that had relied on patronage had few resources to deliver to their clients. Territorially, governments in developing countries risked external intervention, especially if they faced internal rebellion. Since the United States dominated both international financial institutions and the UN security council, these financial and territorial debilities reinforced each other. In the final instance, in the universal language of humanitarianism that the Clinton administration espoused, these democracies confronted an argument against their very existence as sovereign states.[55]

1989–2001: Germany

Of the large European modern democratic nation-states, the British and the Italian had been put to the severest test by the demise of Bretton Woods and the advent of short-term open capital flows. They had survived in part because their governments in the 1980s had eventually chosen to confront the trade unions over inflation. In accommodating rising unemployment, they had reduced the burden of the material expectations that the authority of the state had to bear. In pushing monetary union as a means to increase growth and employment, French governments had appeared more circumspect, but the vehicle on which they had placed their hopes was an ambitious one both in its long-term implications for the language of nationhood and in its practical dependence on the balance of German judgement about the sacrifice it entailed. Since the end of the Cold War transformed the geo-political position of the West German state, it could not but impact both on that judgement and the Bundesbank's monetary policy. In doing so, it opened up a new set of economic difficulties for European governments, in addition to those generated by Washington's new-found power that would put the authority of several states to another severe test.

The demise of communist rule in eastern Europe instantly opened a door to German reunification. Almost immediately after the destruction of the Berlin Wall, Kohl announced a ten-point plan to incorporate East Germany into the Federal Republic and end the formal rights of the four wartime allies over Berlin. With American backing, he persuaded Gorbachev to accept that the unified German state would remain in NATO, that American troops would stay in the old West Germany, and that Soviet troops would leave the former East Germany by 1994. On 3 October 1990, the Parliament established an enlarged Federal Republic of Germany, subjecting 30 million more citizens to the rule of the German state.[56]

In many ways, of course, reunification strengthened that state. Germany no longer confronted a military threat on its eastern border, and it had eliminated that danger without in any way diminishing the American security guarantee from the United States. German governments could now court alliances with the new democracies in eastern Europe and by offering them financial support and a route to EC membership, they would have the opportunity to turn the balance of power in Europe decisively to Germany's advantage. But reunification brought problems too. Whilst the state's new subjects initially accepted its authority readily, and the language of all-German nationhood had survived fifty years of separation, deep differences of interests, experiences and beliefs divided the supposedly singular German people. To contain the consequences of this, the Kohl government had in the short term to find compelling reasons to persuade former east Germans not to leave for the more prosperous part of the country, and in the medium to long term to get former west Germans to make sacrifices so as rapidly to improve the standards of living of their fellow citizens.

In February 1990, Kohl announced that the Deutschmark would become the currency of all Germany five months later and that the old east mark would be converted at a one-for-one rate, seven times above its market value and four times its official exchange rate. Almost all the cost of monetary union, Kohl promised, would be raised by borrowing. The Bundesbank was dismayed, and warned that the introduction of the Deutschmark east of the Elbe would require enormous transfer payments if there were not to be massive social upheaval, as east Germany's state enterprises went bankrupt trying to pay wages way above the productive value of the goods they produced. Kohl prevailed but the Bundesbank was proved right. In the first six months of the monetary union, industrial production in eastern Germany fell by 50 per cent and unemployment soared. Germany was left the most economically polarised state in Europe. By 1993, opinion polls were already showing that more than half of former east Germans wanted a return to reformed communism.[57]

Externally, the restoration of full sovereignty in a world in which the issues generated by the Second World War had formally been laid to rest, appeared to offer the opportunity to recast the German state as a military power. But two days after the Gulf War began, Kohl announced that for constitutional reasons, no German troops would be sent to fight. Stunned by the charge abroad that Germany was free-riding, Kohl called for a new clause in the constitution to provide a legal foundation for German participation in UN security action, and subsequently sent minesweepers to the Gulf. But he did not have domestic support for a radical reversal. In July 1994, the Constitutional Court deemed that German armed force could be used directly to defend the state's territory, to fulfil Atlantic duties under NATO, and in support of UN measures, but no further. Germany could act, it judged, as a military power but only in alliances with others, and by implication any such axis had to include the United States. In no way, the court effectively decreed, could the Bundeswehr be used to further an independent military capability even within the EC.[58]

Within the EC, the opportunities wrought by reunification came at a price. Easily more populous now than any other member-state, and with the opportunity to expand the Community eastwards, Germany was now in a position to assert its leadership independently of its relationship with Paris. Overtly to do so, however, would invite resistance and would require cultivating an entirely different diplomatic language than the European one in which post-war German policy had hitherto been cast. Not wanting to abandon the rhetoric of Europe, Kohl stressed from the outset that German reunification was not an alternative to the Community. Germany, Kohl promised in 1990, was a 'post-national' state that was 'giving up sovereignty in favour of the political unification of Europe'.[59]

Of course, the Kohl government actually had no less a will for its own preferences than any other government and rather more ability than most to realise them. The immediately crucial question was what those preferences now were on monetary union. Whilst Kohl had committed to a three-stage timetable for monetary union before the Berlin Wall came down, reunification and its economic fallout gave him a potential opt-out by which he could claim that circumstances had changed. But he did not hesitate, preferring to extract something from the French government for honouring his commitment to it. In March 1990, he reaffirmed German support for a single currency and suggested that an inter-governmental conference on the issue begin at the end of the year. In return, he persuaded President Mitterrand to support parallel negotiations on institutional reform, which he hoped *inter alia* would lead to far more qualified majority voting (QMV) and some move towards a common foreign and defence policy. When it began, the German government dominated the inter-governmental conference on monetary union. As recompense for abandoning the Deutschmark, it demanded that others accept a European central bank modelled faithfully on the Bundesbank, free from political interference and constitutionally committed to pursuing price stability. The French could have a monetary policy conducted in the name of Europe, but not one that sacrificed one ounce of anti-inflationary rigour. It also insisted that only those states that met tough convergence criteria on inflation, exchange-rate stability, national debt and budget deficits would be able to join monetary union, laying the basis, so it hoped, for a currency that would exclude the poorer Community members, not least Italy. On the institutional structure of the EC and its competencies, the Kohl government was more willing to bargain, settling for only a moderate extension of QMV, and accepting that the Community's foreign and security policy would be determined on an entirely inter-governmental basis.

But in remaining committed to a strategy whereby Germany would exercise its power within the Community in the name of Europe, the Kohl government was taking a domestic gamble. However hard the deal on a single currency that was finally struck at the Maastricht summit in December 1991 seemed to other states, the Bundesbank was unhappy. Contrary to its advice, Kohl had accepted a fixed timetable for beginning monetary union either in 1997 or 1999, had not pressed for any binding fiscal rules on those who participated, and had left it unclear who would decisively decide whether any individual state had met the convergence criteria. In dominating the monetary policy of the ERM states as it did, the Bundesbank had the power to retaliate and did so. Less than two weeks after Maastricht, it raised interest rates, citing accelerating German inflation and the growing budget deficit as the cause of its anxiety, and forcing the other ERM members, which did not have such problems, to act likewise or damage their exchange-rate credibility. Two months later, it published a formal statement attacking the Maastricht treaty and the presumption that a single currency could work without political union. As the Bundesbank's stance became more aggressive, so the tide of German public opinion began to turn against monetary union.

Over the next months, dissent spread beyond monetary union. Some on the left protested that in accepting so little institutional change Kohl had condoned an undemocratic Community. Several of the Länder governments, meanwhile, charged that the EC's structure of decision-making violated their constitutional rights. In persuading the Bundestag and Bundesrat to ratify the Maastricht treaty, the government was compelled to grant Länder a formal role in setting German policy in the Council of Ministers, and promise Parliament a vote on whether other countries had met the convergence criteria. Still some citizens were not satisfied and petitioned the German constitutional court to declare the treaty illegal under German Basic Law. In October 1993, the court ruled that the German Parliament would have the final decision on whether Germany participated in monetary union, flatly contradicting Kohl's previous assertions that Germany had made a binding commitment to give up the Deutschmark.[60]

At the beginning of 1994, with a general election impending later in the year, the Kohl government appeared in a weak position, confronting a Social Democratic party determined to fight on an anti-Maastricht platform. In the event the SPD lacked the economic credibility to exploit effectively their Euro-scepticism, and the CDU-FDP coalition hung on to its majority. But the government still saw monetary union as a liability. To try to reassure the critics, the finance minister, Theo Waigel, proposed in 1995 a set of fiscal rules for the members of the single currency to discipline national budgets. Two years later, the government persuaded the Council of Ministers to accept a stability and growth pact that under the threat of fines prohibited member-states from running budget deficits of more than 3 per cent and committed them to balance their budgets over the medium term.

But if the government had navigated its way by the second half of the decade around a popular backlash against the now renamed European Union (EU), it found the economic impact of reunification and the liberalisation of eastern Europe rather more difficult to contain. Establishing the new German state proved to be far more expensive for the government than it had initially calculated, and by 1994 it was running a budget deficit of 5 per cent. The Bundesbank's monetary policy tipped the economy into recession in 1993, pushing unemployment towards 10 per cent. Whilst West German producers had hitherto been able to export effectively to compensate when domestic demand fell, wage rises well above productivity increases in both halves of the country after 1990 made this difficult, and the current account slipped into deficit. To make matters worse, in the wake of rising wages, low-cost industrial competition to the east, and the social security bill for workers carried by employers, foreign investment in the German economy sharply declined.[61]

After governments had taken economic success for granted for more than forty years, the economy had become a political liability. To try to re-establish Germany as an attractive site for investment and to make it less costly for firms to employ workers, the government promised a major reform of taxes and pensions, but in 1997 the SPD-controlled Bundesrat rejected the proposals. Within the EU, the government's precarious fiscal position during the same year put it in the embarrassing position of missing the Maastricht convergence criteria on budget deficits. Since the CDU's coalition partner, the Free Democrats, refused to countenance any increase in taxes, Waigel was left to revalue Germany's gold reserves and set the profit against expenditure for the fiscal year. This saved Germany's qualification for the euro, but left the government unable to act tough with the states, like Italy, that had failed to meet the debt convergence criterion.

In the general election of October 1998, the CDU-FDP coalition lost to a SPD-Green axis, led by Gerhard Schroeder. Schroeder and his ministers appeared less daunted than their predecessors in overtly using German power abroad. In spring 1999, Schroeder and his Green party foreign minister, Joschka Fischer, committed Germany to the war against Serbia despite fierce Green opposition. By the end of 2002, the government had sent more peacekeepers to various parts of the world than any other state except the United States. Inside the EU, the SPD-Green government was no less assertive, unwilling either to disguise its interests within the Union in the name of Europe or to rely on co-operation with Paris to pursue them. It found its opportunity in the negotiations to write a new treaty to accommodate the expansion of the EU eastwards and southwards that culminated in the Nice summit in December 2000. Determined that votes within the enlarged Union would reflect the size of the new German state, Schroeder pushed in decisions made by QMV for Germany to have more votes than France, Britain, Italy or Spain. Whilst Chirac refused to accept any change to the formal parity between France and Germany, Schroeder persuaded him and the other EU leaders to accept a second set of rules in such votes which ensured that any decision where national vetoes did not apply had to have the backing of states representing 62 per cent of the enlarged Union. Under this provision, Germany would be able to block legisla-tion in alliance with any other two states. Chirac's petulance in trying to deny Germany the influence to which it was entitled under a voting system premised on some principle of the representation of popula-tions, gave Schroeder the chance seriously to threaten Paris over Germany's continuing financial support for the Common Agricultural Policy.

The economy, however, proved just as intractable for the SPD-Green government as it had for the CDU-FDP coalition. After winning the elec-tion, Schroeder appointed the left-wing Oskar Lafontaine as his finance minister. From the outset their relationship was difficult. Schroeder was determined to manage the economy from the centre and press for struc-tural reforms to try to reduce unemployment. Lafontaine was convinced that he could use macro-economic policy to restore growth and jobs and wanted to put more of burden of taxation on business. Reality was on Schroeder's side. With monetary union beginning on 1 January 1999, the government had little monetary or fiscal autonomy. Instead, Lafontaine resorted to rhetorical posturing, demanding that the ECB respond to the needs of the German economy, that the stability and growth pact be reformed, and that the United States accept an interna-tional exchange-rate regime.

In the aftermath of Lafontaine's resignation in March 1999, the gov-ernment won parliamentary support to revise the tax code and liberalise pension schemes, some aspects of employment law and financial markets. Nonetheless, an increasing number of German firms were moving to set up plants abroad where costs were lower, whilst others faced hostile foreign takeovers. The Frankfurt financial markets, which with the launch of monetary union many had hoped would be able to compete more effectively with London, were in the doldrums. By 2001, the German economy was the slowest growing in the European Union, as it had been for the previous seven years, and unemployment was once again rising towards 10 per cent nationally and 20 per cent in the former East Germany.[62]

By the summer of 2001, Schroeder appeared to have reached an impasse in his efforts to resuscitate the economy. Despite the new legislation, German labour markets remained heavily regulated and could only be liberalised by confronting the trade unions and sections of the SPD. Meanwhile, the interest rates set by the ECB were too high for an economy mired in slow growth, and the stability and growth pact ruled out fiscal expansion since the government's budget deficit was already rising towards the 3 per cent limit. To avoid a confrontation with the Commission and the other euro states, the government had to cut public expenditure, but as the German state still needed to transfer the equivalent of around 5 per cent of the former West German's GDP to the five eastern Länder, this could not easily be achieved.

Yet almost a decade of relative economic decline appeared to have produced few serious consequences for democracy and the authority of the German state. For all the huge economic difficulty that had ensued and the significant discrepancies in wages and living standards that persisted, the German modern democratic nation-state had successfully absorbed the former east Germany. In good part, by 2001, Germans in the eastern Länder were voting for the same parties as their western counterparts. The one distinctively regional party that had won representation, the former Communist party, had been neither secessionist nor unwilling to form coalitions with the SPD at the Länder level. However far differences in the material interests, social mores and historical understanding persisted in the different parts of the state – of the kind that had in the past ignited such troublesome political passions – consent to the authority of the enlarged German state and the constitutional rules of democracy were intact.

1989–2001: France

The problems posed by the end of the Cold War to the French modern democratic nation-state stemmed both from the extension of American power and the consequences of German reunification. In the face of the Cold War and the price Washington demanded for a security alliance, de Gaulle had wanted to defend the idea of a sovereign French state as a necessary condition of French nationhood. In his frustration with German monetary power under open capital flows, Mitterrand hoped to rework that conception of nationhood into something perhaps even more ambitious. Now the external world was changing in ways that were unequivocally adverse to both projects.

If American presidents were to press American power under the fiction of an 'international community' and France were to remain detached from the United States militarily, it could only hope to influence the world beyond the EC by overtly opposing American leadership, and its ability to spend more on defence was constrained by the deflationary macro-economic policy required in the ERM. Believing that the price of doing otherwise would be to marginalise France, Mitterrand sent troops to fight in the Gulf War under American command. In December 1995, Mitterrand's successor, Jacques Chirac, announced that France would rejoin NATO. Whilst Chirac appeared to be turning his back on de Gaulle's legacy, he didn't wish to accept American primacy. Inside NATO, he hoped, his government would finally be able to push the EU towards an independent European defence capability, but successive German governments would not commit more resources to the armed forces, and British governments, both Conservative and Labour, remained wed to the Atlantic alliance. Thwarted, Chirac allowed the Clinton administration to bypass the UN over Kosovo, and then saw his protests brushed aside when during the war the NATO operation effectively turned into a unilateral American action. Of de Gaulle's insistence on formal sovereignty over security and external autonomy for the French state little was left. Without the Soviet threat, France's independent nuclear capability meant less, and France was once again a member of a military alliance in which its fate in matters of supposed collective action lay with the decisions of another state. Most of its European allies were not interested in asserting the EU against the United States. Only so long as Washington acted through the UN, where France retained its veto in the security council, could French presidents assert the sanctity of an independent and fully sovereign French state on which a good part of the idea of French nationhood had been fixed since the beginning of the Fifth Republic.[63]

Within the EC, German reunification left French governments with more difficulties. Germany's new-found power meant no French government could hope to retain the freedom of action within the

Community of its predecessors, not least over monetary union. Most urgently, if Kohl were to renege on creating the single currency, France would be left humiliated and trapped in its subordination to the Bundesbank. In 1990 Kohl gave Mitterrand the assurance he immediately needed. But the price was stiff. Germany would still accept a single currency, but only on its own terms: whilst monetary union would ensure a formal parity between France and Germany, practically the ECB would almost certainly produce the same outcomes as the Bundesbank.

Immediately after he returned from the Maastricht summit in December 1991, Mitterrand pretended that the monetary union part of the treaty was something it was not, telling voters in a televised debate that elected officials would establish the economic policy framework in which the ECB would take monetary decisions. After the Danish electorate rejected the treaty in June 1992, Mitterrand called a French referendum to try to prove that there really was enthusiasm for a new European project. During the subsequent campaign, his government was pushed onto the defensive, forced to justify monetary union as it was – the only method left to France to check German monetary power. In the words of the prime minister, Edouard Balladur:

> The rejection of this treaty will not give France more liberty; it will simply allow Germany to act as it desires, without taking heed of its neighbours or its partners, without being constrained by any set of common European rules in its role as a military, economic, financial and monetary power in the centre of the continent.[64]

Mitterrand secured a 'yes' vote by less than 1 per cent, but the clear possibility in the middle of the campaign that he would be defeated put most of the ERM currencies, including the franc, under intense speculative pressure at a time when most European governments were already uncomfortable with the interest rates set by the Bundesbank. Although the franc survived the carnage that took the lira and sterling out of the ERM four days before the French referendum, the credibility of the franc–Deutschmark parity remained in doubt. Since, by 1992, French inflation and its balance of payments were sounder than Germany's, Mitterrand and his prime minister became increasingly frustrated. In March 1993, the Bank of France unilaterally reduced interest rates, forcing them below those set by the Bundesbank for the first time since the ERM began. After another wave of speculation in the summer, and despite massive intervention by the Bundesbank and the Bank of France, the French government, along with all the other remaining ERM members except the Netherlands, had to accept devaluation against the Deutschmark and the suspension of the mechanism.

Confronting the ruins of the decade-old *franc fort,* Balladur declaimed that France couldn't 'allow a situation to continue where so much money can change hands in a very short time and threaten a nation's security'.[65] But the government could do little about it. To allow the franc to continue to fall would cause inflation and put macro-economic decisions even more at the mercy of speculators. It would also put at risk the one exchange-rate alternative to this state of affairs that the French government had, which was monetary union. Accordingly, the Bank of France forced interest rates up until the franc stabilised around its old parity. The result was a recession, which, as expenditure on unemployment benefit rose and tax revenues fell, jeopardised the government's ability to meet the Maastricht convergence criteria.[66]

By 1995 the French budget deficit had risen to around 5 per cent. That May, the centre-right candidate Jacques Chirac beat the socialist nominee, Lionel Jospin, to the presidency. During his first months in office Chirac hesitated, uncertain whether he really wished to invest his political capital in fiscal austerity. As he dithered, the franc weakened. In the autumn, Chirac concluded that there was no substitute for monetary union and instructed his prime minister, Alain Juppé, to do what was necessary to meet the 3 per cent budget-deficit limit. Juppé announced tax increases, an increase in the retirement age, a freeze on public-sector wages and plans to restructure the state's social security, pension and healthcare schemes. Within weeks, striking public-sector workers had paralysed the country, and at the beginning of 1996 Juppé was forced to abandon the majority of his reforms.[67]

For a moment the authority of the French modern democratic nation-state appeared to be in crisis. The government could not persuade large numbers of French subjects to accept its decisions on matters on which it judged the state's whole future within the EU depended. Once more a French president turned to a German chancellor in search of latitude at a moment when none was on offer. Indeed, Kohl now needed Chirac to accept permanent limits on borrowing. In December 1996, Chirac succumbed, accepting in principle what he insisted would be called the Stability and Growth pact, containing a set of binding fiscal rules for the euro. Chirac now had to return to internal reform. When Juppé gradually reannounced most of his reform plans, he met limited resistance. But Chirac over-played his hand and dissolved the National Assembly, hoping to win a direct popular mandate for the action necessary to qualify for the euro. The Gaullists lost the subsequent election to a leftist coalition, and Chirac was forced to appoint Lionel Jospin as his Prime Minister. Jospin and his colleagues had campaigned against fiscal austerity, social security and pension reform, and the terms of the draft

Stability and Growth Pact. Jospin warned that his government would not be bound by the Maastricht treaty. Its priorities, he announced, were creating new jobs, raising the minimum wage, and cutting the working week. At his first meeting of EU finance ministers in May 1995, Dominque Strauss-Kahn, announced that the new government would not sign the Stability and Growth Pact unless Germany made concessions on the independence of the ECB. As Chirac had found in his first months in office, the foreign exchange markets had their own answer to French equivocating, and the franc tumbled. The following month, having offered no serious alternative to monetary union on the terms demanded by Germany but wishful thinking, Jospin signed an unrevised Stability and Growth Pact and committed his government to fiscal tightening, financed by tax increases, to reduce the budget deficit to three per cent.

By the beginning of the twenty first century, the practical and imaginative foundations of the authority and power of the post-war French modern democratic nation-state had in many ways taken a severe battering. Territorially, the end of empire had shrunk the state. Militarily, the French state was a member of a military alliance dominated by the world's only super-power. Economically, French governments did not have authority over monetary policy, they were formally bound by fiscal rules insisted upon by another state, and they provided fewer services to citizens than their predecessors had done immediately after the Second World War. Within the EU, Germany was still financing French farmers, but after the German government had unilaterally tried to increase German votes in the Council of Ministers, no French president could believe that those who led the German state regarded the relationship with Paris as one of equals. Bereft of empire, and subordinated to others within both NATO and the EU, French governments now lacked an international stage from which they could either act as a great power or trumpet the external sovereignty of the French state. The language of nationhood invented by de Gaulle sat very uneasily with this reality, and the rhetoric of Europe to which Mitterrand had turned was making rather less possible than he had imagined.

Yet, at the turn of the century, neither the authority of the French state nor the constitution of the Fifth Republic could be said to be in serious trouble. Governments' inability to reconcile their purposes with American-driven external constraints had destroyed the Fourth Republic. But since then most French citizens had apparently been tamed. Governments could not get some to accept all their decisions without resistance and the authoritarian Fronte Nationale could win a sizeable number of votes in parts of the country, but dissent from policies formed in the face of external constraints was not translating into general opposition either to the state's right to decide authoritatively, or to democracy. Nor was the political class permeated with the kinds of accusations of treachery when others exercised power that had bedevilled the Third and Fourth republics. For all the problems that faced French governments at the end of the twentieth century, the internal authority of the French modern democratic nation-state was not in dispute.

1989–2001: Italy

The authority of the Italian modern democratic nation-state appeared rather stronger in some respects at the end of the 1980s than at any time since its re-creation. The DC-PSI coalition had confronted the trade unions over wage inflation and maintained the lira's membership of the ERM without provoking a rebellion from the industrial working class over unemployment. And in January 1990, it was sufficiently confident to switch the lira to the system's narrow bands and abolish the state's remaining capital controls. But in other respects, the internal authority of the Italian state remained fragile. Much of the south remained poor, suffering a rate of unemployment three times higher than the north. The more prosperous the north became, the more some northern voters resented what appeared to be the permanent redistribution of their taxes to the south. In 1987, a new party intent on protecting northern interests gained representation in parliament. Two years later, its leader, Umberto Bossi, forged a coalition with other northern political organisations, establishing what he termed a 'Northern League' to serve the 'nation of producers' of northern Italy. The League's appeal to disillusioned northern voters in the regional and local elections of 1990 was immediate, leaving the DC with a serious conservative rival. Meanwhile, in the south, the Mafia remained a force. Many in the judiciary increasingly suspected that the DC-PSI patronage networks had begun to extend into those of the Mafia, and wished to break the government's ability to use bribes and kickbacks.

The demise of communism put the Christian Democratic regime under considerable pressure and with it the authority of the state that it had established. When the PCI dissolved in 1991, the DC lost its longest-standing rival, but without the spectre of the left, it and its PSI allies could not so readily justify their command of the state's resources for their blatantly partisan purposes. Internally, the DC began to fragment. In 1991, a junior parliamentary deputy successfully pressed for a referendum on the electoral system. All the major parties opposed reform but, in June 1991, an overwhelming majority of the electorate voted for a change of rules.

By the second half of 1991, the terms of monetary union threatened to wreck the foundations of the state's economic success. Unlike the ERM, they required Italy to move towards German standards of fiscal restraint. To qualify for the single currency, the government had at most seven years to reduce the budget deficit from over 10 per cent of GDP to 3, and its overall debt from more than 100 per cent to 60. Since it was so dependent on delivering patronage, it could not cut public expenditure on the scale required without threatening its power. But if it did not succeed in meeting the convergence criteria, Italy would be pushed out of the inner core of the EU, compromising the whole external support structure that the Union provided to the Italian state.

Over the next year, the Christian Democratic regime disintegrated, and the internal authority of the Italian state was stripped bare. In April 1992, the DC fell to just under 30 per cent of the vote, as large numbers of northern voters abandoned the party for the Northern League, and an anti-Mafia party led by former Christian Democrats won seats in the south. The DC and PSI had just enough seats to retain their parliamentary majority. Whilst the factions of the two parties squabbled over a new president, Milan magistrates served a DC official with notice that he was under investigation for corruption. Over the next three months, the Mafia killed two magistrates and several policemen. Only in June did a new government formally take office, this time under PSI leadership, and the new prime minister, Guilano Amato, gave several of the economic ministries to technocrats. By this time, the lira's membership of the ERM was heading towards crisis as investors began to speculate heavily against the weaker EC currencies after the Danish referendum.

Facing crisis on all fronts, the Amato government tried to salvage what it could without contemplating radical alternatives, sending troops to Sicily to combat the Mafia, negotiating a tripartite pact with employers and trade unions to cut further the *scala mobile*, and introducing an austerity package. But within three months, it had lost the battle to save the lira. After devaluing three days previously, the government was forced to withdraw from the ERM on the same day as Britain, and seemingly abandon any prospect of qualifying for monetary union. On corruption, it was no more successful. In July, magistrates charged Gianni de Michelis, the former PSI foreign minister. By the end of the year, seven of Amato's ministers had resigned, many DC and PSI deputies were under investigation, and the entire regional government of Abruzzo had been arrested for defrauding the EU's regional aid fund. In March 1993, Andreotti, the former prime minister, was arrested as a Mafia suspect.

In less than a year, the magistrates had successfully discredited the entire political class composing the Christian Democratic regime. In desperation, in April 1993, the government issued a decree immediately legalising illicit financing of political parties. When President Oscar Luigi Scalforo refused to sign the act into law, Amato resigned.[68]

The Christian Democratic regime was in ruins. But it was not clear which coalition of parties could assume office in its place. President Scalforo turned to a technocratic solution, asking the governor of the Bank of Italy, Carlo Azeglio Ciampi, to form a new government. Ciampi put together a cabinet of fellow technocrats, Greens and former communists. This government made trying to rescue Italy's bid for monetary union its first priority. In July 1993, it persuaded the trade unions to accept an end to the *scala mobile*, and the major employer organisation to join regular tripartite discussions as part of what it called the 'social pact'. Fiscally, it cut public expenditure and privatised some of the state-holding companies. But despite its immediate success, a technocratic government could not ask the electorate for larger sacrifices to meet the fiscal convergence criteria. Others, meanwhile, saw an opportunity for power via the ballot box. In November 1993, the media and football multi-millionaire, Silvio Berlusconi, formed a new party, Forza Italia, promising a neo-liberal economic policy, social conservatism and an end to the anti-corruption crusade of the magistrates. Forza Italia struck an alliance with the Northern League and the nationalist National Alliance in the south, and in March 1994, this coalition won a general election. Berlusconi's coalition partners were divided over monetary union, and when his proposals for pension reform, without which no Italian government could hope to reduce borrowing, met massive trade-union resistance, he backed down. Eight months after Berlusconi took office, magistrates in Milan charged him with corruption. Bossi withdrew the Northern League's support, and the government fell. Once more Scalforo turned away from the politicians, appointing a second presidential government this time led by Lamberto Dini, another former central banker, supported by a centre-left parliamentary majority. Like Ciampi, Dini's priority was monetary union. Again like Ciampi, Dini found it easier to take radical action to reduce the budget deficit than politicians of the centre-right had done. Where Berlusconi had failed on pension reform, Dini succeeded, appeasing the trade unions with the promise of more co-operation in economic policy through the social pact.

At the beginning of 1996, those upon whom elections conferred power appeared corrupt and incapable of dealing with the problems that threatened the state, leaving the constitutional rules of Italian democracy discredited. But democracy was, as yet, not in crisis. The centre-right had failed spectacularly in its first attempt to re-establish its grip on power through an unstable coalition with a political party determined in one way or another to reconstitute the Italian state territorially. But there was no evidence that the centre-left could not govern, only an unwillingness of the electorate hitherto to bestow power upon it. When a new centre-left alliance, the Olive Tree coalition, built around the social democratic Democrats of the Left (PDS), won the general election held in April 1996, it finally got its chance. Under three different prime ministers, Olive Tree coalition governed for a complete term, and when it was defeated in a general election in May 2001 by Forza Italia, the president was able to ask elected politicians to form a new government.

Like his technocratic predecessors, the first Olive Tree prime minister, Romano Prodi, was convinced that everything depended on monetary union. The outlook remained grim. In five years, successive governments had reduced the deficit by just 2 per cent, leaving Prodi and his ministers at most two years to achieve another 6 percent cut. Fearing that the task was impossible, Prodi met in September 1996 with the Spanish prime minister, José María Anzar, and suggested that the southern EU states jointly press to elongate the timetable for qualification and amend the convergence criteria. Anzar, however, was determined that Spain should not be left behind, and rebuffed Prodi. Soon afterwards, President Chirac professed himself unconvinced that Italy could join the single currency.

Beleaguered abroad, the Prodi government was soon under new internal pressure to find a solution to the problem. In the same month as Prodi had met Anzar, the Northern League leader went to Venice and declared that the north of the country was the independent republic of Padania. Symbolic stunt though it was, Bossi had sensed that the growing crisis of the Olive Tree government over monetary union was his party's chance in a battle for secession. If Italy failed to qualify for monetary union, Bossi hoped that the north could press its claims for participation independently and lay the blame for national failure on the south's financial dependence. Although Bossi's tactics were often muddled, failure on monetary union was now all too likely to risk a crisis of the state's authority. The authority of the Italian modern democratic nation-state appeared to depend on the government being able to hand responsibility for monetary policy to central bankers in Frankfurt.[69]

Nonetheless, the size of the stakes was in one sense the Prodi government's opportunity. The more failure appeared to portend disaster, the easier it was for Prodi to ask the electorate for sacrifices and for his ministers to surrender some controls over the economy. By the end of 1996, the government had introduced a tax 'for Europe', announced that it would divest the state's industrial agency of most of its holdings, and restored the lira to the ERM. The large increase in revenue procured by these actions, and a reduction in interest payments produced by the looser monetary policy that ERM membership allowed, made a huge dent in the budget deficit. In May 1997, the government's external fortune turned when Jospin vowed to fight for Italy's participation in the single currency. By the end of the year, the government was projecting a budget deficit for 1998 under 3 per cent. Although national debt remained around twice that allowed, the German government lacked the credibility to exclude Italy from membership of the euro-zone.[70]

Prodi's government had saved the internal authority of the Italian state from crisis, but had fatally damaged itself in doing so. Under conditions of such severe fiscal austerity, Italy in 1998 was growing more slowly than any of the other euro-bound economies and unemployment had reached 11 per cent. Neither, given the Stability and Growth pact, was there any prospect of a more expansionary fiscal policy in the future. Indeed, since the money from privatisation of state-holding companies came in the form of one-off fiscal injections, the government would need to cut more expenditure to meet its future obligations within the euro-zone. In October 1998, unhappy with another deflationary budget, the Reformed Communist party withdrew its parliamentary support from Prodi. Unable to mobilise a new majority, Prodi handed over power to the leader of the PDS, Massimo D'Alema.

The weakness of the authority and power of the Italian state and the relative feebleness of the idea of Italian nationhood had long made Italian democracy fragile and prone to violence. The Christian Democratic regime tried to contain the consequences of these problems by establishing a dual external support structure through the American alliance and the EC, and commanding the state's resources for patronage. By the early 1990s, American presidents had less to offer and the regime's descent into ever more dubious patronage networks had further damaged the rule of law and destroyed confidence in virtually its entire personnel. Although not always palatable to Berlusconi's governments, the regime's successors had little choice but to rely economically almost exclusively on the EU. In part, the price of that support was less demanding than that extracted by American presidents during the Cold War. No government within the EU would exclude any Italian party from power, even when Berlusconi included former neo-fascists in his coalition. Nonetheless, Italian governments in the 1990s had only been able to maintain the Italian state within the first rank of the EU by dismantling the patronage apparatus through which their predecessors had secured what consent there was to its authority for fifty years.

Some hoped that membership of the euro would also provide an alternative to nationhood by subsuming the idea of an Italian people to a larger idea.[71] But this judgement presumed that the relative failure of nationhood in Italy remained a decisive problem. Strikingly, the territorial crisis that appeared to threaten the Italian modern democratic nation-state halfway through the decade did not come to pass. In qualifying for monetary union, the Olive Tree government took away the Northern League's best argument for secession. In the general election in 2001, the League performed poorly, and by entering a new coalition government with Berlusconi admitted that its independence project had failed. The burden of the adjustment in slashing the state's expenditure had fallen on the south. Yet fiscal austerity produced no real rebellion from those who most directly bore its painful consequences. The one southern-based party in the 1990s, the former semi-fascist National Alliance, moved increasingly closer to the centre ground, cementing its alliance with Forza Italia at the 2001 general election to become the second party in the centre-right coalition above the Northern League. With the Mafia under more control than it had been at any time since Mussolini, the state's internal authority appeared rather robust by the standards of the history of Italian modern democratic nation-states.

1989–2001: Britain

The fallout of the United States' assertion of its power after the end of the Cold War, German reunification and the monetary terms of the Maastricht treaty was perhaps most limited for the the British modern democratic nation-state. The events of 1989 did leave the Conservative government in an awkward position. The Thatcher government had used the end of détente to reassert the idea of Britain as a great power defined by its relationship with Washington. Without any claim to be the guarantor of west European fortitude, Britain was now just another European state, and British troops were not the only European force to participate in the Gulf War. But since the internal authority of the British modern democratic nation-state no longer depended on great-power success, and was not tied to the fate of the Conservative party as that of the Italian state was moored in the Christian Democratic regime, the consequences of the end of the Cold War were confined to party politics.

Economically, the British Conservative government was in difficulty because of sterling's weakness. Earlier in the decade, it had found a political means of living with some of the problems generated by exchange rates under financial liberalisation, not least unemployment. The second and third Thatcher governments, however, pursued a very expansionary policy that eventually severely damaged sterling's credibility in the foreign-exchange markets. In autumn 1990, with the economy sunk in recession and inflation above 10 per cent, Thatcher discarded nearly a decade-long opposition to the ERM and fixed sterling against the Deutschmark. Immediate circumstances were kind. ERM membership injected instant credibility into sterling, and allowed a looser monetary policy. But British interest rates could only fall to just above those set by the Bundesbank, and German rates were on an upward trajectory. To make matters worse, Thatcher had taken sterling into the ERM with a huge current-account deficit at a parity that the Bundesbank judged unsustainable.[72]

When the Bundesbank raised interest rates after the Maastricht summit, Thatcher's successor, John Major, baulked at the prospect of an even tighter monetary policy, having already presided over fourteen months of recession and the collapse of the housing market. But in unilaterally refusing to follow the Bundesbank, he signalled to the foreign-exchange markets that he would not accept the *de facto* rules of the mechanism, and invited speculation against sterling. Benefiting from the ineptness of the Labour party's campaign, the Conservatives held on to office at the general election five months later but with a greatly reduced majority. Flushed with an unlikely victory, Major intensified his rhetoric on the ERM, proclaiming that the anti-inflationary gains were worth the price and that he wanted to make sterling the hardest currency within the Community. But his rhetoric was transparently unreal. Nobody believed that his government could raise interest rates in a recession, and if it could not sustain the sterling parity, it would lose the opportunity to join the euro later in the decade, an option that Major wished to keep open despite having negotiated Britain an opt-out of the final stage of monetary union at Maastricht. After an onslaught of speculation, undeterred by a last-ditch 5 percent hike in interest rates, his government withdrew sterling from the ERM on 16 September 1992.[73]

The crisis destroyed the Major government's macro-economic policy, the time it had bought on monetary union, its internal unity and the loyalty of the parliamentary Conservative party. Over the next ten months, it became locked in siege warfare with its own MPs to ratify the Maastricht treaty. Only after Major turned the matter into a vote of confidence, knowing full well that the Conservatives could not possibly win any general election that ensued, did he secure the bill's passage. Within the EU, Major's government was left bereft of allies and irrelevant to the discussions about monetary union. On the domestic economy, it recovered rather more successfully. It established a new monetary framework that gave a more active role to the Bank of England in decisions on interest rates, and embraced fiscal austerity to reduce the burgeoning budget deficit created by the recession. In doing so, it stabilised sterling and rekindled growth without a return to inflation, something no British government had achieved after a sterling crisis since at least the 1950s. But it reaped no political reward for its achievement. ERM membership had wrecked the government's claim to competence at a moment when the end of the Cold War had eclipsed the Labour party's major weakness.[74]

Issues around sterling had been an almost permanent burden for the British modern democratic nation-state since the introduction of a virtually full franchise in 1918. The response of governments to crises of sterling's value or convertibility had seriously weakened the external power of the British state in Europe and Asia in the 1930s, in the eastern Mediterranean in 1947, and in the Middle East in 1956. Domestically, such crises had proved no less troublesome, triggering in 1926 a direct challenge from the trade unions to the authority of the British state, and ending in 1976 the promise of full employment. Yet the destruction of the Conservatives' competence in government over sterling in 1992 did not even begin to create the conditions for a crisis of the internal authority or constitutional rules of the British modern democratic nation-state. The *quietus* of the Thatcher–Major governments had not been caused by a failure to enforce the state's authority against sections of the electorate who resisted decisions, as had those of the Heath and Callaghan governments. The voters who deserted the Conservatives over the EU appeared to do so not because they were rejecting it, but because the party's self-discipline had crumbled over the issue. Economically, the Conservative government left a legacy from which a Labour prime minister and cabinet who accepted the constraints of the international economy could govern without having to begin in crisis. Territorially, there was little significant political fallout from the economic crisis. Even after the 1992 general election where a substantial majority of Scots were left subject to rule by a party that they had bitterly rejected on four consecutive occasions, no serious threat arose to the authority of the British state over Scotland.

Despite the stability it inherited, the new Labour government, led by Tony Blair, did not intend to leave the British state as it found it, promising early referendums on devolution for Scotland and Wales. Four months later, both electorates voted to establish separate assemblies, the Scottish with some tax-raising powers. In offering autonomy on the terms it did, the government theoretically risked much, allowing Scottish and Welsh members at Westminster to vote on purely English matters whilst protecting legislation for Scotland and Wales from English representatives and retaining a substantial fiscal transfer from London to Edinburgh and Cardiff. But in the subsequent general election in 2001, opposed by an inept Conservative party, the Blair government endured no backlash in England for so arbitrarily compromising the notion of equality in representation that is elemental to the language of representative democracy.

Looking back to 1918, the authority of the British modern democratic nation-state had over eighty years withstood an extraordinary battering. British governments had forfeited an empire and been remorselessly exposed in an American-dominated world, lurched from one exchange-rate-induced disaster to another, and since the 1980s taken what might have seemed inordinate risks over the union that territorially demarcated that authority. As a result, the language of nationhood carried by imperialism and the one defined by full employment and the welfare state had in their essentials passed away, whilst the fiction of a singular British people represented by a sovereign Parliament had been rendered meaningless. But no government since 1919 has confronted a large-scale rebellion against the state's authority of the kind that had hovered in the summer of 1914. The economic test from the 1970s to the early 1990s had been as severe as any since the inter-war years. To succeed, politicians had had to curtail some of the expectations of the modern democratic nation-state that their predecessors had encouraged to reinforce that authority. That a significant number of British citizens were materially disadvantaged and imaginatively disappointed by the outcomes that had ensued is beyond doubt. But, as with the end of empire, the political cost proved strikingly low.

1989–2001: Japan

Like their German counterparts, Japanese governments had not been forced since the end of Bretton Woods to consider the kind of reforms to sustain non-inflationary growth with all their political consequences that the British and Italian governments had undertaken. But they came during the 1990s to face problems on a scale that dwarfed any that a rich state had confronted since the end of the Second World War. Since so much of the Japanese state's authority had been grounded in economic success, unless Japanese politicians could either rework the language of nationhood or politically confront those who would lose from reform, the potential fallout of failure would have seemed enormous.

The Gulf War revealed the consequences for Japan of the United States' post-Cold War power. Japan's material interest in the United States' action and the Bush senior administration's desire to act in the name of the 'international community' exposed the limitations of Japan's military weakness. Although the constitution did not necessarily prohibit Japanese participation in UN collective security action, the government was anxious to avoid divisive domestic disputes about using Japanese power abroad. But whilst the Bush administration accepted the absence of troops, it did expect Japan to make a substantial financial contribution to the war. An LDP spokesperson retorted that Japan could not act as 'a cash-dispensing machine'.[75] In response, the American House of Representatives voted to withdraw 5,000 troops a year from Japan unless Japan agreed to pay all the costs of the American military presence there. Stung, the government offered a large sum and agreed to pay for the yen-based costs and about 70 per cent of the total costs of the American forces in Japan.

Economically, the LDP government entered the post-Cold War world in considerable difficulty. By the end of 1989, the boom let loose by financial liberalisation and accommodation of the dollar was out of control. Worried about an asset and land bubble, the newly appointed governor of the Bank of Japan raised interest rates and effectively terminated the government's support for the weak dollar. As a result, asset prices, property values and the Tokyo stock market crashed spectacularly, radically contracting the capital base of Japanese financial institutions and sending the yen surging upwards against the dollar.[76] In dealing with the collapse, the government was trapped in much the same way as Nakasone had been in allowing the boom. Domestically, it had to keep monetary policy relatively tight to correct the boom, whilst trying to stop asset price deflation going too far. Whilst tighter monetary policy corrected the boom, a continuing fall in prices was likely to push the economy into a huge bad-debt crisis because land and stock-market holdings represented much of the collateral on which financial institutions had made loans. Externally, it risked provoking Washington's wrath if the collapse in domestic demand hurt American exporters. Under threat from the Bush administration, the LDP government was forced in February 1990 to reopen the terms of the security treaty and accept talks on reforming the Japanese economy to facilitate American exports. After Clinton took office, the pressure intensified. Wielding the threat of Super 301, he demanded that the LDP government adopt an expansionary macro-economic policy and liberalise internal markets, foreign investment rules and the banking system. In July 1993, the government succumbed to the pressure, this time accepting institutionalised meetings with Washington to procure more liberalisation.

Electorally, the LDP government had been under pressure since 1989 when it lost its majority in the upper House. Coupled with a series of corruption scandals, the dire state of the economy pushed it towards breaking point. Several reform-minded factions in the party turned against the prime minister, Kichi Miyazawa. After a vote of no confidence, Miyazawa resigned. Some members of the LDP defected to a new party, and the LDP lost the subsequent election. The first ever non-LDP government was composed of all the other parties in the Diet except the communists, and promised electoral reform to try to create a two-party politics that did not revolve around the factional struggles of the LDP. Although it did succeed in creating a new electoral system, it could not get to grips with the economy. Under pressure from Clinton to make swift commitments to specific acts of liberalisation, the coalition government splintered. In spring 1994, the LDP returned to office in coalition with the JSP and a small splinter party of former members. With the socialists abandoning their opposition to the security treaty, the issue that had created more division within the post-war Japanese political class was removed from the domestic political struggle, giving the LDP the chance to reassert that it alone could manage the economy when nothing else mattered. At the first elections under the new electoral system in October 1996, the LDP triumphed and dispensed with the JSP.

Whilst the LDP had survived the fallout of the economic crisis and re-established itself as the unrivalled party of government, it was still, by the middle of the 1990s, searching for a viable domestic and external economic strategy by which it could simultaneously restore growth and appease Washington. The banking reforms demanded by Clinton were drying up the supply of investment capital from financial institutions to corporations. Although successive governments had pursued an expansionary fiscal policy financed by new borrowing to try to resurrect demand at home, the continued appreciation of the yen blunted its impact, creating new incentives for Japanese companies to move production to south-east Asia. Meanwhile, Japanese consumers saved rather than spent their income, fearing that the future would be bleak. In May 1995, the government allowed the yen to depreciate against the dollar, looking to exports as the way back to growth. But when, in 1996, the first signs of a substantial recovery appeared, the government responded too optimistically, raising taxes to try to reduce what had become a large budget deficit, and domestic demand collapsed once more.[77]

The descent into financial crisis of Japan's neighbouring states in the middle of 1997 proved catastrophic because so many Japanese financial institutions had lent heavily around the region. In the first half of 1998, a large Japanese bank crashed, the credit rating agencies downgraded Japanese corporations, and the yen began to plummet. The LDP government was now utterly dependent on the Americans. Fearing a complete financial collapse in Japan, the Federal Reserve Board intervened to support the yen. In return, the American Treasury expected more reform.[78] The LDP government was once again caught. If it could not restore growth, it would embitter Washington more, and compromise the language of shared prosperity that was central to the idea of Japanese nationhood. If it allowed heavily indebted banks and companies to fail and opened the economy to more western capital and goods, it would destroy the fragile construction sector, employing up to 10 per cent of the workforce, and risk its ability to command the state's resources for patronage without having even the semblance of an alternative strategy for rule.[79]

By the end of 1998, the government appeared to have concluded that domestically stability was more important than growth, and that it would not take radical action either to inflate the Japanese economy or to write off bad debts. Externally, it was bolder and tried to assert itself as the decisive state in the crisis consuming east Asia. Most ambitiously, it proposed an Asian Monetary Fund to provide credit to the crisis states with looser conditionality than the IMF. When rebuffed by the Clinton administration, the LDP government announced large assistance packages for the afflicted states, including, to Washington's dismay, Malaysia, which had placed capital controls on short-term flows. In 2000, it struck an agreement with the south-east Asian states, China and South Korea for mutual co-operation in the event of speculative currency attacks through bilateral swap agreements. On trade, it was just as ambitious. Having eschewed any regional trade agreements for fifty years, it also announced in 2000 that it would seek free-trade agreements with ASEAN, and within a year, it had struck its first ever such agreement with Singapore.[80]

But the price of stability at home was deflation. By the beginning of 2001, prices had been falling for nearly three years, despite a huge fiscal stimulus and an interest rate of virtually zero. Whilst the other economies in the region had largely recovered from the troubles of 1997–98, the Japanese economy remained mired in a bad-debt morass and banking crisis. Financial institutions were saddled with around $1 trillion of non-performing loans, and many firms could not service their debts, which were rising in value as prices fell, forcing those that the governments had no political interest in protecting into bankruptcy and pushing unemployment to a post-war high. With the government having issued so many bonds in its failed attempts to reflate the economy, the national debt had risen to 120 per cent of GDP, the highest in the developed world, and the credit-rating agencies had responded by downgrading Japan's debt to the level of far poorer countries.

As deflation and the debt crisis intensified, the LDP's grip on power appeared to wane. In early 2001, the party's power-brokers were seeking to depose the then prime minister, Yoshiro Moro, and find a leader who could pressurise the Bank of Japan to print money without a commitment to banking reform. By March, as the leadership struggle was reaching its climax, the economy appeared to be on the verge of meltdown. The stock market was falling precipitously, leaving the banks, which had huge equity portfolios, unable to dispose of virtually any bad loan. At the beginning of the month, the finance minister pronounced that the public finances were 'quite near a state of total collapse'.[81] Whilst the Bank of Japan responded by making a move towards printing money, its measures were nowhere near on the scale envisaged by the government. Yet while the party bosses succeeded in dispensing with Mori, they were unable to control the succession. Having conceded what they hoped was a minor change to the electoral rules to give party members more of a say in selecting the new leader, they were outmanoeuvred by the reform-minded Junchiro Koizumi, who exploited his grass-roots popularity to beat their anointed candidate from the Hashimito faction. Vowing to pursue 'structural reform without sanctuary',[82] Koizumi declared he would force bankruptcies, cut borrowing and restructure the banks. Within six months, the Hashimito faction had curtailed Koizumi. By the end of 2001, he was left looking for a yen cure for deflation. Theoretically, depreciating the yen made sense. A weaker yen would increase import prices and the resulting inflation would push down real interest rates. But, since imports accounted for only 10 per cent of Japan's GDP, the depreciation had to be large, and the government could not hope to engineer such an adjustment without antagonising Washington, South Korea and China. Caught, the Koizumi government tried to encourage the markets to take the yen down at the turn of the year but nowhere near sufficiently to force inflation.[83]

Thirty years after the end of Bretton Woods, the yen remained a central problem for the Japanese governments. Having tried various strategies for managing it, from switching to higher-value-added exports to shifting production abroad, no government had succeeded in using its relative internal autonomy on the currency to increase its external scope for action. Even holding the largest share of the world's foreign-exchange reserves proved in one respect a liability. Whilst a Japanese government could in principle hurt the United States by selling dollars to press Washington to curtail domestic demand for a reduction in the American current account deficit, it could not afford a radical appreciation of the yen or the loss of export markets across the Pacific. Unable to use the one lever it did have, it remained at Washington's mercy over the domestic economy, as it had always been over security.

The economic price of Nakasone's acquiescence to the Reagan administration over the yen had been the crash of the early 1990s and more than a decade of economic failure. But strikingly, that economic crisis, and the external vulnerability it continually exposed, never appeared seriously to threaten the internal authority of the Japanese state or democratic constitutional rules. Whilst the inter-war experience in Europe might have suggested that a massive fall in asset values where the huge majority of citizens were middle class would cause immense political disorder, the fallout was limited. Certainly the LDP was weaker as the party of government than it had hitherto been, and as Koizumi's earlier woes proved, it could not easily extricate itself from the debt-ridden structure of the economy. Beyond parliament, disillusionment with politicians and corruption appeared to have become rife, and, across the country, regions and cities elected anti-LDP independents as governors and mayors. But nationally the opposition parties failed to exploit the government's difficulties and either mobilise the unemployed and those left out of the LDP's patronage networks, or create a serious issue out of the lines of territorial authority and electoral rules of Japanese democracy. Yoshida, back in 1952, had gambled that economic growth, not full external sovereignty, was the first reason of state for Japanese democracy. His successors had found themselves with neither, but that failure appeared to have far fewer political consequences than Yoshida could possibly have imagined.

1989–2001: India

The problems of modern democratic nation-states in the post-colonial states since the 1980s were of a different kind, revolving largely around questions of external sovereignty. During the second half of the 1980s, the Congress government in India led by Mrs Gandhi's son, Rajiv Gandhi, had fewer problems than most because India had little debt. Nonetheless, the internal authority of the Indian state over parts of the country was far less secure. Most significantly, the Congress government had failed to reduce the burden of violence as the instrument of rule where secessionist pressures were strong. Having agreed an accord on the Punjab in July 1985 on terms that Mrs Gandhi had always rejected, it then reneged on the deal. In the aftermath, violence once again escalated and Pakistan's covert security force, the Inter-Service Intelligence (ISI), infiltrated the region to give support to the rebels. The government relied solely on the security forces and paramilitaries to try to restore order, and in May 1987 imposed presidential rule. In Kashmir, secessionist sentiments among the region's majority-Muslim community were also growing. In March 1986, the government imposed presidential rule on the region. Within a year, ISI forces had crossed the border to train young Muslims to fight. In 1989, the secessionists led armed insurrections in the contested Valley area, prompting the Indian security forces to respond fiercely.[84]

Economically, Gandhi and his ministers had begun ambitiously. In their first budget in 1985, they tried to make a decisive break with import substitution and state planning. But once Congress's electoral prospects declined, as dissent within the party, agrarian agitations and corruption scandals mounted, the political capital Rajiv Gandhi had to invest in the reforms drained away. Unable to break the state's command over much of the Indian economy for fear of the political consequences, the government continued to borrow new money to try to satisfy its supporters within the public sector, to alleviate the pressure on agricultural incomes, and to make interest payments. In doing so, it made the economy increasingly dependent on foreign capital and export earnings to service the debt.

In 1989 an alliance of opposition parties won power, led by V. P. Singh, a former Congress cabinet minister who had parted company from Gandhi in 1987. Singh's government included lower-caste regional parties and was supported in parliament by both the communists and the Bharatiya Janata party (BJP), which argued that the Indian state should act as the agent of Hindu practices. In courting the lower castes and the Hindu nationalists, Singh's government brought into the state two sets of interests and passions that stood in restive relation to each other and were lethal to the imaginative idea of Indian nationhood created by Nehru. Singh's priority was the poor. Having written off the debts of small farmers, adding more to the burgeoning fiscal deficit, he announced, in 1990, that henceforth a quarter of all jobs in the public sector would be set aside for 'backward' classes, with another quarter already set aside for untouchables. Higher-caste Hindus, especially in north India, reacted violently. The BJP seized upon the opportunity to mobilise this group around the idea of religious purity. Its leader, Lal Kishinchand Advani, embarked on a march to the mosque at Ayodha in

Gujurat, leaving a trail of anti-Muslim violence.[85] After police arrested Advani, the BJP withdrew its support in November 1990 and Singh's government collapsed. Not wishing Congress to lead a minority government, Rajiv Gandhi allowed one of Singh's former allies, Chandra Shekhar, to take the premiership with Congress's support.

Whilst Indian governments had hitherto defended the state's external sovereignty effectively, the end of the Cold War and the foreign policies Bush senior and Clinton pursued during the 1990s did create conditions that potentially threatened that sovereignty. The demise of the Soviet Union deprived the Indian government of its most reliable ally. In courting the support of the United States, any Pakistani government would be at a distinct advantage vis-à-vis any Indian government because it could help Washington's relations with the troublesome regimes in Afghanistan and Iran. Since the terms of Indian rule over Kashmir were a defiance of a 1948 UN security council resolution, and Indian security forces had effectively declared war on the secessionists, Washington's embrace of the language of humanitarianism left the Indian state vulnerable to a move by an American president against its sovereignty over the region. During the latter part of the 1980s Pakistan had acquired the military means to launch a pre-emptive attack in Indian territory, so the Indian government also had to accept that Pakistan had the opportunity to alter the strategic balance of power in South Asia. Recognising this reality, the Indian government deployed over half a million troops and security personnel in Kashmir by the middle of the 1990s and closed down substantial lengths of the border with Pakistan.[86]

Most immediately, the demise of the Soviet Union significantly disrupted the preferential trade that India had long enjoyed with Moscow. Iraq's invasion of Kuwait then sent oil prices to levels beyond what exports earnings could withstand and put massive pressure on the foreign-exchange reserves. In response, the credit agencies downgraded India's rating, and the supply of private capital evaporated. With barely sufficient reserves to finance a fortnight of imports, the Shekhar government turned to the IMF, agreeing in January 1991 to a large loan conditional on fiscal retrenchment. But the government was in no position to cut borrowing or curtail the demands from the regions for more spending, and Shekhar soon resigned. During a two-month election campaign, the caretaker government, unable to procure new credit, tottered on the brink of a default.

Congress secured sufficient seats to form a minority government under Narasimha Rao's leadership. Rao's government took office in June 1991 under conditions of immediate crisis and under pressure from the IMF for reforms. With little prospect of reviving private western credit, it was in no position to resist. One month after assuming power, Rao's finance minister, Manmohan Singh, an economist without a political base in Congress, coupled a substantial devaluation with a vow to liberalise the economy. Having used the state to plan industrial production and regulate India's trade for more than 40 years, the new government, Singh promised, would reduce tariffs, eliminate barriers to the import of capital goods, curtail the industrial licensing system, which had placed virtually all decisions on investment in the hands of the state, disinvest government equity in public-sector companies, reform the tax code and invite foreign capital into a range of industries. Over the next year, the financial crisis abated. The current-account deficit fell, and the foreign-exchange reserves more than doubled. During the course of the rest of the decade, inflation fell towards 4 per cent and capital inflows surged. Having taken almost no foreign direct investment before 1991, by 1999 the economy was taking in $2 billion a year. Some parts of the economy grew as quickly as the east Asian economies at their peak. Most spectacularly, the IT sector expanded massively, creating the export base India had never had.

But whilst the Rao government's action on trade, industrial licensing and foreign investment was radical, in other respects it was more cautious and stopped well short of wholeheartedly embracing the post-Bretton-Woods international economy. Unlike its east and south-east Asian counterparts, it did not establish anything like full capital account convertibility. In protecting the rupee from the full brunt of open capital flows, it could continue to control the exchange rate on its own terms, and during the Asian financial crisis capital controls saved the rupee. Neither did the Rao government invest much political capital in trying to reduce the fiscal deficit once the immediate pressure from the IMF had passed. Since it left much of the agricultural sector untouched, it continued to spend large sums of money on food subsidies and farming support. Where the government did push reforms, it established expensive employment-generation schemes to contain the political fallout. As a result, the budget deficit rose back above 7 per cent by 1993–94 and remained above 5 per cent for the rest of the decade.[87]

In several respects, in liberalising parts of the economy, the Congress government strengthened the authority of the federal government. Where the government did cut public expenditure, it was usually in transfers to the states. In other respects, however, the government effectively gave back to the state governments some of the autonomy that previous Congress prime ministers had taken away. Since politicians at the centre were no longer taking decisions about investment, the state governments became crucial agents in determining where private capital was invested, through their discretion over tax, infrastructure and the regulation of land acquisition. In controlling these resources, regional politicians had the means to create their own patronage networks into which they could then entice federal politicians looking for votes. Yet in effectively strengthening the regional governments, the Rao government made it easier to protect the Indian modern democratic nation-state from the grievances of those who were materially hurt by liberalisation and to turn economic expectations away from the state.[88]

The Rao government sustained its reforms for the duration of the parliament without either breaking the Congress party, as Rajiv Gandhi's more moderate efforts had done in the 1980s, or inciting a violent reaction from those citizens who lost out under it. Nonetheless, since some did suffer from liberalisation, the opposition parties were able to exploit the growing inequalities between the states that were beginning to prosper, like Gujurat and Maharashtra, and those, like Bihar, that were not. In passing some *de facto* autonomy to the states, Congress also strengthened its opponents and rather left the field of national politics to those who wanted to battle over religion. In 1996 Congress lost the general election, and the BJP, which had opposed liberalisation, became the largest party in parliament. In less than two weeks, the minority BJP government collapsed, and power passed to a centre-left coalition of regionalist parties, the United Front (UF), which had also campaigned on an anti-liberalisation manifesto. Yet once in power the UF government accepted Congress's economic reforms. Two years later, it too imploded under its internal tensions. After an election in March 1998, the BJP formed another coalition government with fifteen other parties. It also had promised during the election to undo at least some of India's integration into the international economy. But, like the UF, it did not do so when given the chance. Indeed, after it had consolidated its grip on power in a further general election in October 1999, it pushed for further liberalisation, passing a bill allowing foreign equity into more sectors of the economy, introducing patents legislation to meet WTO obligations, and privatising more state-owned firms. By the end of the decade, no major party appeared to have a clear idea of how to govern on any other economic basis.

Beyond the economy, the BJP was much more radical. If participating in the international economy on terms established by more powerful states was unavoidable, this did not mean, the BJP prime minister, Atal Behari Vajpayee, believed, that Indians should accept that they were a subordinate and second-rate state without their own distinctive security interests. In its manifesto in 1998, the BJP had promised to establish Indian sovereignty over the whole of Kashmir and retrieve the territory lost to China in 1962. In office, the BJP government did nothing to advance these claims. But on India's nuclear capability, it was far more determined. In 1995, Rao had flirted with nuclear tests but backed down under pressure from the Clinton administration which was adamant that India should comply with the Nuclear Non-Proliferation (NNPT) and Comprehensive Test Ban (CTBT) treaties. Vajpayee saw no need for such caution, and just ten weeks into office, ordered five underground tests. To defend itself from China, he proclaimed, India had become the sixth nuclear state and should be treated as such by the other powers. The Clinton administration reacted instantly, cutting all aid except humanitarian and all military purchases and licensing. With Japan, India's largest aid donor, following suit, foreign investment waning and the credit-rating agency Moody's downgrading India's credit rating, the government was forced to raise interest rates. By the end of the month, the Pakistani government had tested its own weapons.

The implications of the BJP government's actions were immense. In the party's rhetoric lay a new language of nationhood which stressed that Indian should be a conventional great power. Practically, the BJP government got much of what it wanted. Having effectively ignored India since Mrs Gandhi's battle with Johnson, Washington could now neither dismiss India as a power nor be cavalier in dealing with it in the international financial institutions. The Indian government was also far better able to absorb the economic costs than its counterpart in Islamabad, which was dependent on IMF credit. Realising that neither Russia nor France was prepared to support international sanctions, Clinton soon reversed tack, exempting agricultural production from the embargo within two months and suspending all but military restrictions within six. For its part, the Pakistani government increasingly misjudged the geo-political implications of events, further strengthening India's hand. In February 1999, the two states had agreed to take steps to avoid nuclear war, to settle all disputes between them peacefully and to open new discussions on Kashmir. Three months later, Pakistani-backed guerrillas invaded Indian-held Kashmir. Clinton backed India and told the Pakistani prime minister, Wawaz Sharif, to withdraw. In the aftermath of Sharif's humiliation, the Pakistani military staged a coup and installed General Musharaff in power, making it even easier for Clinton to side with India. In a final stroke of fortune in October 1999, the American Senate voted against ratifying the CTBT, making it more difficult for Clinton to press India to sign. By the beginning of 2000, the American administration was treating India as a *de facto* nuclear power and putting pressure on Musharaff to curtail Pakistani military activities in Kashmir. When in March that year, Clinton then travelled to New Delhi, the first American president to do so for twenty-two years, any pretence that India was a pariah state was over.[89]

In the first decade of economic liberalisation some material benefits had extended to virtually all Indian citizens, and the number of the population living in poverty fell by more than 10 per cent during the 1990s. These benefits were rather unevenly distributed and enriched the middle classes more handsomely than the nearly 70 per cent of Indians who still lived in the countryside and the urban poor. Nonetheless governments of both the major parties had dismantled much of the policy apparatus that most politicians had previously regarded as the best way of improving these citizens' well-being without jeopardising their consent to the state's authority. In retaining capital controls, they had also avoided putting that authority to more radical test, whilst protecting the external sovereignty of the state from the IMF. In then playing the nuclear card, the BJP government had also set some limits to the possible intrusion of the United States and the IMF in the future.

Nonetheless, by the beginning of the twenty-first century, the internal authority of the Indian state was weaker in some regions than at any time since independence. The Indian state's rule in Kashmir rested almost entirely on coercion. Elsewhere those who led the state appeared unwilling to press its claim to a monopoly of legitimate violence. In Gujuarat, local Muslims felt betrayed by a state whose agents were party to violence by Hindus against them, whilst Bihar was descending into something akin to civil war as upper-caste private armies slaughtered untouchables and Maoist militias murdered landlords. Federalism had some political advantages in economic policy, but it could not substitute for impersonal authority at the centre to provide security. Whether Nehru's conception of Indian nationhood could still compensate remained an open question. The BJP government had tried hard to redefine the Indian nation as Hindu and hierarchical. But in order to do so, it had acted domestically as if it led a nineteenth-century European state intent on imposing radical social uniformity on its subjects. Since success at such a task demanded more brutal coercion than governments in democracies can comfortably deploy, it had only undermined the state's authority over the minorities it excluded from membership of the nation without ending the plurality of beliefs and languages among Indian subjects, which Nehru had recognised as the inescapable internal difficulty confronting any Indian state.

1989–2001: Brazil

The external sovereignty of the Brazilian and Indonesian modern democratic nation-states proved far harder to defend, with some far-reaching consequences for their internal authority. The end of the Cold War certainly strengthened the position of Brazil's elected politicians against the army, which in losing the spectre of communism lost a good part of its justification for intervening in domestic politics. The willingness of investors at the beginning of the 1990s to re-engage in the developing world also offered Brazilian governments an appreciable opportunity. If they could succeed in killing inflation, they might, as the largest economy in Latin America, hope to attract a significant share of the capital swilling into the continent, and that money would be free from the kind of political risk that had prevailed during previous decades. Nonetheless, the Brazilian constitution was a serious obstacle to any government wishing to pursue this strategy because it made reducing public expenditure and borrowing, and hence inflation, virtually impossible, and forbade foreign investment in significant sectors of the economy. Any president who wished either to lessen the long-term debt burden or to integrate Brazil into the emerging international economy would have to confront Congress over the constitution.

The presidential election in 1989 was won by Fernando Collor de Mello, who had run as an anti-elite candidate of a newly created party, the National Reconstruction Party (PRN). Whilst much of his rhetoric was directed towards the poor, his primary aim was to liberalise the economy. He wanted to eliminate inflation, deregulate trade, open the economy to foreign capital and develop a trading bloc in South America with Brazil at the centre. His ability to realise this project was from the beginning limited. He did not have even a semblance of a majority in Congress, or serviceable links with most of the state governments. Only in his efforts to set up a trading bloc did he have an effective free hand, reaching an agreement with Argentina at the end of 1990 to create a common market by 1995, which became MERCOSUR, and extending that commitment to include Paraguay and Uruguay six months later.[90] Otherwise he was dependent on the opposition, many of whom had vested political interests in sustaining the resources of patronage provided by the constitution.

In the first instance, Collor tried to govern unilaterally. Taking advantage of the emergency powers the president enjoyed, he issued decrees in March 1990, which froze prices, established a new wage index mechanism, issued a new currency, introduced a capital levy, floated the exchange rate and, most dramatically, seized 80 per cent of the country's monetary and financial assets for the central bank. These decrees had the status of law until voted on by Congress. For the future, he promised privatisation, tariff reduction and tax reform. Three months later, he abolished the department responsible for import substitution. From the outset, Collor struggled to make his programme work. Whilst inflation fell drastically so did production, leaving the economy virtually paralysed. To resurrect the economy, Collor had to make concessions to companies about their assets, which made the whole freeze difficult to sustain, and impaired the ability of the central bank to finance Brazil's debt. Congress, meanwhile, showed little inclination to pass any of the necessary legislation beyond privatisation. To try to secure a base for himself in the legislature, Collor radically increased expenditure on public work programmes in the run-up to the congressional elections in October 1990, which undercut his attempt to reduce the budget deficit, sent inflation back towards 100 per cent and still failed to secure his party seats.

By the end of the year, Collor had turned to the IMF for a new loan, knowing that he could not hope to convince the Fund that he was serious without addressing the fiscal problem. In March, he proposed a set of constitutional changes to increase the federal government's share of revenue and rewrite the tax code. Congress refused to yield and Collor failed in his efforts to mobilise the state governors behind him. Yet even as the prospect of an agreement to end the debt-generating clauses of the constitution slipped away, Collor began to liberalise the capital account thus making the currency vulnerable to the kind of speculative crises that could easily bedevil states with large debts. As the exchange rate depreciated through the second half of the year, inflation, already rising from domestic causes, rocketed, and the cost of interest payments in dollars to foreign creditors escalated. As the premium on a new loan from the IMF rose and Congress put the final nail in his constitutional proposals, Collor demanded an emergency tax increase, which Congress passed on condition that Collar rescheduled the accumulated debts of the states and municipalities. Whilst the IMF granted a new loan, Collor was still in no position to bring about the necessary fiscal reform to stabilise a currency under open financial markets.[91]

During the first half of 1992, Collor's presidency collapsed after his brother levelled corruption charges against him. At the end of the year Congress impeached him and installed his vice-president, Itamar Franco, in office. With Franco having no clear purpose, inflation spiralled towards 2,000 per cent. In May 1993, he appointed Fernando Henrique Cardoso as his finance minister and delegated virtually all power over economic policy to him. Cardoso and his technocratic advisors were convinced that the economy could only return to growth once radical fiscal reform to support a stable currency was in place, and this, they understood, meant dismantling parts of the constitution. Once, they judged, the economy was rid of inflation and open to international trade, it could become the magnet for foreign investment in Latin America, and the Brazilian state could become the dominant regional economic and political power through MERCOSUR.

Within a month of his appointment, Cardoso presented an emergency action plan to Congress, which cut public expenditure at all levels of government and promised to withhold federal loan guarantees from the states until they had made up their arrears in debt payments to the federal government. In December 1993 he presented Congress with a new anti-inflationary programme that pledged to introduce a new currency, the real, seven months later. The real would be fixed in a crawling peg to the dollar and allowed to depreciate by 7 per cent a year, and the exchange regime would be defended by macro-economic policy and reserve intervention. As a demonstration of intent, Cardoso announced an across-the-board tax increase, slashed more spending and established a social emergency fund which for two years recovered around one-fifth of the revenue transferred by the federal government to the states. For the long term, he promised to push constitutional amendments to shift the responsibility for much social expenditure to the states and municipalities, to decrease automatic transfers of federal tax receipts to them, and to end restrictions on foreign investment and privatisation. In April 1994, three months before the real was introduced, Cardoso quit Franco's cabinet to run for the presidency for the Social Democratic party (PSDB), a splinter centrist group from the PMDB. By the time of the election in October, the real plan had produced a very rapid fall in inflation and drawn in foreign capital. Cardoso reaped his reward, easily beating the left-wing candidate to take office in his own right.[92]

Cardoso was forced to confront the risk of external shocks that the real plan entailed almost immediately on taking office. In December 1994 the Mexican currency collapsed. Uncertainty and volatility in the markets soon spread to the other Latin American currencies including the real, forcing the Brazilian central bank to raise interest rates to above 60 per cent. Soon after the crisis had passed, the dollar began its rise against the other major currencies, taking the real with it and leaving the exchange rate uncompetitive against those economies not pegged to the dollar.

To reduce the external pressures on the Brazilian state, Cardoso understood that he had to strengthen its internal authority, and press federal control over economic policy and the exercise of coercion. So long, Cardoso judged, as the constitution gave command over the police and much of the judicial system to the states and municipalities, where local oligarchs and drug traffickers controlled them as private goods, there would be no impersonal rule of law. Without it, those who led the Brazilian state could not expect the poor who were vulnerable to violence to consent to its authority, or perhaps to protect its sovereignty from the human-rights surveillance of the United States. To succeed, Cardoso had to confront the traditional political classes in the states. Yet to secure constitutional amendments, he needed to mobilise a large coalition of parties in Congress, using the very levers of patronage and pork-barrel politics with the state governors that he wished to eliminate. In his dealings with Congress in his first months in office, Cardoso appeared to have constructed a sufficiently large coalition to finesse the problem, and the Congress voted to lift restrictions on foreign companies and permit more privatisation. But, as the year progressed, his alliances waned, and he lost votes on the fiscal relationship between the federal and state governments, the tax code and pension reform. Just to pass ordinary legislation, he became primarily dependent on the conservative Liberal Front party (PFL). Whilst it was supportive of his economic policy, it baulked at other aspects of reform. After the state of Pará's military police shot unarmed peasants in 1996, Cardoso proposed a constitutional amendment to give the federal government some authority over the states' armed forces, but he was unable to mobilise support in the Senate.

Predictably, the more Cardoso failed at home, the more the external financial constraints tightened. By 1997, as Cardoso had achieved virtually nothing to reduce the federal government's spending obligations or increase its revenue, the budget deficit was worsening even before rising interest payments were taken into account. Without any fiscal improvement, high interest rates had to bear the brunt of defending the real parity, which increased the cost of debt servicing and put the budget deficit under more pressure. Exports, meanwhile, stalled in 1996 and 1997 as the dollar continued its rise, and the current account deteriorated. Even whilst foreign direct investment was pouring into Brazil, short-term investors became increasingly nervous, making it impossible for the central bank to loosen monetary policy.

In October 1997, the Asian financial crisis hit Brazil. The central bank responded by doubling interest rates to more than 40 per cent, and Cardoso pushed an emergency fiscal plan on a reluctant Congress. In the first half of 1998, the pressure on the real abated and the central bank was able to reduce interest rates to their pre-crisis level. But the respite was temporary. After the Russian government defaulted on its sovereign debt in August, speculation against the real began again. This time the central bank was desperate not to tighten monetary policy and tried to rely on reserve intervention; but after Moody's downgraded Brazil's debt and the Colombian government devalued its currency, precipitating more capital flight, the central bank succumbed to another massive hike in interest rates, further diminishing the government's ability to service the state's debts. To try to save the real, Cardoso turned to the IMF. He was anxious to avoid striking any agreement prior to the presidential election in the middle of October. But almost immediately after winning an easy victory against the left, he accepted a three-year $41.5 billion loan from the Fund with an additional $14.5 billion in financial guarantees from other states. In striking the agreement, Cardoso committed the government to more fiscal austerity, and to obtaining constitutional amendments on the distribution of tax revenues, the administrative organisation of the state, and pensions. The stakes on reforming the constitution were now higher than ever. Without these measures, the government would lose access to the loan, the real parity would almost certainly collapse, and the Brazilian state and private sector would probably be shut out of commercial capital markets.

But Cardoso's ability to persuade politicians in the states that everything depended on the real surviving remained minimal. In December 1998, Congress passed an amendment on administrative reform but rejected Cardoso's proposal on pensions. Cardoso responded by decreeing more emergency tax rises and spending cuts, which temporarily succeeded in steadying the financial markets. But on 6 January 1999, the governor of Minas Gerais, Itamar Franco, whom Cardoso had abandoned to run as president in 1994, announced a ninety-day moratorium on payments to the federal government. The governor of Rio Grande do Sul followed suit, and capital flew abroad. Cardoso retaliated by blocking federal funds to the states, but he also had to make the federal government responsible for the foreign bond payments of the two states to avoid a total collapse of confidence. As speculation intensified, on 13 January the government moderately widened the terms of the peg. But the selling continued, and two days later the government admitted defeat, devaluing the currency by 8 per cent before floating it.

Cardoso was as caught as ever. The IMF would not release any more credit without a new letter of intent. Franco, meanwhile, appeared determined to lead an assault from the states on Cardoso's efforts to claw revenue back to the federal government. Just after the devaluation, Franco convened a meeting of six other governors to announce that their states were broke and to demand action by the federal government.

Cardoso, Franco charged, had betrayed Brazil's sovereignty: 'so now Stanley Fisher is the finance minister, and Mr Soros runs the central bank. Maybe we should be learning English'.[93] To break the rebellion, Cardoso had to concede compensation to the states for revenues lost under a piece of legislation three years earlier, and even then Minas Gerais and Rio Grande do Sul failed to resume payments. These concessions did nothing to appease the IMF and capital continued to drain abroad. By March, the real had lost over 50 per cent of its value since the beginning of the year, pushing the government to accept tough new conditions from the IMF which included an even tighter fiscal stance.

Eventually the continuing depreciation of the real did strengthen Cardoso's hand. In April he submitted to Congress two bills: a Fiscal Responsibility Law (FRL) which forbade central bank financing of government expenditure at any level and set out rules over budgets at all levels of government, and a Fiscal Criminal Law which made breaking the FRL a crime punishable by a custodial sentence. Within a year, Congress had passed the bills. Once the real steadied, Cardoso finally took on Franco, warning him that the federal government would no longer cover Minas Gerais' bond payments, and won. But pensions proved far more difficult because Congress was reluctant to pass constitutional amendments, and in September 1999 the Supreme Court ruled that two existing pension laws were unconstitutional. Since pension liabilities were a large part of the budget deficit, this failure left the real at permanent risk of renewed crisis. Even after the parity against the dollar had been abandoned, the central bank could not easily lower interest rates. The Cardoso government was still in the same vicious trap in which it had begun. It could not afford to let the exchange rate fall significantly because the inflationary consequences would deter investors and the cost of servicing the dollar-denominated debt would rise, but keeping the exchange rate stable required high interest rates, which increased the cost of financing domestic debt and so sapped confidence in the real. With the currency under pressure again in the summer of 2001, the government turned back to the IMF, agreeing a new loan in exchange for another round of fiscal tightening and new promises of constitutional bills on pensions and tax.[94]

The fallout of the crisis of 1999 left Cardoso's hopes for projecting Brazilian power abroad in ruins. Cardoso had sought to protect MERCOSUR from Clinton's FTAA ambitions, believing these would undermine Brazil's ability to lead South America and its industrial base. Now the volatility of currencies in the region undermined trade within the bloc. Most consequentially, the devaluation of the real hurt producers in Argentina, where the government remained wed to a fixed parity with the dollar. When several large international firms moved to Brazil to take advantage of the cheaper currency, the Argentine government blamed Brazil for worsening its own catastrophic economic problems. As the relationship between Brazil and Argentina degenerated, the smaller Latin American states peeled away. In November 2000, Chile had announced that it would seek full membership of MERCOSUR only to reverse course and begin bilateral talks with the new Bush administration about a bilateral free trade agreement, which prompted Uruguay to hint that it wished to do likewise. As any hope the Cardoso government had of using MERCOSUR to rebuff the expansion of American trade into South America disappeared, in March 2001 Argentina unilaterally increased tariffs on imports in clear violation of the rules of the organisation. Since it had always resisted attempts by others to create a dispute-settlement body for MERCOSUR, the Cardoso government could not resist, and reluctantly agreed to a suspension of the customs union.[95]

As a state-builder, Cardoso's legacy was limited. Although he eventually asserted authority for the federal government over fiscal policy, by the time he did so the public debt had almost doubled as a percentage of GDP, leaving the federal state at the mercy of the financial markets and the IMF as much at any time since Collor had liberalised the capital account. Since Cardoso had failed to reform pensions, the debt was likely to continue to rise. So long as servicing debt absorbed such enormous resources, the prospects for high growth or expensive anti-poverty programmes were slim. Perhaps even more significantly, Cardoso's failure to enhance the federal government's control over coercion had left a space in which violence had escalated dramatically. Since those supposedly responsible for maintaining law and order could be bought, frequently hiring out their services to death-squads, they deprived many Brazilian citizens, especially the poorest, of any semblance of protection from the state.[96] Since no government could take radical action to address the massive income inequality between Brazilians without frightening the financial markets and risking economic collapse, this failure appeared an ominous liability for the Brazilian modern democratic nation-state. Events were showing that failure to procure benefits for all classes of the electorate under conditions of financial liberalisation did not necessarily precipitate a crisis, even when external forces could be blamed for some part of the difficulty, and, although lower than elsewhere in Latin America, tacit support for Brazilian representative democracy remained moderately high.[97] But when that failure was combined with an inability to provide security to the same citizens, its consequences were potentially far-reaching because it left those subjects with no good reason to accept a state's rule. Cardoso's government had probably been more serious about state-building than any in post-imperial Brazilian history. But it had had to act in formidable circumstances. To manage the economy, it had been forced to confront the states and the economic interests that dominated them at just the moment that it needed to reduce the states' power to coerce. Each difficulty that the scarcity of its political capital created simultaneously undermined the state's authority further, and made that authority's repair more urgent. Economically, Brazil could only succeed in the external world by possessing an effective modern state, and the IMF implicitly demanded one through its prescriptions on taxation. Yet in the immediate imperatives created by the currency markets and the relative indifference of the IMF to domestic calculations, the external world had made the project of state-building in Brazil even more difficult than it already was.

1999–2001: Indonesia

In May 1998, the fallout of the Asian financial crisis precipitated the end of General Suharto's thirty-year military rule in Indonesia.[98] Amidst riots in Jakata, Suharto's vice-president, Habibie, assumed office. One month later, he promised competitive elections. In November 1998, after the army had shot demonstrators and more rioting, Habibie announced that there would be an election for the People's Representative Assembly (DPR) in June 1999 under the 1945 constitution retained by Suharto, and that the People's Consultative Assembly (MPR), the formally sovereign authority constituted by the DPR and representatives from the provincial legislatures, the army and various social organisations, would meet to elect a president and vice-president four months later. Subsequently Habibie released political prisoners and lifted restrictions on freedom of speech and the organisation of non-communist parties. When the election came, the opposition party, the Indonesian Democratic party (PDI) led by Sukarno's daughter, Megawati Sukarnoputri, won 34 per cent of the vote and the largest number of seats in the parliament without the votes to guarantee Megawati the presidency.

Circumstances for re-establishing a democracy in Indonesia in the summer of 1999 were perhaps even less propitious than they had been for creating one fifty years earlier. Of all the Asian economies hit by the crisis of 1997–98, the Indonesian economy had suffered the most. During the last months of Suharto's regime, the rupiah had been worth less than 20 per cent of its value a year earlier. The enforced devaluation sent inflation towards 100 per cent, decimated real incomes and made food imports prohibitively expensive for large numbers of Indonesians. In late 1997, the banking system became virtually insolvent, leaving most productive assets belonging to conglomerates that could not service their debts. In January 1998, Suharto's government had established the Indonesian Bank Restructuring Agency (IBRA) to take effective control of the banking sector. To finance this, first Suharto and then Habibie issued a huge amount of domestic debt. After he took power, Habibie launched a subsidised rice scheme, which required more credit. As a result, the budget deficit and accumulated national debt rose dramatically, undermining the confidence of potential foreign investors, putting huge pressure on balance of payments and inviting new speculative pressure. Whilst other afflicted economies in the region began to recover during the first half of 1999, the Indonesian economy did not. Both international financial institutions had extended substantial credit and more would be forthcoming, but the terms on which they lent were fierce. The IMF had demanded that the government restructure both the banking and corporate sectors and end corruption as well as introduce deflationary macro-economic measures, and in good part, Suharto had impaled himself on the contradictions between the IMF's demands and his means of rule.

In retaining the 1945 constitution, Habibie left the government that took office in October 1999 dependent on the army. Although he had cut the army's representation by half in the MPR, since no party had won a clear majority in the DPR, or, given the number of parties that had mobilised for the election, was likely to in the future, the army would have a significant say in determining who became president. Whilst the army had not acted to save Suharto, parts of it remained sceptical about democracy, fearing that it would produce Islamic majority rule, instability and the territorial disintegration of the Indonesian state. As the new president would have to try to retain the support of the army, the generals could hope to exercise a *de facto* veto over developments they deemed adverse.

Perhaps most significantly, those who directly controlled the coercive power of the Indonesian state had little inclination to use it impersonally, and where they were accustomed to using it most arbitrarily, the internal authority of the state was weak. Suharto had worked the legal system and the state's administrative apparatus purely through patronage and corruption, and Habibie had done little to change this. Rather than implementing the rule of law, most judges accepted bribes in exchange for favourable verdicts. Since Suharto's fall, armed gangs of different religious and ethnic groups in Ambon, West Kalimantan and the Molucca Islands had butchered each other without the army intervening. Elsewhere, the army was all too keen to kill. Suharto had courted a secular idea of Indonesian nationhood around a conception of an organic unity between state and society that denied the legitimacy of conflict. Successful economic development had bolstered that idea in many parts of the country, but it had also created severe inequality between the provinces to the benefit of Java. Where the claims of nationhood had failed most acutely – in Irian Jaya, Aceh and East Timor, the former Portugese colony that Indonesia had annexed in 1975 – Suharto had ruled through the army, which had frequently terrorised the local population. Freed from Suharto's regime, the majority of subjects in these of these provinces now wanted independence.

In January 1999, Habibie had promised to deal with the most difficult of the territorial issues, East Timor, by a UN-administered referendum in which the islanders would be offered autonomy on the understanding that if they rejected it, independence would ensue. Fearing that it set a dangerous precedent, neither the army nor Megawati supported the referendum. In the weeks preceding the election in August 1999, anti-independence militias assisted by the army attacked secessionist supporters. After 78 per cent of East Timorese voted against continuing membership of Indonesia, the violence escalated until by the middle of September, 7,000 Timorese were dead and 300,000 had been driven from the territory. Under intense pressure from the army, Habibie declared martial law. In response to the bloodshed, the Clinton administration terminated all military contacts and aid, and threatened economic sanctions if the government did not control the army and the paramilitaries itself or allow the UN to do so. Two weeks after the referendum, Habibie reluctantly agreed to accept a UN peacekeeping force and the army withdrew from the island. Even then, the events in East Timor would cast a long shadow over the new Indonesian modern democratic nation-state. The security council authorised an investigation of the army's activities in East Timor to decide whether to mount an international human-rights tribunal to prosecute the culprits. This put the external sovereignty of the state under acute strain when it was already severely stretched by the demands of the international financial institutions, and left the new government open to the charge that Indonesia had been betrayed to hostile foreign powers. If the government wished to thwart this line of attack, it would have to investigate the army itself and risk the internal consequences.

In October 1999, after protracted negotiations, the MPR elected as president Abdurrahman Wahid, the leader of the Nation's Revival party (PKB), with Megawati as vice-president. Wahid was less immediately beholden to the army than either Megawati or Habibie would have been, and whilst he made General Wiranti, the commander of the armed forces in East Timor, his minister for political and security affairs, he insisted that Wiranti and all other military officers in the government give up their military posts while they served. But in other respects he was politically weak. He was in ill health, his party was only the fourth largest in the DPR, and he owed his success to Megawati's tactical incompetence. To appease the coalition to which he was beholden, he had to offer cabinet positions to a wide array of parties. Meanwhile those who had lost out in the power struggle, not least the PDI, were bitter. Megawati did not appear to accept Wahid's presidency, and his election prompted some of her supporters in Jakarta and Bali to riot.

The Wahid government immediately allowed East Timor to secede. This left unanswered, however, just how Irian Jaya and Aceh would be ruled. Habibie had passed legislation that would over the coming years devolve more fiscal autonomy to local governments, but this approach bypassed the provinces where the brunt of the dissatisfaction lay. Wahid appeared to flirt with federalism, but the army was overwhelmingly opposed. Without a clear strategy for pacifying the rebelling regions, Wahid contrived to infuriate almost everybody. The most immediate threat came in Aceh. Aceh was a resource-rich province that produced most of the country's gas and oil but which because of the government's redistributive fiscal policies was one of the poorest provinces. One month after Wahid took office, the rebels in Aceh organised large demonstrations calling for independence. Whilst travelling abroad, Wahid twice promised that Aceh could have a referendum, only on his return to declare that Aceh remained an integral part of Indonesia and that the army would act if Aceh decided to secede.

Retaining direct rule from the centre increased Wahid's dependency on the army. Domestically, this reduced his ability to exercise power. Externally, it angered the Clinton administration even though that administration supported Wahid's new tough stance over Aceh, fearing Islamic fundamentalism and the fallout for the state's rule elsewhere in the archipelago. In February 2000, after both the UN and Indonesian investigations into East Timor called for General Wiranto to be tried, Wahid had to choose between the competing domestic and external imperatives confronting him. For two weeks Wahid dithered and issued contradictory statements, before sacking Wiranto and restructuring the top of the armed forces. Clinton rewarded him by resuming some military contact. But so long as the violence continued at home, the army had political capital. In March 2000 it stepped up its activities in Aceh. Over the following months, Wahid tried to persuade the rebels to accept some measures of autonomy and secured a temporary ceasefire. But he could not offer enough to quell the secessionist demands, and in April 2001 he gave up and issued a decree giving the army a free hand.[99]

The economic problems that Wahid inherited were similarly enormous and his room for manoeuvre was again externally restricted. The ongoing violence in Aceh and the Moluccas, where the government declared a state of emergency in June 2000, only made matters worse because it deterred new foreign investment and left the rupiah exposed to more capital flight.[100] In February 2000, the IMF approved a three-year $5 billion loan with a set of new conditions about the IBRA's operations, reform of the judiciary, the central bank's independence, fiscal control, energy legislation and anti-corruption measures. But the government was becoming increasingly reluctant to act as the IMF prescribed. It could not simultaneously centralise fiscal authority as the IMF was demanding and use increased financial autonomy to try to appease the dissenting provinces. Whilst the IMF wished the IBRA to sell its accumulated assets, which amounted to around 20 per cent of GDP, Wahid saw them as means to keep his increasingly fragile coalition together. Dissatisfied, the IMF suspended lending, only resuming it in August 2000 after the government signed a new letter of intent.

To make matters worse, during the second half of 2000, a host of foreign and joint investors were attacked. When, in September, East Timorese militias killed three UN workers, the Clinton administration terminated all military contacts again and warned the government that if it did not disarm the militias, it would not be able to reschedule its debt. The IMF once more delayed scheduled credit, and the UN security council threatened a full-scale human-rights court for East Timor. To stave off the pressure, the government reluctantly established an internal tribunal, knowing that to defend the state's external sovereignty, it would have to punish at least some in the army. The IMF, however, was less easily satisfied, and in December 2000 it officially suspended credit, leaving the Wahid government struggling to reschedule its debt with the Paris club and lacking any substantial means of external financial support.[101]

The threat of total crisis that had hung over the Indonesian state since democracy was restored, moved increasingly closer during the first half of 2001. Violence spread across the islands, and Wahid's grip on the army and the police was waning. His opponents, led by Megawati and encouraged by the army, began manoeuvring to impeach him. The prospect that Wahid would fall triggered heavy speculation against the rupiah, requiring higher interest rates just at a moment when growth was returning. Wahid, however, had little intention of going peacefully and exhorted his supporters in west Java to riot and march on the parliament. With the final vote to impeach him beckoning, he tried to declare a state of emergency and suspend the DPR but he could command no power to do so. After desperately calling for a jihad against his enemies, he left office in July, and the MPR elected Megawati president.

Megawati had some means at her disposal to strengthen democracy. Within a year, the MPR had voted to revise the constitution, eliminating the representation of the army, establishing direct presidential elections and creating a Regional Representative Council which, sitting with the DPR, would become the new MPR.[102] Yet in crucial respects the state's internal authority and external sovereignty remained weak. Economically, Megawati appeared, in the summer of 2001, to have an opportunity finally to reconstruct the Indonesian economy. The rupiah rallied against the dollar in the first three weeks of her presidency, and, after her government wrote another letter of intent, the IMF released the credit it had been withholding. But the honeymoon was short-lived. By the end of the year, the rupiah had depreciated to its value at the end of Wahid's time in office, and new investment had fallen to around one-tenth of levels the previous year. Since Megawati was no more inclined to keep to the IMF's terms than Wahid had been, another confrontation with the international financial institutions and Indonesia's official creditors loomed. Without the revenue that the asset sales would have brought, and with public debt continuing to rise, the Megawati government had to make more cuts in the development budget. Territorially, the state's rule over Aceh and Irian Jaya had become almost entirely dependent on brutal coercion. But in banking so much on the army there, Megawati's government left the state even more vulnerable to the power of its creditors and intrusion from the UN, and made it even less likely that nationhood could carry much of the burden of obtaining consent to the internal authority of the Indonesian modern democratic nation-state.

Conclusions

By the end of the twentieth century, there were more democracies in the world than at any time in history. In western Europe and Japan, nowhere had either democracy or the authority of the state collapsed through the interaction of domestic politics and the international economy. In the 1970s the authority of the British and Italian modern democratic nation-states had faced some significant threats as governments struggled against inflation. In the 1990s, the authority of the French and Italian states and the idea of Italian nationhood were put to the test by the demands of qualifying for monetary union. But perhaps only in the case of the Italian modern democratic nation-state during the 1990s can we clearly see through the contingencies how a full-scale crisis was a serious possibility.

In post-colonial states, democracy had become the norm in Latin American, eastern Europe, and parts of Asia and Africa. Compared to the efforts to introduce democracy in the states given their independence in the three decades after the Second World War, these moves to democracy were initially, anyway, relatively successful. By the end of the 1990s, however, some of the difficulties of sustaining democracy in these states were beginning to resurface, as those with power protected themselves by increasingly authoritarian means from genuine electoral competition, or were forced out of office by violence.[103] In contrast to some other Latin American states, democratic constitutional rules have proved relatively robust in Brazil. When in 2002, Cardoso's party lost the presidential election to the left-wing Workers' party candidate, Inacio Lula da Silva, a constitutional transfer of power took place. More surprisingly, given the severity of its territorial and sovereignty difficulties, the legacy of the 1997–98 financial crisis, the Indonesian democratic state survived. Against a backdrop of violence on various islands, Indonesia held three sets of elections in 2004. When Suharto's former party, Golkar, triumphed in the parliamentary elections and a former general, Susilo Bambang Yudhoyono, later won the presidency, Megawati and her supporters in the Indonesian Democratic party accepted the outcome.

Yet the post-war Bretton Woods international economy and the nature of American power after the end of the Cold War left long-standing and new democracies with a myriad of difficulties that had to be contained or conquered. As set out at the beginning of this chapter, after the demise of pegged exchange rates and the American move to liberalise all capital flows, European and Japanese governments had three possible strategies to maintain the state's internal authority and a democratic form of government, none of which was mutually exclusive. First, they could have tried to reinvent their economic success by different means. Second, they could have used the power of the state to defeat those who lost from the new international economy. Third, they could have offered non-economic reasons for subjects to accept the state's authority, especially via foreign policy.

This last option proved the most difficult. The second Cold War reignited issues of sovereignty in security in several western European democracies, but direct resistance in West Germany and Britain could not stop governments accepting the arrival of American missiles, and the parties that opposed the deployments spent the rest of the Cold War out of power. The Thatcher government extracted considerable electoral capital from appearing nationalist on foreign policy and defence issues, but Britain's transparent nuclear dependence on the United States made any radical assertion of independence in de Gaulle's style impossible. Outside NATO and given the place of external sovereignty in the language of French nationhood during the Fifth Republic, French governments had the greatest opportunity to exploit foreign policy. But by the end of the twentieth century, even the French modern democratic nation-state was constructed on practical foundations that included a dependent security alliance with the United States. This did not mean that French governments were ever likely to prove simply subservient to Washington. But, as the fallout within NATO over Iraq in 2003 demonstrated, where President Chirac waited for Schroeder to declare himself before moving to outright opposition to war, French foreign policy had become tightly tied to German. In 2003, Germany, Belgium and France did try to stop NATO responding to Turkey's request for help in the event of war with Iraq, in clear violation of the alliance's founding purpose, and then convened a summit to discuss establishing independent military planning facilities and separate operational headquarters for the EU. But the prospects for such a military capability for the EU look bleak. Two years earlier, the EU states had resolved to have a capacity to deploy 60,000 men with air and sea cover and keep them deployed for at least a year by 2003, but they failed to achieve it, not least because the German government spent the intervening years cutting military expenditure. French hopes of re-establishing security independence from the United States now depend on Germany assuming a new financial burden and entering a kind of politics which has never been part of pre-war or post-war German democracy in which the state takes a significant proportion of taxes for military purposes and has the constitutional authority to act as a sovereign military power.

During the 1970s and 1980s, the West German and Japanese governments were most successful at reinventing a strategy for economic success despite bearing most of the exchange-rate burden of the floating dollar. Within west Europe, West Germany was the most effective at using corporatist practices to control wage inflation. And, in the long term most consequentially, it was the one state that began these years with an independent central bank. As West Germany became the dominant European monetary power, the conditions in which all other west European governments had to take economic decisions were transformed, and most spent the 1980s trying to imitate West German macro-economic policy. By the end of the 1990s, most of the EU states had through monetary union taken monetary policy out of the dynamics of competitive electoral politics and placed apparently serious limits on their fiscal autonomy. Whilst these moves made day-to-day exchange-rate management rather easier and eliminated intra-European currency crises, they represented an extraordinary shift in the place given to macro-economic policy in the post-war conception of nationhood, as well as the scope of elected politicians' authority in these representative democracies.

Having reshaped their economic strategies during the 1970s and early 1980s, Germany and Japan hit difficulties from the early 1990s, which at least in part had their origin in the changing political dynamics of open capital flows from the late 1980s onwards. In Germany's case, the new competition for investment capital and the lure of the cheaper eastern European economies put serious pressure on its labour, welfare and taxation policies at a time when reunification had already extracted its toll on price stability and employment. In the case of Japan, the way that governments in the early 1980s had been able to diffuse the pressure from the United States over the yen ran its course after the May 1984 commitment to full financial liberalisation and the Plaza accord. Once Japanese banks were free from strict LDP control and Japanese monetary policy was set to accommodate the weakness of the dollar, the whole structure of the Japanese economy and the patronage networks it sustained was vulnerable to collapse. Having first found a rather painless way of living with the post-Bretton Woods international economy, German and Japanese governments came to have considerable difficulties in it, albeit at rather less political cost to democracy than might have been imagined during their years of economic success.

During the 1980s the Thatcher governments in Britain and the DC-PSI coalition in Italy adjusted most directly through confrontation after their predecessors had struggled with wage inflation and weak currencies. In both cases the trade unions bore the brunt of the attack and high unemployment and the weakness of opposition parties provided the political cushion. Once the adjustment was secured, however, governments in the two states adopted rather different approaches to the macro-economic dilemmas created by financial liberalisation. Whilst Italian governments embraced ERM membership from the start, and went to immense efforts to qualify for monetary union, successive British governments tried to retain a high degree of exchange-rate and monetary autonomy. Although this autonomy proved unsustainable in 1990 and its consequences precipitated Thatcher into the ERM disaster, since 1993 British governments have demonstrated that it is possible both to produce non-inflationary growth in the post-Bretton Woods international economy without an exchange-rate anchor and to allow elected politicians to choose the level of inflation without wrecking the credibility of a currency. Britain's relative success raised some questions about the political sustainability of the EU's monetary union, the argument for which depends on demanding conditions: no monetary alternatives under conditions of open capital flows; agreement on the untrustworthiness of democratic politicians to make any kinds of decisions about the priority attached to inflation; and some kind of belief in an EU common good in economic policy. As discussed in the next chapter, all of these conditions would appear to pose some difficulties for the EU's modern democratic nation-states.

The issue for the post-colonial developing countries in the post-Bretton Woods international economy was not reinventing a strategy for economic success, but finding a way to achieve it in political circumstances where state-building and ideas of nationhood, and consequently democracy, had frequently failed. During the 1970s the spread of international capital markets provided an immediate opportunity for growth via investment. The price of the end of Bretton Woods, however, was accepting the primacy of American monetary policy and the vagaries of the dollar. Eventually high American interest rates and the rising dollar produced the debt crisis, leaving affected developing countries in desperate need of immediate credit, which could now only be acquired from the IMF. This left these states with radically reduced policy options across every aspect of economic policy.

For states like Brazil, the domestic and international politics of servicing debt became in the 1980s, and remained thereafter, crucial to the possibility of growth and the chances of successfully re-establishing democracy. Most significantly in Brazil's case, the need for fiscal discipline to retain access to credit from the IMF put clear limits on the kinds of constitutional rules that were prudent, turning the territorial politics of the constitution into an issue that could wreak financial havoc and leave Brazilian governments even more exposed to the demands of the IMF. In Indonesia's case the problems went even deeper. Its vexed relationship with the IMF gave Washington some direct leverage over a range of issues crucial to the viability of the Indonesian modern democratic state. It constrained economic choices, the available options to cope with the archipelago's violent territorial politics, the relationship between elected politicians and the army, and the operation of the judiciary. Perhaps unsurprisingly, in 2002 Megawati's government announced that it would not be renewing its IMF loan once it was complete at the end of the year. The economic price of independence, however, appeared high. Whilst the economy had showed signs of recovery through 2002 and 2003, foreign firms were still deterred by the legal uncertainty created by the corruption of the judiciary. Once, at the beginning of 2004, the IMF departed, many existing investors turned away and repatriated their capital.

The depth of the constraints that the debt crisis created for many developing-country governments is well illustrated by the contrasting experience of India. Having largely eschewed borrowing during the first decade of financial liberalisation, Congress governments were able to retain a relatively closed economy longer than virtually any non-communist developing country. This assertion of autonomy came at price in fiscal restraint and when such prudence broke down proved unsustainable. But when Congress under Rao did opt to open up the Indian economy after the 1991 financial crisis, the fact that its debt problems were less pervasive than Brazilian governments' allowed it to shut out the IMF relatively quickly. Indian governments could therefore engage with the international economy much more on their own terms, exploiting cheap labour to attract low-level manufacturing production and service-sector outsourcing without pursuing full capital account liberalisation. In doing so, they demonstrated that foreign investment and liberalised trade can be an effective high-growth strategy for developing countries in democracies, as it had already proved to be for the authoritarian east Asian states and came to be for China.

Nevertheless India still shares serious economic problems with other post-colonial countries, some of which arise out of the politics of the international economy. The scale of rural poverty leaves parts of India with some of the lowest human development indicators in the world, and in 2004, a coalition of left-wing, regional and caste-based parties, led by Congress, mobilised large numbers of rural voters to depose the BJP from office. There are domestic reasons for low agricultural productivity in India, but given the persistence of fierce protectionist practices by the US, EU and Japan, Indian governments cannot use exports as an engine of growth in the way that they could with the manufacturing and service sectors. Since 2003, the Indian and Brazilian governments have led a coalition of developing countries to try to stop further multilateral trade agreements through the WTO without major concessions from the rich states on agriculture, but this cannot in itself change the terms of agricultural trade.[104]

For all its material benefits, the international trading order that has developed since the end of Bretton Woods retains the capacity to generate significant political problems for the states of post-colonial developing countries. In all democracies, relatively free trade creates a temptation to deal with the problem of those producers who lose out to international competition with protectionist measures. For states like the United States the theoretical cost of this approach is mitigated by their ability to extract concessions without reciprocation. For the states of developing countries, this makes trade liberalisation a heavier political burden than it might have appeared at the start of the 1990s. With existing multilateral rules offering no opportunity to exploit their comparative advantages in agriculture, these states are left with swathes of the population disconnected from an international economy from which other citizens are prospering. Meanwhile, their inability to change the WTO's rules on agriculture, rather than simply act together to stop further liberalisations to the advantage of others, draws political attention to the fact that the international economy has been created by the power of richer states and their own external weakness.

Notes

1 See T. L. Karl, 'Dilemmas of democratisation in Latin America', in R. A. Camp (ed.), *Democracy in Latin America: Patterns and Cycles* (Wilmington, DE: Scholarly Resources, 2000).

2 See J. Williamson, *The Failure of World Monetary Reform, 1971–1974* (Sunbury-on-Thames: Thomas Nelson and Sons, 1977).

3 See E. Helleiner, *States and the Re-Emergence of Global Finance: from Bretton Woods to the 1990s* (Ithaca: Cornell University Press, 1994), ch. 5; S. Strange, *International Monetary Relations: Volume Two of International Economic Relations of the Western World 1959–1971* (London: Oxford University Press, 1976); J. Conybeare, *US Foreign Economic Policy and the International Capital Markets: the Case of Capital Export Controls, 1963–74* (New York: Garland, 1988).

4 See P. Terzian, *OPEC: The Inside Story* (London: Zed Books, 1985).

5 See F. Block, *The Origins of International Economic Disorder* (Berkeley: University of California Press, 1977).

6 See B. Cumings, 'The origins and development of the northeast Asian political economy: industrial sector, product cycles and political consequences', *International Organisation*, 38: 1 (1984), 1–40; D. Okimoto, *Between MITI and the Market* (Stanford: Stanford University Press, 1986); R. Samuels, *The Business of the Japanese State* (Ithaca: Cornell University Press, 1986); K. E. Calder, *Crisis and Compensation in Japan: Public Policy and Political Stability in Japan, 1949–1986* (Princeton: Princeton University Press, 1988); M. Kosawa, 'The international economic policy of Japan', in R. Scalapino (ed.), *The Foreign Policy of Modern Japan* (Berkeley and Los Angeles: University of California Press, 1977).

7 See F. Scharpf, *Crisis and Choice in European Social Democracy*, trans. R. Crowley and F. Thompson (Ithaca: Cornell University Press, 1991), ch. 7; M. Kreile, 'West Germany: the dynamics of expansion', in P. Katzenstein

(ed.), *Between Power and Plenty: Foreign Economic Policies of Advanced Industrial States* (Madison: Wisconsin University Press, 1978); C. Lankowski, 'Modell Deutschland and the international regionalisation of the West German state in the 1970s', in A. Markovits (ed.), *The Political Economy of West Germany: Modell Deutschland* (New York: Praeger, 1982).

8 See T. Garton-Ash, *In Europe's Name: Germany and the Divided Continent* (New York: Random House, 1993); J. Joffe, 'The foreign policy of the German Federal Republic', in Roy C. Macridis (ed.), *Foreign Policy in World Politics* (Englewood Cliffs, NJ: Prentice-Hall, 1989).

9 See P. Hall, *Governing the Economy: the Politics of State Intervention in Britain and France* (Cambridge: Polity Press, 1986), chs. 6–7.

10 Quoted in Garton-Ash, *In Europe's Name*, p. 87.

11 See P. Ludlow, *The Making of the European Monetary System* (London: Butterworths, 1982); F. Giavazzi and A. Giovannini, *Limiting Exchange Rate Flexibility: the European Monetary System* (Cambridge, MA: MIT Press, 1989).

12 See A. Prosner, 'Italy: dependence and political fragmentation', in Katzenstein (ed.), *Between Power and Plenty*.

13 See P. Ginsborg, *A History of Contemporary Italy: Society and Politics 1943–1988* (London: Penguin, 1990), chs. 9–10; D. Sassoon, *Contemporary Italy: Economics, Society, and Politics since 1945*, 2nd edn (London: Longman, 1997).

14 See S. George, *An Awkward Partner: Britain in the European Community*, 3rd edn (Oxford: Oxford University Press, 1998).

15 See D. Smith, *The Rise and Fall of Monetarism* (Harmondsworth: Penguin, 1986), chs. 3–5.

16 See Smith, *The Rise and Fall of Monetarism*; Scharpf, *Crisis and Choice*, ch. 5.

17 See J. Joffe, *The Limited Partnership: Europe, the United States and the Burdens of Alliance* (Cambridge, MA: Ballinger, 1987), ch. 1.

18 See R. N. Cooper, *Economic Stabilisation and Debt in Developing Countries* (Cambridge, MA: MIT Press, 1992); I. M. D. Little, *Boom, Crisis and Adjustment: the Macroeconomic Experience of Developing Countries* (New York: Oxford University Press for the World Bank, 1993); M. Kahler, 'The politics of international debt', *International Organisation*, 39: 3 (1985), 357–82; K. Lissakers, *Banks, Borrowers and the Establishment: a Revisionist Account of the International Debt Crisis* (New York: Basic Books, 1991).

19 See M. Kahler, 'The United States and the International Monetary Fund: declining influence or declining interests?', in M. P. Karns and K. A. Mingst (eds), *The United States and Multi-Lateral Institutions: Patterns of Changing Instrumentality and Influence* (Boston: Unwin Hyman, 1990).

20 See L. Hollerman, *Japan Disincorporated: the Economic Liberalisation Process* (Stanford, CA: Hoover Institution Press, 1988), ch. 4.

21 See K. Pyle, *The Japanese Question: Power and Purpose in a New Era* (Washington, DC: American Enterprise Institute, 1992), chs. 5–7; C. Johnson, *Japan, Who Governs? The Rise of the Developmental State* (New York: Norton, 1995), ch. 12; N. B. Thayer, 'Japanese foreign policy in the

Nakasone years', in G. Curtis (ed.), *Japan's Foreign Policy: After the Cold War, Coping with Change* (New York: M. E. Sharpe, 1993).

22 See L. Pauly, *Regulatory Politics in Japan: the Case of Foreign Banking* (Ithaca: Cornell University Press, 1987); F. M. Rosenbluth, *Financial Politics in Contemporary Japan* (Ithaca: Cornell University Press, 1989). For discussion of some of its domestic implications see K. Yamamura and Y. Yasuba (eds), *The Political Economy of Japan Vol. 1: the Domestic Transformation* (Stanford: Stanford University Press, 1987).

23 See Joffe, *The Limited Partnership*; Garton-Ash, *In Europe's Name*, ch. 3.

24 See C. Randall Henning, *Currencies and Politics in the United States, Germany and Japan* (Washington, DC: Institute for International Economics, 1994); R. van der Wurff, 'Neo-Liberalism in Germany', in H. Overbeek (ed.), *Restructuring Hegemony in the Global Political Economy: the Rise of Transnational Neo-Liberalism in the 1980s* (London: Routledge, 1993).

25 On Mitterrand's early foreign policy see Stanley Hoffman, 'Gaullism by any other name', *Foreign Policy*, 57 (Winter 1984–85), 38–57.

26 Quoted in Sassoon, *Contemporary Italy*, p. 73.

27 See J. Bulpitt, 'The discipline of the new democracy: Mrs Thatcher's domestic statecraft', *Political Studies*, 34: 1 (1986), 19–39; Smith, *The Rise and Fall of Monetarism*.

28 See J. Bulpitt, 'Rational politicians and Conservative statecraft in the open polity', in P. Byrd (ed.), *British Foreign Policy under Thatcher* (Oxford: Philip Allan, 1988).

29 See A. Gamble, *The Free Economy and the Strong State: the Politics of Thatcherism*, 2nd edn (Basingstoke: Macmillan, 1994).

30 Unlike many military governments, the Brazilian had governed as a party with one opposition party in formal competition.

31 See F. Hagopian, *Traditional Politics and Regime Change in Brazil* (Cambridge: Cambridge University Press, 1996).

32 See L. Martins, 'The "Liberalisation" of the authoritarian rule in Brazil', in G. O'Donnell, P. Schmitter and L. Whitehead (eds), *Transitions from Authoritarian Rule: Latin America* (Baltimore: Johns Hopkins University Press, 1986); A. Stepan (ed.), *Democratising Brazil: Problems of Transition and Consolidation* (New York: Oxford University Press, 1989).

33 See B. Ames, 'Electoral rules, constituency pressures, and pork barrel: bases of voting in the Brazilan Congress', *Journal of Politics*, 57: 2 (1995), 324–43.

34 See C. Souza, *Constitutional Engineering in Brazil: the Politics of Federalism and Decentralisation* (Basingstoke: Macmillan, 1997).

35 See F. Frankel, *India's Political Economy 1947–77: The Gradual Revolution* (Princeton: Princeton University Press, 1978); V. Joshi and I. M. D. Little, *India: Macro Economics and Political Economy 1964–1991* (Washington, DC: The World Bank, 1994).

36 See P. Brass, 'The Punjab crisis and the unity of India', in A. Kohli (ed.), *India's Democracy: an Analysis of Changing State–Society Relations* (Princeton: Princeton University Press, 1988).

37 See Y. Funabashi, *Managing the Dollar: from the Plaza to the Louvre*, 2nd edn (Washington, DC: Institute for International Economics, 1989); C. R. Henning, *Currencies and Politics in the United States, Germany and Japan* (Washington, DC: Institute for International Economics, 1994).

38 See I. Destler, *American Trade Politics*, 4th edn (Washington, DC: Institute for International Economics, 2005).

39 See T. J. Pempel, 'From exporter to investor: Japan's foreign economic policy', in G. Curtis (ed.), *Japan's Foreign Policy: After the Cold War Coping with Change* (New York: M. E. Sharpe, 1993); R. Doner, 'Japanese foreign investment and the creation of a Pacific Asia region', in J. A. Frankel and M. Kahler, *Regionalism and Rivalry: Japan and the United States in Pacific Asia* (Chicago: Chicago University Press, 1993).

40 See D. Howarth, *The French Road to European Monetary Union* (London: Palgrave, 2000).

41 See K. Dyson and K. Featherstone, *The Road to Maastricht* (Oxford: Oxford University Press, 1999); D. Gros and N. Thygesen, *European Monetary Integration from the European Monetary System to the European Monetary Union*, 2nd edn (London: Longman, 1997).

42 See S. Huntington, *The Third Wave: Democratisation in the Late Twentieth Century* (Norman: University of Oklahoma Press, 1991).

43 See J. A. Thompson, 'Americans and their century', in P. Maitland, *The Future of the Past: Big Questions in History* (London: Pimlico, 2002).

44 Quoted in M. Mastanduno, 'Models, markets, and power: political economy and Asia Pacific, 1989–1999', *Review of International Studies*, 26: 4 (2000), 505.

45 See I. Destler and P. J. Balint, *The New Politics of American Trade: Trade, Labour, and the Environment* (Washington, DC: Institute for International Economics).

46 See M. Cox, *US Foreign Policy after the Cold War: Superpower Without a Mission?* (London: Pinter-Royal Institute of International Affairs, 1995), ch. 3.

47 See E. H. Preeg, *Traders in a Brave New World* (Chicago: Chicago University Press, 1995).

48 See J. Goldstein, 'The United States and world trade: hegemony by proxy', in T. C. Lawton, J. N. Rosenau and Amy C. Verdun (eds), *Strange Power: Shaping the Parameters of International Relations and International Political Economy* (Aldershot: Ashgate, 2000).

49 See N. Bayne, 'Why did Seattle fail?; globalisation and the politics of trade', *Government and Opposition*, 35: 2 (2000), 131–51.

50 See I. Takatoshi, 'US political pressure and economic liberalisation in east Asia', in J. A. Frankel and M. Kahler (eds), *Regionalism and Rivalry: Japan and the United States in Asia-Pacific* (Chicago: Chicago University Press, 1994).

51 See M. Feldstein, 'Refocusing the IMF', *Foreign Affairs*, 77: 2 (1998), 20–33.

52 See I. H. Daadler, *Getting to Dayton: the Making of American Bosnia Policy* (Washington, DC: Brookings Institution Press, 2000).

53 See T. Judah, *Kosovo: War and Revenge*, 2nd edn (London: Yale Note Bene, 2002).
54 See G. Hawthorn, 'The crisis of southern states', *Political Studies*, 42: special issue (1994), 130–45.
55 See C. Clapham, 'Sovereignty and the third world state', *Political Studies*, 47: 3 (1999), 522–37.
56 See P. Zelikow and C. Rice, *Germany Unified and Europe Transformed: a Study in Statecraft* (Cambridge, MA: Harvard University Press, 1995).
57 See D. Marsh, *The Bundesbank: the Bank that Rules Europe* (London: Heinemann, 1992); D. Marsh, *Germany and Europe: the Crisis of Unity*, rev. edn (London: Mandarin, 1995).
58 See J. J. Anderson and J. B. Goodman, 'Mars or Minerva? A united Germany in a post-cold war Europe', in R. Keohane, J. Nye and S. Hoffman (eds), *After the Cold War: International Institutions and State Strategies in Europe, 1989–1991* (Cambridge, MA: Harvard University Press, 1993).
59 Quoted in Marsh, *Germany and Europe*, 150.
60 See Marsh, *Germany and Europe*.
61 See H. Siebert, *The German Economy Beyond the Social Market* (Princeton: Princeton University Press, 2005).
62 See R. Harding and W. E. Paterson (eds), *The Future of the German Economy: an End to the Miracle?* (Manchester: Manchester University Press, 2000).
63 See Stanley Hoffman, 'French dilemmas and strategies in the new Europe', in Keohane, Nye and Hoffman (eds), *After the Cold War*.
64 Quoted in Marsh, *Germany and Europe*.
65 *Financial Times*, 13 August 1993.
66 See D. Howarth, *The French Road to European Monetary Union* (London: Palgrave, 2000).
67 See G. Bonoli, 'Pension-politics in France: patterns of co-operation and conflict in two recent reforms', *West European Politics*, 20: 4 (1997), 111–24.
68 See M. Gilbert, *The Italian Revolution: the End of Democracy, Italian Style?* (Boulder, CO: Westview, 1995); P. Ginsborg, *Italy and its Discontents: Family, Civil Society, State 1980–2001* (London: Allen Lane, 2002); C. Guarnieri, 'The judiciary in the Italian political crisis', *West European Politics*, 20: 1 (1997), 157–75.
69 See B. Dente, 'Sub-national governments in the long Italian transition', *West European Politics*, 20: 1 (1997), 176–93; F. Cavatorta, 'The role of the Northern League in transforming the Italian political system: from economic federalism to ethnic politics and back', *Contemporary Politics*, 7: 1 (2001), 27–40.
70 See Ginsborg, *Italy and its Discontents*; V. D. Sala, 'Maastricht to modernisation: EMU and the Italian social state', in A. Martin and G. Ross (eds), *Euros and Europeans* (Cambridge: Cambridge University Press, 2004).
71 See, for example, F. Mancino, 'The Italians in Europe', *Foreign Affairs*, 79: 2 (2000), 122–35.

72 See H. Thompson, *The British Conservative Government and the European Exchange Rate Mechanism* (London: Pinter, 1996), ch. 6.
73 See Thompson, *The British Conservative Government*, ch. 7.
74 See D. Kavanagh, *The Reordering of British Politics: Politics after Thatcher* (Oxford: Oxford University Press, 1997).
75 Quoted in K. Pyle, *The Japan Question: Power and Purpose in a New Era*, p. 128.
76 See C. Wood, *The Bubble Economy: the Japanese Economic Collapse* (Tokyo: Tuttle, 1993).
77 See R. Boyer and T. Yamada, *Japanese Capitalism in Crisis* (London: Routledge, 2000).
78 See R. Wade and F. Veneroso, 'The Asian Crisis: the high-debt model versus the Wall Street-Treasury-IMF complex', *New Left Review*, 228 (1998), 3–23.
79 R. Taggart Murphy, 'Japan's economic crisis', *New Left Review*, 1 (2000), 25–52.
80 See P. Bowles, 'Asia's post-crisis regionalism: bringing the state back in, keeping the United States out', *Review of International Political Economy*, 9: 2 (2002), 255–8.
81 'Diminishing returns', *The Economist*, 8 March 2001.
82 'Lionheart to the Rescue', *The Economist*, 18 April 2002.
83 See 'The non-performing country', *The Economist*, 7 March 2002.
84 See A. Kohli, *Democracy and Discontent: India's Growing Crisis of Governability* (Cambridge: Cambridge University Press, 1990).
85 See S. Corbridge and J. Harriss, *Reinventing India: Liberalisation, Hindu Nationalism and Popular Democracy* (Cambridge: Polity Press, 2001); C. Jaffrelot, *The Hindu Nationalist Movement and Indian Politics: 1925 to the 1990s* (London: Hurst and Co., 1996).
86 See M. Chadda, *Ethnicity, Security and Separatism in India* (New York: Columbia University Press, 1997).
87 See Corbridge and Harriss, *Reinventing India*; B. R. Nayar, *Globalisation and Nationalism: the Changing Balance in India's Economic Policy* (New Delhi: Sage, 2001); J. D. Sachs, A. Varshney and N. Bajpai, *India in the Era of Economic Reform* (Oxford: Oxford University Press, 1999).
88 R. Jenkins, *Democratic Politics and Economic Reform in India* (Cambridge: Cambridge University Press, 1999).
89 See Matinuddin, *The Nuclearisation of South Asia*. For a more general analysis of Indian foreign policy during the post-Cold War world see B. R. Nayar and T. V. Paul, *India in the World: Searching for Major-Power Status* (New Delhi: Sage, 2001).
90 See L. V. Pereira, 'Towards the common market of the south: Mercosur's origins, evolution and challenges', in R. Roett (ed.), *Mercosur: Regional Integration, World Markets* (London: Lynne Rienner, 1999).
91 See A. R. Moura, 'Stabilisation policy as a game of mutual distrust: the Brazilian experience in post-1985 civilian governments', in M. D'Alva and G. Kinzo (eds), *Brazil: the Challenges of the 1990s* (London: British Academic Press, 1993); P. R. Kingstone, *Crafting Coalitions for Reform: Business*

Preferences, Political Institutions and Neo-Liberal Reform (University Park, PA: Pennsylvania State University Press, 1999).

92 See Werner Baer, 'Illusion of stability: the Brazilian economy under Cardoso', *World Development*, 28: 10 (2000), 1805–19.

93 'Blaming the pilot: Brazil's Cardoso under fire', *The Economist*, 6 February 1999.

94 See G. M. Rocha, 'Neo-dependency in Brazil', *New Left Review*, 16 (2002), 5–33; N. Tingas and P. P. Miguel, 'Capital flows and economic policy in Brazil', in B. N. Ghosh (ed.), *Global Financial Crises and Reforms: Cases and Caveats* (London: Routledge, 2001); Baer, 'Illusion of stability'; A. De Sousa, 'Cardoso and the struggle for reform in Brazil', *Journal of Democracy*, 10: 3 (1999), 49–63.

95 See B. K. Gordon, *America's Trade Follies: Turning Economic Leadership into Strategic Weakness* (London: Routledge, 2001), ch. 4; R. Roett, 'US policy towards Mercosur: from Miami to Santiago', in Roett (ed.), *Mercosur*.

96 See F. Panizza and A. De Brito, 'The politics of human rights in democratic Brazil: a lei não pega', *Democratisation*, 5: 4 (1998), 20–51.

97 See P. Hakim, 'Dispirited politics', *Journal of Democracy*, 14: 2 (2003), 108–22.

98 See R. Mann, *Economic Crisis in Indonesia: the Full Story* (Gateway Books, 1998); H. Hill, *The Indonesian Economy in Crisis: Causes, Consequences and Lessons* (New York: St Martin's Press, 1999); H. Hill, *The Indonesian Political Economy*, 2nd edn (Cambridge: Cambridge University Press, 2000).

99 See R. Sukma, 'Secessionist challenge in Aceh', in H. Soesastro, A. Smith and M. L. Han (eds), *Governance in Indonesia* (Singapore: Institute of South Asian Studies, 2003). On the territorial problems under democracy see J. Snyder, *From Voting to Violence: Democratisation and Nationalist Conflict* (New York: W. W. Norton and Company, 2000).

100 In May 2000, Wahid's economic minister commented: 'if I were a foreign investor, I wouldn't come to Indonesia. The law enforcement is not there.' 'It's the Economy, Wahid', *The Economist*, 6 July 2000.

101 See K. Mizuno, 'Indonesian politics and the issue of justice in East Timor', in Soesastron, Smith and Han (eds), *Governance in Indonesia*.

102 See D. Kingsbury, *Power Politics and the Indonesian Military* (London: Routledge, 2003).

103 See G. O'Donnell, 'Illusions about consolidation', *Journal of Democracy*, 7: 2 (1996), 34–51.

104 See A. Narlikar and D. Tussie, 'The G20 at the Cancun ministerial: developing countries and their evolving coalitions in the WTO', *World Economy*, 27: 7 (2004), 947–66.

5

Conclusions

The two post-war episodes of democracy-building rested on very different understandings of its relation to the international economy. In 1919, the peacemakers put virtually no premium on reconstructing the international economy, and drew up retributive economic provisions that in the circumstances of the American withdrawal from Europe after Versailles proved disastrous. As a result, Europe suffered from a dearth of investment capital and the first five years of the peace were bedevilled with currency and trade problems that fuelled temptations to hyperinflation in some states and to deflation in others, neither of which was domestically or externally conducive to democracy succeeding. In deliberate contrast, the architects of the post-Second World War world believed that creating an international economy that was safe for representative democracy was crucial to the peace. The onset of the Cold War transformed the geo-politics of the Bretton Woods settlement, and the European economic crisis of 1947–48 revealed that the post-war pegged exchange-rate system could not survive without the injection of a large amount of American capital and deferred currency convertibility. In response, the Truman administration rescued the post-war international economy on terms that economically proved even more advantageous to the democracies of Europe and Japan than those agreed in 1944. This change between 1919 and the 1940s was the result both of the conclusions drawn about the consequences of the economic failures of the inter-war years, and the huge political burden, in a world in which imperialism and territorial aggrandisement were discredited, placed on economic prosperity and the distribution of wealth.

The endurance of representative democracy in western Europe and Japan through the first two-and-a-half decades after the Second World War did prove to turn on the economic foundations built at Bretton Woods and reworked by Truman. These made high levels of growth possible and allowed governments to exercise considerable political control over economies for a wide array of purposes without inviting the financial censure of short-term investors. The price of this economic opportunity was paid in external sovereignty over security, a loss of status for the former great powers in international politics, and, in domestic politics, by American-demarcated limits to electoral competition, most conspicuously in Italy. After the failure of the Fourth Republic when financially induced humiliation led to rebellion by part of the army, de Gaulle's unwillingness to accept this bargain on the grounds that the existence of no state could be safe if it handed responsibility for security to foreigners, and his efforts to cultivate a language of nationhood based on absolute external sovereignty, revealed just how historically significant the shift to such a heavily economic conception of the state's purposes was. But beyond France, the price proved more compatible with democracy. The British humiliation over Suez, the Japanese government's struggle to ratify the revised security treaty, and the deflation of West German dreams of reunification, revealed more about the authority of the British, Japanese and West German states for what didn't happen politically than for what did.

That representative democracy proved less robust in post-colonial, developing countries in the three decades after the Second World War is unsurprising. The problems of simultaneously trying to establish representative democracy and a modern state were deep, the post-war international economic order was conceived with the problems of Europe and then parts of east Asia in mind, and the United States proved willing to intervene to support the opponents of democracy in some states. In these contexts, the issues of external sovereignty and autonomy were far less easily contained than in Japan and most west European states. Where weak states, as in Brazil and Indonesia, contributed to high levels of inflation, and where import substitution, as in India and Brazil, depressed exports, severe balance-of-payments difficulties allowed the international financial institutions and other states more purchase over these states' internal affairs than was reconcilable with the weight placed on external sovereignty in post-imperial languages of nationhood. In ways that mirrored de Gaulle, Mrs Gandhi took Indian democracy out of this predicament, but the prudence that her strategy demanded in economic policy left its own set of potentially hazardous problems.

In terminating fixed exchange rates in the early 1970s and moving towards financial liberalisation, the United States undermined the economic foundations that it had previously provided for democracy in western Europe and Japan and created just the kind of policy dilemmas that Keynes had tried to eliminate precisely to make the external economic world safe for representative democracies. Under conditions of open capital flows during the 1920s, many governments had struggled to pursue the kinds of policies that might have strengthened a sense of nationhood. Those citizens who had lost from the high interest rates and public expenditure cuts made necessary by American monetary policy and the pursuit of exchange-rate stability had frequently turned against democracy, and politicians in several states had eventually responded by seizing monetary control. Seen against this history, there were reasons to suppose in the early 1970s that the Nixon administration's actions could inflict potentially grievous harm on modern democratic nation-states. Despite what, after the end of the Cold War, became the mantra that a liberal international economy and democracy naturally reinforce each other and come without the risk of war, any efforts to re-establish democracy in post-colonial, developing countries where it had previously failed would happen in an international economy that had not been shaped with any consideration to the conditions for democracy's success.

By the beginning of the twenty-first century, democracy in Europe and Japan was proving that it could, after all, survive in an international economy where both short- and long-term capital flowed freely. Yet the continuing success of these democracies has not been because Keynes was wrong in his economic judgement about the consequences of financial openness. American monetary dominance did enhance American political power. Politicians did need to find ways to get wages to adjust to exchange rates more rapidly than they had under Bretton Woods. Capital liberalisation and floating currencies did sometimes produce a deflationary bias for governments that made welfare states and patronage more difficult to finance and monetary and fiscal policy redundant as tools of full employment. As the contrasting experiences of Mitterrand's government in 1981–83 and Thatcher's in 1986–88 demonstrated, when each rapidly expanded demand, currency speculation and capital flight were indeed more likely to bedevil left-wing governments than right. And in Japan in the 1990s, the cumulative consequences of financial liberalisation, currency appreciation and fierce American pressure came devastatingly together to precipitate a collapse of the banking system and wreck the entire post-war basis for growth in a way that Keynes could readily have understood.

In dealing with the fallout of these developments, governments in western Europe and Japan were forced back into a set of political difficulties that they had earlier laboured to avoid for motives that could be deemed reason of state in a representative democracy. As the number of unemployed rose, in some countries at some times to levels almost comparable to the inter-war years, whilst the well employed prospered, the economic fortunes of different groups of citizens, especially in Europe,

overtly diverged. Since most European governments struggled to
finance citizens' material entitlements at 1960s levels owing to greatly
increased eligibility, they had to deal with the problem of rising inequality whilst rhetorically disavowing that the state could take direct responsibility for the economic welfare of its citizens. Meanwhile, trying to keep
exchange rates stable against the level of interest rates set by the Federal
Reserve Board and the Bundesbank produced drastic changes. In the
1930s and 1940s, many politicians had fought to make monetary policy
subject to democratic politics, and subsequently used it as a crucial
electoral weapon. But now in turning to monetary union, EU governments asked citizens to accept that elected representatives could not
wisely decide interest rates, and that European price stability was an
incontestable common good in which, whatever the conflict of short-
term interest between them, they all had a long-term stake.

Yet Keynes's political judgement about the consequences of capital
flows and exchange rates has proved considerably less robust than his
economic judgement. Whatever the trepidation of many in the 1970s,
west European and Japanese governments were able to adjust the expectations of their subjects to what Keynes had called the 'economic jug-
gernaut' without damaging the more general presumption that the state
existed for its subjects' well-being. They were able to justify various economic policies by stressing individual responsibility and self-discipline
rather than the shared entitlements of citizenship without leading significant numbers of any electorate to question the authority of a state
that wanted to do less to earn its subjects' consent. And they did assert
that voters were a bad influence on monetary policy without triggering
serious questions either about the accountability of central bankers, or
why the electorate was any better qualified to choose representatives to
judge other issues.

More practically, after the British and Italian governments got into
serious difficulties with wage demands in the 1970s and early 1980s, they
were able to use the state's coercive power to weaken the trade unions
and make resistance to anti-inflationary discipline harder. Eventually,
governments in all developed countries were forced to adjust their
welfare states, and some also their patronage strategies, to the deflationary bias created by the new foreign-exchange markets, and they did
so without precipitating a constitutional crisis or having to legislate by
decree.[1] Even when the governments of the EU member states agreed
to abide by the Maastricht convergence criteria, they still succeeded in
cutting resources to patronage networks and curtailing social security
and pension commitments without, except for more than a few months
in France, jeopardising the authority of the state, or, save perhaps a little

in Italy where they were fragile for other reasons, damaging democratic constitutional rules. Meanwhile in Japan, more than a decade of economic disaster that wrecked the LDP's ability to channel new resources to its clients was not sufficient even to dislodge the ruling party from office. Whereas the economic problems of the 1920s and early 1930s had bitterly divided the political classes of Europe and pushed some towards radical alternatives, few by the 1990s disputed the parameters of monetary policy, or the outcomes produced by a largely open international economy even when it circumscribed the kinds of economic and social policies that centre-left and left-wing governments had in the past considered their *raison d'être*. After Mitterrand's U-turn in 1983, no centre-left government in Europe came into office trying to pursue expansionary macro-economic policies to increase employment, and only a few ministers, like Lafontaine in Germany, dissented. Meanwhile, only in Italy did rising economic inequalities directly produce significant secessionist demands, and few citizens anywhere violently turned against the state's authority or representative democracy. Most clearly in Britain, those who lost from the new international economy were simply politically defeated by governments using the coercive power at their disposal.

Put differently, in the EU states and Japan, representative democracy eventually proved astonishingly robust in the international economy shaped by the United States after the end of Bretton Woods. The experience of the 1920s and early 1930s had revealed something circumstantial about the relationship between democracy and a largely open international economy dominated by one monetary power, not a general truth. States in these countries, more recently, have not just retained their strength in relation to the international economy, as much of the recent literature has demonstrated,[2] but they have found securing consent to the authority of the state much easier than at any time since representative democracy first emerged as a form of government. In part, since numbers are the definitive currency of democracy, the political change between the inter-war years and today is probably a consequence of how many have prospered and suffered on each occasion. But in other ways, the causes of the change have been driven not by questions of relative wealth but by differences in political understanding and judgement that have reduced the sense that there are alternatives to either open capital flows or representative democracy as a form of rule that can provide security and advance prosperity. Whilst many in the political classes in the 1930s had turned to economic nationalism, under the foreign-exchange markets from the 1970s radical assertions of independence from economic realities tended to bring first inflation and then recession with consequences that became all too clearly deleterious. Certainly some politicians in western Europe and Japan were at times tempted by the idea of a tax on foreign-exchange markets, but nowhere has any significant group of them developed a coherent project for trying to resurrect a world of closed capital. And in adopting monetary union, which has been the most radical attempt to face the problem of exchange-rate management under conditions of liberalised finance, governments in some ways embraced more tightly the constraints of the new international economy of their own accord. As the judgements of political classes in western Europe and Japan changed during the course of the 1980s and the 1990s so the passions generated by economic questions appear to have dimmed, to use Carl Schmitt's language,[3] breeding rather fewer friend–enemy distinctions than they did in the 1970s when the post-1945 expectations of what a modern democratic nation-state could deliver began to collide with economic realities. Of course, on occasion, as in France in 1995 and in the Northern League's response to Italy's bid to qualify for monetary union, such passions did still flare. But they did not anywhere induce an enduring rebellion.

Beyond the realm of economic policy, western European and Japanese democracies endured through the 1980s and 1990s in part because by the time they were once again put to the test of open capital flows, they had persisted for the previous thirty years, and in the case of the British much longer. Success in securing consent to the authority of any modern state, whatever the form of government, breeds habits of obedience. In the same way that during the nineteenth century and the first half of the twentieth, some classes of subjects had so frequently plotted against governments and turned to arms against the state that they became conditioned to instability, so the citizens of these states have apparently become accustomed to political stability whatever the economic outcomes produced by their representatives.

At least in Europe, those habits of obedience to authority were undoubtedly reinforced by the historical failure of alternative forms of government to representative democracy. Its competitors in the late eighteenth and nineteenth centuries, monarchy and aristocracy, were destroyed by the decline in Europe of the belief that nature or Christianity ordained the formal superiority of one set of human beings over another without which any form of government that appealed to hierarchy was virtually impossible. Its competitors in the twentieth century, fascism and communism, were then defeated militarily and, in their murderous trajectories, exhausted imaginatively. In some sense in Europe, and indeed in North America, by 1989 no coherent alternative to representative democracy was on offer to tempt anyone to try to over-throw it. Few would deny that as a form of government representative democracy has its problems in dealing with economic questions, and the monetary moves by the EU states have provided stark commentary on some of them. Nor could anyone dispute the dissonance between the appeal of democracy as an idea, supposedly capable of realising the rule of 'the people', and its more mundane and grubby realities. But without an obvious competitor, governments in most of Europe simply had to work less hard to sustain democracy and to prevent discontent turning into armed rebellion than they had in the earlier history of modern democratic nation-states when alternatives carried practical and imaginative weight. Keynes had wanted at Bretton Woods to make the external economic world safe for democracy because he believed that its success against its rivals could not be taken for granted. Without them, the world that he dreaded proved far less dangerous.

For many modern democrats, the success of representative democracy is largely self-evident, something which can be explained by its universal properties and innate superiority. But historically, it is still rather surprising that there could be this much voluntary agreement on any form of rule. As Hobbes insisted, human beings are exceptionally prone to disagree even in the absence of grand passions, and nothing in the circumstances in which the notion of representative democracy took hold on either side of the Atlantic in the eighteenth century suggested that it had any overwhelming advantages in preserving itself as a form of government, or sustaining the authority of the state on which it depends. Outside Europe and North America, this is easier to see even where living standards are comparable. By the turn of the century, Japanese democracy had endured for fifty years, including through the economic meltdown of the 1990s. Yet if the absence of alternatives to democracy in Europe in good part explains why governments there were able to navigate through the difficulties created by financial liberalisation and American monetary power, the same explanation does not suffice here. In East Asia, as the political and economic success of the authoritarian regime in Singapore has exhibited, there are viable alternatives to democracy. The ease with which Japanese democracy absorbed the economic crisis of the 1990s could not have been because nobody within the political class could have imagined an alternative form of rule. Certainly the ongoing American military presence in Japan provided effective external protection against internal threats to democracy without any longer inciting the kind of nationalist passions that had caused difficulty in the 1950s and 1960s. But since at no time during the 1990s did the United States have to support democracy in Japan with coercion, this still leaves something unexplained. Despite the presence of local alternatives, the political class simply fiddled with the rules of democracy in ways that produced much the same outcomes, and those whose lives were damaged, some ruinously, by unemployment and asset deflation did not mobilise, or lash out, against the state. In responding to the economic crisis, successive LDP governments, including Koizumi's, prioritised political stability over restoring growth. Despite the disaffection that sections of the electorate did feel at the methods of the LDP, the majority refrained from letting loose the disorder that radical reform by the other parties would have entailed in the short to medium term. Political order, once achieved even at a considerable price, appeared to have become something that the Japanese political class and a majority of Japanese citizens valued for its own sake.

The political stability wrought in different ways by the modern democratic nation-state in Europe and Japan is by any historical standards a striking phenomenon. As the historian J. H. Plumb said in his account of early eighteenth-century politics in England: 'political stability is a comparatively rare phenomenon in the history of human society. When achieved, it has seldom lasted'.[4] In view of where representative democracy began when it became the predominant form of rule in Europe, its stability is even more remarkable, even allowing for the absence of alternatives. Wide support for constitutional rules in democracy has never been a sufficient condition for its success. The nineteenth century had suggested that such success depended on the possession of both sovereign authority backed by coercive power and a robust conception of nationhood that could convince those subjected to that authority to accept it. When prevailing conceptions of nationhood faltered during the early twentieth century, governments put more of the burden of obtaining consent to the state's authority on coercion than that authority could readily withstand. When this failure was allied to the aggressive foreign policies that the pursuit of nationhood also encouraged, Europe's representative democracies, partial or otherwise, floundered. During the inter-war years most European governments struggled to do much better in an external world that was inimical to reinventing the language of nationhood. After the Second World War, the legacy of German's aggression on national minorities and the international economy fashioned by the United States allowed a more generous external world in which the notion of a nation directed for a single set of economic and social purposes by the representatives of the people carried practical and imaginative resonance. In the wake of the success of this conception of nationhood, representative democracy proved a considerably more internally stable form of rule than it had been almost anywhere hitherto.

When that conception proved untenable after the end of Bretton Woods, there were good historical reasons to suppose that the consequences might have been enormous. That they have not proved to be reveals something potentially very significant: in these states creating and sustaining an idea of nationhood is apparently no longer quite the same general condition for the success of representative democracy as it has appeared in the past. Since the French revolution, an effective language of nationhood had been an attractive instrument for winning consent to authority by creating passions that identified citizens with the states that ruled them. This reduced the need for coercion at a time when older religious beliefs that had previously fulfilled something of the same purpose were faltering or providing justifications for disobedience. By the beginning of the twenty-first century, prevailing conceptions of nationhood were in considerable disrepair and governments had not created anything as potent to replace them, but consent to the authority of states in democracies in the EU and Japan was largely intact. Where governments during the inter-war and Bretton Woods years feared the material expectations of many citizens as hazardous for the state,[5] the economic grievances of particular minorities no longer appear politically dangerous and those tempted, as a result, to break the law are simply punished. In securing consent from citizens to the state's internal authority, far less appears in these states to depend on the collectivist fiction of nationhood than at any time in the history of representative democracy. In place of imaginative justifications of the state's authority that defined a singular people through either external grandeur or economic protection and solidarity, these democracies have offered a mixture of prosperity and stability to the majority of their subjects, whilst trusting that fear, rather than any more demanding reason of state, will suffice for the rest.

This argument might appear to sustain the claim that in these parts of the world representative democracy is now a privileged form of government, relatively immune to serious difficulties. This conclusion, however, would be misleading. First, if democracies in western Europe contained the consequences of the post-Bretton Woods international economy in a way that suggests that rule in democracies is not as demanding, or as likely to fail, as it once was, this simply reinforces the truth that representative democracy is a form of rule that is dependent on the exercise of power. A significant part of the success of these democracies in the 1980s and 1990s depended on politicians changing the expectations of citizens and exploiting their economic fears rather than responding to their explicitly stated interests and preferences. These politicians also bound themselves to exchange-rate and fiscal disciplines and abdicated responsibility for monetary policy to avoid the temptations of governing to please voters in the short term. Some, especially in light of the British experience after 1992, might doubt whether this was a correct judgement about reason of state in the post-Bretton Woods international economy, but nobody could think that this restraint was driven by citizens' understanding of their own interests or their expressed demands for prudence. The tension between the imaginative promise of democracy and its manifestation in modern politics as a form of rule that depends on power has not gone away. The capacity for representative democracy to disappoint remains endless and the exercise of power to contain that will always open up the possibility of conflict because human beings do not like submitting to the will of others.

Second, in the post-Bretton Woods international economy, representative democracy is clearly not the only form of government compatible with economic success. Notwithstanding the ways in which politicians did succeed in crafting economic policies independently of citizens, the likely political fallout of reform did appear to make Japanese and German governments cautious about dealing with the kinds of problems that afflicted their economies during the 1990s. In both states, governments might well have been grateful to have been able to make as radical an adjustment to changing international economic circumstances as Singapore made during the Asian financial crisis by imposing a universal 15 per cent wage and salary cut.

Third, when viewed historically, the contingencies of the success of democracy in the EU states and Japan over the last thirty years are many. So far as this success depended on the absence of alternatives, this was in good part a military outcome, and the defeat of fascism depended on the intervention of the communist Soviet Union. These are also democracies that with the exception of the French have at best taken only partial responsibility for their own security, and in Japan's case virtually none. This is the consequence not of the supposed inherently pacific qualities of representative democracy but of American military guarantees. Unlike the democracies of the inter-war years, these states did not have to confront the need for fiscal and monetary prudence at the same moment as defence against a rising hostile power. One can reasonably argue that the existence of the EU has made its own contribution to an external environment in which regional security concerns can be put at a low premium, but the United States still has military bases in Europe, and the head of US forces in Europe is also Supreme Allied Commander of NATO. Meanwhile Japan does not enjoy such favourable external conditions. Its democracy did indeed endure through the economic tribulations of the 1990s but it did so in conditions where the American security guarantee made the rise of China less threatening than it would otherwise have been, allowing defence expenditure to be very low as annual borrowing to try boost demand rose as high as 7 per cent of GDP. Unlike, for example, British governments during the 1930s, the LDP governments did not have to balance economic and military imperatives at a point of severe financial difficulty, and Japanese democracy was consequently put to far less test.

Fourth, the solutions that governments under any form of rule devise to deal with one set of problems invariably generate new ones. In the late 1980s, most of the EU governments understood monetary union as a solution to the problem of exchange rates and high interest rates under conditions of open short-term capital flows and the power of the Bundesbank. But it was always likely to test the limits of any belief in a European common good that could justify divergent growth outcomes, and with Germany's preference for an independent central bank prevailing, it would strike hard against the idea that democracy allowed the citizens' representatives to choose economic priorities and take decisions to achieve them. In practice it has created problems that are at least as awkward. The stability pact has not held because in 2003 France and Germany so conspicuously disregarded the rules, despite having voted to enforce them two years earlier against Portugal. In so doing, they inflicted grievous damage on any notion that the authority of the EU institutions over monetary union could be impersonal or an agent to realise a European common good. But without some faith among the politicians and citizens of the euro states that monetary union will not produce outcomes determined by relative power, the EU's monetary union in its present form will not survive and the fallout will almost certainly have significant consequences for democracy in some of the present member states. In the summer of 2005, the Italian prime minister, Silvio Berlusconi, lashed out at monetary union, branding it a 'disaster' that had 'screwed everybody',[6] and the possibility of an early full-scale crisis began to loom. Labouring under a near-year-long recession, rising public debt and steadily intensifying competition from China in clothes, textiles and light manufacturing, the Italian economy needs lower interest rates and a weaker euro. If the ECB and the foreign-exchange markets do not oblige, any Italian government, whichever party is in power, will have to decide whether in a representative democracy it can sustain Italian membership of a union that seems radically to curtail policy options for dealing with severe economic difficulties whilst servicing the economies of other euro-zone states rather more successfully. Yet if an Italian government did choose to withdraw from the euro, it would have to contemplate default, compulsory redomination of euro-debts, a systemic bank crisis across the EU (given the losses that a substantial devaluation would inflict on the value of euro-issued bonds and the number of these bonds being held by financial institutions in other European countries), and financial meltdown among heavily indebted corporations. Meanwhile, the failure of the euro for Italy would raise instant questions about the currency's future in other EU states where the absence of room for manoeuvre in monetary or exchange-rate matters was proving politically difficult. The Northern League's reverse of its earlier support for monetary union might well save Italian representative democracy from as much territorial fallout of such events as might have been predicted during the mid-1990s. Nonetheless few could be confident that such a crisis could simply be weathered by a state whose authority has so frequently been contested and a democracy that only a decade ago temporarily proved incapable of meeting its primary purpose of allowing elections to determine who exercises power. The ways in which the EU governments coped with the post-Bretton Woods international economy are far from played out in their political consequences and still have the capacity to put the authority of some of these democracies to severe test.

The fragilities of democracy in developing countries

The domestic consequences for representative democracies in many post-colonial countries of adjusting to the post-Bretton Woods international economy were in some ways as benign as in Europe and Japan, even in far more dramatic circumstances. Governments risked less in the 1990s in deciding economic policy than they had in earlier decades. In India, Congress under Rao successfully pursued far more radical reforms than those Rajiv Gandhi had earlier abandoned in the face of resistance. In Brazil, Sarney's disastrous policies culminating in hyper-inflation provoked neither violent rebellion nor any attempt by the military to recapture power. A decade later, a huge currency crisis and ferocious demands from the IMF had similarly little political fallout. Even more strikingly during the same period, another Latin American democracy, Argentina's, survived four years of recession produced by fierce austerity policies to try to sustain the Argentinean peso's direct convertibility to the dollar, and a catastrophic financial crisis when that currency board collapsed which slashed production and deprived citizens of access to their savings. In some ways, the same phenomenon of reduced alternatives was at work in Latin American as in Europe. During the course of the twentieth century, at least one Latin American or

Caribbean state had experimented with virtually every form of government devised in the modern world, to no uniformly rewarding effect.
Since democracy had succeeded elsewhere, it now enjoyed a certain
premium whatever the vagaries of its practices on the continent.[7] When
its restoration in the 1980s produced calamitous economic outcomes,
this paradoxically reinforced a sense of diminished possibilities because
after the miseries of hyperinflation the expectations of significant
numbers of Brazilian and Argentinean citizens about just what the state
could do economically appeared subdued. In the face of provocation
that was immense by the standards of previous revolts, few rebelled.[8]

Nonetheless, at the beginning of the twenty-first century, representative democracies in many post-colonial, developing countries were substantially weaker than in the EU states and Japan. In some states,
democracy was visibly fragile. In south-east Asia, it did have obvious competitors as a form of government even if most of the region's authoritarian regimes went through the ritual of justifying the power of the
ruling party through the ballot box. In Indonesia, the constitutional
rules were openly contested within the political class; the army, although
squeezed out of parliament by 2002, still had a base from which to exercise influence; and the country's vexed territorial politics was regularly
exacerbated by fiscal and monetary decisions. In Latin America, whilst
Brazilian and Argentinean democracy survived reform, democracy in
some of the smaller states proved less robust. In Venezuela, from 1989
to 1993, economic liberalisation produced serious rioting and an
attempted coup; in Peru, in 1992, President Fujimori closed the
Congress down and concentrated all power in his own hands; and in
Ecuador, in 2000, the military deposed the president after the government had defaulted on its Brady bonds.

Even where representative democracy appeared to have triumphed
over alternatives, for much of the 1980s and 1990s many governments
could not rely on parliamentary legislation to make economic reforms
in the same way that Brüning had had to depend on emergency powers
to secure deflationary measures and reduce wages during the last years
of the Weimar republic. Both Collor's and Rao's governments used
decrees to liberalise the Brazilian and Indian economies, and Cardoso
eventually resorted to criminalising aspects of fiscal policy to try to
reduce borrowing. Meanwhile, in Argentina, between 1989 and 1993
President Menem issued more than 300 decrees on economic issues
without either the legal or constitutional authority to do so, before successfully pressing for a constitutional change to give the president emergency powers to legislate by decree for a fixed period of time.[9] In none
of these cases did regularly substituting overt power for parliamentary

debate produce a constitutional crisis. But Collor's actions did produce a breakdown in relations between the executive and the legislature, which ultimately led to his impeachment, and the more parties in office relied on such means, the more they were likely to undermine support within the political class for constitutional rules.

Externally, capital flows are much the kind of political risk for states in developing countries that had troubled Keynes. Huge outflows of short-term capital can leave poor states and those labouring under high levels of debt with exceedingly high interest rates and within days unable to finance essential imports. The herd mentality of investors and the political fears that democracy can generate about the likelihood of debt repudiation played out for poor states during the 1980s and 1990s much as Keynes would have anticipated. The result has been that governments in these states have to accept 'deflation at the dictate of influences from the outside', just what Keynes had refused to contemplate for Britain in the post-war world.[10] For many states in developing countries foreign direct investment is far more of a risk than for their rich counterparts because new flows can suddenly dry up when the collective investment mood deems emerging markets a liability. After the Asian financial crisis, short- and long-term flows to all emerging markets except China fell massively, and today, contrary to all theoretical understanding of investment dynamics, there is a net capital outflow from developing to developed countries. There are several reasons for this but the most important is that so many governments in developing countries, not just in south-east Asia, concluded after the 1997–99 financial crises that they needed to accumulate large amounts of foreign-exchange reserves in order to exercise more control over their exchange rate and to make themselves less vulnerable to future speculative attacks.

To make matters worse, the claim to external sovereignty of many democracies in post-colonial, developing countries is weak and this frailty cannot easily be politically contained. After the Cold War American presidents began to deploy arguments to justify intervention in another state that could theoretically be used to intervene anywhere where a government resorted to large-scale internal violence. In practice, of course, American and UN interventions were limited: whilst Indonesia became subject to international jurisdiction over its human-rights abuses in East Timor, India was not so treated for similar offences in Kashmir even before it acquired nuclear weapons. But no state that neither possessed a substantial military capability nor was of direct use to Washington could be confident that any part of its external sovereignty was safe. This diminution of external sovereignty under American policies during the 1990s reinforced the dynamics created by debt and the IMF during the previous decade. To reconsider the wisdom of allowing unrestricted short-term capital in the light of these outcomes, the governments would first have had to escape from the IMF, but to do so risked more currency problems, a fall in investment and no prospect of returning to commercial credit markets. Argentina's defiance of the IMF after it defaulted on all its privately owned sovereign debt in late 2001 showed that access to credit does not always require submission, but Argentina crucially benefited from the sheer size of its debt to the Fund and the willingness of the Bush administration and various European governments to overrule the IMF's executive board.[11] Where richer states are not willing to support poor states, the price of foreign debt can indeed be, as Hume had argued about eighteenth-century Europe, 'poverty, impotence and subjection to foreign powers'.[12]

The contrasting experience of the Indian government during the 1990s suggested just how much autonomy was being lost. India's debt at the beginning of the 1990s, although unsustainable, had been accumulated over a rather shorter period of time. When the Congress government began to liberalise the economy, it did not allow full capital account convertibility, and once the IMF loan agreed in 1991 had run its course in 1993, it did not ask for any new credit, giving the Fund no leverage over its policy on short-term capital flows. With the rupee protected from speculation, neither it nor its successors had any need to return to the IMF to cope with a currency crisis. When the BJP government then pushed for India to become a nuclear power in 1998, it was, therefore, in a strong position. Since the IMF had no leverage and since the Clinton administration could not persuade all the other major powers to oppose India, Washington could not inflict the kind of damage on the Indian economy that might have persuaded Vajpayee to reverse course. In possessing as much external sovereignty as it did, the Indian state appeared exceptionally secure by the standards of postcolonial, developing countries with huge insurance against foreign intervention and bargaining capital in the international financial institutions.

Yet even if Indian governments succeeded in shielding the external sovereignty of the Indian state through the 1990s, thanks to the contingencies of time and place they still have to deal with a far more awkward set of external conditions in maintaining Indian democracy than their counterparts in the EU and North America. Indian governments cannot escape paying the utmost attention to regional security. India still has territorial disputes with Pakistan and China, and both states are for different reasons of great geo-political and military interest to the United States. After 9/11, the Bush administration's wish for Pakistani support radically reduced the Indian government's room for manoeuvre over Kashmir, despite India's nuclear capability. After another confrontation with Pakistan in May 2002 in which both governments escalated the nuclear rhetoric, the BJP government responded to pressure from Washington and changed course, re-establishing full diplomatic relations with Pakistan a year later and, in January 2004, beginning new talks on Kashmir's future. So long as the United States remains the dominant power in Asia, India's sovereignty over its own security will not necessarily translate into the kind of autonomy that the grandiose language of great-power status promises. As the historical experience in Europe in the nineteenth and early twentieth century revealed, representative democracy can prove less than conducive to the prudence required by reason of state in foreign policy in these kinds of external conditions. It is perhaps all too easy to imagine future Indian governments having to struggle simultaneously against the patriotic and revolutionary spirits – a feat that Tocqueville deemed impossible.

In the long-established democracies, what were once enormous difficulties posed by state-building and forging an effective language of nationhood to convince large numbers of people that they should accept a particular sovereign authority lie in the past and the cost in human lives of their success casts little visible shadow. In post-colonial, developing countries, by contrast, these problems are acute and the opportunities to address them in the ways that they were in North America and Europe or even Japan seem historically exhausted. Where modern states have been weak, adjusting to the constraints of the new international economy, exploiting its opportunities and absorbing the demands of the IMF have all proved especially difficult. The absence of sovereign authority backed by coercive power made it far harder for the Brazilian and Indonesian governments, for example, to fulfil the conditions of their IMF loans, and for the Indonesian government to create investor confidence in the protection of the rule of law. In Brazil, federalism was a large part of the problem. Even when Cardoso succeeded in curtailing the licence for utter fiscal irresponsibility granted to the states in the 1988 constitution, he could not assert the centre's authority over security, which has put too much of the burden of Brazil's democracy on increasing incomes, whilst diminishing the capacity of any government to exploit international capital for just that purpose.

That state-building has failed in many post-colonial, developing countries and that this failure is a significant economic liability has led some to conclude that a return to some kind of imperial rule is the only way out of the predicament.[13] History suggests that there could be material benefits for the citizens of some countries in abandoning the project of independent statehood, but to presume that this is politically conceivable reduces once again the question of securing consent to authority to the problem of economic development. It just as erroneously assumes that there could possibly be some way of making the direct exercise of power by foreigners bearable to those whose expectations have been shaped by the language of national self-determination. Statehood may be increasingly difficult in some domestic and external conditions, but after fifty years in which achieving an operative modern democratic nation-state has seemed both a right and a political possibility acquiescence to any return to empire is impossible.

Nonetheless, where external sovereignty had been lost to powers that could be deemed imperial, and significant numbers of the state's subjects remain poor, the idea of nationhood that had been cultivated during the first decades of independence has become hollow. Consequently, an enormous amount for these democracies has come to turn solely on questions of power at the expense of consent to authority. In some places, as in Bihar and the poorest neighbourhoods of some Brazilian cities, those who led states have ceded power to private militias, whilst elsewhere they have allowed, as in some regions in Brazil, or encouraged, as in Gujurat, local political actors to use violence at will, leaving any claim to the impersonal rule of law in tatters. In some provinces, as in Kashmir and the Punjab in India and in Aceh and Irian Jaya in Indonesia, governments during the 1990s gambled virtually everything on military power to quell rebellion. But this strategy has little chance of success, and just as the Indian government retreated to new negotiations over Kashmir in 2004 so did the Indonesian over Aceh in 2005. The more brutal the exercise of power in these regions has become the more lethal to any hope of rescuing any idea of nationhood that could encompass all those subject to a state's rule. The longer power is used, the more difficult for anybody leading the state to recreate any semblance of authority that could command consent independent of power. Only Lincoln's apocalyptic strategy of mass destruction of those unwilling to accept the rule of the state before recasting nationhood out of the blood and wreckage stands as a theoretical solution, but even if anyone dared to contemplate it internally, probably not even the Indian state would enjoy sufficient external autonomy to succeed. Just as excessive reliance on coercion undermines the authority of states in most post-colonial, developing countries so it jeopardises what remains of their already flailing external sovereignty and autonomy. Unlike in Europe and Japan, in most post-colonial countries conjuring nationhood is still a compelling reason of state in representative democracy.

The power of the United States and the market dynamics and power relations of the international economy do much to make that task exceptionally difficult just as they punish failures of state-building. There may not be obvious alternatives, at least outside Asia, but it may be that in some states representative democracy can't succeed. This is not a judgement about the suitability of different peoples or political cultures to democracy. It is simply to say that establishing and maintaining representative democracy as a form of government has long been a very difficult exercise, and where, for the moment anyway, the scale of the problems that ensue from it have been successfully addressed, the conditions for that success have been dependent on a host of historical contingencies that cannot be recreated at will.

Notes

1 There was the odd exception. In Belgium, in May 1996, Prime Minister Jean-Luc Dehaene asked the national parliament for special powers to legislate by decree on the next year's budget, after repeatedly failing to win support for a series of austerity measures.

2 See C. Hay, 'Globalisation's impact on states', in J. Ravenhill (ed.), *Global Political Economy* (Oxford: Oxford University Press, 2005).

3 C. Schmitt, *The Concept of the Political*, trans. T. Strong (Chicago: Chicago University Press, 1996).

4 J. H. Plumb, *The Growth of Political Stability in England 1675–1725* (London: Macmillan, 1967), p. xvi.

5 This judgement is articulated forcefully in Bernard Crick's comment in 1970: 'We today might want to consider the economic role of the skilled industrial workers rather than the conscript soldier; quite apart from talk of rights, all modern states depend upon him: he can be granted genuine political rights, or he can be indoctrinated and mobilised in the most elaborate and fantastical manner; but unlike the traditional picture of the peasant, he cannot be ignored. If the object of the state is now held to be his welfare, it is equally true that the safety of the state depends upon his support – on whatever terms.' 'Introduction' in N. Machiavelli, *The Discourses*, ed. B. Crick (London: Penguin, 1970), p. 33.

6 Bloomberg, 28 July 2005.

7 See E. Boeninger, 'Latin America's multiple challenges', in L. Diamond et al., *Consolidating the Third Wave Democracies: Regional Challenges* (London: Johns Hopkins University Press, 1997); P. Hakim, 'Dispirited politics', *Journal of Democracy*, 14: 2 (2003), 108–22.

8 For good arguments from the early 1990s that things were likely to turn out otherwise see A. Przeworski, *Democracy and the Market* (Cambridge: Cambridge University Press, 1991). On the relative political ease of economic reform in Latin America see K. Weyland, *The Politics of Market Reform*

in *Fragile Democracies: Argentina, Brazil, Peru and Venezuela* (Princeton: Princeton University Press, 2002).

9 S. Parrish, 'When the President governs alone: the *decretazo* in Argentina', in J. M. Carey and M. S. Shugart (eds), *Executive Decree Authority* (Cambridge: Cambridge University Press, 1998).

10 Quoted in R. Skidelsky, *John Maynard Keynes: Volume Three, Fighting for Britain 1937–1946* (London: Macmillan, 2000), p. 336.

11 P. Blustein, *And the Money Kept Rolling in (and out): Wall Street, IMF and the Bankrupting of Argentina* (New York: PublicAffairs, 2005).

12 'Of public credit', in *Political Essays*, ed. K. Haakonssen (Cambridge: Cambridge University Press, 1994), p. 167.

13 See, for example, Niall Ferguson, *Colossus: the Rise and Fall of the American Empire* (London: Allen Lane, 2004), ch. 5.

Bibliography

Adamthwaite, A., *France and the Coming of the Second World War* (Cambridge: Cambridge University Press, 1977).

Ambrose, S., *Eisenhower, Vol. II: the President* (New York: Simon & Schuster, 1984).

Ames, B., 'Electoral rules, constituency pressures, and pork barrel: bases of voting in the Brazilian Congress', *Journal of Politics*, 57: 2 (1995), 324–43.

Anderson, B., *Imagined Communities: Reflections on the Origin and Spread of Nationalism*, 2nd edn (London: Verso, 1991).

Anderson, J. J. and J. B. Goodman, 'Mars or Minerva?: a United Germany in a post-Cold War Europe', in R. Keohane, J. Nye and S. Hoffman (eds), *After the Cold War: International Institutions and State Strategies in Europe, 1989–1991* (Cambridge, MA: Harvard University Press, 1993).

Ardant, G., 'Financial policy and economic infrastructure of modern states and nations', in C. Tilly (ed.), *The Formation of National States in Western Europe* (Princeton: Princeton University Press, 1975).

Baer, W., 'Illusion of stability: the Brazilian economy under Cardoso', *World Development*, 28: 10 (2000), 1805–19.

Bartlett, C. J., *The Long Retreat: a Short History of British Defence Policy* (London: Macmillan, 1972).

Bayne, N., 'Why did Seattle fail?; globalisation and the politics of trade', *Government and Opposition*, 35: 2 (2000), 131–51.

Bensel, R. F., *Yankee Leviathan: the Origins of Central State Authority in America, 1859–1877* (Cambridge: Cambridge University Press, 1990).

Bentley, M., *Politics Without Democracy, 1815–1914: Perception and Preoccupation in British Government*, 2nd edn (London: Fontana Press, 1996).

Bhagwati, J., *Free Trade* (Princeton: Princeton University Press, 2001).

Black, J. K., *The United States' Penetration of Brazil* (Philadelphia: Philadelphia University Press, 1977).

Blank, S., 'Britain: the politics of foreign economic policy, the domestic economy and the problem of pluralistic stagnation', in P. Katzenstein, *Between Power and Plenty: Foreign Economic Policies of Advanced Industrial States* (Madison: Wisconsin University Press, 1978).

Blanning, T., *The Origins of the French Revolutionary Wars* (London: Longman, 1986).

Block, F., *The Origins of International Economic Disorder* (Berkeley: University of California Press, 1977).

Blum, J. M. (ed.), *From the Morgenthau Diaries Vol. III: Years of Achievement 1941–1945* (Boston: Houghton Mifflin, 1967).

Blustein, P., *And the Money Kept Rolling in (and out): Wall Street, IMF and the Bankrupting of Argentina* (New York : Public Affairs, 2005).

Boeninger, E., 'Latin America's multiple challenges', in L. Diamond et al. (eds), *Consolidating the Third Wave Democracies: Regional Challenges* (London: Johns Hopkins University Press, 1997).

Bonoli, G., 'Pension-politics in France: patterns of co-operation and conflict in two recent reforms', *West European Politics*, 20: 4 (1997), 111–24.

Borden, W. S., *The Pacific Alliance: the United States' Foreign Economic Policy and Japanese Trade Recovery, 1947–1954* (Madison: University of Wisconsin Press, 1984).

Boyer, R. and T. Yamada, *Japanese Capitalism in Crisis* (London: Routledge, 2000).

Brass, P., 'The Punjab crisis and the unity of India', in A. Kohli (ed.), *India's Democracy: an Analysis of Changing State–Society Relations* (Princeton: Princeton University Press, 1988).

Braun, R., 'Taxation, socio-political structure and state building: Great Britain and Brandenburg-Prussia', in C. Tilly, *The Formation of National States in Western Europe* (Princeton: Princeton University Press).

Brenan, G., *The Spanish Labyrinth: an Account of the Social and Political Background of the Civil War* (Cambridge: Cambridge University Press, 1943).

Breuilly, J., *Nationalism and the State*, 2nd edn (Manchester: Manchester University Press, 1993).

Buckley, R., *US–Japan Alliance Diplomacy 1945–1990* (Cambridge: Cambridge University Press, 1992).

Bulpitt, J., 'The discipline of the new democracy: Mrs Thatcher's domestic statecraft', *Political Studies*, 34: 1 (1986), 19–39.

Bulpitt, J., 'Rational politicians and Conservative statecraft in the open polity', in P. Byrd, *British Foreign Policy under Thatcher* (Oxford: Philip Allan, 1988).

Burke, K. and A. Cairncross, *'Goodbye Great Britain': the 1976 IMF Crisis* (New Haven: Yale University Press, 1992).

Calder, K. E., *Crisis and Compensation in Japan: Public Policy and Political Stability in Japan, 1949–1986* (Princeton: Princeton University Press, 1988).

Calder, K. E., *Strategic Capitalism: Public Policy and Private Purpose in Japanese Industrial Finance* (Princeton: Princeton University Press, 1993).

Calhoun, J., *A Disquisition on Government and Selections from the Discourse on the Constitution* (Indianapolis: Hackett, 1995).

Caenegem, R. C. van, *An Historical Introduction to Western Constitutional Law* (Cambridge: Cambridge University Press, 1995).

Carothers, T., 'The end of the transition paradigm', *Journal of Democracy*, 13: 1 (2002), 5–21.

Carr, R., *Spain 1809–1939* (Oxford: Clarendon Press, 1966).

Cavatorta, F., 'The role of the Northern League in transforming the Italian political system: from economic federalism to ethnic politics and back', *Contemporary Politics*, 7: 1 (2001), 27–40.

Chadda, M., *Ethnicity, Security and Separatism in India* (New York: Columbia University Press, 1997).

Chesterman, S., M. Ignatieff and R. Thakur, *Making States Work: State Failure and the Crisis of Governance* (New York: United Nations Press, 2005).

Clapham, C., 'Sovereignty and the third world state', *Political Studies*, 47: 3 (1999), 522–37.

Claude, I. N., *National Minorities: an International Problem* (Cambridge, MA: Harvard University Press, 1935).

Conybeare, J., *US Foreign Economic Policy and the International Capital Markets: the Case of Capital Export Controls, 1963–74* (New York: Garland, 1988).

Cooper, R. N., *Economic Stabilisation and Debt in Developing Countries* (Cambridge, MA: MIT Press, 1992).

Corbridge, S. and J. Harriss, *Reinventing India: Liberalisation, Hindu Nationalism and Popular Democracy* (Cambridge: Polity Press, 2001).

Costigilio, F., *France and the United States: the Cold Alliance since World War II* (New York: Twayne, 1992).

Cowling, M., *The Impact of Hitler: British Politics and British Policy 1933–1940* (Cambridge: Cambridge University Press, 1975).

Cox, M., 'American power before and after 11 September: dizzy with success?', *Review of International Affairs*, 78: 2 (2002), 261–76.

Cox, M., *US Foreign Policy after the Cold War: Superpower Without a Mission?* (London: Pinter-Royal Institute of International Affairs, 1995).

Crick, B., 'Introduction' to N. Machiavelli, *The Discourses* (London: Penguin, 1970).

Cumings, B., 'The origins and development of the northeast Asian political economy: industrial sector, product cycles and political consequences', *International Organisation*, 38: 1 (1984), 1–40.

Daadler, I. H., *Getting to Dayton: the Making of American Bosnia Policy* (Washington, DC: Brookings Institution Press, 2000).

Dahl, R., *Democracy and its Critics* (New Haven: Yale University Press, 1989).

Dangerfield, G., *The Strange Death of Liberal England* (London: Serif, 1997).

Davies, N., *Heart of Europe: a Short History of Poland* (Oxford: Oxford University Press, 1984).

Dell, E., *A Hard Pounding: Politics and Economic Crisis 1974–1976* (Oxford: Oxford University Press, 1991).

Dente, B., 'Sub-national governments in the long Italian transition', *West European Politics*, 20: 1 (1997), 176–93.

Destler, I., *American Trade Politics*, 4th edn (Washington, DC: Institute for International Economics, 2005).

Destler, I. and P. J. Balint, *The New Politics of American Trade: Trade, Labour, and the Environment* (Washington, DC: Institute for International Economics).

Diamond, L., *Developing Democracy: Towards Consolidation* (Baltimore: Johns Hopkins University Press, 1999).

Diamond, L. and M. F. Plattner (eds), *Economic Reform and Democracy* (Baltimore: Johns Hopkins University Press, 1995).

Doner, R., 'Japanese foreign investment and the creation of a Pacific Asia region', in J. A. Frankel and M. Kahler (eds), *Regionalism and Rivalry: Japan and the United States in Pacific Asia* (Chicago: Chicago University Press, 1993).

Dower, J., 'Occupied Japan and the cold war in Asia', in A. Gordon, *Japan in War and Peace: Essays on History, Race and Culture* (London: Harper Collins, 1995).

Dower, J., 'Peace and democracy in two systems', in *Post-War Japan as History* (Berkeley: University of California Press, 1993), 3–33.

Dunn, J., *Setting the People Free: the Story of Democracy* (New York: Atlantic, 2005)

Dyson, K., *Elusive Union: the Process of Economic and Monetary Union in Europe* (London: Longman, 1994).

Dyson, K. and K. Featherstone, *The Road to Maastricht* (Oxford: Oxford University Press, 1999).

Eckes, A., *A Search for Solvency: Bretton Woods and the International Monetary System 1941–1971* (Austin: University of Texas Press, 1975).

Economist, 'Blaming the pilot: Brazil's Cardoso under fire', 6 February 1999.

Economist, 'Diminishing returns', 8 March 2001.

Economist, 'Lionheart to the rescue', 18 April 2002.

Economist, 'The non-performing country', 7 March 2002.

Eichengreen, B., *Globalising Capital: a History of the International Monetary System* (Princeton: Princeton University Press, 1998).

Eisenberg, C. W., *Drawing the Line: the American Decision to Divide Germany, 1944–49* (Cambridge: Cambridge University Press, 1996).

Epstein, L., *British Politics in the Suez Crisis* (London: Pall Mall Press, 1961).

Feith, H., *The Decline of Constitutional Democracy in Indonesia* (Ithaca: Cornell University Press, 1968).

Feldstein, M., 'Refocusing the IMF', *Foreign Affairs*, 77: 2 (1998), 20–33.

Ferguson, N., *Colossus: the Rise and Fall of the American Empire* (London: Allen Lane, 2004).

Fishlow, A., 'Brazilian economic development in long-term perspective', *American Economic Review*, 70: 2 (1980), 102–8.

Fletcher, G., *Our Secret Constitution: How Lincoln Redefined American Democracy* (New York: Oxford University Press, 2001).

Flynn, P., *Brazil: A Political Analysis* (London: Benn, 1978).

Frankel, F., *India's Political Economy 1947–77: the Gradual Revolution* (Princeton: Princeton University Press, 1978).

Frieden, J., *Global Capitalism: its Fall and Rise in the Twentieth Century* (New York: W. W. Norton, 2006).

Friedman, T. L., *The Lexus and the Olive Tree* (New York: Farrar, Straus and Giroux, 1999).

Fukuyama, F., *State Building: Governance and World Order* (London: Profile Books, 2005).

Funabashi, F., *Managing the Dollar: from the Plaza to the Louvre*, 2nd edn (Washington, DC: Institute for International Economics, 1989).

Gamble, A., *The Free Economy and the Strong State: the Politics of Thatcherism*, 2nd edn (Basingstoke: Macmillan, 1994).

Gardner, R., *Sterling–Dollar Diplomacy in Current Perspective: the Origins and Prospects of our International Order* (New York: Columbia University Press, 1980).

Garton-Ash, T., *In Europe's Name: Germany and the Divided Continent* (New York: Random House, 1993).

George, S., *An Awkward Partner: Britain in the European Community*, 3rd edn (Oxford: Oxford University Press, 1998).

Giavazzi, F. and A. Giovannini, *Limiting Exchange Rate Flexibility: the European Monetary System* (Cambridge, MA: MIT Press, 1989).

Gilbert, M., *The Italian Revolution: the End of Democracy, Italian Style?* (Boulder, CO: Westview, 1995).

Ginsborg, P., *A History of Contemporary Italy: Society and Politics 1943–1988* (London: Penguin, 1990).

Ginsborg, P., *Italy and its Discontents: Family, Civil Society, State 1980–2001* (London: Allen Lane, 2002).

Glenny, M., *The Balkans: Nationalism, War and the Great Powers* (London: Granta Books, 1999).

Godechot, J., 'The new concept of nation and its diffusion in Europe', in O. Dann and D. Dinwiddy, *Nationalism in the Age of the French Revolution* (London: Hambledon Press, 1988).

Goldstein, J., 'The United States and world trade: hegemony by proxy', in T. C. Lawton, J. N. Rosenau and A. C. Verdun (eds), *Strange Power: Shaping the Parameters of International Relations and International Political Economy* (Aldershot: Ashgate, 2000).

González, F. E. and D., King, 'The state and democratisation: the United States in comparative perspective', *British Journal of Political Science*, 34: 2 (2004), 193–210.

Gordon, B., *America's Trade Follies: Turning Economic Leadership into Strategic Weakness* (London: Routledge, 2001).

Gros, D. and N. Thygesen, *European Monetary Integration from the European Monetary System to the European Monetary Union*, 2nd edn (London: Longman, 1997).

Guarnieri, C., 'The judiciary in the Italian political crisis', *West European Politics*, 20: 1 (1997), 157–75.

Gupta, A., 'The political economy of post-independence India: a review article', *Journal of Asian Studies*, 48: 4 (1989), 787–97.

Gurr, T. R., 'War, revolution and the growth of the coercive state', *Comparative Political Studies*, 21: 1 (1988), 45–65.

Haggard, S. and R. R. Kaufman, *The Political Economy of Democratic Transitions* (Princeton: Princeton University Press, 1995).

Hagopian, F., *Traditional Politics and Regime Change in Brazil* (Cambridge: Cambridge University Press, 1996).

Hakim, P., 'Dispirited politics', *Journal of Democracy*, 14: 2 (2003), 108–22.

Hall, P., *Governing the Economy: the Politics of State Intervention in Britain and France* (Cambridge: Polity Press, 1986).

Harding, R. and W. E. Paterson (eds), *The Future of the German Economy: an End to the Miracle?* (Manchester: Manchester University Press, 2000).

Harper, J. L., *America and the Reconstruction of Italy, 1945–1948* (Cambridge: Cambridge University Press, 1986).

Hawthorn, G., 'The crisis of southern states', *Political Studies*, 42: special issue (1994), 130–45.

Hawthorn, G., *The Future of Asia and the Pacific* (London: Phoenix, 1998).

Hay, C., 'Globalisation's impact on states', in J. Ravenhill (ed.), *Global Political Economy* (Oxford: Oxford University Press, 2005).

Heiber, H., *The Weimar republic*, trans. W. E. Yuill (Oxford: Blackwell, 1993).

Helleiner, E., *States and the Re-Emergence of Global Finance: from Bretton Woods to the 1990s* (Ithaca: Cornell University Press, 1994).

Heller, F. H. and J. R. Gillingham (eds), *The United States and the Integration of Europe* (New York: St Martin's Press, 1996).

Henning, R. C., *Currencies and Politics in the United States, Germany and Japan* (Washington, DC: Institute for International Economics, 1994).

Hess, G. R., *The United States' Emergence as a Southeast Asian Power 1940–1950* (New York: Columbia University Press, 1987).

Hewlett, S. A., *The Cruel Dilemmas of Development: Twentieth Century Brazil* (New York: Basic Books, 1980).

Hill, H., *The Indonesian Economy in Crisis: Causes, Consequences and Lessons* (New York: St Martin's Press, 1999).

Hill, H., *The Indonesian Political Economy*, 2nd edn (Cambridge: Cambridge University Press, 2000).

Hirschman, A. O., *A Bias for Hope: Essays on Development in Latin America* (New Haven: Yale University Press, 1971).

Hobbes, T., *Leviathan* (Cambridge: Cambridge University Press, 1996).

Hobbes, T., *On the Citizen*, trans. M. Silverthorne (Cambridge: Cambridge University Press, 1998).

Hobsbawm, E., *Nations and Nationalism since 1780: Programme, Myth, Reality* (Cambridge: Cambridge University Press, 1992).

Hoffman, S., 'Gaullism by any other name', *Foreign Policy*, 57 (Winter 1984–85), 38–57.

Hoffman, S., 'French dilemmas and strategies in the new Europe', in R. Keohane, J. Nye and S. Hoffman (eds), *After the Cold War: International Institutions and State Strategies in Europe, 1989–1991* (Cambridge, MA: Harvard University Press, 1993).

Hollerman, L., *Japan Disincorporated: the Economic Liberalisation Process* (Stanford, CA: Hoover Institution Press, 1988).

Hont, I., *Jealousy of Trade: International Competition and the Nation-State in Historical Perspective* (Cambridge, MA: Harvard University Press, 2005).

Horsefield, J., *The International Monetary Fund, 1945–1965*, 3 vols. (Washington, DC: IMF, 1969).

Howarth, D., *The French Road to European Monetary Union* (London: Palgrave, 2000).

Hull, C., *The Memoirs of Cordell Hull* (New York: Macmillan, 1948).

Hume, D., 'Of public credit', in *Political Essays*, ed. K. Haakonssen (Cambridge: Cambridge University Press, 1994).

Huntington, S., *The Third Wave: Democratisation in the Late Twentieth Century* (Norman: University of Oklahoma Press, 1991).

Huntington, S., 'After twenty years: the future of the third wave', *Journal of Democracy*, 8: 4 (1997), 3–12.

Jackson, R., *Quasi-States: Sovereignty, International Relations and the Third World* (Cambridge: Cambridge University Press, 1990).

Jaffrelot, C., *The Hindu Nationalist Movement and Indian Politics: 1925 to the 1990s* (London: Hurst and Co., 1996).

James, H., *The Roman Predicament: How the Rules of International Order Create the Politics of Empire* (Princeton: Princeton University Press, 2006).

Jenkins, R., *Democratic Politics and Economic Reform in India* (Cambridge: Cambridge University Press, 1999).

Joffe, J., *The Limited Partnership: Europe, the United States and the Burdens of Alliance* (Cambridge, MA: Ballinger, 1987).

Joffe, J., 'The foreign policy of the German Federal Republic', in R. C. Macridis (ed.), *Foreign Policy in World Politics* (Englewood Cliffs, NJ: Prentice-Hall, 1989).

Johnson, C., *MITI and the Japanese Miracle: the Growth of Industrial Policy, 1925–1975* (Stanford, CA: Stanford University Press, 1982).

Johnson, C., *Japan, Who Governs? The Rise of the Developmental State* (New York: Norton, 1995).

Joll, J. (ed.), *The Decline of the Third Republic* (London: Chatto and Windus, 1959).

Joshi, V. and I. M. D. Little, *India: Macro-Economics and Political Economy 1964–1991* (Washington, DC: The World Bank, 1994).

Judah, T., *Kosovo: War and Revenge*, 2nd edn (London: Yale Note Bene, 2002).

Kahil, R., *Inflation and Economic Development in Brazil* (Oxford: Clarendon Press, 1973).

Kahler, M., 'The politics of international debt', *International Organisation*, 39: 3 (1985), 357–82.

Kahler, M., 'The United States and the International Monetary Fund: declining influence or declining interests?', in M. P. Karns and K. A. Mingst (eds), *The United States and Multi-Lateral Institutions: Patterns of Changing Instrumentality and Influence* (Boston: Unwin Hyman, 1990).

Kaiser, W., *Using Europe, Abusing the Europeans: Britain and European Integration 1945–1963* (London: Macmillan, 1996).

Kaplan, J. and G. Schleiminger, *The European Payments Union: Financial Diplomacy in the 1950s* (Oxford: Clarendon Press, 1989).

Katzenstein, P. J., *Small States in World Markets: Industrial Policy in Europe* (Ithaca: Cornell University Press, 1985).

Kavanagh, D., *The Reordering of British Politics: Politics after Thatcher* (Oxford: Oxford University Press, 1997).

Kaviraj, S., 'Crisis of the nation-state in India', *Political Studies*, 42: special issue (1994), 115–229.

Kennedy, P., *The Realities Behind Diplomacy: Background Influences on British External Policy, 1865–1980* (London: Fontana Press, 1985).

Kent, J., *British Imperial Strategy and the Origins of the Cold War* (Leicester: Leicester University Press, 1994).

Kershaw, I., *The Nazi Dictatorship: Problems and Perspectives* (London: Edward Arnold, 1985).

Khilnani, S., *The Idea of India* (London: Hamish Hamilton, 1997).

Kindleberger, C., *The World in Depression 1929–1939* (Berkeley: University of California Press, 1973).

Kingsbury, D., *Power Politics and the Indonesian Military* (London: Routledge, 2003).

Kingstone, P. R., *Crafting Coalitions for Reform: Business Preferences, Political Institutions and Neo-Liberal Reform* (University Park, PA: Pennsylvania State University Press, 1999).

Kissinger, H., *Diplomacy* (London: Touchstone, 1994).

Knock, T. J., *To End All Wars: Woodrow Wilson and the Quest for a New World Order* (Oxford: Oxford University Press, 1992).

Kocs, S., *Autonomy or Power? The Franco-German Relationship and Europe's Strategic Choices, 1955–1995* (Westport, CT: Praeger, 1995).

Kohli, A. (ed.), *India's Democracy: an Analysis of Changing State–Society Relations* (Princeton: Princeton University Press, 1988).

Kohli, A., *Democracy and Discontent: India's Growing Crisis of Governability* (Cambridge: Cambridge University Press, 1990).

Kosawa, M., 'The international economic policy of Japan', in R. Scalapino (ed.), *The Foreign Policy of Modern Japan* (Berkeley and Los Angeles: University of California Press, 1977).

Krasner, S., 'United States' commercial and monetary policy: unraveling the paradox of external strength and internal weakness', in P. Katzenstein (ed.), *Between Power and Plenty: Foreign Economic Policies of Advanced Industrial States* (Madison: Wisconsin University Press, 1978).

Krasner, S., *Sovereignty: Organised Hypocrisy* (Princeton: Princeton University Press, 1999).

Krasner, S., 'The case for shared sovereignty', *Journal of Democracy*, 16: 1 (2005), 69–83.

Kreile, M., 'West Germany: the dynamics of expansion', in P. Katzenstein (ed.), *Between Power and Plenty: Foreign Economic Policies of Advanced Industrial States* (Madison: Wisconsin University Press, 1978).

Krüger, P., 'The Federal Republic as a nation-state', in J. S. Brady, B. Crawford and S. E. Wiliarty, *The Post-War Transformation of German Democracy, Prosperity and Nationhood* (Ann Arbor: University of Michigan Press, 1999).

Kuisel, R., *Seducing the French* (Berkeley: University of California Press, 1993).

Lampe, J. R., *Yugoslavia as History: Twice there was a Country* (Cambridge: Cambridge University Press, 1996).

Lankowski, C., 'Modell Deutschland and the international regionalisation of the West German state in the 1970s', in A. Markovits (ed.), *The Political Economy of West Germany: Modell Deutschland* (New York: Praeger, 1982).

Leffler, M. P., *A Preponderance of Power: National Security, the Truman Administration and the Cold War* (Stanford: Stanford University Press, 1992).

Leffler, M. P., *The Struggle for Germany and the Origins of the Cold War* (Washington, DC: German Historical Institute, 1996).

Levi, M., *Consent, Dissent and Patriotism* (Cambridge: Cambridge University Press, 1997).

Linz, J., 'Early state building and late peripheral nationalisms against the state: the case of Spain', in S. N. Eisenstadt and S. Rokkan (eds), *Building States and Nations: Analysis and Data across Three Worlds* (Beverly Hills: Sage, 1973).

Linz, J., 'From great hopes to civil war: the breakdown of democracy in Spain', in J. Linz and A. Stepan (eds), *The Breakdown of Democratic Regimes: Europe* (Baltimore: Johns Hopkins University Press, 1978).

Linz, J. and A. Stepan (eds), *The Breakdown of Democratic Regimes* (Baltimore: Johns Hopkins University Press, 1975).

Linz, J. and A. Stepan (eds), *Problems of Democratic Transition and Consolidation: Southern Europe, South America and Post-Communist Europe* (Baltimore: Johns Hopkins University Press, 1996).

Lipset, S., *Political Man: the Social Bases of Politics* (New York: Doubleday, 1960).

Lissakers, K., *Banks, Borrowers and the Establishment: a Revisionist Account of the International Debt Crisis* (New York: Basic Books, 1991).

Little, I. M. D., *Boom, Crisis and Adjustment: the Macroeconomic Experience of Developing Countries* (New York: Oxford University Press for the World Bank, 1993).

Ludlow, P., *The Making of the European Monetary System* (London: Butterworths, 1982).

Luebbert, G. M., *Liberalism, Fascism or Social Democracy: Social Classes and the Political Origins of Regimes in Inter-War Europe* (Oxford: Oxford University Press, 1991).

Lundestad, G., *'Empire' by Integration: the United States and European Integration, 1945–1997* (Oxford: Oxford University Press, 1998).

Lynch, F. B. M., 'Resolving the paradox of the Monnet Plan: national and international planning in French reconstruction', *Economic History Review*, 37: 2 (1984), 229–43.

Macartney, C. A., *National States and National Minorities* (London: Oxford University Press, 1934).

Macaulay, Lord, 'Hallam's constitutional history', in *Critical and Historical Essays* (London: Longmans, Green, and Co., 1877).

Mack-Smith, D., *Italy: a Modern History*, rev. edn (Ann Arbor: University of Michigan Press, 1969).

Madison, J., A. Hamilton and J. Jay, *The Federalist and the Letters of Brutus* (Cambridge: Cambridge University Press, 2003).

Maier, C. S., 'The vulnerabilities of inter-war Germany', *Journal of Modern History*, 56: 1 (1984), 89–99.

Maier, C. S., *Recasting Bourgeois Europe: Stabilisation in France, Germany, and Italy in the Decade after World War I* (Princeton: Princeton University Press, 1988).

Maier, C. S. and D. S. White, *The Thirteenth of May: the Advent of De Gaulle's Republic* (New York: Oxford University Press, 1968).

Malley, M., 'Regions: centralisation and resistance', in D. K. Emmerson (ed.), *Indonesia Beyond Suharto: Polity, Economy, Society, Transition* (Armonk, NY: M. E. Sharpe, 1999).

Mancino, F., 'The Italians in Europe', *Foreign Affairs*, 79: 2 (2000), 122–35.

Mandelbaum, M., *The Ideas that Conquered the World: Peace, Democracy, and Free Markets in the Twenty-First Century* (New York: Public Affairs, 2002).

Mann, R., *Economic Crisis in Indonesia: the Full Story* (Toronto: Gateway Books, 1998).

Manor, J., 'How and why liberal representative politics emerged in India', *Political Studies*, 38: 1 (1990), 20–38.

Marquand, D., *The Unprincipled Society: New Demands and Old Politics* (London: Jonathan Cape, 1988).

Marsh, D., *The Bundesbank: the Bank that Rules Europe* (London: Heinemann, 1992).

Marsh, D., *Germany and Europe: the Crisis of Unity*, rev. edn (London: Mandarin, 1995).

Marsh, P., *The Discipline of Popular Government: Lord Salisbury's Domestic Statecraft* (Aldershot: Gregg Revivals, 1978).

Martins, L., 'The "liberalisation" of the authoritarian rule in Brazil', in G. O'Donnell, P. Schmitter and L. Whitehead (eds), *Transitions from Authoritarian Rule: Latin America* (Baltimore: Johns Hopkins University Press, 1986).

Mastanduno, M., 'Models, markets, and power: political economy and Asia Pacific, 1989–1999', *Review of International Studies*, 26: 4 (2000), 493–507.

Matinuddin, K., *The Nuclearisation of South Asia* (Oxford: Oxford University Press, 2002).

Macfarlane, S. N., *Superpower Rivalry and Third World Radicalism: the Idea of National Liberation* (London: Croom Helm, 1985).

Mayer, A., *Political Origins of the New Diplomacy*, 2nd edn (New York: Meridan Books, 1964).

Mayer, F., *Adenauer and Kennedy: a Study in German-American Relations, 1961–63* (London: Macmillan, 1996).

Mazower, M., *Dark Continent: Europe's Twentieth Century* (London: Allen Lane, 1998).

Mcdonough, P., *Power and Ideology in Brazil* (Princeton: Princeton University Press, 1981).

Mckay, D. and H. M. Scott, *The Rise of the Great Powers 1648–1815* (London: Longman, 1983).

Meinecke, F., *Machiavellism: the Doctrine of Raison D'état and its Place in Modern History*, trans. D. Scott (London: Transaction Publishers, 1998).

Milward, A. S., *The Reconstruction of Western Europe 1945–51* (London: Methuen, 1984).

Mizuno, K., 'Indonesian politics and the issue of justice in East Timor', in H. Soesastro, A. Smith and M. L. Han (eds), *Governance in Indonesia* (Singapore: Institute of South Asian Studies, 2003).

Moggridge, D. (ed.), *The Collected Writings of John Maynard Keynes, Volume VII: The General Theory of Employment, Interest and Money* (London: Macmillan, 1973).

Moggridge, D. (ed.), *The Collected Writings of John Maynard Keynes, Volume XXV, Activities 1940–1944, Shaping the Post-War World: the Clearing Union* (London: Macmillan, 1980).

Mommsen, W., *Imperial Germany, 1867–1918: Politics, Culture and Society in an Authoritarian State*, trans. R. Deveson (London: Arnold, 1995).

Mosca, G., *The Ruling Class: Elements of the Science of Politics*, ed. A. Livingston, trans. H. D. Kahn (New York: McGraw-Hill, 1939).

Moura, A. R., 'Stabilisation policy as a game of mutual distrust: the Brazilian experience in post-1985 civilian governments', in M. D'Alva and G. Kinzo, *Brazil: the Challenges of the 1990s* (London: British Academic Press, 1993).

Mouré, K., *Managing the Franc Poincaré: Economic Understanding and Political Constraint in French Monetary Policy, 1928–1936* (Cambridge: Cambridge University Press, 1991).

Murphy, R. T., 'Japan's Economic Crisis', *New Left Review*, 1 (2000), 25–52.

Narlikar, A. and D. Tussie, 'The G20 at the Cancun ministerial: developing countries and their evolving coalitions in the WTO', *World Economy*, 27: 7 (2004), 947–66.

Nayar, R. B., *Globalisation and Nationalism: the Changing Balance in India's Economic Policy* (New Delhi: Sage, 2001).

Nayar, R. B. and T. V. Paul, *India in the World: Searching for Major-Power Status* (New Delhi: Sage, 2001).

Newman, K. J., *European Democracy Between the Wars*, trans. K. Morgan (London: Allen and Unwin, 1970).

Nicholls, A., *Freedom with Responsibility: the Social Market in Germany 1918–1963* (Oxford: Oxford University Press, 1994).

Ninkovich, F., *The Wilsonian Century: US Foreign Policy since 1900* (Chicago: University of Chicago Press, 1999).

Notermans, T., *Money, Markets, and the State: Social Democratic Economic Policies since 1918* (Cambridge: Cambridge University Press, 2000).

Nurske, R., *International Currency Experience: Lessons of the Inter-War Period* (Geneva: League of Nations, 1944).

O'Donnell, G., 'On the state, democratisation, and some conceptual problems: a Latin American view with some glances at some post-communist countries', *World Development*, 21 (August 1993), 1355–69.

O'Donnell, G., 'Illusions about consolidation', *Journal of Democracy*, 7: 2 (1996), 34–51.

Okimoto, D., *Between MITI and the Market* (Stanford: Stanford University Press, 1986).

Oppenheim, H., 'Why oil prices go up: the past: we pushed them', *Foreign Policy*, 25 (Winter 1976–77), 24–57.

O'Rourke, K., *Reformasi: The Struggle for Power in Post-Soeharto Indonesia* (Crows Nest, NSW: Allen and Unwin, 2002).

Osiander, A., 'International relations and the Westphalian myth', *International Organisation*, 55: 2 (2001), 251–87.

Palmer, N. D., *The United States and India: the Dimensions of Influence* (New York: Praeger, 1984).

Panizza, F. and A. Barahona de Brito, 'The politics of human rights in democratic Brazil: a lei não pega', *Democratisation*, 5: 4 (1998), 20–51.

Parrish, S., 'When the president governs alone: the *decretazo* in Argentina', in J. M. Carey and M. Soberg Shugart, *Executive Decree Authority* (Cambridge: Cambride Univeristy Press, 1998), 33–61.

Pauly, L., *Regulatory Politics in Japan: the Case of Foreign Banking* (Ithaca: Cornell University Press, 1987).

Paxton, R. O. and N. Wahl (eds), *De Gaulle and the United States* (Oxford: Berg, 1994).

Pereira, L. C. B., *Development and Crisis Within Brazil, 1930–1983* (Boulder, CO: Westview Press, 1984).

Pereira, L. C. B., J. M. Maravall and A. Przeworski, *Economic Reform in New Democracies: a Social Democratic Approach* (Cambridge: Cambridge University Press, 2003).

Pereira, L. V., 'Towards the common market of the south: Mercosur's origins, evolution and challenges', in R. Roett, *Mercosur: Regional Integration, World Markets* (London: Lynne Rienner, 1999).

Pempel, T. J., 'Japanese foreign economic policy: the domestic bases for international behaviour', in P. Katzenstein (ed.), *Between Power and Plenty: Foreign Economic Policies of Advanced Industrial States* (Madison: Wisconsin University Press, 1978).

Pempel, T. J., 'From exporter to investor: Japan's foreign economic policy', in G. Curtis, *Japan's Foreign Policy: after the Cold War Coping with Change* (Armonk, NY: M. E. Sharpe, 1993).

Plumb, J. H., *The Growth of Political Stability in England 1675–1725* (London: Macmillan, 1967).

Pocock, J. G. A., *The Machiavellian Moment: Florentine Political Thought and the Atlantic Republican Political Tradition* (Princeton: Princeton University Press, 1975).

Preeg, E. A., *Traders in a Brave New World* (Chicago: Chicago University Press, 1995).

Prosner, A., 'Italy: dependence and political fragmentation', in P. Katzenstein (ed.), *Between Power and Plenty: Foreign Economic Policies of Advanced Industrial States* (Madison: Wisconsin University Press, 1978).

Przeworski, A., *Democracy and the Market* (Cambridge: Cambridge University Press, 1991).

Przeworski, A. (ed.), *Sustainable Democracy* (Cambridge: Cambridge University Press, 1995).

Przeworski, A., 'Minimalist conception of democracy: a defence', in I. Shapiro (ed.), *Democracy's Value* (Cambridge: Cambridge University Press, 1999).

Przeworski, A., 'Democracy and economic development', in E. D. Mansfield and R. Sissons (eds), *The Evolution of Political Knowledge* (Columbus: Ohio State University Press, 2004).

Przeworski, A., et al., 'What makes democracies endure?', *Journal of Democracy*, 7: 1 (1996), 39–55.

Przeworski, A., S. C. Stokes and B. Manin, 'Introduction', in A. Przeworski, S. C. Stokes and B. Manin, *Democracy, Accountability and Representation* (Cambridge: Cambridge University Press, 1999).

Pyle, K., *The Japanese Question: Power and Purpose in a New Era* (Washington, DC: American Enterprise Institute, 1992).

Rickliefs, C., *A History of Modern Indonesia* (London: Macmillan, 1981).

Rioux, J. P., *The Fourth Republic 1944–1958*, trans. G. Rogers (Cambridge: Cambridge University Press, 1987).

Rocha, G. M., 'Neo-dependency in Brazil', *New Left Review*, 16 (2002), 5–33.

Roett, R., *Politics in a Patrimonial Society*, 3rd edn (New York: Praeger, 1978).

Romero, F., 'Migration as an issue in European interdependence and integration: the case of Italy', in A. S. Milward, F. M. B. Lynch, F. Romero, R. Ranieria and V. Sörensen, *The Frontier of National Sovereignty: History and Theory 1945–1992* (London: Routledge, 1993), 33–48.

Rosenbluth, F. M., *Financial Politics in Contemporary Japan* (Ithaca: Cornell University Press, 1989).

Rothschild, J., *East-Central Europe between the Two World Wars* (Seattle: University of Washington Press, 1974).

Rueschemeyer, D., E. H. Stephens and J. D. Stephens, *Capitalist Development and Democracy* (Chicago: Chicago University Press, 1992).

Sachs, J. D., A. Varshney and N. Bajpai, *India in the Era of Economic Reform* (Oxford: Oxford University Press, 1999).

Sala, V. D., 'Maastricht to modernisation: EMU and the Italian social state', in A. Martin and G. Ross (eds), *Euros and Europeans* (Cambridge: Cambridge University Press, 2004).

Samuels, R., *The Business of the Japanese State* (Ithaca: Cornell University Press, 1986).

Sassoon, D., *Contemporary Italy: Economics, Society, and Politics since 1945*, 2nd edn (London: Longman, 1997).

Scammell, W. M., *International Monetary Policy: Bretton Woods and After* (London: Macmillan, 1975).

Schaller, M., *The American Occupation of Japan: the Origins of the Cold War in Asia* (New York: Oxford University Press, 1985).

Scharpf, F., *Crisis and Choice in European Social Democracy*, trans. R. Crowley and F. Thompson (Ithaca: Cornell University Press, 1991).

Schmitt, C., *The Concept of the Political*, trans. T. Strong (Chicago: Chicago University Press, 1996).

Schmitter, P. and T. Karl, 'What democracy is . . . and is not', *Journal of Democracy*, 2: 3 (1991), 75–88.

Schumpeter, J., *Capitalism, Socialism and Democracy* (London: Routledge, 1994).

Seton-Watson, C., *Italy from Liberalism to Fascism 1870–1925* (London: Meuthen, 1967).

Seton-Watson, H., *Eastern Europe between the Wars* (Cambridge: Cambridge University Press, 1962).

Sfikas, T., *The British Labour Government and the Greek Civil War, 1945–1949: the Imperialism of Non-Intervention* (Keele: Keele University Press, 1994).

Siebert, H., *The German Economy Beyond the Social Market* (Princeton: Princeton University Press, 2005).

Sieyès, E. J., *What is the Third Estate?*, trans. M. Blondel and ed. S. E. Finer (London: Pall Mall Press, 1963).

Simmons, B., *Who Adjusts?: Domestic Sources of Foreign Economic Policy During the Interwar Years* (Princeton: Princeton University Press, 1994).

Skidelsky, R., *John Maynard Keynes: Volume Three, Fighting for Britain 1937–1946* (London: Macmillan, 2000).

Skidmore, T. E., *Politics in Brazil 1930–1964: an Experiment in Democracy* (New York: Oxford University Press, 1967).

Skinner, Q., *The Foundations of Modern Political Thought, Volumes One and Two* (Cambridge: Cambridge University Press, 1978).

Smith, D., *The Rise and Fall of Monetarism* (Harmondsworth: Penguin, 1986).

Smith, G., *Democracy in West Germany: Parties and Politics in the Federal Republic*, 3rd edn (Aldershot: Dartmouth, 1990).

Snyder, J., *From Voting to Violence: Democratisation and Nationalist Conflict* (New York: W. W. Norton and Company, 2000).

Soesastro, H., A. Smith and M. L. Han (eds), *Governance in Indonesia* (Singapore: Institute of South Asian Studies, 2003).

Sousa, A. de, 'Cardoso and the struggle for reform in Brazil', *Journal of Democracy*, 10: 3 (1999), 49–63.

Souza, C., *Constitutional Engineering in Brazil: the Politics of Federalism and Decentralisation* (Basingstoke: Macmillan, 1997).

Stampp, K., *The Era of Reconstruction 1865–1877* (New York: Knopf, 1975).

Steinmo, S., *Taxation and Democracy: Swedish, British and American Approaches to Financing the Modern State* (London: Yale University Press, 1993).

Stepan, A., *The Military in Politics: Changing Patterns in Brazil* (Princeton: Princeton University Press, 1971).

Stepan, A., 'Political leadership and regime breakdown: Brazil', in J. J. Linz and A. Stepan (eds), *The Breakdown of Democratic Regimes in Latin America* (Baltimore: Johns Hopkins University Press, 1978).

Stepan, A. (ed.), *Democratising Brazil: Problems of Transition and Consolidation* (New York: Oxford University Press, 1989).

Stern, F., 'The new democracies in crisis in inter-war Europe', in A. Hadenius (ed.), *Democracy's Victory and Crisis in Inter-War Europe* (Cambridge: Cambridge University Press, 1997).

Stern, F., 'Bethmann Hollweg and the war: the bounds of responsibility', in *The Failure of Illiberalism: Essays on the Political Culture of Modern Germany* (New York: Columbia University Press, 1992).

Stone, N., *Europe Transformed 1878–1919* (Oxford: Blackwell Publishers, 1999).

Strange, S., *International Monetary Relations: Volume Two of International Economic Relations of the Western World 1959–1971* (London: Oxford University Press, 1976).

Strange, S., *The Retreat of the State* (Cambridge: Cambridge University Press, 1996).

Sukma, R., 'Secessionist challenge in Aceh', in H. Soesastron, A. L. Smith and H. M. Ling (eds), *Governance in Indonesia: Challenges Facing the Megawati Presidency* (Singapore: Institute of Southeast Asian Studies, 2003).

Sundhaussen, U., *The Road to Power: Indonesian Military Politics 1945–1967* (Kuala Lumpur: Oxford University Press).

Takatoshi, I., 'US political pressure and economic liberalisation in east Asia', in J. A. Frankel and M. Kahler (eds), *Regionalism and Rivalry: Japan and the United States in Asia-Pacific* (Chicago: Chicago University Press, 1994).

Terzian, P., *OPEC: the Inside Story* (London: Zed Books, 1985).

Thayer, N. B., 'Japanese foreign policy in the Nakasone years', in G. Curtis (ed.), *Japan's Foreign Policy: After the Cold War, Coping with Change* (Armonk, NY: M. E. Sharpe, 1993).

Thomas, H., *The Suez Affair*, 3rd edn (London: Weidenfeld and Nicolson, 1986).

Thompson, H., *The British Conservative Government and the European Exchange Rate Mechanism* (London: Pinter, 1996).

Thompson, J. A., 'Americans and their century', in P. Maitland, *The Future of the Past: Big Questions in History* (London: Pimlico, 2002).

Thompson, J. A., *Woodrow Wilson* (London: Longman, 2002).

Thorne, C., *The Approach of War* (London: Macmillan, 1982).

Thorp, R., 'A reappraisal of the origins of import-substituting industrialisation 1930–1950', *Journal of Latin American Studies*, 24: supplement (1992), 181–95.

Thucydides, *The Peloponnesian War*, trans. T. Hobbes (Chicago: University of Chicago Press, 1989).

Tilly, C., *Coercion, Capital and European States, AD 990–1990* (Oxford: Blackwell, 1990).

Tingas, N. and P. P. Miguel, 'Capital flows and economic policy in Brazil', in B. N. Ghosh (ed.), *Global Financial Crises and Reforms: Cases and Caveats* (London: Routledge, 2001).

Tombs, R., *France 1814–1914* (London: Longman, 1996).

Tomlinson, B. R., *The Economy of Modern India: the New Cambridge History of India* (Cambridge: Cambridge University Press, 1993).

Tomlinson, J., *Democratic Socialism and Economic Policy: the Attlee Years 1945–1951* (Cambridge: Cambridge University Press, 1997).

Treverton, G. F., *The Dollar Drain and American Forces in Germany: Managing the Political Economies of Alliance* (Athens, OH: Ohio University Press, 1978).

Tsuru, S., *Japan's Capitalism: Creative Defeat and Beyond* (Cambridge: Cambridge University Press, 1993).

Van Dormael, A., *Bretton Woods: Birth of a Monetary System* (London: Macmillan, 1978).

Vannicelli, P., *Italy, NATO, and the European Community* (Cambridge, MA: Harvard University Centre for International Affairs, 1971).

Wade, R. and F. Veneroso, 'The Asian crisis: the high-debt model versus the Wall Street-Treasury-IMF Complex', *New Left Review*, 228 (1998), 3–23.

Weber, E., *Peasants into Frenchmen: the Modernisation of Rural France, 1870–1914* (London: Chatto and Windus, 1977).

Weber, M., 'The nation-state and economic policy', in *Weber: Political Writings*, ed. R. Speirs and P. Lassman (Cambridge: Cambridge University Press, 1994).

Weber, M., 'Politics as profession and a vocation', in *Weber: Political Writings*, ed. R. Speirs and P. Lassman (Cambridge: Cambridge University Press, 1994).

Weber, M., 'Suffrage and democracy in Germany', in *Weber: Political Writings*, ed. R. Speirs and P. Lassman (Cambridge: Cambridge University Press, 1994).

Weingast, B., 'The political foundations of democracy and the rule of law', *American Political Science Review*, 91: 2 (1997), 245–63.

Weyland, K., *The Politics of Market Reform in Fragile Democracies: Argentina, Brazil, Peru and Venezuela* (Princeton: Princeton University Press, 2002).

Whitehead, L., *Democratisation: Theory and Experience* (Oxford: Oxford University Press, 2002).

Williamson, J., *The Failure of World Monetary Reform, 1971–1974* (Sunbury-on-Thames: Thomas Nelson and Sons, 1977).

Willis, F. R., *Italy Chooses Europe* (Oxford: Oxford University Press, 1971).

Windsor, P., *Germany and the Management of Détente* (London: Chatto and Windus, 1971).

Wolf, M., *Why Globalisation Works* (New Haven: Yale University Press, 2004).

Wolfe, M., *The French Franc between the Wars, 1919–1939* (New York: Columbia University Press, 1951).

Wood, C., *The Bubble Economy: the Japanese Economic Collapse* (Tokyo: Tuttle, 1993).

Wood, R., *From Marshall Plan to Debt Crisis: Foreign Aid and Development Choices in the World Economy* (Berkeley: University of California Press, 1986).

Wurff R., van der, 'Neo-liberalism in Germany', in H. Overbeek, *Restructuring Hegemony in the Global Political Economy: the Rise of Transnational Neo-Liberalsim in the 1980s* (London: Routledge, 1993).

Wynia, G. W., *The Politics of Latin American Development*, 3rd edn (Cambridge: Cambridge University Press, 1990).

Yamamura, K. and Y. Yasuba (eds), *The Political Economy of Japan Vol. 1: the Domestic Transformation* (Stanford: Stanford University Press, 1987).

Zeiler, T. W., *American Trade and Power in the 1960s* (New York: Columbia University Press, 1992).

Zelikow, P. and C. Rice, *Germany Unified and Europe Transformed: a Study in Statecraft* (Cambridge, MA: Harvard University Press, 1995).

Zysman, J., 'The French state in the international economy', in P. Katzenstein (ed.), *Between Power and Plenty: Foreign Economic Policies of Advanced Industrial States* (Madison: Wisconsin University Press, 1978).

Index

Aceh 119, 121, 235–8
Adenauer, Konrad 90–3, 154
Ali, Sastroamidjojo 121
Amato, Guilano 207–8
Andreotti, Giulio 147–8, 161, 170, 207
Argentina 9, 85, 172, 226, 231–2,
    262–3, 265
Asia-Pacific Economic Co-operation
    189
Asian financial crisis 191, 222, 229,
    233, 260, 264
Asian Monetary Fund 217
Attlee, Clement 98
Austria-Hungary 34, 35, 42–3

Balladur, Edouard 185, 203–4
Bank of Japan 94–5, 181, 215, 218
Berlusconi, Silvio 209–11, 261
Bethmann Hollweg, Theobald von 34
Bevin, Ernest 98
Bismarck 30–4, 37, 46
BJP government 220–5, 243, 265–6
Blum, Léon 66–7, 103
Bossi, Umberto 208–9
Brady plan 188, 193
Brandt, Willy 134, 136, 153–4
Brazil
    (1945–64) 12, 15, 85, 123–30,
        137–8, 144–5
    (1973–89) 173–7, 178, 181
    (1990–2001) 226–33, 239, 242–3,
        246
Bretton Woods
    creation of 75–81

end of 131–135
years of 75–138
Brissot, Jacques-Pierre 29–30
Britain
    18th century 22–3, 28–9
    (1815–70) 31
    (1870–1914) 32–5, 37–8
    (1919–39) 44–5, 48–9, 54, 56, 67–9
    (1945–71) 75, 77, 79, 81, 83, 85,
        91, 97–102, 103, 107, 108, 264
    (1973–78) 148, 156, 158–61
    (1979–84) 166, 169, 171–3, 239–42
    (1989–2001) 200, 207, 211–14
Brüning, Heinrich 12, 60–1, 263
Bülow, Bernhard von 33–4
Bundesbank 91, 134, 146, 154–5, 158,
    167–70, 181, 184–6, 195–9, 203,
    212, 254, 261
Bush junior administration 12, 232, 265
Bush senior administration 187–9,
    215, 221

Callaghan, James 160–1, 213
capital controls 78–9, 84, 100, 132,
    135, 146–7, 150, 163, 168, 171,
    217, 222
capital flows 1, 7–8, 13, 115, 62, 77–8,
    135, 150, 153, 164–5, 169, 172–3,
    195, 202, 222, 239, 241–2, 252,
    255, 261, 264–5
Cardoso, Fernando Henrique
    227–33, 239, 263, 266
Carter administration 149, 153–4,
    158, 162, 164

Chamberlain, Neville 65
China 9, 12, 33, 69, 75, 77, 94–5,
    115–16, 134, 144, 152–3, 189,
    191, 217–18, 224, 243, 261, 264–5
Chirac, Jacques 184, 200, 202, 204–5,
    209, 240
Churchill, Winston 70, 75, 97–8
Ciampi, Carlo Azeglio 208
Clinton administration, 189–95, 202,
    215–17, 221–5, 231, 235–7, 265
Cold War 108, 115–6, 125, 128, 134,
    137, 162, 166, 169, 186–8, 192,
    210
Collor, Fernando 226–7, 263–4
constitutions 24, 26, 36–7, 63, 71, 89,
    93, 103, 105, 114, 119, 122, 124,
    144, 176–7, 226–31, 238, 242,
    266
Coty, François 105
Crispi, Francesco 33
Cromwell, Thomas 20
Czechoslovakia 9, 14, 65–6, 70, 86, 191

debt 6–8, 23, 30, 32, 44, 46–8, 51, 56,
    68–9, 95, 98, 102, 122, 148–50,
    156, 162–3, 170, 174–9, 187–8,
    194, 197, 199, 207, 210, 217–20,
    226–43, 261–5
de Gasperi, Alcide 108–11, 171
de Gaulle, Charles 92–3, 100–7 132,
    136–7, 169, 202, 205, 240, 252
d'Estaing, Giscard 107, 155, 168
Delors, Jacques 185
Delors report 185–6
developing countries 85–8, 144–5,
    173, 187–90, 193–5, 239, 242–4,
    262–8
Dini, Lamberto 208
dollar-gold convertibility 107, 131–2,
    134–5, 146
Dulles, John Foster 94
Dutra, Eurico Gaspar 125

East Timor 235–7, 264
Eden, Anthony 99–101

Eisenhower administration 81, 90,
    96, 99–100, 105, 123, 126
England 19–22
Erhard, Ludwig 91–3
European Atomic Energy
    Community 91, 104
European Coal and Steel Community
    81, 90, 104, 110
European Community 158–9, 168–9,
    172, 180–1, 185–6
European Economic Community 91,
    100–1, 104, 106, 110–11, 131
European Union 199–200, 202,
    204–5, 207, 209–13, 240–3, 254,
    257, 260–3
Exchange Rate Mechanism 155,
    157–8, 161, 168–70, 184–6, 198,
    202–3, 206–7, 210, 212–13, 241

Federal Reserve Board 55, 57, 132,
    135, 148–9, 162, 167, 181, 21, 254
Fischer, Joschka 200
France
    16th-17th centuries 19–20
    (1870–1914) 35, 40
    (1919–39) 43, 45, 48–9, 50, 56–60,
        69, 71
    (1945–71) 81, 85, 91–2, 98–9, 102–
        7, 112, 132, 136–7, 145, 252
    (1973–78) 154–6
    (1979–84) 148, 153, 166–9, 255
    (1985–88) 184–86
    (1989–2001) 200–4, 224, 240, 254,
        256, 261
    Louis Napoleon 31
    Louis Philippe 30–1
    Revolution 23, 26–7, 29–30
Franco, General 64–5
Franco, Itamar 227–8, 230–1
Free Trade Area of the Americas
    189–90, 231

Gaillard, Félix 105
Gandhi, Indira 116–17, 137, 178–80,
    220, 224, 252

Gandhi, Rajiv 219–23, 262
General Agreement on Tariffs and
    Trade 87, 131, 147, 180–2, 188–90
Germany
    (1870–1914) 31–5
    (1919–33) 8–9, 12, 42–6, 48, 50–4,
        56, 58–62 64–7, 69–71
    (1945–71) 75, 77, 79–84, 88–93,
        102–4, 107, 110, 112, 131, 134,
        136–8
    (1973–78) 146, 148–9, 151, 153–6,
        157–8, 160–1
    (1979–84) 166–9, 170, 172
    (1985–88) 181, 183–5
    (1989–2001) 193, 195–201, 202–5,
        207, 210–12, 214, 239–41
Giolitti, Giovanni 35, 49, 50, 109
Gladstone, William 33
gold standard 7, 44, 54–5, 57–9, 61–2,
    68
Goulart, João 129–30

Habibie 233–6
Hatta, Mohammad 119–20, 122
Healey, Dennis 159–61
Heath, Edward 158–9, 213
Henri IV 19–20
Henry VII 19
Henry VIII 19–20
Hitler, Adolf 9, 12, 61, 64–7, 69–70
Hobbes, Thomas 21, 46, 257
Hume, David 23, 265
Hungary 48, 65, 66, 70, 191

import substitution 123, 125–7, 130,
    143, 227, 252
India
    (1945–71) 9, 14–15, 97, 113–18,
        119, 133, 137, 144, 252
    (1973–88) 173, 178–80
    (1989–2001) 219–25, 243,
        262–7
Indonesia
    (1945–64) 13, 15, 87, 118–23,
        136–8, 145

    (1989–2001) 191, 233–8, 239, 242,
        252, 263–4, 266–7
International Monetary Fund 78–80,
    99, 128–31, 135, 146–7, 149, 156,
    160, 163, 174–9, 188, 191–4, 217,
    221–2, 224–5, 227, 230–4, 237–8,
    242–3, 247, 249, 262, 265–6
inter-war years 7–9, 11–12, 42–71,
    77–8, 82, 85, 145, 150–2, 214,
    219, 251, 25, 255, 258–60
Irian Jaya 118, 120–2, 235–6, 238
Italy
    (1870–1914) 27, 32–3, 35–7
    (1919–39) 49–50, 54, 59, 67, 69–70
    (1945–71) 107–13, 145
    (1973–78) 156–8
    (1979–84) 169–71, 173, 241
    (1989–2001) 197, 199–200, 206–11,
        255– 6, 262

Japan
    (1870–1914) 20
    (1919–39) 69
    (1945–71) 75, 77, 80–5, 93–7, 118,
        120–1 131, 133–4, 137–8, 145
    (1973–78) 146–9, 151–3, 156
    (1979–84) 164–6
    (1985–88) 80–4
    (1989–2001) 189, 193, 214–19,
        224, 238–41, 243
Johnson administration 93, 101, 107,
    116–17, 130–4

Kashmir 11, 220–1, 224–5, 264, 266–7
Kennedy administration 92–3, 100,
    112, 126, 128–30
Keynes, John Maynard 1, 15, 47, 69,
    72–9, 150, 252–7, 264
Kishi, Nobusuke 95–6
Kissinger, Henry 133–5
Kohl, Helmut 167, 184–5, 195–8, 203–4
Koizumi, Junichiro 218–19, 258
Korean war 80–1, 90–1, 94, 120
Kosovo war 192, 202
Kubitschek, Juscelino 127–8

Lafontaine, Oskar 200
Latin America 15, 59, 81–2, 85–6, 128, 136, 144, 179, 187, 226, 228, 232, 239, 262–3
Lincoln, Abraham 36–7, 267
Louis XIII 19
Louis XIV 21
Louis XVI 16, 29
Louis Napoleon 31
Louis Phillipe 31
Louvre accord 182–4

Maastricht treaty 186, 198–9, 203–5, 211–12
MacDonald, Ramsay 68
Machiavelli, Niccolò 6, 18, 27
Macmillan, Harold 99–101
Madison, James 24–5, 87
Mafia 109, 206–7, 211
Major government 212–13
Marshall plan 87, 98, 104, 109, 118
Mauroy, Pierre 168, 172
Megawati Sukarnoputri 233, 235–9, 242
Mercantilism 22–23
MERCOSUR 226, 228, 231–2, 249
Mexico 163, 188–9, 228
Mitterrand, François 166–9, 172, 184, 197, 202–3, 205, 253
Miyazawa, Kichi 216
modern state 4–6, 13, 18–27, 33, 44–5, 82, 86, 144–5, 256, 266
and representative democracy 23–6, 36–8, 86–87, 252, 258, 260
monetary union 136, 185–6, 196–201, 203–5, 207–13, 239, 241–2, 247–8, 254, 256, 261–2
Monnet plan 103–4
Morgenthau, Henry 77–80, 87, 103, 132
Moro, Aldo 112–13, 156–8
Moro, Yoshiro 218
Müller, Hermann 58–60
Mussolini, Benito 12, 35, 50, 56, 64, 108, 211

Nakasone, Yasuhiro 165–6, 182–4, 215, 219
Napoleon 27, 30
nationhood 4, 13 18, 23 26–8, 31–8, 44–6, 70–1, 82–3, 85–6, 88, 136–8, 145–6, 150–1, 238, 240–2, 252–3, 258–9, 266–7
Natsir 120–1
Nehru, Jawaharlal 113–16, 121, 180, 220, 225
Neves, Tancredi 174–5
Nixon administration 132–5, 138, 146–8, 150, 152, 158, 163, 177, 253
North Atlantic Treaty Organisation 36, 81, 90, 93, 98, 104, 106, 109, 112,162, 166, 172, 177, 182, 191–3, 195–6, 202, 205, 240, 260
North Atlantic Free Trade Area 189–90

Okinawa 94, 96, 97, 134
oil price shock (1973) 147–8, 150, 156, 159, 162
oil price shock (1978–9) 151, 162–4 168–9, 174, 178

Pakistan 113, 116, 133, 187, 220–1, 224–5, 265–6
Pflimlin, Pierre 105
Pildsuki, Marshall Jozef 56
Plaza accord 181–4
Poland 8, 14, 42–4, 55–6, 59, 65–6, 77, 88, 134
Prodi, Romano 209–10

Quadros, Jânio 128–9

Rao, Narasimha 221–4, 243, 262–3
Reagan administration 151, 162–7, 169, 172–3, 179, 180–3, 219
real plan 228
reason of state 2, 5–6, 23, 25, 28, 32–3, 45, 49, 70, 78, 95, 98, 106, 165, 167, 171, 253, 266–7
Roosevelt (Franklin) administration 65, 67, 69, 75–80, 85, 97, 131, 133

Salisbury, Lord 32
Sarney, José 174–7, 262
Schmidt, Helmut 153–5, 166–7
Schroeder, Gerhard 199–201, 240
Schumpeter, Joseph 3, 15, 25
Shastri, Lal Bahahadur 116
Shekhar, Chandra 221
Sieyès, Abbé 23, 26
Singapore 9, 217, 257, 260
Singh, Manmohan 222
Singh, V. P. 220–1
Snake, the 136, 154–6, 159
South Korea 80, 181, 187, 191,
    217–18
Soviet Union 43, 48, 65, 67, 70,
    75–80, 82–3, 87–9, 92, 94–5, 108,
    115–17, 129, 133–4, 137, 144–5,
    148, 153–4, 162, 166, 172, 178,
    187–8, 192, 195, 202, 221, 260
Spain 8, 14, 20, 62–5, 144, 200, 209
Stability and Growth pact 201, 204–5,
    210
Stresemann, Gustav 53, 58
Suez crisis 98–101
Suharto, General 123, 233–5, 239
Sukarno 13, 119, 121–3, 233
Sukiman, Wirosandjojo 120–1, 123
Suzuki, Tadakatsu 164–5
Sweden 14, 20, 61–2, 71

Tanaka, Kakuei 134, 152
Thatcher government 161, 166,
    171–3, 186, 211–13, 240–1
Thiers, Adolphe 31
Thucydides 38
Truman administration 75, 79–81,
    85–7, 90, 93–5, 98, 102, 104, 109,
    118, 120, 123, 126, 131–3, 139,
    251, 278

unemployment 9, 58–61, 68, 154,
    157, 159, 169, 170–3, 183, 184,
    195–6, 199–201, 206, 212, 218,
    241, 253, 258
United Front government 223
United States of America 7–8, 24–5,
    36–7, 42–4, 48–9, 54–5, 67–70,
    75–88, 131–8, 144–51, 180–2,
    186–95
  civil war 36–7
Uruguay 226, 232
Uruguay round 181–2, 189–90,
    194
US-Japan security treaty 94–6, 153,
    215–16, 252

Vajpayee, Behari 223–4, 265
Vargas, General 123–9
Venezuela 17, 144, 263
Versailles treaty 20, 30, 43–6,
    48–52, 54, 58–9, 65, 67, 69, 71,
    251
Vietnam war 93, 96, 103, 105, 117,
    131–3

Wahid, Abdurrahman 235–8
Weber, Max 10, 40
White, Harry Dexter 77, 87
Wilson, Harold 101, 159–60
Wilson, Woodrow 42–4, 70–6
Wiranti, General 236
World Bank 78, 87, 95, 104,
    116–17
World Trade Organisation 189–91,
    194, 223, 243–4

Yoshida, Shigeru 94–5, 219
Yugoslavia 14, 45, 49–50, 55–6, 65, 71,
    187, 192